D1524133

SEVEN JEWISH CULTURES

SEVEN JEWISH CULTURES

A REINTERPRETATION OF
JEWISH HISTORY AND THOUGHT

EFRAIM SHMUELI

TRANSLATED FROM THE HEBREW BY GILA SHMUELI

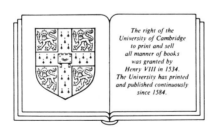

The right of the
University of Cambridge
to print and sell
all manner of books
was granted by
Henry VIII in 1534.
The University has printed
and published continuously
since 1584.

CAMBRIDGE UNIVERSITY PRESS

Cambridge
New York   Port Chester
Melbourne   Sydney

Published by the Press Syndicate of the University of Cambridge
The Pitt Building, Trumpington Street, Cambridge CB2 1RP
40 West 20th Street, New York NY 10011, USA
10 Stamford Road, Oakleigh, Melbourne 3166, Australia

Originally published in Hebrew as *Sheva tarbuyot Yisrael*
by Yachdav United Publishers, Tel-Aviv, 1980
and © Yachdav United Publishers, 1980
First published in English by Cambridge University Press 1990 as
Seven Jewish Cultures: a Reinterpretation of Jewish History and Thought
English translation © Cambridge University Press, 1990

Printed in Great Britain at the University Press, Cambridge

British Library cataloguing in publication data
Shmueli, Efraim, 1908–88
Seven Jewish cultures.
1. Judaism, history
1. Title   11. *Sheva tarbuyot Yisrael*, English
296.'09

Library of Congress cataloguing in publication data applied for

ISBN 0 521 37381 6

SE

For Karny, Hanan, and David Jacoby –
to whom their Saba wished to dedicate this book.

CONTENTS

BIOGRAPHICAL NOTE

It is a sad task, and really an impossible one, for me to attempt the kind of evaluative summation that I believe my father's work merits. I can only express the hope that one of his readers may wish to do this one day. I will venture to provide here no more than a brief biographical sketch.

On his tombstone, under his name, we inscribed in Hebrew the epithet: "A man of wondering and thinking." These words echo the title of the book which he considered his most important philosophical work, *Pli°ah va-hashivah be°olam hiad a°i technologi* "Wondering and Thinking in a Techno-Scientific Age" (1985), and we deemed them a fitting title for his life, perhaps a hint and a clue to its secret and substance. The allusion to "thinking" is a natural choice when characterizing a man whose intellect was not only his livelihood but the source of his deepest personal joy. His background presaged little of this – until the age of twelve he could not even read the Latin alphabet. He came from a poor Ḥassidic family in the industrial city of Lodz, Poland (Europe's third largest Jewish community at the time), a background which he described in his semi-autobiographical book *Ba-dor ha-yehudi ha-aharon be-Polin* ("With the Last Generation of Jews in Poland") (1986). His father, seeing he had a young *ilui* (brilliant scholar) on his hands, took him out of the *ḥeder* and placed him, with the help of scholar-ships and the boy's own earnings from tutoring jobs, in Dr. Mordechai Braude's new, progressive, Zionist-oriented Hebrew *Gymnasium*. His father, pious Ḥassid though he was, already sensed that the old world of his own traditional faith was no longer capable of stimulating and holding an inquisitive and penetrating young mind. My father himself always retained a painfully lucid awareness of the great spiritual drama confronting his father, and his father's entire generation, as a result of the disintegration of traditional faith. An echo of this experience can be heard in *Seven Jewish Cultures*, especially in the last chapter.

It was at the Hebrew highschool in Lodz that the foundations were laid for his Zionist world view, his mastery of the Hebrew language and literature, and the breadth of his general education in the humanities (Latin, German,

Polish, world and Jewish history and literature). Later in life he taught himself Greek, Italian, and Spanish. "With the Last Generation of Jews in Poland" describes the great sociological and cultural ferment generated in Lodz by the Socialist and Zionist movements in the twenties. The "court" of the Ḥassidic *rebbe*, by whom his father's life and that of hundreds of thousands of pious Jews was still guided at the time, is depicted with the deep sympathy and understanding of a native son, but without sentimentality. Lively portraits of my father's highschool teachers attest both to his phenomenal memory and, where memory failed him, to his uncanny skill at reconstructing scenes and situations based on his later historical knowledge and on his psychological insight. Much to his amused satisfaction, readers often found difficulty in determining where personal memory ended and reconstructive work began. In that same vein, he used to have great fun when traveling in engaging strangers in conversation on the bus or in the train; after a very short exchange, he could relate to them their life history in considerable detail, much to the listeners' amazement, if not alarmed suspicion.

In 1928, upon finishing his secondary education, he left Lodz for the richer intellectual pastures of Germany, a country which exercised magnetic attraction for thousands of bright young Jews from eastern Europe and Russia at the time. He himself had experienced the world of his childhood in Poland as an environment of material and spiritual poverty, and felt at parting, besides the normal regrets of leaving home and childhood, that he was leaving behind an environment in stagnation and decline, a world destined to be destroyed. He wished this old world to be spared, but he also felt it was necessary to grasp that something new was in the process of being formed. In Jewish and humanistic studies he wished to rediscover the world's charm, to embrace with love, to mend the tears.

The first step in this direction was the departure from Lodz, an industrial city of smoking chimneys which had mushroomed with unnatural speed, a city of impatience, of people frenetically scratching together a livelihood, to the baroque town of Breslau, with its large established middle class, its settled and comfortable tradition, its beautiful layout and landmarks.

The Jewish community in Breslau was composed of transients and denizens, newly arrived "Ostjuden" and more established "western" Jews, Orthodox, and Liberals. It was the home of the Rabbinical Seminary founded by Zacharias Frankel in 1854. Some of its illustrious teachers in the nineteenth century, besides Frankel himself, had been historians, such as Heinrich Graetz and Mordechai Brann. Moses Güdemann, David Kaufmann, Hermann Cohen, and many excellent rabbis who served congregations in Germany and elsewhere, had graduated from here. Its academic prestige and intellectual importance far outstripped its actual size: its peak enrollment (in 1930) was seventy students. The four chief instructors

("Dozenten") in the 1920s and 1930s were renowned scholars, among them Yehiel Michael ha-Cohen Guttmann, who taught Talmud and the Poskim (Codifiers). He was one of the great experts in this field, a man of encyclopaedic knowledge and the author of *Mafteah ha-talmud* ("The Key to the Talmud")

Isaak Heinemann taught medieval Jewish philosophy as well as methods of interpretation of the *aggadah*, as these compared to Hellenistic exegesis. He was a brilliant lecturer and excellent teacher, a man who charmed his students with his wisdom and sense of humor. Heinemann translated Philo and Stoic writers from Greek to German, and edited the *Monatsschrift*, the leading journal of the Science of Judaism in Germany, founded by Frankel and Graetz. Both these instructors, especially Heinemann, are mentioned more than once in *Seven Jewish Cultures*.

By the time my father enrolled in the Rabbinical Seminary he had already abandoned the religion of his childhood, or any form of primitive religion so often ridiculed by atheists and heretics such as Marx and Freud. He knew what an adult religion was. The *rebbes* that he had known in Lodz were no childish believers in a castigating father, in a vulgar anthropomorphic materialization. They apprehended God as a religious principle, an abstraction; inasmuch as He was endowed with elements of personality, it was for the sake of metaphorical discourse. I mention this because even though my father became a secular Jew, the transcendent dimension always remained his deepest preoccupation, and what he heard from Paul Tillich in Frankfurt, namely, that God is someone in whom one's interest is absolute, was what he had also imbibed from his Hassidic rabbis back in Lodz. He learned quite early (or perhaps this was the intuitive side of his personality) to recognize the distinction between knowledge of objects by way of scientific investigation and philosophical conceptualization, and the comprehension of that which is of the essence of wondering and the wondrous, beyond what is revealed to human perception or apprehended through symbols.

He left the Rabbinical Seminary after two years and went to Frankfurt (1930–1), where he attended lectures by some of the luminaries of the age: theologian Paul Tillich and sociologist Karl Mannheim. He returned to the Friedrich Wilhelm University of Breslau to complete a degree in philosophy in 1933. His Ph.D. dissertation was tilted "Individualism and structure of society in Hegel's ethics and social philosophy." His instructors in Breslau were M. Horckheimer, E. Kühnemann, Richard Höngiswald, and S. Marck. All his life he felt he had been blessed with seminal instructors, teachers who left him charged with enough intellectual current to energize his entire career.

He left Germany for Palestine in April 1933, three months after Hitler's rise to power, and shortly after the departure of Thomas Mann and a large group of writers and intellectuals who escaped in the first big wave of emigres, people who, like himself, did not believe that things were going to change quickly. In later years he remarked sadly that the only fully accurate prediction he had ever made was contained in the articles he published in the German Jewish press of the time, warning Jews to get out of Germany.

Having established himself in Haifa, he began his long career as a teacher, lecturer, and writer. He held a number of teaching jobs simultaneously and taught whatever was required: history, Hebrew language, Hebrew and world literature, Bible, pedagogy, sociology. He turned out to be a most gifted teacher, in the fine tradition of those educators and scholars who had made his own student days so memorable.

Shortly after his arrival in Palestine he was encouraged by the poet Yitzḥak Lamdan, editor of the literary monthly *Gilyonot* (established 1933), to become a regular contributor. *Gilyonot* passionately argued that the young generation of Hebrew writers and scholars in Palestine should play an active role in shaping the social, political, and intellectual development of the emerging Jewish national entity. It rejected both the detachment of those who believed in art for its own sake, and the shallow, over-politicized articulations of the left. It sought to challenge such fashionable rebellions by emphasizing the importance of intellectual continuity, combined with a critical evaluation, of the past. The monthly journal was also very open to fresh evaluations of the great treasures of world culture, and it is in this sphere that my father diligently pursued his interest in the Renaissance. He studied and wrote on Montaigne, Cervantes, Thomas More, Giordano Bruno, Macchiavelli, Paracelsus, and, eventually, produced his two-volume book *Anshei ha-Renaissance* ("Men of the Renaissance") (1948–52). He was equally interested in Jewish figures of that period: Don Isaac Abravanel, Judah Arie (Leone) of Modena, Uriel Acosta, Sabbatai Zevi, Spinoza, and others.

The objects of his attention in these studies had, I believe, several elements in common. He was intrigued by these early expressions of the struggle "between faith and heresy" (as one of his books was titled) and by the development of individualism in modern society as it had evolved since the Renaissance. His immersion in the Renaissance surely reflected more than an academic interest: a culture which set out to reinterpret an antecedent culture, to invigorate the ancient model with its own new meanings, was unfolding under his very eyes in the National-Israeli endeavor. His interest in political theorists – Thomas More, Machiavelli and, later, Max Weber – was surely also spurred by the political reality he was experiencing. The birth of the Jewish state was on the horizon, and it was imperative to study, clarify, and consolidate the legacy of western political thinking.

My father always considered himself a Holocaust survivor, for, although he was not physically present in that hell, he easily could have been. It was a subject that preoccupied him deeply in the last years of his life. One of the most moving pieces he wrote appears in his last book *Ha-yahadut bein samchut le-hashra*ʾah* ("Judaism between Authority and Inspiration") (1988) in a chapter titled, "*Kiddush ha-shem*: the problem of faith during the Holocaust", where he attempted to reconstruct the reflections of a believer on the way to the gas chambers of Treblinka. He took as his prototype Rabbi Yitzḥak Menaḥem Mendel Danziger, the last Ḥassidic rabbi of the Alexander dynasty, the "court" near Lodz that he had frequented with his father in his youth. It was his intention to devote his next book to the rise of European liberalism and its eventual debacle in the totalitarian regimes of the twentieth century and the Holocaust.

My father spent three periods of his life teaching in the U.S.: – two short periods in Chicago and Detroit in the early and mid-fifties, and a period of thirteen years, until his retirement, in Cleveland, Ohio. While teaching and lecturing in Haifa, he did not have the opportunity to engage in the subject for which he had initially trained himself and which was closest to his heart, philosophy. The years spent in Cleveland (1963–76) were very happy. American hospitality and generosity engulfed him and he basked in the respect and recognition that was showered upon him. First he taught at the Cleveland College of Jewish Studies and later was appointed a professor of philosophy at Cleveland State University. He found his American students and colleagues eager and receptive and this stimulated him to be his most expansive, giving, communicative self. He initiated interdepartmental public seminars, lectured throughout the U.S., Latin America, and Canada, entertained frequently at home, and made many warm and lasting friendships.

He produced only one book during the Cleveland period: *Beit Yisrael u-medinat Yisrael* ("The House of Israel and the State of Israel": Studies in American Jewish Life, Changes, and Trends) (1966). However, he published a number of articles and studies in English, resulting from his observation of life in America (for example, "Ancient Cynics and modern hippies," "Freedom and the predicaments of self-realization in a techno-scientific age") and from his professional philosophic endeavors. Some of the latter, on Spinoza, Hegel, Marx, Husserl, and Mannheim, later appeared in book form under the title *Crossroads of Modern Thought* (in English, 1984). After his official retirement and return to Israel in 1976, at the age of sixty-eight, another period of phenomenal productivity began. Book followed book, almost every two years. Much of the material had been developed during the Cleveland years, but was drawn together and finalized when retirement gave leisure for these kind of comprehensive summations.

Morashah u-maʾ avak ba-shirah uva-hagut ("The Struggle for Continuity in Hebrew Poetry and Philosophy") (1978), contained extensive monographs on the poetry of Bialik, Zalman Shne ʿur, and Lamdan, and the philosophy of Zvi Diesendruck, Julius Guttmann, Zvi Voislavski, and Martin Buber. *Seven*

Jewish Cultures, which he considered his most important contribution to the understanding of Judaism, both methodologically and philosophically, appeared in 1980. Themes from this work (for example, on the historic strength of the Rabbinic culture and its recent resurgence in modern Israel) were further developed in *Ha-yahadut bein samchut le-hashra'ah* which appeared posthumously in 1988. The latter was somewhat more combative and political than the theoretical and scholarly *Seven Jewish Cultures*. In both books, however, the author's discussion of ongoing cultural and political issues evoked criticism from two directions: some modern professional scholars committed to academic "objectivity" faulted his conception as too personal and too partisan. Cultural or political activists, on the other hand, felt it was too reticent. He himself addressed the issues of objectivity and the social and moral commitments of the historian in chapter 8 of *Seven Jewish Cultures*. The practical implications were also spelled out: study of the heritage, reinterpretation of its symbols, openness and tolerance.

Adam be-matzor ("Homo Angustus") (1981) was a collection of studies in literature, existentialism, and the philosophy of hermeneutics highlighting works by Thomas Mann, Kafka, Camus, Heidegger, Gadamer, Schleiermacher, and Dilthey.

"Wondering and Thinking in a Techno-Scientific World" was, next to *Seven Jewish Cultures*, the work he valued most. It presented a "philosophy of wondering" and contained his statement on man's identity and individuation, on the limits and possibilities of rational thinking, on the uniqueness of selfhood, and the source of all possibilities, which included, as he put it, "the possibility of the appearance of wonders."

He continued to teach as an adjunct professor of philosophy at Haifa University until the day of his death on June 9, 1988. He was still remarkably active and vigorous as he entered his eightieth year. Certain aspects of Israel's political, social, and moral development distressed and pained him, and some of this is expressed in the concluding chapter of *Seven Jewish Cultures*. However, none of the disillusionments so often attendant upon old age seemed to erode the hard core of his natural optimism and his tremendous faith in Israel's creative potential. Emotionally, he never indulged in nostalgia about better days in bygone times; he had no doubt that the Israel of the future would be quite different from that he had known in the past, but he believed that this change held unforeseeable positive possibilities. He was not afraid of the future. He paid little heed to political fashions; he was much too serious a thinker to fall for the rhetoric of the right or the left, or to embrace extreme positions of any shade or tone. He believed Jews had a right to settle in Eretz Israel, but that not all rights could or should be realized. The historic position of the Zionist movement in favor of territorial compromise or partition of the land between Arabs and Jews appeared to him the only possible solution.

He lived a full and happy life. He met, corresponded, and interacted with most of the literary, scholarly, and intellectual "whos's who" of Israel from the mid-1930s onward. He was intellectualy preoccupied with the major themes and personalities of the modern era, with issues of faith, the capabilities and limits of knowledge, science and thinking, the dilemmas of freedom and self-realization, the Renaissance, humanism and western culture, Judaism and the Jewish people, modern Hebrew literature and the giants of world literature and thought. He wrote countless articles over the half century of his prolific activity. Compiling his bibliography will be a daunting undertaking.

Finally, a word about the translation. He had full and intimate knowledge of the Hebrew language in all the layers and cultures he describes in this book, and was a consummate master of Hebrew style. In his later years, in fact, his style became simpler and less ornate than in his early years when he, like many young writers of the thirties and forties, vied for Bialik's linguistic and stylistic inheritance. When I undertook to translate this book we agreed that I would not try to do justice to the literary qualities of his style, but simply to render his ideas in English as clearly as I could. We also agreed that some editing would be required to trim the book's size to dimensions palatable to an English editor and reader. Three entire chapters have been omitted in this English version: a chapter on language and symbols, and two chapters devoted to a theory of historical change. The new introduction provides a summary of the book's main ideas. I often suggested to my father that his work should be translated and that he should devote some energy and attention to this task. He could write adequately in English, as he had done during the Cleveland years, but he was not interested. Writing in Hebrew, with an exclusively Hebrew readership in mind, was always one of his deep commitments. Thus he did not go over the English manuscript with the kind of painstaking attention he devoted to "his own" works, and any errors that plague it must be attributed to the translator's shortcomings.

He remained up until his death a voracious reader and had no trouble in keeping up with new publications, especially in philosophy and Jewish studies. *Seven Jewish Cultures* (published in 1980), however, expresses his thoughts as they were in the 1970s. He did not share my worries that the book might be outdated by the time it appeared in English, now some fifteen years after its conception. He was satisfied that major new insights into the understanding of Jewish or world history did not occur every year, or even every decade, and that the issues and scholars he had chosen to discuss and to debate with would continue to be of interest for some time to come.

Gila Shmueli

ACKNOWLEDGMENTS AND
TRANSLATOR'S NOTES

For his painstaking reading and insightful comments, the translator wishes to thank Dr. Arthur Lagawier of Seattle, Washington – a learned scholar, a wise and gentle critic, a dear friend.

Thanks also to Rabbi Theodore Friedman of Jerusalem and to Professor Leon Goldstein of SUNY Binghamton for encouraging the translation of this book.

Quotations from the Bible are taken from the *New English Bible*, New York, Oxford University Press, 1971. The version of the Talmud used is *The Babylonian Talmud*, trans. and ed. Rabbi Dr. I. Epstein, London, Soncino Press, 1940.

ABBREVIATIONS

Tractates of the Mishnah

Ab.Zar.	*Abodah Zarah*
Bab.B.	*Baba Batra*
Bab.K.	*Baba Kama*
Bab.M.	*Baba Metzia*
Ber.	*Berachot*
Erub.	*Erubin*
Git.	*Gittin*
Ḥag.	*Ḥagigah*
Ket.	*Ketubbot*
Kid.	*Kiddushin*
Meg.	*Megillah*
Men.	*Menaḥot*
M.K.	*Moʿed Katan*
Ned.	*Nedarim*
Pes.	*Pesaḥim*
Sab.	*Shabbat*
San.	*Sanhedrin*
Sot.	*Sotah*
Suk.	*Sukkah*
Taʿan.	*Taʿanit*
Tem.	*Temurah*
Yad.	*Yadaim*
Yeb.	*Yebamot*

INTRODUCTION

Throughout the ages theologies, theories of culture, and historical interpretations have attempted to provide satisfying answers to the mystery and exigencies of the enduring Jewish existence. Perhaps the very persistence of the question, both in Jewish scholarship and as a Jewish preoccupation in the larger sense, testifies to the elusiveness of any one answer. Certainly this persistence serves as a caution against the temptation to seek but one, definitive, all-encompassing notion of Judaism. We may find such definitions of Judaism convenient, often very persuasive. Nonetheless, they are more often than not articulations of wishful, non-existent constructs, a figment of the imagination of scholars and theologians.

One may legitimately wonder: what did Judaism mean to Maimonides? What did it mean to the late medieval Mystics–Kabbalists? What does it mean to us? Surely, meanings have changed. If we were to assume that they have not, if we thought, for example, that Maimonides' concept of God was identical to that held by the Mystics, or that the latters' concepts were identical to the notion of God as presented in the Bible, how are we to explain even such seemingly innocuous idiosyncrasies in our culture as the curious fact that God is described by entirely different appellations in the Bible, the *Guide for the Perplexed*, and the *Zohar*? In the Bible He is known as the Lord of Hosts (*ʾel tsvaʾot*), the Almighty (*ʾel shaddai*), the Most High (*ʾel ʿelion*); to Maimonides He is the Primal Cause, the Incorporeal that no corporeal entity can apprehend; and to the Mystics of the *Zohar* He is the Hidden One, the Boundless One (the *ʾen-sof*). Is it possible that these three seminal books, each representative of a separate and unique culture in our history, incorporate radically different concepts, as different as their vocabulary, of something so axiomatic, so undisputed, as Israel's God?

Until the last century, Jewish scholarship rarely showed interest in historical research. With the exception of Josephus, no Jewish historiographer of stature comes to mind. One may well wonder why. Perhaps Jewish scholars and leaders in the ages of traditional faith found comfort in a Jewish history whose meaning could be viewed as a monolithic, unchanging, eternal, God-given destiny, and that historical inquiry, with its unsettling tendency to reveal the contingent and the accidental, was pushed aside as a distraction from the serious pursuit of meaning. There were, no doubt, other causes for this view, which require a serious theory of change and stability that would account for the traditional belief of many Jewish generations in the undisrupted continuity of their history, and the unity of its meaning.

Serious attempts to grapple with the meaning of Jewish history have, of course, been made, but most interpretations of history have generally fallen into one or more characteristic fallacies. One has been *pars pro toto* – taking one set of ideas from one significant period (which will shortly be redefined as a "system of culture"), and making it representative of *all* Jewish cultures, for example, to argue, as modern liberalism did, that Judaism is essentially ethical and prophetic, or that it is legalistic-*halachic* (Talmudic, Rabbinical), or Mystical, or that it transcends history altogether. Some prominent theorists guilty of this error are Naḥman, Krochmal, Aḥad ha-ʿam, Yeḥezkel Kaufmann, Martin Buber, Franz Rosenzweig, Yitzhak Baer, and Benzion Dinur.

A second fallacy has been to view the totality of tradition as transhistorical, i.e. each idea in Judaism is as valuable as any other; the whole heritage is equally holy (an Orthodox fundamentalist view). Yeshaʿayahu Leibowitz is a well-known proponent of this concept.

In modern times yet a third error has arisen: a radical relativism rejected the continuity that had hitherto been perceived as endemic to Jewish history and stressed its precise antithesis – lack of consistency, a diversity of sources incapable of forming a unity. Everything that a Jew thinks or does is intrinsic to Judaism, the Israelitic prophet of Baʿal is no less "Jewish" than the "true" Prophet of the Lord. Berdyczewski exemplified this approach.

It is not, I believe, unfair to say that theological interpretations tend to suffer from a lack of historical understanding, leading to a total neglect of the distinct historical and religious character of the different articulations of our heritage and the imposition of one set of meanings on all of them alike. Indeed, theology is fundamentally inimical to history. We recognize that Christian theology, for example, stamped its own brand of meaning on Jewish history: the Bible became the "Old Testament," and Israel's past a mere prelude to a new covenant. Post-Biblical Jewish theology has been no less audacious in interpreting the Bible according to the changing religious requirements at different periods. Regrettably, the gap between theological doctrine and the results of historical research has not narrowed in recent times, in spite of our legitimate expectation for a more objective approach in modern Jewish historical research. The "essence" of Judaism is still frequently viewed as though it were an entity in itself, rather than a complex struggle of historical situations. Leo Baeck, for example, professed that the tragic experiences of the Holocaust had deepened his previous theological conceptions, yet in the face of the most shattering, disruptive cataclysm, he too still sought Judaism's timeless essence as the consistent, logical center of all Jewish experience. Even today one still encounters a revival of the "essential" tunnel-view of Jewish history.

It is not difficult to arrive at an essential theology that exemplifies one aspect, or one layer, or one system of culture in Judaism, but it is impossible, in my view, to construct a theology that encompasses *all* of Judaism's systems of culture except in very general and superficial terms. The reason is obvious: even the superordinating concepts of Jewish history – God, Torah, Israel's chosenness – have different meanings and functions in each culture. It is impossible, according to my view, to sum up the totality of Jewish religious truth, and even less the complexities of historical Jewish life, in a Hegelian fashion. That is, there is no principle of unity which would illuminate the true essence of Judaism as the ultimate synthesis, once and for all. This must be said against all neo-Hegelian attempts in Jewish theology and history, from Naḥman Krochmal and Samson Raphael Hirsch to Yitzhak Baer. We merely find optimal expressions of Jewish creativity, i.e. some systems have been more creative than others, and not all cultural diversities in the Jewish world are self-sufficient entities. In religious terms one might say that it is impossible to fence God into any of the notions that have been construed of Him at any particular period, or in any one of the seven systems of culture presented in this study. Jews everywhere – in Jerusalem, in Babylonia, in Cordoba and in Cracow – molded their experiences in different constructs or modes. If we insist on seeking those trends or expressions which were *common* in all our history, we should not be surprised, or disappointed, when we find that these trends share only very general characteristics. This paucity in satisfying generalizations with which to rationalize our history will, I trust, be amply redeemed by the wealth that our new theory uncovers: not one Jewish culture, but seven.

I propose that Jewish history be considered as an unfolding of seven successive systems of cultures. These systems (or cultures, for short) are conceived as organized sets of meanings in the practical, as well as in the theoretical and soteriological (redeeming) realms, of human endeavor. By culture I mean a set of shared symbols which represent an organized collective attempt to express the meaning, or meanings, of life and to make the world habitable by transforming its impersonal vastness and frightening dimensions into an understandable and significant order. Through culture, a chaotic and opaque environment becomes a meaningful world. Clearly, then, by this definition culture does not merely designate the sum of men's "adjustment to their surroundings," in Sumner's and Keller's famous phrase, but rather the reshaping of life's conditions by adapting them to man's search for practical, theoretical, and redeeming knowledge.

The ontological uniqueness of each culture produces quite distinct

interpretations of the superordinating concepts that govern Jewish existence – God, Torah, Israel's chosenness – and of the nation's archetypal
collective experiences – the exodus, the kingdom of David, the destruction of
the Temple, etc. The fact that these concepts and experiences have abided
throughout Jewish history contribute to the impression of unbroken Jewish
continuity and permanence. Our point is that while the concepts have
endured, their meanings have changed, the inevitable result of the changes
occurring in the ontologies underlying these concepts and experiences.

A culture implies a grouping of elements in which inconsistencies have
been minimized. In reality, incompatibilities never disappear altogether.
Three principal tensions characterize each Jewish culture: between
universalism and particularism (relations to other nations and religions);
between the individual and the nation (rights and duties, who gets what,
and how much); between the different elements constituting culture
(language, land, temple, economy, army, leadership, etc.). It is the nature of
cultural systems that what is intelligible and "normal" in one culture ceases
to make sense in another. Paradoxes, contradictions and inconsistencies,
hitherto tolerable as only seeming, not real, difficulties, become opaque and
intolerable. It is not without some amusement that we read in the major
writings produced by each culture earnest protestations about the logical,
emotional, and moral poverty, the regrettable human lacunae of the
heretofore venerated bearers of the former system. Incoherences and
antinomies no longer go unnoticed.

The struggle between the cultures involves socio-political forces. Leader-
ships assign roles, status, and sanctity. When a leading group becomes
dominant by establishing its system of meanings as valid and redeeming, it
tries to legitimize its interpretations vis-à-vis its opponents. Enemies, then,
are those thinkers whose influence must be removed, whose interpretations
must be wiped out. It is, of course, hard to find in any of the older Jewish
cultures (as in most traditional cultures) fair accounts of the ideologies of
adversaries. The Bible is far from stating fairly the ideas of pagan religions;
the Pharisees hardly mention the Sadducees or the Essenes. Censorship and
bans were common devices for combatting ideological adversaries in
Judaism. Analogous conflicts in the non-Jewish world often involved far
harsher methods. Adversary movements are sometimes known to us by the
derogatory labels they were given by their more powerful opponents: the
Jesuits in Spain named their foes "Liberals" to connote licentiousness, in
contrast to the "Serviles," the loyal ones. The uncomplimentary name
"Pharisee" was probably coined by the Sadducees.

Needless to say, the renewal of each system occurs within a specific
material framework. A culture confronts a new power structure within its
environment and expresses the dynamics of political events and socio-
economic institutions. The pattern of these confrontations and struggles is

reflected in each culture. However, I do not believe that each culture is an adaptation of these patterns and even less that it is derived from socio-political structures. On the contrary, each system selects those elements which are adaptable to its principal valuations, and no system is identical with any previous or with any subsequent system. The Rabbinic culture, for example, is by no means identical with the Talmudic culture, for the very reason that it came later and that it unquestioningly accepted the authority of the Talmud. Regardless of its innovations, each system accepted Judaism's superordinating concepts and strengthened the traditional view that all of its new developments stood safely within the framework of the true heritage. It maintained the identity of the perennial themes in Jewish life and continued the dialogue with previous generations in an attempt to innovate and preserve, to adopt and modify, to reject and integrate. The nature of the differences and innovations depended upon the leadership's creative powers, and upon the peculiar circumstances surrounding the development of cultural formations.

Each system of culture creates its own language of images, concepts, and symbols, which distinguishes it clearly from that of its predecessors: a generation raised in the Hebrew language of one culture, such as the Biblical, would barely comprehend the meaning of images and symbols used by the Talmudic or Mystic cultures. The famous *midrash* about Moses who was unable to understand a discussion among the Rabbis illustrates this point. The thinking of a people within a historical culture is circumscribed by the imagery it employs; only within the range of this imagery can terms be used meaningfully. In each culture a certain set of experiences had a decisive impact upon the imagery and conduct which became unique to that particular culture. The central new experiences were articulated in an innovative terminology, new images, reinvigorated symbols.

Different Hebrew systems of language have struggled for the expression of the central experiences of the five traditional cultures (from the Biblical to the Rabbinic). The existence of a large mass of inherited words and phrases cannot obscure the fact that the dominant meanings are the new ones. They are powerful enough to reinterpret the old meanings in the climate of the emerging central experience of a new culture. The new symbols color the whole inherited imagery. Even the names of God, as we mentioned earlier, are not identical in each of the traditional cultures. The same is true for the denomination and description of Torah and Israel. These, too, are given new names which necessarily convey new connotations. A Biblical man could not have understood the first *mishnah*, and a Talmudic man would similarly have failed to understand a chapter in the Hebrew translation of the *Guide for the Perplexed*.

The convergence of at least five systems of language is most evident in the Daily Prayer Book. The efforts of the Rabbinic culture to merge the previous four languages into its own is a unique phenomenon. It resulted from this culture's sense of piety which inhibited open legitimation of its own innovations. The Rabbinic culture accepted the Talmudic Sages as its highest authority, and related to them as they, in turn, had related to the Bible. But, whereas the Talmudic Sages innovated freely, the scholars of the Rabbinic culture seldom abandoned or cancelled Talmudic pronouncements by aggressive reinterpretations of their own.

Even in times of relative political and economic stability, a cultural system was preserved only through intense efforts of cultivation. The preservation of a culture is part of the creative process of its evolution and diffusion. Its producers and preservers are its co-creators, for without preservers to nurture it, no system can sustain itself. This idea is at the core of the commandment to study the Torah. Each system renewed this commandment, though always adapting it to the study of its own particular concepts and innovations. For medieval philosophers like Saʿadiah Gaʾon and Bachya Ibn Paquda, for example, the study of philosophy became a religious duty.

The Talmudic culture saw paramount importance in making Torah-study not merely a religious and intellectual discipline, but also a means of establishing personal identity associated with a social role, and especially with a new occupational role. Originality notwithstanding, ideas by themselves often have no historical consequences, and great powers of creativity may be lost when not effectively communicated. Ideas require carriers, disciples, teachers, and schools. It has often been said that the inherent qualities of an idea or a set of teachings do not by themselves render such ideas fertile or consequential. The transmission and diffusion of ideas is decisive for the increase or decrease of their influence. The study of Torah became a social role and created a social identity for many individuals who in ancient times were known as Sofrim (Scribes), and later as Hachamim (Sages) and Rabbis. Torah-scholarship became widespread only after the destruction of the Temple. Here we may apply Tocqueville's thesis, given in the context of the French Revolution, that the real changes, or the tendencies toward change, had actually been evident as early as fifty years prior to the revolutionary outburst: Hillel the Elder fought unsuccessfully for the popularization of Torah-study in his day (c. 30 BCE to 10 CE). The results of his efforts, however, were only felt after the destruction of the Temple, when the Pharisaic revolution had firmly established the dominance of the Talmudic culture.

No nation is totally segregated from other groups, but probably no other nation was as involved in the history of so many other groups and cultures as was Israel. In this historical-geographical sense the Jewish people is indeed a "people of the world," a universal nation, in Dubnov's famous phrase. There was little in human history that was entirely alien to Judaism.

Its history is interlocked and interwoven with events and ideas of various peoples and, in a way, it refracts the changing character of itself and its neighbors by a variety of modes of participation and segregation. The influences were manifold. Yet despite this involvement with the history of so many nations, the Jewish people was able to preserve its identity, a phenomenon which long ago became a focus of wonderment, as well as of scholarly effort.

Jewish creativity consists of a remarkable ability to embrace new elements. For example, Jewish Halachah incorporated Hellenistic and Roman law, and changed a number of legal constructs of ancient Judaism, and yet the Talmudic culture was clearly distinct both from Hellenism and from ancient Judaism. New ideas from without were admitted and incorporated into the overriding constructs in order to cope with events more effectually and to anticipate them where possible.

But what is it that makes Judaism unique? By unique I mean distinct, not in a sense of being arrayed against other nations and civilizations, or being superior in an evaluative moral context. Jewish history is unique for better or for worse, as is every individual and culture, and its problem has always been how to communicate its individuality and how to co-operate with other unique individualities. The idea of Jewish history as a series of successive renaissances, or restorations, views the core of Jewish cultures as a meeting-ground between history and theology, where the restatements of religious constructs became strategies for defending and preserving Jewish life and its significant meanings. The "response" to hard "challenges," to use Toynbee's terms, was aimed at restoring authentic Jewish selfhood, a strategy against the alienation, anomie, and apathy resulting from the intermittent attempts to be "like all nations." Although the Jewish people cultivated its distinction and uniqueness, there were also powerful drives toward assimilation. (For early literary references, see I Sam. 7.20; Ezek. 20.32; I Macc. 1.11–12, or Maimonides' epistle to the Jews of Yemen.) The struggle between identification with Jewish selfhood and alienation from it is the essence of the Jewish drama. The ordinating religious constructs, like the covenant, sin, reward and punishment, the remnant of Israel, the day of judgment, the Messianic idea, martyrdom, served as the very instruments whereby the authentic could be distinguished from the alienated. The struggle between the two was the perpetual theme of theology and history alike. The *mishnah* Ḥelek is a case in point: it comes closest to defining principles of Jewish faith, and it is obviously polemical against Sadducees, Gnostics, and apocalyptic believers. It sets standards for distinguishing what it considers authentic in Judaism from the irrelevant and dangerous.

Like creators of other systems, Maimonides too was critical of his forerunners, whom he characterized as incoherent and impoverished. (Despite such scathing critique, however, the forerunners remained for

Maimonides part and parcel of Jewish history.) Maimonides consciously attempted to offer a new theological creed and a definitive theory for daily conduct, thereby presenting Judaism as a unified body of intellectual doctrine and moral discipline. He expressed the intellectual doctrine in principles of faith, a credo, and the moral discipline, in his reformulated precepts of the law. Leon Roth rightly saw in Maimonides' system all the elements of a complete apologia. Here was an attempt to respond to the challenge of the outside world by rationally expounding the grounds for a Jew's unique mode of life, while at the same time participating in intellectual endeavors of global interest. No wonder the *Guide for the Perplexed* was hailed enthusiastically and acclaimed as a great new revelation.

One avenue of access to the past was never neglected: each system was a new opening leading back to the Bible. The Bible was the only written book which was never deprecated by any system of Jewish culture (unlike some of the books representative of other cultures). It has always occupied a central position as the Holy Writ in which the divine word was recorded by Moses and the Prophets. It became the cornerstone of all subsequent systems, with each phrase and word inspiring hosts of new ideas. Even the purely narrative portions of the Bible were made to convey profound, often hidden, messages. The Kabbalah attempted to reinspire not only every word, but every letter, and this in *all* the books comprising the Bible. Other cultures generally felt varying degrees of affinity with different verses, chapters, or books of the Bible, but each renaissance of the Bible that constitutes the emergence of a new culture was also a rebellious disruption of the continuity, a revolt against the previous system. These reinterpretations of the Bible were by no means simply a matter for the ingenuity and skills of individual exegetes, but an effort by the new culture to establish, through its exegesis (homiletical, allegorical, anagogical, or mystical), the "true" meaning of the holy text, according to its own ontological presuppositions. The conceptual and evaluative frameworks used by the individual exegetes are based on distinct cultural systems. Characteristically, each system raised objections to interpretations which did not coincide with its own aims, and confidently claimed that only its own modes of exegesis could elicit the true meaning of the Bible or of any later system. The controversy was waged not over minor details of interpretation, but over the significance of the total framework of conceptual and evaluative principles.

Our awareness of the various perspectives by which the meanings of the Bible were ascertained in each culture no longer permits us to adopt any of the hitherto established modes of Biblical interpretation. Our approach to cultural hermeneutics calls for a new comparative method, one that attempts to supplement the critical-scientific approach of modern exegesis by clarifying the presuppositions underlying the various cultures in their efforts to interpret the Bible. The exegesis of the Song of Songs is a prime example of cultural hermeneutics.

Jewish history thus conceived as a series of conflicts and reaffirmations of culture is dramatic, innovative, and full of surprises. Unfortunately, its fascinating character is obscured both by the normative-sanctifying historiography and by the functional approach. The former sees only the sacrosanct continuity; no controversy, if it is within the framework of accepted premises, ever presents a contradiction to the norms. The functionalist approach looks at all the elements of culture as interdependent and mutually adjusted. Both are inadequate approaches to an understanding of historical reality.

Of course, reality is more than knowledge of reality; it may suggest many forms or systems of knowledge. It is difficult to find a transhistorical absolute standpoint from which historical reality can adequately be described. We comprehend different perspectives; this does not mean, however, that we can only affirm a relativism of values. The multiplicity of these perspectives, as it is expressed in the different Jewish cultures, is a sign not of fragmentation or defeat but of the wealth and generosity of Jewish life. Perspectivism as a historical view is a modest model, in comparison to the sweeping aspirations of the theological and idealistic approaches. It does not attempt to speak in the name of providence, transhistorical guidance, the invisible hand, or the "objective" universal structure of history. For this reason, I believe it is a more appropriate model for our life experiences and for the intellectual and scientific climate of our times. The balanced perspectives allow us to uncover the fulness of historical experience. As every great piece of literature seeks to provide insight into the complex fabric of contesting forces, so Jewish historical writing must now discover the orchestration of the disparate notes which constitute Jewish culture in its dialectical continuity.

I

A WEALTH OF CULTURES

Continuity and break – a historical approach

It is with awe and astonishment that we contemplate the wonder of Israel's unbroken existence of three millennia. Rarely did Israel know the taste of political liberty; most often it suffered oppression, persecution, and catastrophes, the likes of which no nation had ever endured. And yet, it has survived in extraordinary dynamism and creativity. An existence at once so brilliant and dark has often appeared to observers as if it were exalted beyond the transmutations of time, beyond the reach of the laws of nature, as though the "eternality of Israel" could persist throughout the ages immune to destruction. Indeed, traditional religious historiography saw in Israel's history a continuity of sacrosanct values, transmitted in an unbroken chain of legators and inheritors. No controversy, if it was deemed to be "in the name of Heaven," could undermine these hallowed values; one could say about adversaries like the House of Shammai and the House of Hillel that "both are the words of the living God" (*Erub.* 13b). But if a controversy was thought *not* to be "in the name of Heaven," it was pronounced a deviation, a "heresy." Those who would break the bounds, be they individuals or entire sects, were ejected from the fold of Israel, their writings buried, their names forgotten. In this view of history, Israel's past is enveloped in a hallowed cloak of divine providence, impervious to conflict or change.

But not only traditional historians have glided over contradictions and conflicts in Jewish history. Secular Jewish historiography has also neglected the study of the dynamism of change and innovation. It has adopted the modern structural-functional approach that prizes the permanent over the transitory. For this school of historiography, Israel's greatest accomplishment in its history is the sheer triumph of national survival in the midst of an environment that relentlessly exacted from an exiled community both resistance and adjustment. In this view, beliefs, institutions, customs, and ordinances were necessary for the preservation of the nation, even if some of their functions may no longer be clear to us today.

Appealing as these two historic views may at first appear, both suffer from a very major flaw: they largely disregard change. The fact that in the course of its history Israel underwent prodigious changes, both internal and external, changes that were nothing less than revolutionary, is hardly accounted for. It is my contention that the history of Israel has been a dramatic arena of conflicts and accommodations, of controversies partly settled, often left unresolved, of fundamental contradictions in beliefs, valuations, and opinions, all of which brought about change that eventually forged entire cultures which were distinct from one another in substance as in style.

Furthermore, in neither of these two prevailing conceptions do we catch even an echo of the colossal events which have molded the experience of the past generation. Our contemporaries have had the shattering experience of a history that is not a continuity of slow, organic evolution, but a series of ruptures and upheavals, breaches, and surprises. Historical time, unlike the "even flow" of physical time ("tempus quod equabiliter fluit," in Newton's phrase), no longer appears to us as a continuous flow of events and acts, but as an outburst of things that had never before been considered, or even imagined. In contemporary eyes, the nature of history looms as catastrophic in its very essence, irrational temporariness descends without warning, cataclysmically, disasters abound, and the chain of reasonable causality is snapped. This has been the fundamental experience of our generation, and of Jews especially; it impels us to re-examine our attitude to Jewish history. Whoever has experienced a catastrophic outburst which so utterly disconnects all lines in the adventures of experienced time and is so astounding in its manifestations, cannot but contemplate the past through a prism of disruptions and shocks. Whoever has experienced the Holocaust of European Jewry, the rise of the Jewish center in the United States, and especially the rebirth of the State of Israel, whoever has personally witnessed the hitherto unimaginable, can no longer cling to an image of an uninterrupted historic structure. He need not necessarily believe in miracles, but he clearly needs to rethink the image of our world and of our history.

The establishment of the State of Israel was a revolutionary act of liberation, one which imprinted not only the future face of the Jewish people, but its past image as well. In the light of this revolutionary transformation we try to grasp the events transpiring within us, and around us, to comprehend the marvel of our dark existence in this remarkable form of a past that is shouldered and carried on. What is the meaning and the purpose of our years of freedom in ancient times and of our 2,000 years of exile? We ponder our past in perplexity, in admiration, also in shame, and we seek to mend the faults that were inflicted upon us during our long exile by the nations of the world, and by our own shortcomings of thought and deed.

The new era now begun in the history of the Jewish people does not diminish, but rather intensifies our wonderment over the nature of Jewish identity today and over all those countless generations of heroes and saints, sufferers of exile, expectant of salvation, over all that eternality of Israel for which Jews were slaughtered, then and now. I believe it is possible for us now, at an early stage of this era, to attain a new historical understanding, one which will fully meet the rigors of scientific inquiry and yet will also express our own spiritual values, the life-experiences of our own times, so fraught with change and horror.

Seven Jewish cultures

I distinguish in the history of the Jewish people seven units of acts and events, each charged with its own weight of meanings and symbols, and each a recognizable culture unto itself, unique in its characteristics. Every culture is a set of meanings articulated in the language of its own experiences and concepts, painting a picture of the world based on the specific experiences of the generations it encompasses. A culture in this study refers mainly to a unit of organized meanings that grasp and organize the multifarious manifestations of reality in three ways: through the practical sciences, via theoretical knowledge, and by offering a plan for personal and collective salvation. Each culture witnesses struggles between the originators of the new meanings and those who subsequently interpret them, but in each period a dominant trend emerges, which eventually determines the character of the entire cultural unit. Expressed in contradictory ideas and acts, in controversies and wars, overtly and in secret, these tensions-struggles resolve themselves in different ways, depending on the times, on the strength of the creators, and on the nature of the entire culture.

These are the seven cultures in the history of the Jewish people:

1 Biblical
2 Talmudic
3 Poetic-Philosophic
4 Mystical, and its later offshoot, the Ḥassidic movement
5 Rabbinic
6 The culture of the Emancipation
7 The National-Israeli culture

Naturally, each culture dominated at a particular period in history, but neither the periodization that we find in the history books during the ages of tradition faith, nor the periodizations prevalent in modern historiography (First Temple, Second Temple, Israel in its Land, Israel in Exile, etc.) correspond to this division into cultures. The theory of cultures requires a new periodization.

Periodization basically does two things: it organizes meanings into complete units, and it ascribes particular importance to certain events. Regarding its first function, one can say that periodization divides time into segments on the basis of certain differences it distinguishes between these segments, thereby defining the character of each period – by no means an easy task. But at the same time that it distinguishes periods based on the differences between them, it also determines how common meanings of the historical subject are carried forward, and how divisions and differences in these same periods occur. When the boundaries of meanings are delimited by a clear differentiation between those that belong to an earlier period and those belonging to a subsequent period (on the background of a physical sequence, but from the viewpoint of continuity and consecutiveness), distinguishable units are created, each of which is characterized by a certain integration, as we explain in chapter 5 in our discussion of tensions and their equilibrations.

The second step in periodization is the determination of the event or events which delimit the boundary between two units of meanings. This task, which at first glance appears the easier of the two, is in fact very difficult, and many historians and philosophers have wrestled with it, as witnessed, for example, by the endless debates on when the modern era, both in world and in Jewish history, can be said to have actually begun. One should be able to designate an event, or a series of events, purporting to delimit periods, as revolutionary in their salience and importance, and as roadsigns pointing to incontestably great changes. But, since the concept of period is essentially a heuristic aid, a diagnostic method, i.e. a methodological tool for the study and understanding of history, occasionally the roadsigns designating a period may be dislodged from their former positions, when a new method of research is introduced and a new understanding of the units of meanings is gained. A scholar's periodization scheme unmistakably reveals his historical conception. The roadsigns designate the importance he attributes to the units of meanings – where they begin and where they end.

The basic and central unit in our study is not a period but a culture. It is even more difficult to set time-limits for cultures than for periods, for cultures constantly invade each others' domain, as vanguards, rearguards, or as rivals. That this is frequently the case in Israel's cultures is due to a number of reasons inherent in the history of a nation dispersed in many lands, and lacking a single organizing political center sufficiently powerful to impose one culture on all its diasporas.

One can say that the Biblical culture and its various sub-cultures continued to the time of Simeon the Just (c. 300 BCE) and Joshua Ben Sirah (known in the Apocrypha as Ecclesiasticus, the author of *The Wisdom of Sirah*; c. 190 BCE), perhaps even extending down to the early Hasmoneans (c. 165 BCE). This was followed by the vigorous growth of the Talmudic culture, which expanded and spread until its first consolidation at the time of Yoḥanan ben Zakkai (70 CE) and his disciples. This culture remained dominant until the eruption in the seventh century of anti-Talmudic social-religious ferment, some of which culminated in the Karaite movement. The Arab conquest (c. 640 CE) is perhaps the dividing line between these periods. The Poetic-Philosophic culture reached its zenith in the eleventh and twelfth centuries, in no small measure as a function of the spread of Arab influence. The Mystical culture consolidated during the thirteenth century and reached its peak in the sixteenth century, attaining its maximal spread in the Sabbatean movement (mid-seventeenth century). The Rabbinic culture reigned for a few hundred years. It achieved almost exclusive dominance in the sixteenth century, successfully rivaling the Mystical culture and completely supplanting the Poetic-Philosophic culture. In the Ḥassidic movement a blending of the Rabbinic and the Mystical cultures was eventually achieved. In the nineteenth century the Rabbinic culture still ruled in eastern Europe and in Muslim lands. The Emancipation culture, which next displaced preceding cultures, first germinated in seventeenth-century Holland, unfolded in the eighteenth century, and reached its first apex in the nineteenth century. The granting of equal rights in France as a result of the French Revolution is one of its outstanding landmarks. It reached eastern Europe in the form of the Haskalah, but its days there were short-lived. Its main thrust was felt in western and central Europe, and today it has reached a peak in the United States, France, England, and some other smaller Jewish communities. The National-Israeli culture arose in the late nineteenth century in eastern Europe and was subsequently carried forward by the Zionist movement in Israel.

The distinctions between these cultures do not lie in valuations of minor or trifling points; they are fundamental. Each culture carved out its own path into the very heart of the Jewish faith, into the superordinating concepts that govern Judaism – God, Torah, Israel – and into the nation's archetypal collective experiences: the exodus, the making of the covenant, the kingdoms of Judaea and Ephraim, exile and destruction, personalities of saintly or wicked men, expectation of the Messiah, and so forth. The cultures diverged over the most decisive and momentous issues, over life-styles and articles of faith. Each culture perceived itself as a new revelation of God's truth, bestowing a new comprehension of divine providence and of human and societal conduct (an insight its members denied, of course, to the antecedent cultures). Each such revelation, each new culture at its inception, was accompanied by an exuberant outburst of creativity and enthusiasm, a marveling at the miracle of innovation and an intense zeal. The Jewish soul could indeed rejoice in the bounty of distinct, seminal literary creations, each of which clearly embodied a new culture: the Bible, the Talmud, the *Guide for the Perplexed*, the *Zohar*, *Shulḥan ʿaruch*, the writings of Moses Mendelssohn, Herzl's *Jewish State*. Those who experienced the vigor of these great works felt as though their authors had shed a new light over the world and over Israel.

Let us briefly list ten points, out of many more that we must ignore for the sake of brevity, upon which Jewish cultures disagreed:

1 The nature of human happiness: the description of the garden of Eden and of the first man prior to sin; sin-free man in the Messianic age.

2 The nature of sin and its cause: the evil inclination; the entire issue of the presence of evil in the world; crime and punishment.

3 Death: the uncleanness of the dead; the survival of the soul and the world to come; Judaism's attitude toward the dead and toward dying.

4 The giving of the Torah at Sinai, so central an event yet one barely mentioned in the Prophetic literature. What happened to the giving of the Torah in the Mystical literature? How did Maimonides view this event?

5 Signs and miracles: the power of divine will to alter nature's course and the abidingness of nature's elements; the meaning of belief in miracles; opinions on faith and the attitude toward the heretic.

6 The Jewish people: its character, mission, and fate among the nations; the nature of Israel's chosenness; the significance of the exile.

7 *Ta'amei ha-mitzvot*: the reasons, or rationale, for the Bible's commandments.

8 The freedom of man's will: free choice and the decrees of providence; attitude toward the individual, tensions between individual and collective.

9 Images of the patriarchs and of the nation's leaders: we find very diverse evaluations of Moses, King David, the Prophet Elijah.

10 The idea of redemption: the image of the Messiah and the Messianic age. Is redemption a natural process, or a radical upheaval that entirely cancels history?

In subsequent chapters some of these points will be examined in a systematic fashion as we analyze how each culture diversely interpreted the Bible, understood the *mitzvot*, and legitimated its authority. It will become clear that in each of these weighty issues the differences distinguishing each culture are far from trivial. Although each culture rests on the same superordinating concepts – God, Torah, Israel – and on the same archetypal collective experiences – the exodus, the covenant, etc. – each is bold in its innovations. How bold depends, of course, on the vigor of its creators, the breadth of their creation, and the depth of its penetration.

Culture and ontology

Three dimensions of ontology

Our study rests on the assumption that each one of Israel's cultures is anchored in its own sense of reality, i.e. that each culture is nurtured by its unique ontology. Ontology is defined, briefly, as the concept of the reality of beings, events, and acts, the sense of what is important or inconsequential, true or vain, permanent or transitory in these beings, events, and acts.[1]

In keeping with its unique ontology, each culture makes a determination of what it considers real and what, within the real, is significant. Reality encompasses all beings, events, and acts that are revealed to consciousness, be they sensory or merely imaginary (as in the case of myths, idle fears, or phantoms of faith; phantoms, too, are a reality if they are taken seriously). But reality also directs consciousness outwardly at that which it yet lacks, at the dimensions of objectivity. In each ontology a tension is evident between subjective valuation and the desire to grasp reality "as it is." Ontology's sum of meanings can be classified in three main categories:

1   The significance of all the tools and methods with which society succeeds in maintaining itself, providing for its daily needs, ordering, and organizing its environment. The latter meanings include a society's relation to its land and to the nations that surround and influence it, as well as the ways in which both individual and group view and conduct themselves, i.e. the entire organized system of roles and statuses that endows a society with relative stability. This dimension of the sense of reality may be termed pragmatic ontology, or utilitarian knowledge, or the practical wisdom responsible for shaping men's acts and life-styles, their work and tools, their interpersonal relations, and their governing institutions.

2   In addition to developing practical wisdom for daily life, a culture must have a framework of meanings with which to render intelligible the nature of the world and the universe. This knowledge does not necessarily have a utilitarian purpose and is not apprehended through varieties of technology (magic being one variety of technology). This set of meanings includes opinions and beliefs about the nature of the universe – the heavens and the earth, the sun and the moon, oceans and storms – and about life's major phenomena that lie beyond man's control – birth and death, disasters, and horrors. This cosmological dimension of the sense of reality is theoretical knowledge. It is the source of philosophy and the sciences.

3   But in most cultures ontology has yet another, transcendent dimension. This encompasses that portion of culture-building meanings which offers salvation, relieves individuals and nations from distress, redeems from oppression, and "mends the world." This is the soteriological (redeeming)

dimension of ontology, also known in Jewish history as the "Messianic" dimension.

All three dimensions of the sense of reality are interrelated. Practical knowledge – the skill of the craftsman, the wisdom of the laborer – is aided by theoretical knowledge, and theory, in turn, is eager to enter the realm of action and public utility. Knowledge of the world combines with soteriological beliefs; for example, the belief that the Creator of the world is also its Redeemer. The Prophet Jeremiah already associated the knowledge of natural phenomena with the knowledge of a redeeming God: "God made the earth by his power, fixed the world in place by his wisdom, unfurled the skies by his understanding" (Jer. 10.12). "Israel is the people He claims as his own" (Jer. 10. 16); He is the Creator, He leads the world, and He redeems. Thus life, knowledge, and faith are inseparably fused. Together they penetrate progressively into a culture's subconscious until they become self-evident and understood as the "way of the world."

Each culture embodies in the daily acts of individual and society specific interpersonal meanings which direct, organize, and explain life. It sketches for its members a map of their natural and social environment, explains existing reality, and marks the limits of possibility. A culture also provides the means for attaining desired goals: tools and methods of work, principles and laws of behavior, as, for example, the uses of property and possessions. Every culture creates a framework of priorities deeply anchored in emotions and desires; these are known as values. It also furnishes the criteria necessary for judging these values.

The obligations imposed by an ontology are accepted by the individual and the group as if they carried the force of an objective reality, capable of inflicting injury or bestowing benefit, a force to be reckoned with in every decision. The sense of reality spreads over all acts and opinions; any attempt to assail its foundations is akin to stabbing the natural intelligibility of common sense; it is the arbitrary act of a lost soul, a heretic perhaps, warranting banishment, expulsion, or yet a worse fate. Since beliefs and principles of knowledge also draw upon feelings and imagination, one may say that all valuations and determinations are nurtured by the prevailing ontology, or, at the very least, are strongly influenced by it (for in each culture there are also remnants of the prior ontology and intimations of the ontology to come). Whether an individual is enriched by his culture's ontology, which is so much subsumed in all his reactions, or whether he is impoverished as a result of a shrinking ontology, is indeed a complex problem. This problem is perhaps best illustrated by the dual power of language.

It is not surprising that the Talmudic Rabbis thought of "nation and language" as one unit. They defined "nation" as a community of people that hold in common language, origin, and territorial sovereignty. They understood that when the Assyrian King Sennacherib "long ago went up and mixed up all the nations" (*Ber.* 28a), he abolished both their kingdoms and their languages. Yet it is precisely through language that man can articulate much more than he alone, with his limited knowledge and life experiences, could ever come to know by himself. The language he employs automatically bestows upon him the knowledge gained by countless predecessors; thus, his understanding is expanded and enhanced with borrowed riches. Of course, the opposite can also be said: that language is limited and that man knows more than he is capable of articulating. He perceives countless impressions that cannot all be expressed in his limited daily vocabulary. The same is true of his skills and everything we call practical wisdom, all of which do not readily lend themselves to scientific formulation. We may say, therefore, that the prevailing culture and its formats both expand and contract the individual's capacity for expression.[2]

What is true of language holds also for all other forms of individual self-realization. Intellectually and emotionally the individual leans on this relatively safe and stable entity we call culture, which, in turn, both aids and encumbers him. Man acquires a measure of confidence by virtue of a relatively uniform and generally accepted tradition of meanings, i.e. a complete ontology comprising all three dimensions we have described.

Ontology, then, imparts the daily practical wisdom a community needs in order to deal with its physical-biological and social environment. This practical wisdom provides technological means for cultivating the world. But an ontology also ponders the central problems of life: birth and death, body and soul, creation and its creatures. And finally, it endeavors to answer the anguished cry: "Where shall I find help?!" (Ps. 121.1). This kind of overall ontology pulls together all the individual characteristics of a culture into one relatively stable entity. Like any other organized framework, a culture operates according to the dictates of its own logic: it permits and prohibits, selects and rejects. Those customs, traditions, deeds, and beliefs that ensue from its premises are allowed to prevail; contradictory premises are forbidden and rejected. Permanent modalities to which individual and community may attach themselves thus crystallize, thereby allowing the individual to join thousands of unknown members of his culture in a kind of ontological communion that imparts the comfort of a secure sense of belonging.

The sense of reality, or comprehensive ontology, or theory of reality, is not an unknown phenomenon in the study of cultures. Giambattista Vico spoke of "a common nature of nations." Oswald Spengler described the soul of nations and the "fateful ideas" that are at the foundation of each culture: the idea of order and harmony guided the Apollinian Man and shaped the destiny of the Graeco-Roman civilization. Ambition, struggle, and a yearning for the infinite created the Faustian Man and determined the cast of European culture. Ruth Benedict gave examples of how primitive cultures were based on various orientations: one tribe's culture was geared to a life of sharing, while another tribe inclined toward competitiveness and hostility. In contrast to the theories of Vico, Spengler, Benedict, and others, our theory of cultures does not postulate a permanent, fixed sense of reality, a sort of immortal soul animating a community's mortal body. Consequently, we avoid any anticipation of future events as though these were but the preordained outcome of the past.[3]

The soteriological (redeeming) dimension of ontology

On the day of judgment a Jew is asked: "Did you hope for salvation?" (*Sab.* 31a). That dimension of the sense of reality which offers a plan for the redemption of man and nation, i.e. the soteriological part of every public ontology, seeks to relieve human anguish in a number of ways. Many and varied are the troubles that afflict mortal humanity, their boundaries stretch anywhere from ills that afflict with the force of impending catastrophe to lacunae and absences of perfect goodness. Let us list here four main categories of human afflictions.

The first category is anchored in the very finitude of human life. It includes the withering of the body, old age, diseases, and final extinction. Man is but a creature of flesh and blood, an object made of clay who, from time to time, is reminded of his own inescapable mortality: "Man was not joined but to be parted," lamented Moses Ibn Ezra. The partings and ruptures owed to the impermanence and the decay of human relationships are acutely painful. In ages past and down to the formulation of the second law of thermodynamics, this fate loomed in the imagination of nations in dramatic and terrifying imagery. The evil spirits were headed, of course, by the Angel of Death. How to escape the torments of finitude and unpredictable chance? How to flee that woeful day of our passing and final extinction? How to gain eternal life? To these anguished questions the soteriological dimension of ontology applies itself, providing answers that reflect the entire public sense of reality.

A second category of human afflictions arises from the wearying stress of human conflict. Individuals and nations are forever in a state of strife of one kind or another, from the private squabbles and disputes of individuals, all the way to global war. This category includes the entire public and personal pathology of discord and discontent. Jealousy and animosity fuel quarrels and disputes, the world is shredded and torn. Man yearns for a respite, for a remembrance of eternal peace and a dream of a serene future: "Seek peace and pursue it" (Ps. 34.14).

A third category of woes comes from sin and the sense of guilt. The sinner knows that he has acted wrongfully, that he does not merit the position he holds among men, that he has failed to achieve the goals his own elevated self-image had dictated. The discrepancy between actual behavior and desirable conduct prompts a yearning for improvement and amendment, for the innocence and perfection of a lost paradise in a blissful future, free of the demands and obligations that so often give rise to feelings of remorse and guilt. Individual and society sense that they have failed to reach the state of perfection commensurate with their status, with their self-image or with a self-imposed hallowed code. They scrutinize their doings, find fault, bring various ailments upon themselves and upon others, and look for scapegoats to atone for imaginary or real sins. The soul's distress is not, therefore, limited to the private distress of the lone individual; it quickly spills over into the public domain, there to subvert and distort with mutual recrimination and strife. The fear of sin in bourgeois society gives rise to no lesser feelings of guilt than did the fiery invocations of hell during the ages of faith.

The fourth category of afflictions arises from the fear of a world devoid of meaning. The absence of meaning, the vanity of all things, is experienced as a tear in the fabric of meanings to the point of chaotic disintegration and dissipation. Man fears the hollowness of the soul that magnifies the emptiness of the world. He fears disorder in the surrounding phenomena and bewilderment in his own heart, so irrevocably immersed in the transitory. Without some kind of anchor in the permanent, he cannot even grasp the transitoriness of these disorders. This category of troubles was, of course, the potent subject-matter of modern existentialist writers. Doubt, boredom, and emptiness are the symptoms of the non-being hidden in being. From this dualism of our existence we wish to be redeemed to a life of fulness, a life of meaning, purpose, dignity, and pleasure, a life free of absurdity and nausea.[4]

Modern man has tried to escape these doubts by embracing the facile peremptoriness of a catechism; better to have a jumble of narrow, circumscribed meanings than an absence of any coherent meaning at all. By surrounding himself with myriad shreds of meanings, man escapes from the terrifying silence of the void into the ear-splitting din of proliferated meanings, thus blocking out the torments of boredom and hollowness.

During the periods of religious faith, Israel's God was described in its cultures as a Redeemer from all four of the above categories of afflictions. He Himself is conceived and depicted as the complete substitute and opposite of these troubles: He lives forever, He makes peace, He is utter perfection, His name is certain, His seal is true, He showers plenty upon the world, including the plenty of purpose, which fills all lacunae. But the Messianic dimension in Jewish ontology is distinct in each culture. As we shall see, the soteriological methods of the Biblical, Talmudic, or Mystical cultures are by no means identical. The Messianic dimension is clearly the choice element in every framework of culture-building meanings; however, since it entails a fundamental transformation of an earlier ontology, it cannot be identical in each culture, except in a very superficial way. Only the emotional force that accompanies it is consistently sustained in all generations.

Not without reason, therefore, has it been observed that the secret of Israel's endurance as a nation lies in its high level of expectancy, in its faith in redemption, and its belief that history is not haplessly abandoned to the powers of evil. The symbols of hope in Israel's cultures are multifaceted, and all express the faith that there is a Master to the City, a watchful, though not always intrusive, Ruler over men and nations, who will, by virtue of performed *mitzvot* and good deeds, fulfill His promise according to the faith of His people.

Typical development of cultures

Polemics and birth pangs

Clearly discernible, if not always immediately apparent to the eye, an identifiably distinct visage characterizes each Jewish culture. Each culture embodies a defiance of those trials and tribulations (the four categories of afflictions, or Israel's exile, or specific catastrophes) from which it hopes, by virtue of its own new creations, to deliver. Every culture wages war against some "idolatry," not only the idolatry of Gentile cultures, but also against mask and graven image within Judaism's own fold. The cultures rage against "heresy," or "atheism," against any who would liken themselves to God in the manner of the Gentiles, by glorifying strength and courage, wealth and fortune. They would like to take these notions of preceding cultures, now become intolerable, and simply pound them to dust. Thus, in addition to the battles waged against idolatrous foreign cultures, disputes abounded within Judaism itself; for no culture simply accepted unchanged and unchallenged the legacy of its predecessors.[5]

The complex problem of how a Jewish culture arises, maintains itself, and finally disintegrates is compounded by the fact that many of the political, social, and economic forces that shaped cultures originated outside the nation itself and were often, in fact, quite beyond its control. On the other hand, each new cultural system wished to brand upon the age the mark of its own special political, social, and economic program. Thus it simultaneously reflected and directed, expressed and sustained, commanded and elevated, in order to magnify Israel's selfhood as it saw it. In each culture battle was waged over power: who rules? Who determines the nature and importance of the meanings that bestow power and honor? The political and intellectual leadership was charged with combatting the competing meanings propounded by hostile sects (*minim*, i.e. atheists, and heretics), and unorthodox definitions of its own meanings; it had to counteract harmful beliefs. This struggle was also waged by way of omission and suppression. Jesus, for example, is seldom mentioned in the Talmud, an omission that antedates the Christian censorship, hence a conscious Jewish intention. Similarly, the Bible makes no effort to throw any light on the tenets of idolatrous religions. Hebrew sources do not enlighten us on the Sadducees, the Essenes, and the Gnostic sects. The Talmudic Rabbis excluded from the Bible the extensive body of apocryphal literature, that sequel to the Prophetic style. In the seventeenth and eighteenth centuries the Rabbinic literature concealed the character and strength of the Sabbatean movement. Moreover, it takes many years for a new culture to prevail. The adherents of the Talmudic culture, for example, did not gain widespread influence until long after the early generations of *zugot* ("pairs" of pre-Tanna'itic scholars and leaders), and not without heavy battles, especially during the reign of Alexander Jannaeus, the last strong Sadducee to occupy the Judaean throne.[6]

The champions of each culture invest a tremendous amount of mental and emotional labor in the culture-building endeavor, in order to confer upon all its members the knowledge and conduct that befit a Jew in God's world. They also realize that the Torah does not pass in automatic inheritance from generation to generation; rather, it is acquired in anguish, it has "seventy faces," it is a spirit in man, a live spirit, through which he yearns to individuate and express himself. The cultures of religious faith dressed this spirit in the guise of *mitzvot*, those stringent norms of hallowed and accepted conduct, and cemented it in permanent molds. But they also infused it with fervor and enthusiasm, carrying it beyond the narrow possession of an exclusive, scholarly élite to become an inspiration for the individual to take upon himself willingly and lovingly the "yoke of Torah," the "yoke of the Kingdom of Heaven." Both of these aspirations, however, created tension, and each generation produced not only its innovators and ground-breakers, but also its own version of "perplexed," "heretics," and "atheists."

The charge of heresy accompanied all the great controversies in Jewish history: between the Pharisees and Sadducees; in the polemics surrounding the Karaites; in the disagreements between Maimonides and his opponents; in the polemics over the false messiahs; in the arguments between Ḥaredim and Maskilim; between Ḥassidim and Mitnagdim; and today between Orthodoxy and modern secularism. Politics did not cease in Israel with the destruction of the commonwealth in 70 CE. Indeed, if no effective disciplinary power could be wielded from within Judaism, the "guardians of the walls" would activate forces from without, as happened during the controversy over the *Guide for the Perplexed*, when the Jews themselves asked the Dominican inquisitors in southern France: "Why go to such lengths to ferret out heretics? They are right in your midst – the adherents of this very book of heresy."[7]

Creativity and the urge to renew the original

From dawn to decline each one of Israel's cultures passes through certain identifiable stages. The study of this development, however, has not yet yielded conclusions that can be considered certain and valid for each culture; for the time being, therefore, we limit ourselves to some general comments on how a culture evolves.

Generally, each culture embarks on its course with all the boldness of creative innovation, eager to do battle with the old, trumpeting triumphantly its own novelty as elevating, exalting, and redeeming. Witness the creators of the Talmudic culture who unabashedly crow: "A Prophet may henceforth [i.e. after Moses] make no innovations!" (*Sab.* 104a). And elsewhere: "A Sage is better than a Prophet" (*Bab. B.* 12a). Whence do the wellsprings of spiritual creativity arise, and what causes them eventually to dry up and vanish? The mystery of our creative power is never completely revealed to us. Two well-known attempts to explain the nature of creativity can be cited here.

Freud believed that spiritual creativity resulted from the sublimation of certain instincts, primarily the sexual instinct, when their avenue to immediate gratification is blocked. When emotions and sexual desires ("erotic" in the larger sense of the word) are suppressed and inhibited, they seek an outlet through channels of creativity. Hermits, saints, and ascetic mystics, for example, transformed the fire of carnal desire into a passion for God, which they expressed in sublime creations. In essence, then, this theory hypothesizes that deprivation spurs creativity. Sublimation of the instincts is the ennoblement enjoined upon us by the ever-present danger of our unbridled libido intruding into the public domain. Creativity, therefore, is a compensation for gainsaid pleasures.

A second theory – let us call it an idealistic-religious theory – makes quite the contrary assumption: powers beyond human understanding and control radiate and descend upon a base world from above, in order to elevate it and confer upon it a spark of the divine spirit. This ennoblement is an inspiration from above – not, as it was with Freud, from below – a reward, not a compensation. Creativity, according to this theory, originates from an abundance of internal powers that seek active outlets, an excess of that plenitude and generosity which God alone can bestow.

It is difficult to decide between these two opinions; no doubt there is an element of truth in each. For on the one hand, the creative power depends, so it would seem, on arduous efforts to free oneself from negativities, from private and collective distress; yet there is also a need for the positive, for elevation, for the creative spark which works its way from distress to relief. It seems to me that both these sources of creativity, the negative and the positive, if we may thus call them, are quite evident in the development of Jewish cultures.

Be that as it may, the beginning of a culture is to be found in the creative power itself. Whenever creativity is intensely experienced, as in the first unfolding of a new culture, one can be sure to find important changes taking place; it is the unmistakable sign that great events and acts require new elucidation and interpretation, that decisive breakthroughs can no longer be ignored or left unchallenged. In these instances a joyful awakening makes itself felt. Bergson's words are appropriate here:

Partout où il y a joie, il y a création: Plus riche est la création, plus profonde est la joie ... La vie humaine a sa raison d'être dans une création ... la création de soi par soi, l'agrandissement de la personnalité par un effort qui tire beaucoup de peu, quelque chose de rien, et ajoute sans cesse à ce qu'il y avait de richesse dans le monde.[8]

How deeply felt was the joy of anyone who had the good fortune to cleave wholeheartedly to the creations or to the creators of a new culture! The soul was inspired, the new work and its originators were exalted above all preceding works. New vistas seemed to open up, a kind of foggy veil was lifted from reality to reveal holiness in all its glorious brilliance; darkness rolled away before light. Witness how the Rabbis spoke of the Oral Law, the Poet-Philosophers about the *Guide for the Perplexed*, the Kabbalists about the *Zohar*, and the members of the Rabbinic culture about the *Shulḥan ʿaruch*. Our literature abounds in testimonials to the euphoria evoked by a cultural creation, especially at the beginning of its development, or at the zenith of its achievement.

Every culture rises and endures in the joy of creativity; indeed the justification for its existence is this very creativity, especially the ability to create dramatic symbols that not only delight the heart and the mind, but also contribute to a soteriology. The startling Talmudic metaphor picturing God engaged in the study of Torah is an example of just such a symbol. In the famous *aggadah* about Moses in heaven, we hear that God not only sits and studies the Written Law of Moses, but also all its subsequent exegeses, refinements, and innovations, the authority of which has now become as compelling as that of the original Written Law. The notion that the Torah had pre-existed Creation, that it had always contained that unique Talmudic brainchild, the Oral Law, was a bold claim indeed. It was staked by the champions of the new Talmudic culture as part of their struggle to justify and legitimize their own creation.

Another word yet on creativity: the individual creator often does not know from what source his work emanates, for he frequently absorbs influences, the nature and limits of which he is unaware; even when the source of influence becomes known to him, he stamps his own imprint on whatever he has absorbed to the point of obliterating the external source of influence. So, too, does a culture *vis-à-vis* the sources that bear upon it. The hallmark of each culture is the forcefulness with which it can shape and formulate, so that even when external influences are absorbed, its own unique stamp obliterates those externals. There are numerous examples of this phenomenon in our cultures.

Influence indeed is not the essence of creativity. At most, it is a stimulus and an incentive. One should not, therefore, judge a culture by the influences that worked upon it, but by the uniqueness of its experiences, opinions, and beliefs. In this uniqueness is its ontology crystallized. The wonder of ontological renewal in all three dimensions we have described certainly merits serious attention. Even when the surrounding circumstances and influences have been studied and made known, the renewal itself remains an astonishing and exhilarating phenomenon.

However, before we arrive at a culture's consolidation, we should first take a look at an important phenomenon in the unfolding of each new culture: innovation, so we see, is not brought about by a complete break with the past; it results rather from the infusion of new blood and spirit into an already existing creation. Each of the post-Biblical cultures was borne on the crest of a revitalization movement in an attempt to renew and refurbish that which had lost its vigor and prestige. We venture to say that Israel owes its survival to this ability to both eradicate and revitalize its past. Each of the redemption-seeking, post-Biblical cultures attempted to acquire its knowledge of reality by reopening the wellsprings of creativity which had dried up in the previous cultures, always returning to that primary source of blessing: God's word revealed in the Bible. Not unlike the Renaissance movement in its day, the cultures of Israel sought to cleave again to the original source, to take new possession of the original intent of the nation's fathers. This they did, however, in the spirit of their own experiences and concepts. We shall elaborate on the revitalization of Scriptures later on. Here we merely note that every culture yearns to recapture that blissful moment of Judaism's peak creativity. Its creations attempt to breathe new life into Scriptures, to partake again of that first sweetness of creativity, and to have the good fortune of seeing their own new ideas being savored as much as the prefigurations of these ideas, originally given at Sinai, had been.[9]

The creators of each culture believe that there exists a permanent inexhaustible fund upon which one may continue to draw, even though its principal has been largely consumed and much depleted, or, to echo a *midrashic* metaphor, as if glass vessels that have been shattered could still be restored.

In cultures that venerate the old and mistrust the new, a movement of new awakenings is forced to assume the guise of venerable antiquity. The Romans, too, preferred the old to the new (unlike the Greeks, who relished novelty), as Cicero reminds us: "Nihil mihi antiquius est" ("Nothing is as dear to me as the ancient"). Our Sages voiced a number of stringent prohibitions against new ideas, whether innovations in Torah itself, or merely in life-styles. Generally, they drew no distinction between mundane matters and matters pertaining to faith and doctrine. Only in the seventeenth century did a new avenue open for the study of writings dealing with worldly matters, for example, with *midrashic* legends and anecdotes, where the Rabbis addressed non-*halachic* issues. That such a distinction could and should be made was the argument put forth by Azariah dei Rossi in *Meʾor ʿeynaim* (Ferrara, 1574), and this was, in fact, the focal point of the dispute engendered by that controversial book. The generations of faith clung to the notion that whoever was pure in conduct and thought, would keep and cherish the Torah; a true believer would not presume to adulterate in any way the sterling coin minted by the ancients. We know, of course, that in violation to this pious intention, every one of our cultures brought forth men who propagated startling new ideas. This, however, was done cautiously, by ascribing new insights to venerated old names, to early codifiers (Poskim), to the fathers of the nation, and directly to Scriptures, by way of "creative interpretation." In this manner they swept out their own inhibitions and the strict rules against innovation; they threw out the old, because they had discovered something newer and better.

The revitalization of Scriptures took various forms, but its purpose was always the same: if the previous culture no longer satisfied, if it failed to ensure redemption, its dying flame had to be salvaged from the embers, a new altar would be erected, and the eternal light rekindled. Every culture thus linked itself to the chain of tradition, preserving and destroying the antecedent in keeping with its own needs, and with a care not to let the burden of the past hamper its own forward march.

The period of consolidation; legitimation via exegesis

The second period in the development of each culture is its consolidation and institutionalization. This is the time for more precise formulations of its authority and the proper organization of its functionaries. In the Talmudic culture, academies (*yeshivot*) are established and rulings are promulgated. The Mishnah preens with the might of an authority scarcely inferior to that of the Bible itself. A new class of scholars is created which sets itself apart from the ʿamei haʾaratzot (the unschooled, the ignoramuses). Learning Torah is deemed an obligation incumbent upon every Jew, and the merit of erudition now sweeps aside the authority of the traditional ruling classes, for it bestows equal rights (and more) upon the lowliest, even upon the bastard, provided he be a scholar. This consolidation of a culture depends to a large extent on the historic conditions surrounding its development. The spread of the Talmudic culture, for example, would surely have been impeded if Jewish communities had not been drawn together within the fold of the great Islamic empire, whose political center, Babylonia, was the metropolitan home of the Talmud's disseminators. As long as this entity remained unified, the Geʾonim's word was heard in the far-flung confines of the empire. On the other hand, the same political cohesion which bulwarked the authority of the Exilarchs and the Geʾonim also favored the spread of skepticism and heresy within the Talmudic culture and gave birth to the Karaitic movement. Similarly, the violent expulsions from Spain and Portugal, more than any internal decline, forcibly ended the spread of the Poetic-Philosophic culture. The very nature of this culture required for its flowering a climate of rationalism and tolerance, an adherence to humanistic-universal wisdom. These were not the qualities nurtured by the political conditions prevailing in Spain and Portugal at the time, and they inevitably withered and died, thus expediting the demise of the entire Poetic-Philosophic culture.

Many dangers imperil a culture from within and from without; it must be cultivated with devotion, wisdom, and purpose. The study of its meanings and the preoccupation with their preservation and development are therefore an integral part of a culture's creation, making whoever labors on cultivating its meanings an important partner in its creation. The Talmudic Sages frequently expressed this idea when they spoke in praise of Torah-study, placing it even above prayer. They liked to emphasize the verse: "If a man turns a deaf ear to the law, even his prayers are an abomination" (Sab. 10a, commentary on Prov. 28.9). Similarly, Maimonides in *Mishneh Torah* expressed this idea with the zeal of a true believer: "Of all precepts, none is equal in importance to the study of the Torah. Nay, study of the Torah is equal to them all, for study leads to practice. Hence, study always takes precedence of practice."[10] In the same spirit, Saʿadiah Gaʾon, Bachya Ibn Paquda, and other creators of the Poetic-Philosophic culture, recommended the study of philosophy and the sciences. In the following example, we encounter an exhortation to study something which would undoubtedly have been unthinkable in the previous culture: Rabbi Bachya prefaces his book *Duties of the Heart* with these words:

I once questioned a man counted among the learned in the law, concerning some of the topics I have mentioned to you as appertaining to the Science of Inward Duties; and he replied that on this and like subjects, tradition takes the place of independent thought. "This," I rejoined, "can only apply to those who, on account of their small powers of perception and intelligence, lack the capacity for reflection; as, for example, children and feeble-minded persons. But surely, one whose intellect is able to attain certainty on what he has received by tradition, and who refrains from investigation owing to sheer indolence or because he holds God's commandment and His Law in light esteem, will be punished and held guilty of negligence."[11]

In its second stage, a culture disseminates its own interpretation of the Scriptures; this newly revitalized version then becomes institutionalized. We have said that while it is true that every one of Israel's cultures is a new opening, a vital explosion of bold creative forces yearning to revive the cultural domain with its own fresh waters of salvation, each culture also aspires to be a renaissance of something older than itself, a restoration of the Biblical culture. The Scriptures were held to be God's revealed word, or Israel's spirit revealed in its purity: only the first generations were privileged to see God and His world in their original luminance. The rest of us are burdened with the task of rediscovering the light of their early, bright vision. Even though each culture manipulates the Scriptures (by way of "creative exegesis," as explained in chapter 2) with great freedom and claims for itself definitive authority, the Biblical literature always remains "Holy Writ," the cornerstone of Israel's very existence. Yet the builders of each new culture stress that Scripture is to be properly understood, and this, of course, in their way. The Mystical culture goes so far as to claim that without its interpretation, the Bible in its literal meaning (peshat) is nothing but a barren desert. How so? The letters of the word "בראשית" (in the beginning) are the same letters as those that make up the words "אתר יבש" (a dry place). Removing Kabbalistic wisdom from the understanding of the Written Torah, says Tikkunei ha-Zohar,[12] is like removing the fountain from the spring, reverting the universe to chaos, impoverishing the world and prolonging the exile. Thus, the Kabbalistic interpretation to the first words of the Bible boldly informs us that the written Torah, unaided by Mystical knowledge, is but a barren desert.

This kind of interpretation transposes one culture into the sphere of another in the belief that this transposition, though an adaptation to life's new requirements, actually unveils the essential core of that other, original culture, and removes from it any hint of latterly acquired corruption and blur. Indeed this exegesis attempts a new view of life, a new thought, a vision of God, Torah and Israel, which transcends the historical guise of these superordinating concepts. The generations of faith feared deviations from the divine source embodied in Scripture: the new and the recent, being farther removed from the divine source, were inevitably inferior to the more ancient. The possible compromise in this struggle between early generations, with their outdated strategy of salvation, and the changed horizons of the new age, was exegesis.

The problematics of exegesis and the ways in which it reflects not only Scripture itself, but the literal sense as well, is discussed in chapters 2 and 3. Here we merely point out the tactics of a culture in its second phase, in the stage of solidification and institutionalization, when it employs a variety of means in order to strengthen its authority. Foremost among these, as we have said, are the revitalization of Scripture by way of "creative exegesis," drawn from the new ontology, and the dissemination of the exegetical version of the newly dominant culture.

Stagnation and collapse

In its third phase of development, a culture becomes routinized in a self-evident ontology, a reality that now feels like "second nature" and no longer elicits wonder. The matter-of-fact overcomes, then silences, the enigmatic and the querying. A culture into which creators have poured their energies, whose life's blood has watered its network of meanings for the redemption of the world, now becomes a unit of given facts, a heritage that stands on its own, seemingly impervious to change, to be accepted as it is, as in the first bloom of its youth. Objectivization and dogmatization are symptoms of this stage. The gnawing from within, however, grows more insistent, and the meanings begin to decay and disintegrate. New creative forces are waiting to rise from the underground. It should, however, be reiterated that we cannot expect to find a clear, straight line of progression from one phase to the next. History is full of disjunctions and fluctuations, and leaps are more often the rule than slow evolution. Nonetheless, we can distinguish in the development of a culture at least those three phases we have listed. The third phase deserves particular attention, and we shall elaborate on it now, as we summarize the entire theory of cultures.

No culture undertakes to build its edifice without a proper strategy for the successful resolution of the problems and anxieties that afflict the times. Every historical document, whether a written text or an archeological finding in clay or stone, hints at the entire strategy, or at least at a part of it. Every document embodies the effort to overthrow the burden of defects stacked upon a culture; it can be understood in the light of the transactions carried on at the time by the members of the culture with one another and with their predecessors. The novelty of a culture is that, armed with its strategy, it opens up new avenues of salvation for its builders-members. It is not easy, however, to find candid formulations of the proposed strategies. Israel's cultures do not always openly acknowledge the need for change or adjustment. But even in the Talmudic and Rabbinic cultures, there evolved a number of rules that were meant to justify, even demand, a strategy of change. These were known as "instructions for the hour," "the need of the hour," "the times require it," and the like.

No culture can emerge from naught; if the forerunning culture has been utterly destroyed, a new one cannot simply arise from its ashes. Yet, clearly, the convulsions of crisis and destruction do open up new opportunities. Every new culture is buoyed precisely when faith in the ability of the preceding culture to console and redeem begins to falter. This progressive undermining lays bare the failings of the previous strategy and of the entire

preceding ontology. And in this respect there is no difference whether faith
has been undermined by external or internal causes. Every culture struggles
to rise from its underground position as a counter-culture into conditions
that will promote the penetration of its consciousness, its ontology, into the
hearts and minds of the general public.

Attempts to salvage from the ruins

Each culture is first triggered by a real experience of conflagration and
collapse, or by the perception of imminent conflagration and collapse. The
builders of the new culture seek to salvage whatever they can, or need, from
the ruins of the old culture. They may congratulate themselves upon the
sacred rescue-mission they have performed and may ascribe their motives
to dutiful devotion to the fathers and reverence for the system of meanings
the latter had erected. Indeed it is notable that aside from occasional
acrimonious outbursts of controversy in times of extreme crisis, Israel's
cultures generally did not ill treat each other.[13] What the members of a
culture do not like, they simply leave to oblivion; whatever appeals to them
as a life-giving draught, they utilize, their aim being to draw unto their
fledgling culture the sanctity and authority of venerated predecessors. Every
one of Israel's cultures luxuriates in the past; it gathers, preserves, and
remembers. But, as we have explained, it also scatters, forgets, and buries.
No matter how hard a culture fights for its life, no matter how insistently it
keeps claiming that it is a unified, complete entity, no single element of
which may be rejected (like that stone-structured dome in the Rabbis'
famous metaphor of the Torah, where the dislodgement of a single stone
brings about the collapse of the entire dome), these claims now go
unheeded. This kind of disregard for a ruling culture's directives, the
disregard that ventures to pick and choose at its convenience ("the whole
Torah is from Heaven, except a single point, a particular *ad majus* deduction
or a certain *gezerah shawa*," *San.* 99a) elicited from the Talmudic Rabbis the
sharp rebuke contained in the verse: "He has brought the word of the Lord
into contempt" (Num. 15.31).[14] These admonitions notwithstanding, new
cultures always seemed bent on undermining the entire dome, so that some
building-blocks could be thrown out and others reused for their own new
edifices.

The cultures of Israel may at first glance appear as an accretion of
meanings, many of which have been relegated to deepest oblivion. Yet
Israel's cultural heritage is not a graveyard in whch meanings lie buried in
the dust of ages with not a hope of resurrection. Rather, meanings lie side by
side, or one on top of another, awaiting the sound of the trumpet that will
awaken them to return and serve the needs of the living, either in their
original meaning, or in a changed form, according to the needs of
subsequent ages.

Final eclipse

Tradition refers to the collapse of a culture as "forgetting" ("When the Torah was forgotten from Israel"), whereas the building and buttressing of a new culture is referred to as "establishing." The Talmud mentions a number of "forgettings" and "establishments" in the history of Israel: "For in ancient times when the Torah was forgotten from Israel, Ezra came up from Babylon and established it. (Some of) it was again forgotten, and Hillel the Babylonian came up and established it" (*Suk.* 20a). I interpret these expressions as hints that empower the superordinating concepts of Judaism (i.e. God, Torah, Israel) to assume new meanings in accordance with the changed needs of the age, in other words, as hints at a culture's collapse and the beginnings of a new one.

The chasm that separates between the Talmudic and Biblical cultures is nowhere better illustrated than in the *aggadic* story we mentioned earlier about Moses who ascended to Heaven and found the Holy One, "engaged in affixing coronets to the letters of the Law" (*Men.* 29b). The idea here is that the Torah cannot be placed in the hands of Moses without these "coronets," because Rabbi Akiba will in the future "expound upon each tittle heaps and heaps of laws." When Moses wishes to hear what Torah scholars, post-dating him by many generations, are talking about, he seats himself in a distant back row and listens to their discourse upon the law. But he is unable to "follow their arguments." So wide has the gap grown between his Torah and theirs that his spirit is weakened, his strength deserts him, and he is not consoled until he hears Rabbi Akiba say, in response to his pupils' challenge as to the source of a certain *halachah*: "It is a law given unto Moses at Sinai".[15]

And indeed how could a member of the Biblical culture, one of its chief architects no less, understand the thought processes, the language and style of a member of the Talmudic culture? The entire language of the Mishnah is alien to a member of the Biblical culture, the language of the Gemarah even more so. For language is not merely a tool or a form. It is a most fundamental construct in the organization of knowledge and wisdom, and a change in language entirely alters not only cognitive conception, but also sense perception. Language enters into the very marrow of experience and thought, and imbues the latter's capacity to conjure sights and crystallize general concepts. The *aggadah* story cited above makes clear that each culture speaks its own language of concepts, metaphors, and symbols, and that consequently it is difficult for its members to understand the language of another culture, and virtually impossible to grasp finer nuances and deeper meanings. This is the reason for corrupted meanings and for misunderstandings between cultures.

Another observation about the disintegration and collapse of cultures is, I believe, that not one of Israel's cultures vanished from the world as a result merely of internal exhaustion. True, after a certain period of time, every culture begins to show signs of fatigue, its power to console and redeem wanes. But more often than not, closure came upon a culture due to ravages, expulsions, and catastrophes from without. It is difficult, of course, to calculate accurately the true relationship between an end resulting from a depletion of energies, an arrival at an impasse, and an end that descends, unforeseen, from without. Perhaps both modes of decline are interconnected. This is how the author of *Seder olam zuta* ("Brief Order of the World," a chronicle of unknown date, probably from the sixth to eighth centuries) described the end of the Talmudic culture: "After the court of Rav Ashi, Israel was dispersed a great dispersion, and disputes increased, and the roads fell into disrepair, and the study of Torah declined."[16] Internal and external factors are indistinguishably interwoven in this statement.

I myself tend to believe that certain cultures, especially the Biblical and the Poetic-Philosophic, had their lives cut short before realizing their full creative potential. In contrast, the Rabbinic culture has arrived at an impasse: its output continues to pile up with no fertilization from without and with little inspiration from within. The tremendous forces it commanded in its heyday, which could, in the midst of harsh exile and debilitating persecutions, brighten and lend dignity to the life of east European Jewry, began to ebb in the eighteenth century. For a while it revived again when Ḥassidism injected the vitality and enthusiasm of the Mystical soteriology into the waning Rabbinic ontology. But when the foundations of the Jewish reality upon which the Rabbinic ontology was based began to weaken, the Rabbinic culture could no longer rule as before. I attempted to prove elsewhere[17] that this undermining of Rabbinic supremacy had occurred well before the actual collapse of the guardian walls of tradition in the French Revolution. The earth-shaking events that occurred outside the ghettos did not come as a surprise to western European Jews. True, the Emancipation was the product of non-Jewish visions, but the transformation that had paved its way in the Jewish world was the result of internal choices. Some time later, I was gratified to find my analysis supported by Benzion Dinur,[18] who, contrary to commonly held belief, thought that the changes taking place in European Jewry did not result from the onslaught of the Jewish Enlightenment, the Haskalah. The Maskilim's critique, according to Dinur, sought to salvage a world that was already disintegrating. The internal Jewish world had begun to break down earlier, following the failure of the Sabbatean movement, and as a result of the new ontology that had begun to penetrate certain circles in the upper stratum of western European Jewry. These became the creators of the Emancipation culture. Once the foundations of the new ontology were embraced by a large public, the Rabbinic tradition lost its status in western countries. But it continued to exist, and in the State of Israel it has even experienced a recent revival.

The wealth of Jewish cultures

The age-old Jewish world stretches before us in richness and breadth, embracing in its generous fold at least seven large provinces, which we have designated as the cultures of Israel. It is tempting, of course, to gloss over the glaring discrepancies between one culture and another by insisting, as tradition has so often done, that whatever appears novel is simply a facsimile of an older original, which alone is worth preserving. Indeed, the gates of interpretation were never closed, but historical honesty requires that we note both sides of the coin: the seven cultures have much in common, to be sure, but the distinctions separating them cannot be disregarded; the continuity is there, but the ruptures must be taken into account too. It is precisely because these distinctions amount to such fundamentally different ontologies that the question must be posed: what is it that sets Judaism apart as a unity within diversity and as a continuity amidst change (if indeed it possesses a unique essence). The term "unique" used here conveys neither a complimentary nor a pejorative connotation, but simply suggests a sense of difference and distinction, in the spirit of the Rabbis' testimony about Israel that "Israel are distinguished by their ways from all other nations" (*M.K.* 16b).[19] Every culture is "distinguished" from its neighbors and Israel, clearly, did not quite resemble any other nation. Even if we do not appreciate the opinion that "*all* of Israel's deeds are stranger than those of all the nations of the world" (*Pesikta Rabbah*, 15), many of its deeds are clearly "separate unto themselves" (*Exod. Rabbah*, 15), unlike the ways of other nations, separate and unique. Similarly, the same recognition of distinctness must be accorded to Israel's seven cultures. From this wealth of cultures stems the uniqueness of the *totality* of Jewish history.

The pity of it is that over the ages much of this wealth has been lost. Time and time again Israel's treasure houses were plundered and decimated. Just as in the Middle Ages Jewish property and financial capital seldom endured in Jewish hands for more than three generations, so too the heritage of the spirit seldom survived intact. Catastrophes and persecutions precluded steady accumulation. But there was a deeper reason for the absence of accumulated spiritual capital, one which our theory of cultures readily accounts for: although each culture preserved and cultivated previous achievements, it also disqualified and rejected much of the old, to the point of transforming, often quite beyond recognition, even uncontroversial elements. It is a privilege of the modern historian to be able now to survey all seven cultures "as they were" and as they fancied themselves to be, together and individually; he alone is able to restore to long-buried and rusted treasures their brilliant luster of old.

Our theory of cultures should forestall the facile optimism of historical functionalism as it has occasionally appeared in the social sciences, especially in sociology and anthropology, whereby whatever serves the community in its struggle against adversaries or natural catastrophes is thought to be preserved in its culture, while that which is ineffective is supposedly rejected and forgotten. The Rabbis of the Talmud had already unwittingly propounded this kind of functionalism: whatever the generation required, they said, was preserved, and whatever it did not require, disappeared. More recent historians like S. Dubnov and R. Mahler held a similar view.

My observation has been that every culture also preserved gross misjudgments, retrogressive notions, and withered wisdoms that were of little benefit to the living in their day, much less so after they had passed, while the excellent was not always cherished. The creative momentum of each culture was not spared blunders and absurdities, and these too continued their existence, to the detriment of the inheritors who now wish to take possession of their complete heritage. Moreover, we see plainly in Israel's history how difficult it was to bury anything with finality. That which had once been apocryphal literature, something external and contradictory to "Torah," was revealed in another culture as being of paramount importance. Those apocryphal visionary books shook off their dust in the Mystical culture and experienced a remarkable revival. We note, however, that in their second incarnation they made a more cautious appearance, hiding under the safe screen of great Talmudic names like Rabbi Simeon bar Yoḥai, Rabbi Israel the High Priest, Rabbi Akiba, or Rabbi Ḥanina ben Hakaneh.

Politics and culture: conflicts and tensions

The concept "culture" in this study refers to a framework of various types of meanings which are embodied, with a certain measure of permanence and in relative uniformity, in the deeds and institutions of the individual and the society, all geared toward the ultimate goal, redemption. We have explained that every culture is a network of meanings which shape personal and collective life-experiences by addressing the four main categories of human distress. Every culture is, therefore, in its essence soteriological, that is, it seeks to mend and to redeem, and this explains why religion figures so largely in culture, even when it takes a secular form: God, the supreme symbol of religion, is "the One performing grand salvation in the midst of the earth" (Ps. 74.12).[20]

But every culture is also a political phenomenon. Human beings forge their life-experiences in the inter-personal relations that activate their economic and political behavior, and in the prototypes they create for their thoughts and actions. This forging cannot take place outside the framework of existing meanings. Human beings find the fabric of their culture spread before them. It antedates their birth and it continues after their death. Nonetheless, their culture hinges on them, on their experiences, on their solution to the distresses of their existence. The relationship is therefore dialectic, complex, and bristling with tensions between the prerogatives of the individual and the public exigency. Superficially, it may appear that politics, which attempts to organize this relationship, is nothing but the battlefield upon which rights and privileges, properties and possessions, freedoms and servitudes are fought over. But the essence and source of this battle in our theory of cultures is the struggle over the right to define the cultures' meanings – their nature, their worth, their relative rank. The adversaries in the political arena fight over the organization of meanings; for a meaning must signify something, i.e. it does not deal so much with the private, narrow acts of individuals as with institutionalized public acts, such as a hand outstretched in greeting, or a public office. In this ceaseless battle, politics endow the meanings manifested in a society's conduct with relative stability, until it triumphs as a regnant meaning, accepted voluntarily by the majority, or imposed upon it. Aristotle already pointed out that politics was, due to its power to exercise authority, the most decisive "art" in life, "chief of all the arts."[21]

We conclude from all this that the controversies that animated Israel's cultures were political in nature, i.e. they were disputes over the interpretation of meanings: what do the superordinating concepts and the archetypal collective experiences mean, and how are they to be organized into a coherent system capable of exerting control in all spheres of life? Examples of these struggles can be found in all our cultures. The example I shall bring here, while it is perhaps political by its very nature in that it concerns the relations between Israel and the nations, nonetheless adequately illustrates, I believe, the point we wish to make.

We know that the early Hasmoneans waged war not only against the Seleucian rulers, but also against aliens residing in the Land of Israel, mainly in the Hellenistic towns surrounding Judaea, forcing upon them conversion to Judaism or exile. A town whose residents refused to accept Israel's Torah was destroyed and its people banished. A new concept emerged at this period: the "cleanness" of Eretz Israel versus the "uncleanness" of heathen lands. "Jose ben Jo'ezer of Zereda and Jose ben Joḥanan of Jerusalem decreed uncleanness in respect of the country of the heathens and glassware" (*Sab.* 14b).[22] Here we have the first Tanna'itic "pair," two of the early creators of the Talmudic culture, decreeing and instituting the Pharisaic notion that the Land of Israel was to be preserved "clean." On many issues the Hasmonean kings, in particular Alexander Jannaeus, failed to see eye to eye with the Pharisees, but this decree they gladly adopted: there was room in the Land of Israel for none but Jews and Judaized aliens. The extended meaning of the notion "uncleanness" was thus exploited to vindicate the Hasmonean conquests. The very extension of the concept was a political act that carried with it a number of important consequences during the Second Temple and thereafter.[23]

Trailblazers and rearguards

The creative endeavor engages a range of talents: innovators, renovators, vanguards, always some romantics, and also parasites feeding on crumbs left over from earlier creators. The concept of culture proposed here explains the phenomenon of van- and rearguards by clarifying the methods advocated by a culture for its soteriological strategy. We see plainly how some of the bold innovators ventured far out ahead of the pack to define and organize meanings into a new cultural framework, yet their message remained unheeded – the hour was not ripe, or their strategy ineffectual. Others, no less innovative, enveloped their message in venerable old trappings, which seemed at the time to contain no novelty at all; only some time later was the seemingly conventional message recognized as having blazed forth a trail toward a new culture.

An example of this phenomenon may be drawn from the history of the Poetic-Philosophic culture. We know that Jews in antiquity, i.e. in the first two cultures, did not incline toward rational cognition, the kind that is acquired through "objective" observation and abstraction. In this their creativity differed from that of the Greeks, who had invented the concept "theory" (from the verb *theiatei*, meaning to observe phenomena, as also in the word "theater," another word derived from that same root). The man of theory observed the unfolding events of existence, but refrained from intervening in them. The ancient Hebrew also acquired wisdom, but this wisdom expressed itself in affinity for his family, his people, and his God, a spiritual affinity of religious devotion. During the first two cultures he thought in terms of the perceptible. His abstract concepts were few, although in one such concept the early Jew arrived at the summit of abstraction, in breadth and in power. That, of course, was the idea of a God entirely inconceivable by means of the sense perceptions. Generally, however, knowledge was acquired by a Jew in ancient times as something he experienced "in all his bones," in his body and soul, in love and in fear, in anger and in joy. As a result of the strong imprint left by the first two cultures on the entire history of Israel, this early mode of non-abstract cognition is apparent in subsequent cultures as well.

It is possible, of course, to speak of "Jewish philosophy" during Biblical and Talmudic times, and many scholars have indeed presented the basic concepts of the Prophets and the Rabbis as systematic creations. Scholars have especially admired the abstraction of certain Talmudic aphorisms which seem to encapsulate a comprehensive theology, sayings like: "Everything is in the hands of Heaven, except fear of Heaven" (*Ber.* 33b).

The keenness and succinctness that characterize conceptual definitions in a number of Talmudic sayings bear witness to an experienced use of fine-tuned conceptual tools, resembling those used by the Greeks. Best known perhaps for the vigor of their conciseness and abstraction are the maxims in the *Ethics of the Fathers* (*Pirkei ʾavot*). But, in general, one may safely say that Jewish thought prior to the Poetic-Philosophic culture had not acquired systematic form. Problems were conceived disconnectedly, with little thought of fusing them into a comprehensive intellectual unity. There had been some early attempts at systematization, but failing to gain recognition as innovations, they had left little mark. The prevailing strategy of their culture did not permit such innovators to sail out and chart new courses, and they were thought in their time to be no more than an additional prop to the already existing cultural edifice.

Philo of Alexandria (*c.* 20 BCE–40 CE) was an exception. This seminal thinker devised a theological system not unlike those created in a later period by the Poetic-Philosophic culture. But he himself, despite the influence he exercised over the development of Christian thought ("from Philo to Spinoza," in H.A. Wolfson's famous thesis),[24] was little known among his own people and was not revealed as a precursor of the Poetic-Philosophic culture until that culture belatedly discovered him in the sixteenth century. During his lifetime Philo had no influence on Jewish thinking; the Talmudic culture, in the upward momentum of its swing to power, rejected and buried any work tainted by the encounter with Greece. Thus, it was only upon the second encounter between Greek thought and Judaism, through the mediation of Islam, that a Jewish Poetic-Philosophic culture was finally created. In ancient times, the conditions for its development were more favorable in the Hellenistic diaspora than in Eretz Israel, where the soteriological strategy of the Pharisees had already become entrenched.

This kind of reintroduction of ancient, previously ignored, sources occurs also in the Mystical culture. It is possible that the roots of the Mystical culture go back to antiquity. In the Talmudic culture one finds strong intimations of opinions that became prevalent in the late mysticism, which would explain why the *Zohar* was attributed to Rabbi Simeon bar Yoḥai and his son, and to their disciples. But the Mystical culture did not become a full-fledged and large-scale ontology until those early intimations had undergone major transformations. Those who were later thought of as the initiators of the Mystical culture were not recognized as such in their day, and it is quite possible that they had never intended to initiate this culture at all.

The concept "culture" as a heuristic tool

Thus far we have given preliminary explanations on the theory of Israel's seven cultures. It is difficult, however, to conclude this introductory chapter without some additional elucidation of the primary concept in our study, namely the concept "culture." Our theory is anchored on an understanding of the comprehensive context of historical research in general and of the research methods used. This theoretical basis radiates in many directions. The following deals with the methodological aspects of the concept "culture" and with its meanings in a number of research areas. This explanation will, I believe, bring out the unique nature of our theory.

The nature of the model

Immersed in the tide of historical processes, man is ill equipped to grasp the entire meaning of human (or Jewish) history, for history is never at a standstill point of conclusion and consummation. It is forever in flux toward an unknown future. Those who view the whole of history as one completed unit of the past, lacking an outreach toward the future, invariably drift into foggy speculation and vain casuistry. On the other hand, even though it is unwise to seek one meaning for the whole of history, it is difficult to observe its phenomena and proceedings without wishing to endow them with meaning: what "really" happened, we ask, and what was the nature and purpose of these deeds and events? But while it is vain, in my opinion, to pursue "the meaning of history," it is certainly quite legitimate to look for the meanings of specific events and acts. In particular, we can seek and discover those meanings and intentions that the participants themselves saw in their history, we can examine and find out how they explained to themselves and to others the occurrences of their lives. On this point it is surely possible, based on the sources, to arrive at some kind of "true" assessment. How to interpret sources accurately is in itself a difficult problem, and we shall have occasion to return to it in chapter 8. Here we merely wish to stress that the idea that there could be a meaning for the whole of history is a dubious and hazy ideological concept, and we have no use for it except by way of negation: to distance ourselves from its fallacy and from those who have embraced it and lost their way in its labyrinth. But we do have a keen interest in the meanings that former generations imputed to the events of their own times, to their ontology, to their institutions and actions. In this kind of empirical research, it is possible to discover units of meanings and arrangements of orders and disorders that I have labeled cultures.

The concept "culture" is used here as a heuristic model for the study of Israel's history. Theories of scientific method, as well as theories of cognition and of language in the philosophical systems current today, distinguish different types of models. There is, for example, a model that is meant to represent the modeled object, but in altered proportions, such as a miniature airplane. Then there is a model which, by its attributes or actions, sets out to imitate the original, as when a private act of charity serves as a metaphor of the entire idea of charity. In religious language it was said that a man must imitate the attributes of the Holy One: "Just as He is gracious and compassionate, so be thou gracious and compassionate . . . as He clothes the naked . . . so do thou also clothe the naked" (*Sab.* 133b). For the uses of research, however, it is the heuristic model that is particularly useful; it is a construct that guides the researcher in acquiring knowledge, as, for example, Bohr's model of the atom, or Freud's model of the psyche. Whatever its type, the model parallels certain qualities of the original, but it never itemizes or exhausts them all. Hence the rather extreme claim of one thinker: "There is no such thing as a perfectly faithful model; only by being unfaithful in *some* respect can a model represent its original."[25] Disregard of this basic fact leads to an erroneous interpretation of the model's behavior. In some measure the model resembles all human means of expression that attempt to elucidate the enigmatic and the arcane by way of "transference." These linguistic forms are called metaphors, i.e. comparisons that "lend" or "transfer" the meanings from a tangible item to an abstract object, or vice versa. "The model functions as a more general kind of metaphor."[26]

Thus "culture" is for us a symbolic representation of a very specific reality, contrived for the purpose of describing and explaining the history of Israel. The unit "culture" is a construct devised for the purpose of understanding, and the researcher labors to bring it as near as possible to "reality as it was," fully aware all the while that it is quite impossible for it to be reality "as it was" in its entirety. Absent this awareness, he falls into an error in categorization, stripping the model of its metaphoric character as though it were entirely materialized in reality. The concept "culture" as it is used here, is akin to Max Weber's concept of the "ideal type."[27]

Hegel proffered the concept of the state as a heuristic model of this kind. His philosophy of history postulated the state as the primary historical unit and in this context Hegel discussed the kingdoms of China, India, and Persia, as well as the Napoleonic empire. These states were in his view both the patent subjects of history and the units of meanings through which one could understand the historical process. The error in this construct was that it ignored whatever was not state, and lumped together in one state the history of many nations over a very long period of time. Hegel's Kingdom of Persia, for instance, included, through the entire millenium of its existence, all of Assyria, Babylonia, Egypt, Judaea, and Samaria.

Other well-known heuristic models have been postulated, usually, as in the case of Hegel, with little discrimination as to their nature and functions, by Oswald Spengler ("Kultur"), Erich Voeglin ("configuration") and Arnold Toynbee ("civilization").[28] Toynbee's concept of "challenge and response" is reminiscent of Hegel's thesis, antithesis, and synthesis, but they are less dialectical and more emotional. In fact, they are rooted in Scripture. The Bible, remarked Toynbee, is deeply ingrained in our hearts, though we may not be aware of this. The Bible frequently addresses the individual in calls, commandments, warnings, or as Toynbee puts in, in challenges: the first man is challenged not to eat from the Tree of Knowledge; Noah is challenged to build an ark; Abraham is called to "go forth," etc. Success is obtained by a straightforward response; failure results from a distorted response (also known as sin). The challenge–response model is quite different from the model of cause and effect in natural phenomena.[29]

In one respect the soteriological concept of culture that I have presented here coincides with Toynbee's view that the essence of history is always the story of religion, for example, that the rivalry between paganism and Christianity in Greece and Rome, and the eventual conversion of the pagans to the Christian faith, was a decisive factor in ancient history. Metaphysical philosophers of history have always set their hearts on analyses of world history that would encompass in their grand sweep the entire historical horizon revealed to them. The study of the details they left to historians. They assumed that history indeed revealed a coherent structure, not a chaotic hodge-podge of countless order-resistant details. History was basically a forward-march which might be experienced as progress or evolution, as a cyclical recurrence, or at some other rates of change, or any other combinations of the above, as, for example, that history repeated itself partly in cycles and partly in forward motion, like the revolving of a wheel that swiftly propels the vehicle forward while spinning around itself in cycles.

Closest to our own model of culture is Pitirim A. Sorokin's concept of "systems of culture,"[30] of which there are basically three: the ideational, the sensate, and the idealistic. There are also mixed systems of cultures. Both the basic systems and the satellite combinations have highs and lows, whose rate and occurrence Sorokin calculated with precision. All the cultures of the world are built on the basic system or on a combination of systems.

Two concepts in the study of culture today

The concept "culture" is set forth here in contradistinction to the two definitions of the term that are most current today in scientific discourse and in everyday language: the humanistic definition and the anthropological-sociological definition. Each is based on a different conception. The humanistic conception reserves the word "culture" for only one set of human creations. Not every individual or group action, not every public institution can be considered a product of culture. Culture and public activity are not synonymous notions. The humanistic conception holds it as self-evident that a community can produce a variety of required tools and artifacts, as well as opinions and beliefs. The question is, what are the special qualities that make these a unit worthy of the designation "culture." Not every human proceeding can be dignified by this name.

The humanistic concept is normative-evaluative: good manners and refined taste, works of art and thought, everything beautiful and noble belongs to culture. It makes sense, therefore, to say that absent a literature or art, certain people, and even entire nations, have no culture. Being normative, the conception distinguishes between high and low levels of culture. The humanistic conception, consciously or unconsciously, presupposes (but seldom concedes openly) that there exists a world of universal, general, and human values operative throughout all the expanses of geography and the transformations of history, and that it is possible to determine objectively who generates and supports such values and who rejects and subverts them. Certain details of this objective evaluation may fall prey to disagreements, but the prevailing rule declares: wherever there are no universal values, there you find a low culture, even barbarism, regardless of tools and artifacts. The concept "culture," therefore, stands in opposition to barbarism, lack of culture, primitiveness, etc. Furthermore, some groups possess a high culture while others have inferior cultures. A group that has embraced universal values and lives by them is said to possess a high culture, whereas a group that seals itself off in ethnocentric tribalism has a culture of the inferior sort, if it can be thought to have a culture at all.

Art, literature, philosophy, and religion are the foundations of culture, according to the humanistic concept; some in this school of thought emphasize in particular the religious element. T.S. Eliot, for example, believed "that no culture has appeared or developed except together with a religion." Moreover, only religion imparts order and tradition, without which a culture cannot achieve any kind of internal spiritual integration. Because of the decline of religion in our day, western society lacks a true culture, according to Eliot.[31]

The anthropological-sociological concept emphatically rejects the normative-evaluative approach. In this view, works of art, religion, and philosophy are only a portion, and not necessarily the choice portion, of culture as a whole. They may be noble in the eyes of its members, but in the eyes of the examining researcher they deserve no preference and should be treated no differently from other more prosaic components of culture. Culture, said the great anthropologist A.L. Kroeber, is "the mass of learned and transmitted motor reactions, habits, techniques, ideas and values – and the behavior they induce."[32]

The anthropological-sociological concept recoils from evaluation: everything human belongs to culture and there is no basis for any preference of one element over others. Culture is beyond good and evil, beauty and ugliness. The notion that culture is the totality of all life's experiences, rather than the result of exerted powers and talents, produces a neutral and tolerant conception of culture. This conception has had a long intellectual history, originating from the polemics between biological determinism and speculative philosophy (such as Hegel's). Culture is the totality of a group's actions, and the outcomes of its actions, in relation to its environment, everything that individual and society acquire and organize through their power and talents in accordance with their needs. This is how the concept was defined by Tylor and other early anthropologists and most sociologists have followed this definition. The need for neutrality in scientific inquiry contributed to the spread of this concept in our times.[33]

The new approach

The concept "culture" that I employ in this study is neither humanistic nor anthropological-sociological. It shares with both concepts the emphasis on the special dimension of human endeavors in history, which are not products of instinctual automatism, as biological determinism would have it. It holds that even though culture belongs to the realm of the living and requires a corporeal body and world in which to reveal itself, beliefs and principles, art and technology, language and institutions are not transmitted from generation to generation via biological channels. The Torah, as we know, is not passed on in inheritance, but is acquired in the exertions of creativity and perseverance. But in contrast to these two primary theories of culture, the concept we have offered here distinguishes in culture three dimensions. The entire concept has been labeled "soteriological" in order to emphasize the third, most important, dimension. A soteriological conception which defines culture, any culture, as a system of meanings expressing a three-dimensional public ontology that includes individual and corporate redemption, cannot be narrowed to a definition of culture as the sum of men's "adjustment to their surroundings," as Sumner and Keller proposed.[34]

The emphasis on the struggle waged by human beings in order to change the conditions of their life so as to mend the world and to redeem themselves does not disregard the minutiae of everyday living, or economic and political issues, nor the evil and the ugly that require mending. The mundane tools, the clothes, and methods in which meanings are embodied are not dismissed in aristocratic disdain, for in this concept culture is not the outcome of an ethereal spirituality hovering in rarefied spheres of abstraction.

The proof of a concept's strength is in its fecundity. The test for this new conception of Israel's history is, therefore, its power to understand and to illuminate. The principal thesis of our study, as it has been presented in this introductory chapter, now requires proof and illustration. This the following chapters propose to do as they deal with methods of Scriptural exegesis, with conceptions of the *mitzvot* in the different cultures, with problems of tensions and legitimation, and with historical perspectivism. We begin with the Bible, that cradle of all Jewish cultures, how its interpretations changed and how it was changed by interpretation.

2

INTERPRETATION OF SCRIPTURE
IN ISRAEL'S CULTURES

Our study postulates that each one of Israel's cultures understood Scripture in its distinctly unique way. The profound differences in how the Bible was interpreted, and how its sanctity was valued, clearly demonstrate that any notion of there being but one single Jewish culture cannot be entertained except metaphorically. Nothing could better illustrate the fundamental differences between the seven ontologies than the wide variance in interpretations of Scripture itself. Before we begin our discussion of exegetical methods in a number of Israel's cultures (not all can be analyzed in the limited space of this study), we shall classify the methods of interpretation into five types. A clearly defined classification of interpretational approaches should help us understand the nature of interpretatio in general, and of Biblical interpretation in particular, and should reveal the originality of the comparative method we are advancing here. Our method sets out not only to explain texts; it aspires to a "hermeneutics of cultures," to an understanding of how each one of Israel's cultures relates to the Bible itself, and how it relates to the preceding cultures' understanding of the Bible. We thus venture beyond Scriptural exegesis into a realm where entire cultures comprehensively interpret each other. This cultural hermeneutics is the foundation of the comparative method that I propose.

Five types of interpretation

How the Bible was interpreted in each of Israel's cultures can first teach us something about interpretation in general. Let us consider these five major major types of interpretation:

1 *Reconstructive* interpretation sets out to explain a text without straying beyond the boundaries of the assumptions underlying that text or, to use Abraham Ibn Ezra's (1092–1167) famous metaphor in the introduction to his commentary on the Bible, "If the truth is like the center point inside the circle," then this kind of interpretation strives toward the "center point of

the circle,"[1] to reconstruct the intention of the writer as it had originally been conceived. Modern interpretational theory would say that this interpretation is situated inside the "hermeneutic circle." The image of the circle in textual criticism has become a basic conceptual tool for scholars of hermeneutics, from Schleiermacher and Dilthey in the nineteenth century down to Heidegger and Gadamer more recently.[2] Schleiermacher maintained that it was impossible to interpret an individual verse without comprehending the full text, just as the full text could not be grasped without understanding the individual verse. The whole is understood through its parts, and the parts can only be understood in the context of the whole. The reconstructive interpretation penetrates this circle, enters within the horizon of the writer's culture, embracing the assumptions that underlie his opinions and beliefs, and the modes in which these are expressed. This interpretative work has registered varying degrees of success and failure, and one should be careful to distinguish the simplistic from the sophisticated, the innocently credulous from the critical-scientific. But regardless of their level of sophistication, these reconstruction methods are all within Ibn Ezra's "circle," within the hermeneutic circle, or within the horizon of assumptions underlying the interpreted text. This is illustrated by Scriptures interpreting one another, Talmudic Sages interpreting their peers, Biblical scholars attempting to reconstruct texts and their meanings.

2   The second type of interpretation is one I have called *creative* or *constructive*. We have already had occasion to refer to it in chapter 1 and shall elaborate on it a little further on. This interpretation is, in Ibn Ezra's words, "outside the circle's periphery": it is an interpretation that invades the horizon of the subject-text from the realm of another culture, and is nurtured by the assumptions underlying that other culture.

In scriptural exegesis this interpretation can be *midrashic*, or philosophic, or mystical, or rabbinic, depending on the culture doing the interpreting, as we shall see in a moment. The creative interpretation sets out to correct the underlying assumptions of the interpreted text, to alter and adapt them, but not to destroy them altogether.

3   In contrast to the creative-constructive interpretation, the *destructive* interpretation entirely uproots the underlying assumptions of the interpreted text, virtually turning the text inside out, or upside down. In the generations of traditional faith, interpreters of this brand were labeled *minim* (heretics); Ibn Ezra calls them "distorters," and to this category he assigns the Sadducees, the Karaites, and "whoever does not believe in the words of the bearers of religious tradition." For a modern example of this kind of interpretation, we will take a look at Freud's theory on Moses and the origin

of monotheism. The concept of a destructive interpretation is, of course, somewhat polemical; we must bear in mind that every upbuilding of a new culture was attended by subversion and destruction from an opposing culture.

4   The fourth type of interpretation is the *critical-scientific* method current today. This method, too, hopes to reconstruct the text, but the underlying assumptions of the text, especially as they relate to opinions and beliefs, are regarded as factual "givens." Their value is neutralized and put, as it were, between parentheses. The values themselves are material for objective research. The modern scholar and secular reader of the Bible regards the beliefs and opinions as a sort of *epoche*, i.e. he shrinks from judgmental valuations, because he believes that preference accorded to one value over another will invalidate his effort to view the text in complete objectivity.

Here we see a deflection of interest from the literal and syntactical deciphering of words, verses, chapters, and books (which had been paramount to the reconstructive interpretation), toward an interest in the texts themselves and the stages of their development. The text is analyzed and broken down into components in a philological-historical manner, in order to penetrate the original version and identify earlier and later renditions. By sifting through various versions, one hopes to arrive at the "original."

5   As a sequel to this type of interpretation, I wish to propose a *comparative-perspectivistic* approach, which takes into account the interpretational methods employed in *all* of Israel's cultures: their assumptions, their methods, and their relation to one another. What I have in mind is a new and extensive plan – a study not only of how the Bible was interpreted, but also of how each culture interpreted itself and its fellow cultures. The following chapters will illustrate this new method of interpretation by showing how three traditional cultures – the Talmudic, the Poetic-Philosophic, and the Mystical – interpreted the Song of Songs (chapter 3) and how they explained the rationale for the commandments (chapter 4).

The essence of the new method is that at the foundation of a culture's interpretation of the Bible there lies a certain conception of reality, one which embraces the meaning of Jewish history, its superordinating concepts – God, Torah, Israel – and its archetypal collective experiences and the meaning of human existence in general. This conception of reality is not an intellectual construct. It is nurtured by specific historical, physical and spiritual events and deeds, which are drawn into the focus of attention in accordance with their relative significance in that culture's ontology. But, before we go into the details of the new method, let us consider for a moment the essence of the other four types of interpretations we have listed. The reconstructive interpretation is perhaps the least interesting of the five; much more intriguing is the creative-constructive approach. The new method, I hope, will prove to be the most fruitful of all.

Secular vs. religious interpretations

It is a commonplace that every source and written document that comes down to us from the past undergoes the winnowing process of interpretation. We need hardly say that this is all the more true where the Bible is concerned. Clearly, a wide gulf separates traditional Biblical exegesis from modern secular interpretations. In a secular age, the first and second types of interpretations we have described, the reconstructive and the creative, will recede to make room for the destructive, the critical-scientific, and the comparative-perspectivistic methods. In fact, the differences in our five types of interpretation provide an accurate index of the nature and the workings of secularization. The generations of traditional religious faith – Talmudic, Poetic-Philosophic, Mystical, Rabbinic – enshrined the Bible at the center of their culture; the Bible, inspired by the Holy Spirit, was a true testimony of God's will, and the highest wisdom revealed to man. They saw their own world reflected in it. Their opinions, beliefs, and all their life-styles were validated in the Biblical inspiration. The Bible, as far as they were concerned, taught an ontology that was valid for its own time and for all times, conveying eternal truth and the precise demands enjoined by this truth in ever shifting circumstances. Answers to the personal and collective dilemmas of human existence were to be sought, and found, in it. Secularism, on the other hand, does not look to the Bible for these answers and does not accept its commandments, warnings, and admonitions as absolutely binding. The Bible is regarded as an important work in the history of cultures, its special status as a book hallowed throughout the ages may even be acknowledged, but it remains essentially a book created by and for human beings, and is subject to interpretation like any other historical document.

The great transformation from faith to secularism is reflected in the attitudes toward the assumptions underlying each culture. The cultures of traditional faith accepted the basic premise that the Bible was a divinely inspired book of laws and wisdom, which they were bound to observe and preserve. They disagreed over the rationale for these laws and over the nature of the wisdom, but the underlying assumptions remained unchallenged. In contrast, the secular interpretation has no interest in the underlying assumptions. It stands outside the hermeneutic circle, and discusses Scripture objectively, taking care not to usurp the past. Aided by linguistic, grammatical, and rhetorical tools, it seeks to uncover the text's literal meaning, as it was intended by its early writers, without passing judgment on the validity of this meaning.

Creative interpretation in the cultures of faith
Ezra and Neḥemiah – a beginning of Biblical interpretation

Let us now look at the principal features of the creative-constructive interpretational method. The beginning is actually found in the Bible itself, in the Books of Ezra and Neḥemiah, but the first truly exemplary application of this method is to be found in the Talmud. The adjective "creative" in this context was coined by my teacher, Professor Isaak Heinemann,[3] who characterized the Talmudic-Midrashic interpretational method as "creative philology." I take the liberty of borrowing this phrase for my purposes.

Exegesis of the Bible properly began in the period of the Second Temple, at the early stages of the emergent Talmudic culture. True, the word ‎"פרש"‎ itself appears in the Bible on two earlier occasions, but in the sense of "explanation" and "elucidation," as the Rabbis used it, this word appears only in the Book of Neḥemiah: "They read from the book of the law of God clearly [and] made its sense plain" (Neḥ. 8.8). The Book of Neḥemiah relates that after the return from the Babylonian exile, Ezra (*c.* 430 BCE) and the heads of the re-established Judaean community read the Torah in Jerusalem "clearly, made its sense plain and gave instruction in what was read." When they came to the verse "that no Ammonite or Moabite should ever enter the assembly of God" (Neḥ. 13.1), they proceeded to separate "all who were of mixed blood" from the body of Israel. Now, the Bible had indeed commanded: "No Ammonite or Moabite, even unto the tenth generation, shall become a member of the Assembly of the Lord" (Deut. 23.3), but did this mean that *no* foreigner, of any ethnic extraction whatsoever, could ever intermarry with Israel?

Here is a vivid illustration of the tremendous power exercised by Biblical exegesis on the nation's life. Clearly, Ezra was not simply a quick "scribe," a sort of nimble copier of old scrolls, but a Sage and a teacher, driven to instruct his people and to make the Bible the law of Israel: "For Ezra had devoted himself to the study and observance of the law of the Lord and to teaching statute and ordinance in Israel" (Ezra 7.10). We know that Ezra had been authorized by the Persian rulers to appoint judges to assist him in this task, an authority which he apparently successfully wrenched from the priests, whom he regarded as having led the nation astray in the practice of the law. Ezra replaced the priests with a new brand of religious intelligentsia, trained under his tutelage to lead the people in the light of his own ideas.[4]

Disagreements on how the Bible was to be construed immediately cropped up: the leaders and magistrates, even the sons of the High Priest, had been "the chief offenders" (Ezra 9.2), freely marrying into Ammonite

and Samaritan families. The returning exiles from Babylonia did not regard
the contemporary inhabitants of the land of Ammon and Moab as
descendants of the ancient Pentateuchal Ammonites and Moabites, and,
consequently, did not view intermarriage with these and other "foreigners"
as contrary to the law. Moreover, Jews at this period had little reason to fear
the spread of idolatry through intermarriage (this had been the foremost
reason given by Scripture for the prohibition). Ezra's dire warning, "The
land which you are entering and will possess is a polluted land, polluted by
the foreign population and their abominable practices, which have made it
unclean from end to end" (Ezra 9.11), seems overstated when we consider
that many aliens marrying into Jewish families at this period sought to
convert to Judaism and there was nothing in the Law of Moses that stood in
the way of such adhesion.

Yet Ezra thought otherwise. *All* the nations of the world, ancient and
modern, were to be shunned. Heathen abominations were all equally
reprehensible. The Torah had forbidden intermarriage with the "seven
nations" of ancient Canaan:

When the Lord your God brings you into the land which you are entering to occupy
and drives out many nations before you – Hittites, Girgashites, Amorites,
Canaanites, Perizzites, Hivites, and Jebusites – seven nations more numerous and
powerful than you – when the Lord your God delivers them into your power and you
defeat them, . . . you must not intermarry with them (Deut. 7.1–2).

The Torah then added the prohibition of intermarriage with the Ammonites
and Moabites (in Deut. 23.3, as we read above), and there were also
restrictions with respect to Edomites and Egyptians. These Pentateuchal
extensions of the original prohibition against the "seven nations" allowed
Ezra to deduce that it had been the Lawgiver's intent not only to ban
intermarriage with the original seven nations of Canaan, or with the
ancient Ammonites and Moabites, but to oppose any mixing of the "holy
race" with aliens.

This is an example where interpretation goes far beyond the limits of
philological inquiry, elucidation of facts, translation of rare and difficult
passages, or any similar treatment of a text. The new interpretation becomes
the law of the land, a powerful new force that henceforward determines the
nation's life and its entire self-image: "Judah has violated the holiness of the
Lord by loving and marrying daughters of a foreign god" (Mal. 2.11). The
interpretation of Scriptures is instrumental in shaping fundamental
judgments and decisions of the entire body politic.

Motives for Biblical interpretation

Let us distinguish here four basic motives that throughout the ages gave
impetus to Biblical interpretation. First, there was the understandable desire
to elucidate obscure points in the texts, to explain the grammar and syntax

of difficult passages, and to deal with the questions they raised. A second motive was the desire to resolve contradictions within the Bible itself. Personalities, opinions, and chronology in the Bible's various books did not always agree, yet the Bible was held to be one holy unit. The need, therefore, to settle contradictions and to explain discrepancies within the Holy Book was urgently felt. This motive inspired attempts to tie together disconnected ends and to associate often quite disparate matters, eventually welding them all into a cohesive new culture. The third motive was the need to derive from Scriptures guidelines for actual practice, either by pronouncing new *halachot*, or by drawing upon existing allusions and corroborations. The Torah was held to be a legal code and, as such, it had to contain the innumerable details, instances, and nuances required for application to daily practice. But, of course, not all of these details could be found in the Book, or at least, not in sufficient clarity. At times, too, the plain meanings of the text simply did not support any of the eductions the Rabbis had derived from it, and it served merely as a corroborative reference. This third motive prompted the promulgation of new commandments, necessitated by "the times" and an infusion of new meaning into the reasons for the *mitzvot*. This point will be explained in greater detail in chapter 4. The fourth motive was the desire to vindicate the new, interpreting culture with direct reinforcement from Scripture, endowing it thereby with the authoritative halo of sanctity.

These important motives gave impetus to the increasing use of interpretation in educing both *halachah*, laws, and *aggadah*, homiletic material. The purpose of the homiletic method was to validate the ontology of the Talmudic culture. Subsequent cultures sought the same kind of validation in their own version of homiletic interpretation.

The hermeneutic rules

The philological and logical tools with which the Torah was interpreted were referred to as *midot*, or hermeneutic rules. As Saul Lieberman pointed out, the word *midah* and the names for these hermeneutic rules were influenced by Hellenistic grammarians and rhetoricians who, not unlike the Talmudic Rabbis, painstakingly labored over the explanation and elucidation of their written heritage, the works of Homer and Hesiod. *Midah* means "canon," i.e. an exposition in logic. *Gezeirah shavah* (an argument by analogy) is "syncresis," a term used for the reconciliation of dissimilar principles (small with large, or large with small). The *kal va-ḥomer* (*a fortiori*) argument is a rule belonging to this type of syncresis. In brief, the seven hermeneutic rules espoused by Hillel, the thirteen rules developed by Rabbi Ishmael, or the thirty-two rules attributed to Rabbi Eliᶜezer, are all established hermeneutic rules in the theory of logic and exegesis used by the Hellenistic interpreters in the study of their own ancient texts.

How this influence reached the Rabbis, how it assisted them in developing a "kind of Talmudic logic," and whether it actually attained the scope claimed by S. Lieberman, or was a considerably more modest endeavor, as claimed by A. Schwarz, is a question I leave to the experts.[5] For our purposes here, an examination of some hermeneutic rules used in the exposition of both *halachah* and *aggadah* will suffice. Clearly, some of the interpretations collected in *Midrash Rabbah* seem quite plausible, while others appear far-fetched and contrived. The hermeneutic rule known as *ribui* (pluralization), for example, applies to, among others, the Hebrew words, "the," "also," "too," i.e. words whose function it is to pluralize the noun or verb in question. Now, while it is perhaps possible for us to accept the pluralization principle in a case like, " 'Honour your father and your mother' – also your eldest brother" (*Ket.* 103a), it is difficult to swallow statements like, " 'The Lord showed favour to Sarah' – and also to all other barren women" (*Yalkut Shimóni*, 92). Or, to cite another example, the comparison by analogy, *gezeirah shavah*, generally does not attempt a thoughtful comparison of texts, but engages in a superficial verbal comparison only, such as: "It is said in Samuel: 'No razor shall ever touch his head' (I. Sam. 1.11) and in Samson it is said: 'and no razor shall touch his head' (Judg. 13.5). As the razor in the context of Samuel refers to a Nazarite, so the razor in the context of Samson refers to a Nazirite" (*Ned.* 10a). "Razor" here, "razor" there, the analogy is clear. From the words "men of renown" mentioned both in connection with the generation of the flood (Gen. 6.4), and in the incident of Koraḥ (Num. 16.2), the Rabbis deduced the severity of Koraḥ's rebellion, otherwise it would not have been described in the same words that had been applied to the evil generation of the flood. This actually happens to be an appealing commentary, but the external correspondences on which it is based are clearly arbitrary. In order to avoid the arbitrariness inherent in this hermeneutic rule, the Rabbis decided that an analogy was not permissible unless its use in a particular context had been sanctioned by earlier tradition.

That Scripture had many meanings could be proven from Scripture itself: "Do not my words scorch like fire? Are they not like a hammer that splinters rock?" asks Jeremiah (23.29). To which the Rabbis commented: "Just as [the rock] is split into many splinters, so also may one Biblical verse convey many teachings" (*San.* 34a). In this context, in an example of *a fortiori* reasoning, they also compared the words of Scripture (Eccles. 5.2) to a dream: if dreams, which "have no effect either one way or the other" (*Git.* 52a), have more than one meaning, then surely this is all the more the case when we deal with the weighty words of the Torah, where one verse has many meanings. We, who read these words today, know that all these meanings merge into one large overriding meaning, one that strengthens and vindicates the interpreting culture.

The entire method of Talmudic homiletic or *halachic* commentary is a philological-logical undertaking of rather ambiguous intentions. In fact, it is a complex and, to our taste today, a somewhat bizarre spiritual creature: partially explanation of texts, partially literal (in the writer's view) derivations of moral lessons or *halachot* based on intentions the interpreter reads into the text. Rabbi Yehuda and Rabbi Simeon, Rabbi Ishmael and Rabbi Akiba often debated whether the sense of a verse should or should not be derived by *derash* (homiletically). There is, however, no disagreement among them about the paramount importance of innovating *halachot* via textual interpretation, or of defending *halachot* introduced by earlier commentators. This is the fruitful ambiguity that arises when the belief that an interpretation is, in fact, the plain, literal meaning of a text confronts the desire, seconded by the slightest of allusions in the text, to innovate and infuse new meaning into the old frame.

The Talmudic method

Interpretation culminated either in new *halachah* (law) or it took the form of *aggadah*. In the case of the former, the prohibition against taking the written text out of its literal meaning was scrupulously observed, and even though in the end, of course, the texts were deliberately manipulated to suit the Rabbis' needs, we cannot doubt their earnest attempt to adhere as much as possible to the literal meaning, as they construed it. In the case of the latter, the Sages took considerable liberty with Scriptures, even according to their own understanding of the texts. We need only recall, for example, the startling declaration that our Patriarch Jacob was not dead. How so? Was it then for nought that he had been bewailed, embalmed, and buried? To which the ingenious exegist replies, "I derive this from a Scriptural verse" (*Taʿan.* 5b), that is, I am introducing this meaning into the text and I believe that it can teach us a lesson, or delight the listener.[6]

Worthy subject-matter for homilies was not only presented by difficult texts, of which the Rabbis said, "This text clamors for interpretation," but all texts of Holy Scriptures, and even Apocrypha, like the Wisdom of Ben Sirah, or the *Megillat taʿanit* ("the Scroll of Fasts"), a historical document from the time of the Second Temple were likewise analyzed: why was the word, "בהון" (in them), repeated twice (*Taʿan.* 18a), they queried, as if this historical text too were fit subject for exegesis, capable of suggesting, through this seemingly needless duplication of words some kind of lesson. Azariah dei Rossi likened some of the homiletic flights of fancy to light-engulfed angels who recited poetry in earlier times.[7] Clearly, there are interpretations which appear simple and natural, and others which are contrived and strained. Joseph Solomon Delmedigo (1591–1655) compared the latter to wine that will not flow out of the flask except by squeezing and forcing. More recently, scholars have systematically analyzed the methods of the homiletic interpretation; the homiletic literature serves as our prototype for the type of interpretation we have labeled "creative-constructive."

Isaak Heinemann opens the chapter, "The methods of creative philology,"[8] with an exposition of the rules governing the Talmudic interpretational method. The Rabbis believed that a Book so different from any other human creation required special methods of interpretation. These were: first, all its particulars were to be meticulously studied; the Bible contained no insignificant details. While they acknowledged the existence of different Prophetic styles, and even conceded at times that the Scriptures contained textual redundancies, the Rabbis maintained that the Holy Spirit permeated each and every verse. Thus, even word duplications or repetitions of individual letters had to be interpreted. Second, the Bible sought neither to entertain the reader nor to shock him. Its aim was to teach a lesson, instruct a commandment, convey a warning. Finally, parts of speech in Scripture had an autonomous power, and it was permissible to interpret individual letters and words, and their various combinations. Save for the philological method of the Poetic-Philosophic culture, the traditional cultures all employed these three rules, which, in Heinemann's view, were the basis for the Talmudic exegesis.

We said earlier that the ages of traditional faith opposed conscious innovations. "A text cannot be taken out of its literal meaning," was the rule. On the other hand, as we have seen, they also said: "One verse can be interpreted in a number of ways." The resultant tension between these two rules accompanies the entire history of the creative interpretation, and thus, the entire body of Biblical commentary in the cultures of traditional faith. But these same cultures also produced forerunners of the modern critical-scientific method, climaxing in the remarkable accomplishments of Jonah Ibn Janaḥ and Abraham Ibn Ezra. Ibn Ezra indeed kept much of what he had promised in his introduction to the Bible: "First I shall investigate with all the power at my command the grammatical form of each word and then I shall explain its meaning to the best of my ability."[9] But even this extraordinary commentator, who could be very critical of the fanciful homiletic methods, knew that the Torah had "seventy faces" and that the prohibition against taking a verse out of its literal meaning obtained only in matters of strict *halachah*.

Complaints about texts being taken out of their literal meanings were already voiced during the Talmudic culture itself. The most famous protest was the outraged cry of the ʾAmora, Rabbi Yossi ben Dumeskit: "Why do you distort Scriptures so?!" This interesting passage in the *Sifre*[10] deals with a homily of Rabbi Yehuda on the verse: "He has come to the land of Ḥadrach and established himself in Damascus" (Zech. 9.1). The word "Ḥadrach," which combines sharp (*ḥad*) and soft (*rach*), naturally piques the preacher's imagination. And he expounds: "This refers to the Messiah, who will be sharp to the nations of the world and soft to Israel." To which the said Rabbi Yossi responded: "Why do you distort the Scriptures so?! I call Heaven and earth to witness that I come from Damascus and there is a place there called Ḥadrach." Needless to say, however, homily frequently triumphed over geography, and on another occasion we find the very same Rabbi Yossi expounding freely on unfamiliar geographic names just as had been done in the case of his own Ḥadrach.

Interpretation in the Poetic-Philosophic culture

We suggested earlier that the Spanish Biblical scholars be viewed in a sense as the precursors of the critical-scientific method that is generally espoused today. Undaunted by the biases and prohibitions of the Talmudic and Rabbinic cultures, these scholars energetically probed and investigated Holy Scriptures, and attempted to authenticate the text's plain, accurate, and, at times, unorthodox meanings. As we read these scholarly works, philological and philosophic treatises alike, it is difficult to contain our amazement at the independence of spirit and breadth of thought they reveal. Explicitly or circuitously (by way of fine grammatical analyses), a great spirit of criticism animates these pages. Particularly striking for their perspicacity and penetration are the interpretations of Abraham Ibn Ezra and David Kimḥi. Great courage was surely required even to hint that the Scriptures might contain texts not authored by Moses. Ibn Ezra cryptically alluded to the twelve closing verses of Deuteronomy, claimed by the Rabbis to have been written by Moses in tears, as having rather been written by Joshua: "If you understand the secret of the twelve, and of 'and Moses wrote,' and of 'and the Canaanite was then in the land' and of 'In the mount where the Lord was seen,' and of 'Behold his bedstead was a bedstead of iron,' you will discover the truth."[11] Ibn Ezra's allusions were, of course, vehemently contested, to the point of imputing him with Karaitic leanings. His defenders, and there were such even in the Middle Ages, generally resorted to somewhat awkward arguments. Even Naḥmanides, who admitted in the introduction to his own interpretation that he had overt reproof for Ibn Ezra, "but hidden love," saw no need to criticize his colleague in the matter of the "secret of the twelve," and apparently sided with him on another controversial issue.[12]

In this area of Biblical scholarship a galaxy of spiritual freedom seekers came together to challenge accepted norms. Kimḥi writes: "Things that reason negates cannot be accepted." And elsewhere about Talmudic commentaries that strayed from the plain meaning of the text: "They who said those things, knew what they were speaking of,"[13] implying that he, Kimḥi, is not thus privileged. Biblical scholarship sent a fresh breeze blowing down through the age and widening its horizons. In Judaism, as with other nations, serious Biblical scholarship often carried an implied critique of the established order. It had about it a special pathos, an ardent desire to magnify life and enhance wisdom.

The exegetical method used by the Jewish Poet-Philosophers resembled that of their contemporary Islamic thinkers. Verses from Holy Scriptures were taken as demonstrations of philosophical theories. A great effort was made to banish the literal meaning from texts that alluded to the Creator's corporeality. The premise of a Creator who could not be likened to His creatures, whose speech was not human, necessitated allegorical solutions, in the manner of the Islamic Muʿtazilah sect, which sought to remove any hint of God's incorporification by explaining the Koran with the aid of "figure and parable," "transposition," and "metaphor" (tawil). The Hebrew interpreters in the Middle Ages acknowledged that the Torah spoke in the tongue of men, yet they endeavored to separate, as far as they could, the language of mortals from the divine speech, within the boundaries permitted by the grammar, style, and spirit of the Hebrew language.

The problem of exegesis in this culture was complex indeed. In all the cultures of traditional faith it was believed that the whole Torah, Oral and Written, had been received by Moses from the divine source. Maimonides formulated this as his eighth princple of faith in his commentary to the Mishnah. But what exactly was the precise nature of the Torah-giving and how far did it go? There is no disagreement among scholars, says Maimonides, over those interpretations which are universally accepted as having been given by Moses. But there is disagreement over the conclusions drawn by the Sages from the hermeneutic rules given to Moses at Sinai. Maimonides proposes, therefore, the following distinction: whatever is uncontroversial in the Talmud was received from Moses; whatever is debated was not received from Moses.[14]

Many scholars have objected that this distinction was difficult to entertain. But, in a more general context, it may serve as a helpful guide to Maimonides' method of interpreting the Talmud. The distinction he drew was as follows: interpretations in the Oral Torah directly attributed to Moses explain meanings of words, over which there is no disagreement as, for example, that "the fruit of the citrus-tree" (Lev. 23.50), to be used during the festival of Sukkot,' refers to a citron (ʾetrog), or that "frontlets between your eyes" (Deut. 6.8) refer to phylacteries (tephilin). These meanings are clearly understood in the light of tradition, and it is universally acknowledged that they derive directly from the literal meaning of the text. On the other hand, we have ordinances called halachah le-Moshe mi-Sinai (a law given to Moses at Sinai), which have no base in Scriptures: no allusion, no reference, no reasonable basis for eduction. However, both types of mitzvot, those derived from the interpretation of Scriptures, and those that have no hint or precedent in the Holy Book, were given at Sinai.[15] The disagreement is only about the conclusions that are derived, through study and conjecture, based on the hermeneutic rules and the commentaries.

The Poskim (codifiers) dealt at length with Maimonides' method and most of them found its logic strained. There had been disagreements over commandments attributed to Moses at Sinai, as indeed over all other commandments, and even over "eye for an eye," which, Maimonides thought, referred in its *literal* meaning to monetary damages. He claimed this had been the accepted explanation handed down from Moses, and, consequently, there was no disagreement over it. But we know that there had been dissenters, as, for example, Rabbi Eliʿezer, who said: "Eye for an eye literally refers to the eye [of the offender]" (*Bab. K.* 84a). The fact that there were many disagreements regarding *halachot* which, according to Maimonides' system, were inconsistent with the accepted tradition, presented a difficult problem to the great Halachah-scholars of the day and to researchers in our times.

An emphatic articulation of the belief that most commentaries, as Rav Tzaʿir said, are derived from the inherent logic of the texts, can be found in the Talmudic notion that certain hermeneutic rules for interpreting the Torah were given to Moses at Sinai. In other words, the *tools* for interpreting the Torah and their logic were given with the Torah itself, and with their aid, by penetrating into the logic of the texts, the Sages derived their commentaries. In their commentary on the verse, "The Lord gave him [Moses] two tablets" (Exod. 31.18), the Rabbis call attention to the giving of these rules to Moses: "Could Moses have learnt the whole Torah? Of the Torah it says: 'The measure thereof is longer that the earth, and broader than the sea' [Job 11.9]. Could then Moses have learnt it all in forty days? No, it was only the principles thereof which God taught Moses."[16] But to which rules they were referring, whether to the thirteen rules or to the thirty-two rules, whether to all or only to a part, or whether they meant other rules altogether, this they did not specify.

The Poet-Philosopher scholars generally believed that only the hermeneutic rules, not the entire Oral Law, were given to Moses at Sinai. Joseph Albo, for example, observed that the interpretations derived from the hermeneutic rules were new according to details that varied in every generation, and that the Oral Torah was not, therefore, all given at Sinai:

The law of God cannot be perfect so as to be adequate for all times, because the ever new details of human relations, their customs, and their acts, are too numerous to be embraced in a book. Therefore Moses was given orally certain general principles, only briefly alluded to in the Torah, by means of which the wise men in every generation may work out the details as they appear.[17]

In fact, Judah ha-Levi had already expressed this view in *The Kuzari*. Vowelization, accents, and the masoretic signs convince us that the Oral Torah was also given from above, for without the commentary of the Oral

Law, *halachot*, such as those pertaining to the sanctification of the new moon and the inauguration of the new month (*rosh ḥodesh*), or the exact definitions of labors proscribed on the Sabbath, are quite unintelligible. "This month shall be unto you the beginning of months" (Exod. 12.2) looks like a simple enough verse to understand. Yet how are we to know whether God "meant the Calendar of the Copts – or rather the Egyptians – among whom they lived, or that of the Chaldeans, who were Abraham's people in Ur-Kasdim; or solar, or lunar years?"[18] "For that which appears plain in the Torah, is yet obscure, and much more are the obscure passages, because the oral supplement was relied upon."[19] The Oral Law is complementary to the Written Law and is indispensable. The commentaries it contains are true, for the authors "employ secret methods of interpretation which we are unable to discern, and which were handed down to them, together with the method of the 'Thirteen Rules of Interpretation,' or they use Biblical verses as a kind of fulcrum of interpretation in a method called Asmakhta, and make them a sort of hall mark of tradition."[20]

Indeed ha-Levi claims that *all halachot* were received from the Prophets, for "prophecy had scarcely ceased, or rather the Bath Qol [the heavenly voice], which took its place."[21] In brief, commentaries of Sages post-dating Moses and the Prophets are to be thought of as prophecy too; their dicta are to be considered as *mitzvot*, even when they depart from the Torah's own words or when they consciously innovate, or even when they appear at first glance, as did Solomon in his Ecclesiastes or Song of Songs, downright contradictory to Torah. The tradition was transmitted from the Prophets to the members of the Great Assembly, from the Great Assembly to the Tannaʾim and from the Tannaʾim it passed on to the Amoraʾim. Therefore it could be said that everything rested upon Prophecy.[22] For Maimonides' opinion on the matter, see chapter 4 on the commandments.

The Poetic-Philosophic method in Biblical interpretation, and Maimonides' method in particular, have been studied in detail.[23] Man's perfecting of himself, it was thought, was the true purpose of both Torah and philosophy. This perfecting was to be attained in contemplating God, His attributes and deeds, and by mending one's conduct in acts of justice and righteousness. Intellectual contemplation did not contradict divine revelation: "Heaven forbid that I should assume what is against sense and reason."[24] Torah should be studied with the tools of logic and science, for it is "through the understanding [that] we are confirmed in our faith in the truth of the Book of God's Law."[25] No contradiction existed between divine and human truth; this was a basic underlying assumption of the Poetic-Philosophic culture. To be sure, there were important distinctions between the scholars on this point. For some, the point of departure was faith in the Torah, for which they sought support in human wisdom and its tools; others celebrated human wisdom first and foremost, making it the touchstone for the Bible's veracity. Gersonides felt strongly that nothing in the Torah could be contrary to reason. "Our practice," he says in the introduction to his commentary, "is first to examine matters from the rational angle, and then it will become obvious that this was also the view of our Torah." Truth should be sought as it ensues from rational contemplation, "for the Torah is not a law which compels us to accept falsehoods; rather, its purpose is to direct us to the attainment of truth, insofar as this is possible."

It was no easy task to transpose the language and symbols that articulated the ontology of Biblical man into language and symbols capable of expressing the conceptions of the Poetic-Philosophic culture. Maimonides envisaged, so he says, writing a "Book of Prophecy" and a "Book of Reconciliation."[26] The *Guide for the Perplexed* was to a large extent the fulfillment of that intention. The introduction declares that the "primary object in this work is to explain certain words ... and certain obscure figures which occur in the Prophets"[27] and in certain Talmudic commentaries, as the author had promised he would do in the "Book of Harmony." That book was to have dealt with harmonization, or rational settling of discrepancies or, as in al-Ḥarizi's Hebrew translation of the Arabic original, with "the relation of things to reason," in order to resolve the doubts that arose when Talmudic commentaries appeared remote from rational truth.

The following is a characteristic example, one of many, of the method used by the creators of the Poetic-Philosophic culture in interpreting both Scripture and *aggadah*. Rabbi Yoḥanan is cited in the Talmud as follows: "The Shechina rests only on a wise man, a strong man, a wealthy man, and a tall man" (*Sab.* 92a), or "on the mighty, the rich, the wise and the humble, all this from Moses" (*Ned.* 38a). This saying and its subsequent discussion are included in a give-and-take about the carrying of burdens on the Sabbath and about the placement of accents for the reading of the Torah. Let us follow this logic: we know that Moses was tall of stature and physically strong from the verses, "he spread the tent over the Tabernacle" (Exod. 40.19), and "I took the tablets and flung them down and shattered them" (Deut. 9.17). Other verses tell us the height of the Tabernacle and the weight of the tablets. Thus his strength is established. As to his wealth, the verse, "I have not taken from them so much as a single ass" (Num. 16.15), proves Moses took nothing from others. The Gemara here also says that Moses became rich from the debris of the tablets. The said Rabbi Yoḥanan concludes, then, that "all the Prophets were wealthy," and cited further proofs from Samuel, Amos, and Jonah. In Jonah (1.3) we read, "He paid its [i.e. the ship's] fare," evidence that Jonah was wealthy enough to pay the 4,000 dinars required for the wages of the entire ship. There can be no doubt that the Sages spoke here of might and wealth in an entirely literal sense.

But Maimonides in his commentary on the Mishnah says something quite new:[28]

Know that no prophet began prophesying until he had attained all the intellectual and most of the character requisites for it is said, prophecy descends only upon the wise, the mighty and the rich; rich is he who is content with his portion, for the Sages read "content" as rich ("Who is a rich man? He that is content with his portion"). Mighty is he who uses his power according to reason, as it is said: "Who is mighty? He that subdues his evil impulse."

It is not difficult to see that Maimonides has taken the words "mighty," "rich," and "wise," far out of their literal meaning "by way of metaphor and allegories,"[29] in order to infuse them with the substance of the new ontology.

And indeed those reconstructing interpreters who wished to clarify the plain meaning of Scriptures or of Talmudic sayings protested against the philosophers' intellectualizations. Thus, Nissim ben Reuben Gerondi (1320–80) in his *Derashot* wrote:[30] "Those who explain 'strong' as one whose reason conquers his inclination, or 'rich' as one who is content with his portion . . . are wrong, for the Sages understood 'strong' and 'rich' literally."

The real problem lay in the Biblical conception of reality which was expressed in terms and metaphors that were problematic for a later ontology. Maimonides included in the concept *shem* most of the words in the language. Thus he undertook to explain not only nouns, such as *tzelem* (image) and *demut* (likeness), *temunah* (similitude) and *tavnit* (pattern), *yad* (hand) and *regel* (foot), *nefesh* (soul) and *ruaḥ* (spirit), but also adjectives like *ram* (high), *ḥai* (living), *ḥacham* (wise), and verbs, such as *kam* (rose), *ʿamad* (stood), *halach* (went), etc. Of these, he claims, some are homonyms, one word with multiple meanings, like the word *ruaḥ* (signifying air, wind, breath, and spirit,), some are metaphoric, like the word *kanaf* (literally, wing, figuratively, corner, end, cover, and protection), and some are amphibolic, i.e. ambiguous words like *adam*, which can refer both to a living and a deceased person, and to a human image made of wood or stone. It is the object of the *Guide* to establish that the Torah's wisdom is its truth; this requires clarification of the accurate sense of the Biblical terminology and avoidance of any misunderstanding of its meaning, as it was conceived by the philosophers. The same is true for the metaphors and riddles in which it was believed the Torah spoke. These too require "comparison," i.e. reconciliation with reason. The believer must teach himself the symbolic language of the Torah, not through terms and metaphors borrowed from the material world, but according to its truth, its inner meaning, its moral. Adherence to the literal sense of Scriptural metaphors leads to contradictions, especially to the gravest contradiction of all, the apparent inconsistency between Torah and reason. The explanation of the "seven causes of inconsistencies and contradictions" in the introductory remarks to the

Guide for the Perplexed is indeed an extraordinary masterpiece, "a light dispelling all darkness" in Shem Tov Ibn Falaquera's words, a clear example of cultural hermeneutics, when cultures collide with one another.[31]

Our medieval philosophers wished to liberate the language of Holy Scriptures from the limitations of sense perception and the vagaries of the imagination, in order to make it suitable for intellectual-spiritual cognition. They were shocked and scandalized by the concrete idiom in which Biblical symbols were articulated. "Intellectual perception, in the exercise of which he does not employ his sense, nor move his hand or his foot"[32] – this is the definition of human reason in the *Guide for the Perplexed* – cannot accept literally the language of, "Let us make man in our image" (Gen. 1.26). Such metaphors, derived from close or distant similarities, and whose ideational core is frequently obscured and overwhelmed by the external husk, draw too heavily upon the tangible and the imagination, and fail to enlighten the mind. On the contrary, these metaphors confuse us by blurring the distinctions that exist between concepts. The vestments of language, be they ever so lovely, can be heavy and cumbersome, like the armor of some Goliath, unsuited to do battle for the living God.

Moreover, symbols are products of their time and their culture and of the methods and metaphors adopted by a culture for making itself tangible; from this viewpoint they are accidents of history, not a necessity. What makes certain symbols more legitimate than others? And finally, while the Biblical metaphors have already been interpreted by the Talmudic Sages, the Sages' commentaries have raised new barriers between ourselves and Scriptures. Their commentaries are themselves stumbling blocks, and in need of commentary. Only an "ill-formed Theologian" would find the Talmudic homiletic method unproblematical.[33]

The hermeneutic theory of the Poetic-Philosophic culture sought to overcome the historic concreteness and randomness of the Biblical idiom that "spoke according to the language of man," to redeem it from subservience to Talmudic interpretations and to decipher its anthropomorphic symbols in a manner that would lead to supreme spiritual apperception.

We have learned, therefore, that the "gates of interpretation were not closed," not in the Talmudic culture, nor in the Poetic-Philosophic culture, which, as we have said, frequently interpreted the Bible by "the use of parables and figures,"[34] nor, of course, in the Mystical culture. Indeed all the pre-set rules were broken. For example, Abravanel decreed that whatever is written bears witness that "it was and did occur, and we must not budge from its literal meaning" (commentary on Isa. 20).[35] However, as I already demonstrated in my book on Don Isaac Abravanel and the expulsion of the Jews from Spain, he himself did not adhere to his own rule in this matter.[36]

The Mystical interpretation

The interpretational method of the Mystical culture was characterized, albeit polemically, by Abraham Ibn Ezra in the above-mentioned introduction to the Bible:

Every precept of the Torah, whether great or small, must be measured in the balance of the heart into which God has implanted some of His wisdom. Therefore if there appears something in the Torah which seems to contradict reason or to refute the evidence of our senses then here one should seek for the solution in a figurative interpretation.[37]

Then Ibn Ezra boldly declares the "Magna Carta" of the Poetic-Philosophic commentary:

For reason is the foundation of everything. The Torah was not given to men who cannot reason and man's reason is the angel which mediates between him and his God. It follows that wherever we find something in the Torah that is not contrary to reason, we must understand it in accordance with its plain meaning and accept it as saying what it seems to say, believing that it is its true meaning . . . Why should we understand as mysteries things which are perfectly clear as they stand?[38]

Originally the Biblical commentators distinguished only between *peshat* (literal meaning) and *derash* (homiletics), but in the Middle Ages they adopted (apparently from the Christian commentators) the "squared system": *peshat, remez, derash, sod* (literal, allegorical, homiletic, mystical), hence, according to W. Bacher and G. Scholem, the anagram *PaRDeS*. The word *sod* (mystery) signified to the Mystics not only a deciphering of the parable, but also a supreme "illumination." Bachya ben Asher already lists in the introduction to his commentary on the Torah (Saragossa, *c.* 1291) four methods of interpretation: "Some pursue the way of *peshat*, others yearn for the ways of the *midrash*, some, like the philosophizing scholars, choose the way of reason, and the chosen few who mount the path to the House of the Lord contemplate the inner heart."[39]

The *Zohar* views the Torah not merely as a collection of commandments, laws, and ordinances, or of accounts of deeds and prophecies, but rather as an assembly of divine forces and lights, which assumed the form of letters and words and were revealed in human script. The Torah encapsulates the hidden life of the Creator. Nahmanides thought the entire Torah consisted of the names of God; that most commonly known version of His name, the name revealed to Moses, is only one of many possible combinations in the weaving of holy names, which mirror the deity in the Torah. The Torah's commandments embody the secret of the deity in the world and therefore the omission of even one *mitzvah* from the Torah is likened to a detraction from the image of the deity itself. Every single letter and word in the Torah is regarded as a symbol, a mystery supreme and sealed to all but the chosen few. Mystical exegesis desires to lift the veil spread over the Torah and to reveal the divine essence shimmering through the symbolic envelope; this is the high favor and the special privilege of the chosen.[40] In chapter 4 we shall elaborate on the extraordinary role the Mystical culture ascribed to the commandments.

Like the philosophic exegetes, many Kabbalists warned against the incorporification of God when symbols like God's hand, foot, face, etc., were taken as indications of the deity's actual essence. Incorporification, they thought, was idol worship, a making of mask and graven image, yet they often failed to guard against careless anthropomorphisms, especially in the sexual symbolism that describes the life of the deity as a male–female relationship and in the description of "a body of the Godhead" (shi'ur komah).

The destructive interpretation

As we have seen in some detail, the creative interpretation innovates, and it is in the nature of innovation both to uproot and to preserve. But this is a form of interpretation that leaves intact the Jewish superordinating concepts and the archetypal collective experiences, as well as the sacredness of Scriptures. Every culture's Biblical commentary contains an element of destruction, but none of Israel's cultures sets out to destroy the foundations of Biblical faith itself, as it understands them. On the contrary, each culture is very confident that it illuminates these foundations with a new, radiant light, although it is always suspended in the dialectical tension between preserving certain assumptions and extirpating others.

Diametrically opposed to the creative interpretation is the destructive type of interpretation. (Needless to say, the terms, "creative" and "destructive" carry no value judgments as to the superiority of any one form of interpretation over another.) Nietzsche, Marx, and Freud are examples of interpreters who set out to demolish the foundations of religion, to undermine Scriptures, and to shock the faithful. This destruction results from a repudiation of all the underlying assumptions of the interpreted text and an adoption of contrary assumptions. In this instance, the horizons of cultures do not meet; instead, the newcomers uproot and demolish the entire Biblical culture. Freud, for example, endeavored to explain the development of monotheism and the destiny of Israel on the basis of psychoanalytic theory. In *Moses and Monotheism*,[41] Freud boldly hypothesized that Moses was an Egyptian nobleman by birth, an attendant in the court of the Pharaoh Ikhnaton, founder of the monotheistic sun worship. Moses was murdered by the Israelites, and Israel's religion, its faith in one God, is the resultant neurosis. After they murdered their Prophet and leader, in whom they recognized an awesome father-image, the Children of Israel repented of their misdeeds. This great repentance reinforced their yearning for the single god, the primordial father. This, Freud explained, is the story of Moses and the basis for the faith in God's unity. The desire to utterly destroy traditional beliefs is obvious, although this does not invalidate the claim that Freud, too, used an essentially interpretative approach. By seeking in Scriptures corroboration for psychoanalytic theories he, like the practitioners of the creative interpretation, looked to Scriptures for a lesson that would serve his own goals. Thus, the opposing interpretations – the creative and the destructive – have at least this in common: they both take Scriptures seriously. Paradoxically, Freud's posture here is that of a Jew who, though guilty of heresy, still believes the power of Scripture to be sufficiently compelling that he should seek support therein for his own theories.

The critical-scientific interpretation

The critical-scientific interpretation with which one is most familiar today attempts to reconstitute the text and its meanings, to correct it, and to restore its ancient form in order to draw forth, sometimes from the very depths of oblivion, its original pristine meaning. This kind of textual criticism bears little resemblance to the traditional creative interpretation founded on immense erudition, and on a long tradition of transmitted commentaries, which so often neglected plain meanings in favor of new underlying presuppositions.

In its attempt to rehabilitate and reconstitute the text, the critical-scientific method must enter into the same hermeneutic circle wherein the text was first created. A high degree of reflection and criticism is required for the interpreter to arrive at the literal meaning of significations, a task which only a very sophisticated interpreter can competently accomplish. It is not difficult to reconstruct the underlying presuppositions of a text when the interpreter and the interpreted are both within the same hermeneutic circle, but in order to reconstruct meanings that are outside the interpreter's own circle, a sense of perspective, and the resultant differentiation between the interpreter and the interpreted are required. This is the task undertaken by the critical-scientific interpreter both in Scriptural exegesis and in the study of other texts, like the Talmud and the literature of the Oral Law. Using modern methods of source analysis, such as comparative philology, and aided by a plethora of information about the social, legal, political, economic, and artistic order of the times, the scientific scholar attempts to arrive at an explanation of the text, as its author had construed it, and as it was understood when it was first uttered or written. The researcher must be knowledgeable about the dynamics of the text's formation and its evolution throughout the ages. Painstaking investigation and examination eventually yield the text's correct, purified, and refined meaning. In Biblical research this method is aided by archeology, history, comparative philology of neighboring nations, and other auxiliary disciplines, for the establishment of the accurate literal meaning of the texts in their widest possible contexts. This interpretation seeks, therefore, to determine the exact nature of both text and context, of the *peshat* and of the symbol, which together convey the full meaning. It utilizes all the techniques and methods that can be applied to decipher a text, resolve difficulties and construe meanings in the context of the time and milieu in which they were conceived. The premise underlying this interpretation is that religious faith and scientific explanation are two entirely separate domains.

Spinoza in his *Theologico-Political Treatise* was the first to chart the course of this interpretation (see especially his seventh chapter, "Of the interpretation of Scripture"). His main argument was that whatever we claim to know from Scripture should be contained in Scripture itself, just as our knowledge of nature derives solely from nature itself. We must not distort the meaning of Scripture to accommodate our own reasoning as, for example, when we find in Scripture things that in their literal sense are inconsistent with what we consider reason. We cannot comprehend the meaning of Scripture without a profound knowledge of the Hebrew language, of Jewish history, and of the lives of the Prophets and other Biblical writers: "Such a history should relate the environment of all the prophetic books extant; that is, the life, the conduct, and the studies of the author of each book, who he was, what was the occasion, and the epoch of his writing, whom did he write for, and in what language."[42]

An important principle, according to Spinoza, was the care not to confuse the intent of Scripture with what we believe to be the intent of the Holy Spirit or the truth of the matter. In this way Spinoza thought to secure for Biblical research a neutral position in matters of faith. Whether Spinoza himself, in this and in other works, adhered to the principles of the method he advocated ("the only true method") is a separate problem. There can be no doubt, however, that he was a pioneer in the application of modern science to Biblical research.

As Yeḥezkel Kaufmann and other Hebrew scholars pointed out when they analyzed the Biblical scholars of the German school, especially Wellhausen and his followers, this method too was not free of bias and prejudice. It was at times quite far from the objectivity and neutrality to which it pretended. Clearly, the critical-scientific approach could not escape the limitations inherent in its peculiar perspective, even when it applied its tools to the literal meaning of the texts, or to their comprehensive meaning. This scientific method too grew out of certain presuppositions underlying a historical ontology which was peculiar to a specific time and place.

The comparative-perspectivistic method

The comparative study of cultures, i.e. how each culture interprets the Bible and the history of Israel in their generality and in their details, considers the following four basic questions:

1   How was the Bible interpreted literally in each one of our cultures and how was its meaning, as expressed through symbols, parables, mysteries, and allegories, understood by the commentators?

2   To what degree did these commentaries reflect the ontology of their authors, and what is the implication of these commentaries in the larger religious, historical, and philosophical context, i.e. what characterizes these commentaries as prototypical expressions of a culture, and how did the commentators themselves view their works as contributing to the individuation of their culture?

3   How do the commentaries of one culture differ from those of other cultures in the eyes of one who surveys the Jewish historical landscape in all its breadth? In other words, as we look today at our history, to what extent do we find it characterized by continuity in our cultures, or by ruptures and breaks? In the final analysis – and this is our argument here – it is impossible for meanings to continue shining as brightly as "when they were given;" for the world of the interpreter intervenes to create a distance and to place the interpreted text in the historical perspective of its own time.

4   And finally, as we, members of the National-Israeli culture, attempt to find in the Biblical culture a foundation for our own culture, we cannot disregard the relevance that the interpretations advanced by previous cultures carry for us today; no real understanding is possible without an appreciation of self-understanding and its limitations. The critical and reflective research which is imbedded in historical perspectivism does not profess to have arrived at definite conclusions, only to attempt them, as far as possible. The new method is, for the time being, more of a mission and a charge. It is fascinating, for example, to compare commentaries from different cultures to the same Biblical work, for example, the Song of Songs. Let us consider the Talmudic commentary, Gersonides' Philosophic *Commentary on the Five Scrolls*, Moses Alschech's Mystical *Shoshanat ha-ʿamakim*, and commentaries from the Enlightenment period down to our own day. This comparison will demonstrate how the new method applies to Biblical study in particular and to the study of differences between cultures in general.

3

SONG OF SONGS –
A PARADIGM OF CULTURAL CHANGE

Johann Gottfried Herder – at a crossroads of cultures

Commentaries on the Song of Songs furnish a most revealing illustration for the comparative approach to the study of Jewish cultures and their divergent conceptions of God, man, and the world. No other Biblical book so patently exemplifies each culture's unique interpretation of the spiritual and vital forces which fashioned the nation's character. In fact, the variety of commentaries of the Song of Songs should constitute not one, but two subjects for study, a subject within a subject. The first question we might consider is this: when viewed through the prism of their interpretations of the Song of Songs, how do the cultures of traditional faith as a whole compare with the last two secular cultures, i.e. the Emancipation and the National-Israeli cultures? Secondly, and no less importantly, what are the varieties of views on the Song of Songs within the cultures of traditional faith themselves? Our main interest in the following pages lies with the second topic, but let us begin with the first, which encompasses the entire framework.

One is hard pressed to find among all the books of the Bible a work whose interpretations better illustrate than the Song of Songs the fundamental differences between the cultures of faith and the last two secular cultures. Is the scroll a "holy of holies," or is it a collection of popular love-songs? Is it a metaphor of God's relation with the Congregation of Israel, or are these songs erotic profanities, over which the Sages, in their dramatic style, lamented: "The Torah, dressed in a sack, stands before the Holy One, blessed be He, and says: Lord of the Universe, thy children have made me a fiddle on which frivolous persons play" (*San.* 101a).[1]

The early Maskilim did not seek to comment on the Song of Songs. We may attribute this reticence to the embarrassment and doubt raised by the book's erotic nature. Even Herder's declaration that the Song was of divine inspiration in its content, but the handiwork of a great, albeit human, lover-poet, did not resolve their doubts. Herder is never mentioned by Mendelssohn in his treatise on the "subject of poetry and its nature in the holy books," contained in the *Bi*ʾ*ur's*[2] preface to the Song of Moses. Mendelssohn, who rightly considered himself the first Hebrew exponent of the formal aspects of Biblical poetry, "for [he had] not found in any of the commentaries of the Torah a statement that adequately explain[ed] the matter," failed to acknowledge that Herder had preceded him on this subject with more than an "adequate" treatment (in German, however).[3] Let us briefly examine Herder's thoughts on Hebrew poetry in general, and on the Song of Songs in particular. For they represent a crossroads in European civilization, a point at which the modern secular cultures part from the cultures of traditional faith.

We know that Christian commentators, like their Jewish counterparts, viewed the Song of Songs as an allegorical dialogue. Jesus Christ was the lover, the church, his beloved and bride. Her two breasts were the Old and New Testaments. The "threescore valiant men" of Solomon (3.7) were the Fathers, from Adam to Jesus. Indeed the Song of Songs had frequently been commented upon in Christian theology as a book of sacred love, revealed in the Holy Spirit. This tradition was broken when Johann Gottfried von Herder (1744–1803) ventured an interpretation of the Holy Scriptures devoid of a Christian theological bias. He no longer saw references to Jesus in those famous verses from the Old Testament which had so often been taken out of context and stripped of their literal meaning. For Herder, the Song of Songs was strictly a collection of love-poems. No German theologian has ever matched Herder's appreciation for the unique artistry of the Bible.[4]

In 1778 Herder published his treatise on the Song of Songs entitled *Lieder der Liebe* ("Songs of Love"), followed in 1782–3 by his great book *Vom Geist der Hebräischen Poesie* ("On the Spirit of Hebrew Poetry"). Since much has been written on these books, I shall devote our discussion here to one of his lesser known essays entitled *Über die Wirkung der Dichtkunst auf die Sitten der Völker in alten und neuen Zeiten* ("On the Influence of Poetry on the Morals of Nations in Ancient and Modern Times"), published in 1778 as a prize-winning entry in a competition.[5] That essay summarizes the views of this extraordinary theologian, historian, thinker, and poet.

The Holy Scriptures, says Herder, were inspired by the Holy Spirit and there is no doubting their divine origin. They are God's revelation of Himself through the spirit of the Prophets and poets of Israel: "This people was poetic in its very origins. Indeed it was the divine blessing of poetry that set apart the seed of Shem, Abraham, Isaac, and Jacob and his sons."[6] Moses was a poet, not only a lawgiver. The first grand impression that he imprinted on Israel's soul stemmed from the power of poetry – the Song at the Sea, which is the song of the exodus, a song that still stands like a rampart in the midst of the sea. Moses' last song (Deut. 32) is another mighty fortress, a poetic monument:

Where was there a lawgiver who desired more than Moses to wield a profound influence upon the morals of his people? Even Lycurgus pales beside him, and when he [Moses] attempts now to summarize in words his life's work, a song bursts forth . . . His whole heart and soul, his law, his life, the heart and morals of the nation, its destiny, joy, and tragedy, and all its history are encompassed in this magnificent song. It is to be an eternal monument to the law-giver, a song that will shape the nation's character and its heart for ever.[7]

King David too, the "lyre of Israel," worked "kingly deeds" by virtue of the poetry of his Psalms. These poems were a "crowning glory at the end of his life." His son Solomon has patently demonstrated how laws and good manners influence poetry and how poetry, in turn, implants these in the hearts of men. On the Song of Songs Herder wrote: "These Songs of Love are the most delicate and mysterious lilies of the dawn; no royal hand ever plucked their like in the vale of joys. His court was magnificent, full of poets and singers, lovers of the royal muse."[8] Hebrew poetry was composed and sung in the Holy Spirit; it was "divine" in that it aimed at moral improvement and spiritual refinement and awakened the love of God. In all of these qualities the Song of Songs notably excelled.[9]

We have noted that Mendelssohn did not mention Herder in his own writings on the poetry of the Holy Scriptures, and that other Maskilim seem to have been reluctant to render an unequivocal opinion on the Song of Songs even after Herder's ground-breaking insights into the "divine" intent but "profane" form of the songs of love. They seem to have recognized that love-songs to the bride-the beloved need not resemble the "fiddling of the frivolous," and that they could indeed be holy. Yet with the sole exception of Naftali Hertz Wessely (or Hartwig Weisel, 1725–1805), who attempted an audacious excursion into Biblical poetry in an epic poem on the life of Moses, *Shirei tif'eret* (influenced, apparently, by Herder and Klopstock), a long time would pass before a Hebrew Maskil expressed an opinion on the Song of Songs in Herder's new spirit. Solomon Loewisohn (1788–1821), historian, grammarian, and linguist, embraced Herder's approach, but with a difference: in his *Melitzat Yeshurun*,[10] he ascribed to the Song a new plot, one that was to become a distinct hallmark of interpretations in the Emancipation culture. In Loewisohn's view, the Song of Songs was a collection of fourteen poems recounting the love of King Solomon for the Shulamite, a rustic maiden who did not return the King's love because her heart was given to a young shepherd. She was taken against her will to the King's court, but remained faithful to her swain. Finally, she fled the palace, and that is the meaning of the book's last verse: "Make haste, my beloved, and be thou like a roe" (8.14). This Maskil poet still attributed the Song of Songs to King Solomon, but the songs themselves were no longer an allegory.

Herder's views attained great popularity with later Hebrew Maskilim, because his approach opened up for the creators of the Emancipation culture vast possibilities of new blendings of Torah with *derech ʾeretz*, or of the holy and traditional with the secular and modern. His interpretation was not entirely novel; some German Biblical scholars had preceded him in these innovations, but none had grasped the implications of the new interpretation more fully, so that if he was not the sole originator of this view, he undoubtedly endowed it with unprecedented impetus and vigor. For both Jews and non-Jews of his generation Herder's method of interpretation facilitated the transition between cultures; for that reason he has merited our special attention in this study.

Later scholars who maintained that this small volume of poems was simply the love-song of a youth and a maiden, a work devoid of any distinct religious idea, have nonetheless asserted that the love it described was no ordinary passion; not only was it "as strong as death" (8.6), but also pure and radiant with sanctity. Simon Bernfeld declared that there simply was no place for such a work in any religious anthology, even if we enlarge the concept of religion to encompass doubts and misgivings about religious truths (as in the books of Job and Ecclesiastes). In Bernfeld's opinion, the Song of Songs is a "profane work that does not belong in the Holy Scriptures. The book owes its preservation and inclusion in the Holy Scriptures entirely to an accident, i.e. to its attribution to King Solomon."[11] But although Bernfeld does not share the opinion of earlier scholars on the divine nature of these poems, he explicitly agrees with Herder that they are holy in their "natural and simple truthfulness, in their delicacy. This is the pure love of two innocent souls . . . the words are so endearing in their beauty and natural innocence that they do not impress us as the expression of vulgar passion; the erotic is ennobled by the poetic naturalness."[12]

Similarly, and even more ardently, Aaron Kaminka wrote in the introduction to his commentary on the Song of Songs: "True, the book contains no explicit idea of holiness. From beginning to end it is an amatory dialogue that appears entirely profane. But this great and consuming love, depicted without inhibition, is enveloped by clouds of glory in which a revelation from a higher sphere, as it were, may be sensed." The name of God is not once mentioned in the book (if we exclude the last syllable of the word *shalhevetiah*, literally "flame of God," 8.6), yet God's presence pervades it throughout. Moreover, although the book makes no allusion to the nation, to its vision, and its life,

early Hebrew readers probably as far back as the Second Temple must have felt in the soft images that so lovingly cling to the mountains and hills of Judaea and Israel, in the poetic metaphors that embrace Lebanon and Carmel, Jerusalem and Tirzah, the Tower of David and the valiant men of Israel, a distinct awareness that it was not the individual soul that was here consumed with love, but the soul of the entire nation. They must have sensed that the song was merely a symbol and a vision, and that all its words were like burning embers on the altar of the Lord God of Hosts.[13]

An interpretation that sees in the Song of Songs an expression of the nation's love for its ancestral land clearly identifies its author as a member of the modern National-Israeli culture.

Let us proceed now with our second and most important topic of examination wherein we compare how the cultures of faith that preceded the Emancipation each related in its own way to this love-poem. This comparison seeks to strengthen the principal thesis about the multiplicity of cultures in our history.

The Talmudic interpretation of the Song of Songs

In order to educe allegorical and figurative insights from every verse, the Rabbis were wont to take certain liberties with the holy texts. Nonetheless, they were careful to insist that their interest lay with the plain, literal text. Rashi too pointed out in his introductory comments to the Song of Songs that, while each verse of the Torah could be interpreted in more than one way, a verse always retained its most simple meaning and could not be divorced from it. The Rabbis were particularly wary of allegorization, lest the arbitrariness and playfulness of allegory trifle with the Torah and the commandments. It is therefore all the more remarkable that of the entire Holy Writ, one book alone was not subject to this inhibition: from the very outset the Song of Songs was regarded as a purely symbolic text. This book would undoubtedly have been excluded from the canon had its meaning not been divorced from a literal reading as a secular love-poem. According to tradition, the book was pronounced admissible when the Rabbis of the Great Assembly finally alighted upon the allegorical device: the book was to be interpreted symbolically as an intimate dialogue between the Holy One and the Congregation of Israel.[14]

The Tanna'im still debated the nature of the book: was it truly holy (in their words, did it "defile the hands," or "render the hands unclean"),[15] or was it profane? They were well aware that the Song of Songs had initially been found unfit for canonicity, as were other problematic works like Proverbs and Ecclesiastes, until the men of the Great Assembly pronounced it a dialogue between God and the Congregation of Israel. The *mishnah Yadaim* (3.5) presents a debate among the Tanna'im which is pervaded with doubts and hesitations about the nature of the Song of Songs, but also contains Rabbi Akiba's ardent exclamations on this "holy of holies." Rabbi Akiba declared: "God forbid that it should be otherwise! No one in Israel ever disputed that the Song of Songs does not defile the hands. For all the world is not worthy as the day on which the Song of Songs was given to Israel, for all the Writings are holy, but the Song of Songs is the Holy of Holies." And he was not content until he had elevated the Song of Songs to a level of importance rivaling that of the entire Torah. The following admiring utterance is found in a later *midrash*: "Rabbi Akiba said, 'Were there nothing given in the Torah except Song of Songs, it would be enough to guide the world.'"[16] To such an extent did he value this scroll! He also refuted opponents like Rabbi Yosse, a disciple of Rabbi Ishmael, who had maintained that while Ecclesiastes was definitely profane (did not "render the hands unclean"), the status of the Song of Songs was arguable. These and similar sayings are veiled testimonials, spoken in a code that was easily intelligible to Akiba and his contemporaries, to the many hesitations and doubts about the Song of Songs that the Rabbis had to overcome through considerable efforts of faith.

The dispute was finally settled with the general acceptance of the interpretation that the Song of Songs was a parable of the love between God and His chosen people, and of the longing of each for the other, particularly during Israel's exile. This was, then, a love-song about God and Israel, the Torah and the Temple, exile and redemption, a spiritual and holy love. Once this allegorical interpretation was firmly established by the Talmudic Sages, subsequent Jewish cultures of faith embraced the basic premise that the Song of Songs was not to be read literally. Our main interest here is to examine the nature of this allegory in the Talmudic, the Poetic-Philosophic, and the Mystical cultures. We have alluded earlier to the interpretations promulgated by the culture of the Emancipation and by the subsequent National-Israeli culture.

The Song of Songs was widely popular in the Talmudic culture and was generally attributed to King Solomon.[17] King Solomon, according to this tradition, had composed the songs in his youth: "When a man is young, he sings songs. When he becomes an adult, he utters practical proverbs. When he becomes old, he speaks of the vanity of things."[18] Thus, after writing the Song of Songs in his youth, Solomon composed the book of Proverbs in his maturity, and Ecclesiastes in his old age. But some Sages found in the opening verses, "The song of songs which is Solomon's," a reference to God (the root of the name Shlomo, Solomon, is the same as that of the word *shalom*, peace, hence: "the song of songs by Him who has peace"), i.e. the song of God Himself to whom peace pertains. Every reference to Solomon was to be read as an allusion to God (with only two exceptions).

The first thing that strikes us in the Talmudic approach to the Song of Songs is that the Sages wished to elevate the work, to which they had imparted new symbolic meaning expressive of the relationship between God and the Congregation of Israel, to the highest grade of sanctity. They said: "The Song of Songs – the best of songs, the most excellent of songs, the finest of songs."[19] The Holy One in all the glory of His greatness had spoken it. Rabbi Yoḥanan said: "It was spoken at Sinai." Rabbi Meir said: "It was spoken in the Tabernacle."[20] Whoever reads the Song of Songs as a profane work commits a sin: even one who "trills his voice in the chanting of the

Song of Songs," (i.e. sings it as one would a profane song), admonished Rabbi Yoḥanan ben Nuri, "has no share in the world to come."[21]

Echoing Rabbi Akiba, Abraham Ibn Ezra warned in the introduction to his commentary to Song of Songs: "Far be it that it should be understood as an erotic poem, but it is to be taken allegorically."[22] Ibn Ezra explained the Talmud's interpretation: the Song of Songs referred to the Congregation of Israel and to God. The Prophets had often compared Israel to a woman, and Israel's Lord to a loving husband. Isaiah says, "A song of my beloved touching his vineyard" (Isa. 5.1), and "As the bridegroom rejoiceth over the bride, so shall thy God rejoice over thee" (Isa. 62.5). Hosea said, "I will betroth thee unto me for ever" (Hos. 2.19), and "Go, take unto thee a wife" (Hos. 3.1). In Ezekiel we read, "Thy breasts are fashioned, and thine hair is grown, whereas thou wast naked and bare" (Ezek. 16.7), and so forth in that chapter. These erotic images and metaphors are stripped of their literal meaning and made to assume the guise of a strictly spiritual love. Countless examples could be added to Ibn Ezra's enumeration. It was the prevalence of such references throughout Scriptures that allowed the Rabbis not only to include the Song of Songs in the sacred texts, but to elevate it to a supreme level of sanctity.

The second striking feature that emerges from a study of the Talmudic exegesis is that the Song of Songs was viewed, in the words of Rabbi Elʿazar ben Azariah, as a means of inculcating "the fear of God and the acceptance of His yoke." The "yoke," of course, was the burden of the commandments. The verse, "Thy love is better than wine" (1.2), was interpreted as a reference to Torah and commandments, as explained by both Rashi and Sforno, in the spirit of the Midrash: "Thy love, that is the Torah and the commandments which, in Your great goodness, You have written down for our instruction, is more pleasant and desirable to me than wine" (Sforno).

The third outstanding characteristic of the Talmudic commentary to the Song of Songs is the tendency to direct the Song to the eschatological future. It is taken out of its setting in the time of King Solomon and is generalized into a reference to the entire Congregation of Israel (*Knesset Yisrael*), as the Jewish people is called in Talmudic parlance. Exiled, afflicted by foreign oppressors, the Congregation of Israel yearns to return to the home of its youth, to its "first husband" (Rashi, in the preface to his commentary on the Song of Songs, based on numerous Talmudic *midrashim*). Rabbi Akiba expounded the verse, "Therefore do the virgins love thee" (1.3), as follows: "They have loved you even unto death; for Thy sake are we slain every day." From its exile and bondage the Congregation of Israel longs for redemption and beseeches God to fulfill His promise: "Draw me, we will run after thee" (1.4). The Song of Songs is viewed as Solomon's divinely inspired foreshadowing of the impending and catastrophic exile.

These three main features, then, characterize the interpretation of the

Talmudic Sages: the Song of Songs is read as a metaphor of the love between the Congregation of Israel and God. The bond between Israel and its God is the study of the Torah and the observance of the commandments. The Song is felt to be a cry from the anguish of exile and a foreshadowing of the great destiny intimated by the Torah and the Prophets. The conclusion that these are indeed three cardinal features of the Talmudic interpretation can be substantiated by additional examples. In the interest of brevity, however, we now proceed to a different interpretation of the Song of Songs and a radical antithesis to the entire Talmudic commentary.

Song of Songs in the Poetic-Philosophic culture

Among the many Poetic-Philosophic interpretations of the Song of Songs, that of Gersonides merits our particular attention as an outstanding illustration of the underlying assumptions of this culture. His interpretation comes closest to typifying the elements of this culture's conception of the superordinating concepts and the archetypal collective experiences, as it saw them.

Rabbi Levi ben Gershon, Gersonides (1288–c. 1344), a native of Bagnols in southern France, was a versatile personality: philosopher, Bible commentator, mathematician, Talmudic scholar, astronomer, astrologer, inventor of a device for calculating the motions of the heavenly bodies, author of astronomical tables, engineer, and physician. He was one of the greatest Jewish minds of all times, both in the profundity of his thought and in the scope of his scientific and technological interests, an *uomo universale* in the Italian Renaissance mold. His grandfather, Levi ben Abraham, a Bible and Talmud scholar and an expert in engineering, physics, and astronomy, had been harassed by Rabbi Solomon Adret during the controversy over Maimonides' *Guide for the Perplexed* at the beginning of the thirteenth century. It appears, however, that his illustrious grandson, the most radical Aristotelian in Jewish philosophy, did not suffer persecution, as there is no record of severe controversy surrounding him during his lifetime. After his death, as the world-view of the Poetic-Philosophic culture gradually waned and was shunted to the sidelines of spiritual creativity by the new Mystical culture and by a fortified Rabbinic culture, his views came to be opposed, notably by Rabbi Ḥasdai Crescas (1340–1410), whose *Or Adonai* ("The Light of the Lord") was aimed against Gersonides' *Milḥamot Adonai* ("The Wars of the Lord"). But Gersonides continued to retain a following of loyal admirers.

Like other thinkers of his day, Gersonides believed that not only could there be no internal inconsistency within the Torah – the Torah of God being perfect – but that no contradiction between Torah and true science or philosophy was possible, as the intellect, like the Torah itself, was a gift of

God from above. In the introduction to his Torah commentary, Gersonides argues that the Torah is intended to guide us toward true perfection, which is none other than perfection of the intellect, albeit moral perfection is an important preliminary stage leading to intellectual perfection. Knowledge of nature leads to knowledge of God, which, in turn, leads to the true love of God. The "benefits" (to ʿalyot) with which Gersonides summarized the ethics derived from each section of Biblical narrative or prophecy, endeared him to his readers. In the nineteenth century, Adam ha-Kohen Lebensohn wrote that, were the collection of Gersonides' to ʿalyot to be published as a book in its own right, it would constitute a more noble work of ethics than all other ethical treatises hitherto produced by the Jewish people.

We mentioned in chapter 2 that the Biblical exegetes of this culture shared some of the problems which occupied Muslim interpreters of the Koran, stemming from the need to eliminate from Scriptures anthropomorphisms of God, which were to be explained in true philosophical spirit by each school according to its own concept of truth. The conflicting schools of Muslim commentaries on the Koran are clearly reflected in the works of these Jewish scholars.[23] Even later thinkers such as Gersonides, who lived outside the Islamic sphere, in Provence, and no longer wrote in Arabic, continued to be influenced by Muslim thought. Maimonides was influenced by Avicenna (Ibn Sina), while Gersonides, a more radical Aristotelian, accepted many of the views of Averroes (Ibn Rushd). Moreover, even though Gersonides wrote his works in Hebrew, he imitated the Arabic-patterned Tibbonite style.

Many medieval Biblical exegetes begin their works with lengthy expressions of regret that they can find no simple and credible interpretations among their predecessors. Whenever we encounter such prefaces, generally accompanied by considerable polemics and argumentation, there is good ground for suspicion that the *peshat* (literal meaning) of this new exegete, who has audaciously nulled the work of his predecessors, will itself prove to be one of far-fetched *derash* (homiletics). Gersonides opens his commentary to the Song of Songs[24] with the complaint that a correct and seemly interpretation of the scroll was not to found: "We have not seen a plausible commentary which clarifies the words of this scroll." All of the commentators who had preceded him had strayed from the plain meaning of the verses in "the way of sermonics," and had thus expressed the antithesis of what the book itself intended. Gersonides believes that if an exegete wishes to say certain things which are, in themselves, worthy and correct, he ought to say them in a work of his own, and not artificially attach them to Scripture by way of exegesis, for "it is not right that he should mix together with commentaries words of his own sermons." This creates a confusion and a mixing of literary types which bewilders the readers and misconstrues the subject. In light of the many failures in the interpretation of Song of Songs, including the *midrashim* of our Sages, which may appear reasonable, yet in fact fail to interpret the scroll properly, he comes to "write what seems to us the correct meaning of this scroll, without mixing into it other things which do not fulfill this intent."

Gersonides then proceeds to explain his interpretation of the book, its general subject-matter, and how one ought to interpret its details "according to its true intention." Following this introduction the reader learns to his astonishment that Song of Songs is intended to guide the intellect on its path towards perfect apprehension of divine wisdom. As understood by Gersonides, in the spirit of Averroes and others, Song of Songs is an allegorical presentation of Aristotelian philosophy. The intellect is called "King Solomon in Jerusalem," the faculties of the soul are the "daughters of Jerusalem," while the activities of the intellect are the "daughters of Zion." The ripe fruits are the perfection of speculative science, while the flowers and lilies are the fruit "in potential." The entire scroll is an allegory of man's effort to attain the intelligible forms, the apprehension of which bestows eternal life or the survival of the soul. The intellect "grazes in the lilies" when it is in an imperfect stage, influenced by the power of imagination, wherein the intelligibles are only found in potential. The conclusion of Gersonides' "literal" commentary is that Song of Songs is intended to guide man "towards complete perfection, to approach it and make every possible effort to attain it."[25]

The details of Gersonides' philosophy are not our concern here. It is sufficient to note that although Gersonides follows with only minor changes the Averroistic school and thus exaggerates a certain trend within Aristotelianism, his general direction is typical of the dominant view of the entire Poetic-Philosophic culture. What interests us is Gersonides' belief that Song of Songs in fact provides, in poetic form, instruction of a certain philosophical approach. He believes that the entire book is an "allegory and metaphor" for the path that the hylic human intellect must take in order to receive the fulness of the "active intellect," thereby acquiring comprehension of the universe in all its lawfulness and regularity, and, particularly, knowledge of the divine wisdom. A man ought not commit the error of thinking that the meaning of this scroll is transparent.[26] It was written in its present form in order to hide from the eyes of the unworthy, while revealing to the worthy, how they may attach themselves to the Object of their desire and attain perfect knowledge. "Let him kiss me with the kisses of his mouth" refers to spiritual attachment. Intellectual love "is more desirable and honorable than bodily pleasures." "For the kiss indicates attachment, and it is concerning this that it is said of Moses, Aaron, and Miriam that they died by the divine kiss, meaning that at the time of their death they were attached to God." Further on, he observes, "However, it is written 'let him kiss me,' and not 'may I kiss him,' for in reality God is the active party in this, for whatever knowledge we have of Him is due to the fulness which is poured upon us from God, by means of the active intellect."[27]

The phrase, "I am black but comely" (1.5), is explained as the words of the hylic intellect addressed to the soul, "which is originally black, lacking all intellect, but is comely in terms of its readiness to receive the intelligibles [pure ideas] when there is something to arouse it to this." There are many difficulties on the way to attaining perfection of divine wisdom, and the commentator enumerates the various "obstacles" to perfection, even to the longing for perfection, in his explanation of the verse, "I sleep but my heart waketh," (5.2).

This is what the loved one said: although her will and heart were awake to do the will of her beloved to the best of her ability, she was asleep in terms of the deeper [metaphysical] level of these matters and [in terms of] the difficulty of being intellectually prepared for this wisdom, until her beloved called upon her, but she was too indolent to rise and open to him.[28]

It is impossible to attain the level of speculative perfection without a great deal of knowledge.

Here is a philosophical interpretation of two other key verses: "A garden inclosed is my sister, my spouse, a spring shut up, a fountain sealed" (4.12). The spring is the abundance of the active intellect, which is free of matter, "as explained in *De Anima* that the active intellect cannot affect our intellect, unless the phenomena have first been perceived by our senses . . . as Averroes mentioned in his abridged version of *The Book of the Sense and the Sensed*." This and more is alluded to in this verse. He concludes: "'Make haste, my beloved, and be thou like to a roe or to a young hart upon the mountains of spices!' [8.14] She told him that she had already prepared what is needed, and that he should try to ascend the mountains of spices, which is divine wisdom, with diligence and greatest possible haste."[29] The Song of Songs demonstrates, like the well-known Platonic parable, how one may ascend from the cave of folly, sense, and imagination, to the spice-hill of speculative perfection (which includes ethical perfection) where the acquired intellect may attach itself to the active intellect. The Song alludes to the manner in which the human spirit clings to the spiritual entity with which God guides the world and determines its order. The Talmudic symbolism has disappeared without a trace: neither the Congregation of Israel nor the Shechinah, not even the happiness or redemption of the nation, are the subject-matter of Song of Songs, but rather the redemption of the individual soul and the supreme joy which it experiences when it approaches perfection and enters its halls – "the king hath brought me into his chambers" (1.4) – "for the most perfect joy and pleasure is the full, true comprehension of the honored [One]."[30]

We have taken Gersonides as an outstanding example of the dominant type of interpretation of the Song of Songs in the Poetic-Philosophic culture. One may certainly find in the interpretations of other thinkers, such as Joseph Ibn Aknin, a friend and student of Maimonides, differences of detail and nuance, but not of substance. For purposes of comparison, it should be noted that in the *Guide for the Perplexed* Maimonides quotes only six verses of Song of Songs, all of which are explained in a manner quite similar to that of Gersonides. The three principal quotations are at the end of part 3, in which he discusses the highest level of human perfection and how it may be attained. Like Gersonides, it is clear to Maimonides that Song of Songs was meant to instruct human understanding in the path toward perfection; this is the ultimate end of "eternal success" or "eternal beatitude." Moses alone ascended to a level where, "whilst speaking with others, or attending to our bodily wants, our mind is all that time with God; when we are with our hearts constantly near God, even whilst our body is in the society of men."[31] This is alluded to in the verse: "I sleep but my heart waketh" (5.2). He explains the verse, "Let him kiss me with the kisses of his mouth," and the Talmudic simile of "death by a kiss" in connection with Moses, Aaron, and Miriam, like Gersonides.

The meaning of this saying is that these three died in the midst of the pleasure derived from the knowledge of God and their great love for Him. When our Sages figuratively call the knowledge of God united with intense love for Him a kiss, they follow the well-known poetical diction, "Let him kiss me with the kisses of his mouth."[32]

The Song of Songs thus speaks of knowledge of God, which is both apprehension and love of Him; it "allegorically represent[s] the state of our soul"[33] and points to

the true perfection of man; the possession of the highest intellectual faculties; the possession of such notions which lead to true metaphysical opinions as regards God. With this perfection man has obtained his final object; it gives him true human perfection; it remains to him alone; it gives him immortality, and on its account he is called man.[34]

The verse ". . . mine own vineyard have I not kept" (1.6) refers to the abandonment or neglect of this perfection.[35] Thus, despite differences in their understanding of Aristotelianism or in interpretations of individual passages in the Song of Songs, there is general agreement between Gersonides and Maimonides, the foremost, if not the first, thinker of the Poetic-Philosophic culture.

The Mystical commentary – Alschech's Shoshanat ha-ʿamakim

The Mystical writers embroidered the Song of Songs with esoteric meanings: it was the Song, they said, that the Holy One Himself recited each day.[36] The book was not only a paean to God, but also, as it were, God's own song. It "contain[ed] all mysteries of the Torah and of divine wisdom; the song wherein is power to penetrate into things that will be; the song sung by the supernal princes (*sharim = sarim*)."[37] Its praises abound: "When on earth we living terrestrial creatures raise up our hearts in [this] song, then those supernal beings gain an accession of knowledge, wisdom, and understanding, so that they are enabled to perceive matters which even they had never before comprehended." He who is deemed worthy to grasp the depth of all its mysteries and allusions "becomes adept in the doctrine and obtains wit to discern what has been and what will be." King David was already cognizant of and inspired by it to "compose hymns and songs, many in number, in which he hinted concerning future events." His son Solomon then "made a book of the song itself."

What the Talmudic Sages had only hinted at, the Kabbalists developed into a full-fledged theory: the Song of Songs was the song of the deity and the celestial attendants; King Solomon had brought it down from heaven, or had used it as a model. The book contained all matters of Torah and wisdom and prefigured future events, mainly mysteries of the exile and the redemption. More precisely, the Song of Songs was first sung here on earth on the day that Solomon erected the Temple in Jerusalem as a true replica of the celestial Temple. The day when the Song was unveiled to the world was a day in all ways perfect: "The Shekhina came down to earth, and Solomon spoke the Song in the Holy Spirit."[38] The song contains the secrets of Creation (*ma'aseh bereshit*), the mysteries of the deity (*ma'aseh merkavah*), the deeds of the Patriarchs, the bondage in Egypt and the exodus, the Song at the Sea, the giving of the Ten Commandments at Sinai, Israel's exile among the nations, the future redemption, and the resurrection of the dead.

In brief, the book alludes to everything that has been, is, and shall be, as foreseen by King Solomon through divine inspiration. The *Zohar* summarizes all this in one long sentence:

This song comprises the whole Torah; it is a song in which those that are above and those that are below participate; a song formed in the likeness of the world above, which is the supernal Sabbath, a song through which the supernal Holy name is crowned. Therefore it is a holy of holies. Why so? Because all its words are instinct with love and joy.[39]

The Song, then, is more than a parable. It is also mystery and allegory. The physical imagery alludes to lofty spiritual matters. As to the details of the similes, the Kabbalists produced quite a variety of commentaries. But they all agree that the kiss alluded to the adhesion of the soul to the source of life, and an influx of the Holy Spirit that derives from this adhesion. "I am black but comely" (1.5) are the words of the Shechinah "which went down to Egypt with our Patriarch Jacob and was in exile with Israel . . . and was lamenting and fretting over her exile, walking about darkly with the other powers charged over the nations, saying: the exile has rendered me black and gloomy."[40] The perfumes ("the savour of thy good ointments," 1.3) represent the flux from the upper to the lower worlds, the holy perfume of annointment which emanates from the Holy Ancient One. The chambers ("Bring me into your chambers," 1.4) are an allusion to the hidden mysteries of the soul when it cleaves to the source of life. His right and left ("His left hand is under my head, and his right hand doth embrace me," 2.6) designate the two substances, the upper substance, the simple and pure, and the lower, the polluted. The lover is the divine intellect, the crown ("the crown wherewith his mother crowned him in the day of his espousals," 3.11) is divine providence, and the espousals, the true supreme goal.

The above summarizes briefly the approach to the Song of Songs in the early generations of the Mystical culture, primarily in the thirteenth century, before it had gained widespread currency. When the efficacy of the Poetic-Philosophic culture began to wane, the Mystics gained ascendancy, so that even before the flowering of Lurianic Kabbalah, the great codifier Rabbi Moses Isserles could testify that Kabbalah was steadily spreading among the people, and that not only scholars, but everyone, even simple, ignorant folk, who could barely distinguish between their right and their left, were jumping on board and learning Kabbalah.[41] Thus by the mid-sixteenth century the writings of the Mystics were already accessible to a wide public.

Among the many Kabbalistic commentaries to Song of Songs, one that gained considerable popularity was *Sefer Shoshanat ha-ʿamakim* ("The Book of the Lily of the Valley") by Moses Alschech.[42] It is interesting to compare Gersonides' philosophic interpretation completed in 1326, with this Kabbalistic work of 200 years later.

Rabbi Moses Alschech was born in Adrianopolis in 1507. He settled in Safed and was an important Kabbalist there until the advent of Rabbi Isaac Luria (the "Holy Ari"). According to tradition, the Holy Ari refused to teach Alschech the mysteries of his lore. Alschech became known primarily as a Biblical exegete, preacher, and codifier (Posek). *Torat Moshe*, his commentary on the Pentateuch, attained great fame and endeared him to readers who eventually came to call him "the Holy Alschech." He also composed homiletics and commentaries on the Prophets and the Five Scrolls. His commentaries were in no small measure responsible for the popular spread of Kabbalah. He explained the literal meaning of Scriptures based on the Rabbis and Rashi and on his own insights, but mainly he let himself be guided by the *Zohar* and other Kabbalistic writings.

Alschech, too, believed that the Song of Songs was superior to all other songs found in the Bible, including the Song of Moses,[43] and that only in the days of King Solomon, when the Temple was erected, did joy spread throughout the world by virtue of the Song of Songs. Alschech thought that the Scroll's essence is a dialogue between the exiled Congregation of Israel and its Lord, a proclamation of the reciprocal love between Israel and God. In lovely parables the Scroll compared Israel to "a princess, loved by a great king, replete with wisdom and beauty. The king took this maiden, who found favor before him more than all other women, for a wife and went out to war against her enemies; she too loved him." But later he found fault with her, "because she made love to one of the courtiers; the king was very angry, and he banished her from his house." Ever since the queen has been wandering from house to house and from court to court finding no rest for her weary feet; in her painful wanderings she recalls her "first love . . . and she weeps . . . the king too remembers his wife and her fate." In the end, the king takes his spouse, his beloved, back to his bosom. This is the story-line of the Song of Songs, a dramatic tale of love, sin, exile, return, reconciliation, and consolation, more or less in keeping with the Talmudic *midrashim*. The difference is in the *sodot*, the mysteries.

Alschech does not wish to stray too far from the literal meaning, the *peshat*, but we have already noted that such well-intentioned promises by the exegetes are seldom kept. The *peshat* and the *sod* (mystical meaning) fuse in *Shoshanat ha-ᶜamakim* to produce some truly bizarre commentaries. A critical reader of this commentary will readily identify its author as an active participant in the revolutionary Mystical spiritual transformation, which undertook to reveal, via theurgic-cosmic symbolism, a new truth in both the inner content and the outer shell of the Torah. The Song of Songs contains, in Alschech's opinion, symbols of the inner, hidden life of the deity; whoever can grasp this system of mysteries and allusions may attain a high degree of personal perfection, may actively assist all of Creation, and may add strength to God – this being the ultimate goal of man's service. Every Jew is required to participate in "mending the world" and precipitating redemption. Israel's exile is but one revelation of the reign of "shells" in the world. Therefore, mending the world and Israel's redemption are a single holy endeavor, the essence of which is giving strength to God. There are many expressions in the Kabbalah to this giving. The Song of Songs, according to Alschech, introduces the intelligent reader into the knowledge of the *sodot* and brings him closer to the redeeming act.

How so? Let us look at the details of the commentary as they relate to the soteriological dimension, i.e. to personal salvation, to the redemption of Israel, and to the mending of the Shechinah and the world. The name Song of Songs itself testifies to a twofold praise: the Congregation of Israel lauds the Holy One, and He lauds Israel: "And perhaps this is what our Sages meant when they said: 'All the writings are holy, but the Song of Songs is the Holy of Holies.'. . . This Song contains two holies, the praise of the Holy One and the praise of the Congregation of Israel."

"Let him kiss me with the kisses of his mouth" (1.2) refers to *devekut*, mystical cleaving to God; to address him "mouth to mouth," as did Moses, is ultimate perfection. "Thy love is better than wine" (1.2) – those who drink wine are in need of sleep, to rid themselves of the effects of the liquor. But with their drunkenness, the sweetness of the wine they have tasted will also wear off:

Not so is Your love, for when You brought us to the place our Sages called "the winecellar of Torah" and gave us Your love and rejoiced in our love for You, we knew then too that the Temple would be destroyed because of our sins; since then You have been sleeping because of our evil doings, until You awake, O God, to redeem us . . . Your sleep has not removed Your friendship from us, for although You exiled us to another land, You have not despised us and our union has not been broken, unlike wine which sours.

A bold metaphor indeed! God has fallen asleep from an excess of the wine of love and must be awoken. When He wakes, His sweet love for Israel will never depart again.

Alschech comments at length on the verse, "Look not upon me, because I am black" (1.6). The Gentiles accuse Israel of double blackness, inside and out, in its soul and in its material being, in sinfulness and in miseries inflicted upon it from without:

This nation has sold out its honor. But Israel replies that the darkness of its sins is not its natural hue, for "I am scorched by the sun," and darkness clings to me as something unnatural, which is not the case with you [Gentiles], whose blackness is intrinsic . . . No evil has clung to the part that is my soul.

In brief, the darkness of the soul is unnatural and temporary. Moreover, when the Temple still stood, the Congregation of Israel watched not only over the vineyard of the Lord God of Hosts, i.e. over the House of Israel, but also over the vineyards of other nations, by offering sacrifices for their welfare. When Israel ceased cultivating its own vineyard, the Holy One punished it and destroyed the Temple, but this He did only as a father would chastise a son. The Gentiles reprove Israel that it still clings to its Beloved and believes itself superior to other nations, when in fact it is black and dark-spirited because of their oppression. To this Israel replies that it suffers only from external afflictions, from the stroke of the sun, and is likened to the "tents of Kedar" (1.5), "because the Holy One did not inflict these [evils] on the inner soul, only on the outer form, in order to protect the inner soul, as the tents of Kedar suffer to be blackened from without from the heat of the sun in order to protect that which is within."

"Thy two breasts are like two young roes" (4.5, 7.4) allude to the two interpretational methods, *peshat* and *sod*, which should be applied to the study of the Torah as the two most important of the four methods for interpreting Torah. The exegete assumes, as do all the Mystical commentators, that "each and every *mitzvah* has a source of holiness above, each according to its mystery; when a man performs a *mitzvah*, he awakens its holy source and root; the light increases, and his soul cleaves to the Supernal." Every person can draw down the divine light from above when he fulfills a commandment. In the sequence of the four methods for comprehending the Torah: literally, allegorically, homiletically, and mystically, there is an ascending order, the last being nearer to the Blessed One than the three underlying levels. But all four levels are interconnected, and it is possible to draw down the spirituality of the Torah from above by any one of these methods. The Mystical Sage knows how to proceed from the literal meaning to the allegorical, from there to the homily and thence to the profound mystery of the Torah. Thus he makes the connection between the upper and the lower worlds "until the fire of the upper world invades the earth below . . . and that is the purpose of this world's existence."

Like Gersonides, Alschech concludes on an eschatological note. But whereas the philosopher mobilized all of Aristotelian philosophy, as he understood it, to prove that the Song of Songs provided instruction in personal salvation by the acquisition of "intelligibles" and a cleaving unto the "active intellect," the popular Kabbalist ends with the redemption of Israel. In this he is certainly closer to the Talmudic Sages. We are again reminded that every culture was enchanted by the road leading to the "mountains of spices" (the final words of the Song of Songs), but that the paths to salvation taken in each culture were quite different.

The influence of Mystical commentaries, as illustrated by Alschech's *Shoshanat ha-ʿamakim*, was varied and profound. The Ḥassidic movement founded by the Baʿal Shem Tov had a very special regard for the Song of Songs, and its adherents used to chant it with intense enthusiasm and concentration on Sabbath eves, after ritual immersion, as though it were a prayer, and a prayer of particular sanctity at that, which combined the study of Torah and the observance of the commandment of prayer. The *Zohar*, Alschech's commentary, and other exegeses contributed to the transformation of Song of Songs into a book used in prayer. The Mystical culture triumphed over the Poetic-Philosophic culture and swept aside the latter's world-view. Scriptural commentaries of the kind offered by Gersonides fell into discredit.

4

THE COMMANDMENTS IN ISRAEL'S CULTURES

Introduction – the problem in the State of Israel

The problem of the *halachic* laws – their underlying reasons, the manner of their observance, and, especially, their formal status in the State of Israel – arose as an intensely emotional issue immediately upon the state's establishment. Were the laws of the new state going to reflect the ideas of a secular legal system, in keeping with the ideology of its largely non-observant citizens, or would the reborn Jewish state be governed by the Rabbinic legal system, the Halachah? Or, by way of compromise between these two opposing positions, should a fusion or mixture of both systems, some kind of hybrid or synthesis between democracy and theocracy, be attempted? Many pondered the dilemma: in what manner and to what extent should the *halachic* legal system be reactivated in the diverse spheres of modern life? The Halachah, it was argued, had insured Jewish survival throughout the long periods of oppressions and catastrophes. One could not deny, of course, that as the nation's independence diminished, the jurisdiction of Jewish law had contracted correspondingly. (Talmudic rulings like, "The law of the kingdom is the law," acknowledged the precedence of Gentile law over Jewish law in secular matters and testified to the Halachah's subordinate legal status.) Nonetheless, the Halachah continued to govern both private and communal aspects of a Jew's life in exile. Moreover, even before the founding of the state, the Rabbinate in Palestine exercised jurisdiction in family law. Should all Jewish courts in Israel, then, be required to enforce the laws of the Torah, or should Rabbinic courts exist side by side with secular courts?

Both the Ashkenazi and the Sephardi Chief Rabbis at the time gave the matter much thought. Ashkenazi Chief Rabbi Herzog recognized that the Jewish state would be neither quite theocratic nor entirely democratic. Separation of "church" and state was out of the question, but, he acknowledged, the realization of the desirable structure would demand of the Rabbinic authorities profound study and care. Sephardi Chief Rabbi Uziel wrote in much the same vein: the task before us, he said, was to find a way of fusing the Torah with the exigencies of the state, of indelibly imprinting the Torah upon the state in a manner fitting the character of the Holy Land and the Jewish people.[1] Opinions diverged widely precisely over the "fitting" manner in which religion and the new political reality could be reconciled. These ranged from rigidly uncompromising Orthodoxy to advocacy of *Torah im derech ʾeretz* (Torah-rule combined with worldly approaches), in the neo-Orthodox style, to still other positions favoring the preservation of the Torah's tradition based only on the *ideas* embodied in its laws, rather than on the literal sense of the laws themselves. And, of course, there are many in Israel today who wish to minimize the status, authority, and scope of the Halachah or to separate entirely between state and Halachah.

I submit that our theory on the multiplicity of Jewish cultures may shed new light on this dilemma. Perhaps by gaining a better understanding of how differently the commandments were conceived in the ages of faith, we can expand the horizons within which our choices in this "church–state" dilemma must ultimately be made, and thus add clarity to a difficult issue.

The commandments in the Biblical versus the Talmudic culture

The transition from the Biblical world to the Talmudic framework was one of the most decisive transformations the Jewish people was destined to undergo in its long history. So momentous was the change that it is evidenced even in seemingly external-semantic clues. Take, for example, the imagery applied to Israel itself in these two cultures. In the Bible Israel is depicted as a youth, a beloved son, sometimes as a bold warrior, or as a young virgin, a daughter of Zion, a bride and betrothed, or even as a young she-camel. In the Talmudic culture the central image is that of the yoke – the "yoke of *mitzvot*" and the "yoke of the Kingdom of Heaven." The Biblical author who laments over the destruction of the First Temple knows that the youth that is Israel will not brook the terrible yoke thrust upon him; Israel balks at the harsh judgment. The author's heart aches for the young man who "sit[s] alone and sigh[s]" over the yoke that lies heavy upon him (Lam. 3.28). In what seems to be an attempt to glean some sort of lesson from the terrible disaster, the author of Lamentations comments despondently on the young Judaean sitting amidst the ruins of Jerusalem awaiting mercy: "It is good, too, for a man to carry the yoke in his youth" (Lam. 3.27). How is it, then, that in the Midrash (*Lamentations Rabbah*) this yoke is embraced without reservation as a thing to be desired, a holy burden ordained by God? The Daughter of Zion, Israel the boy and man, the valiant warrior, have been metamorphosed into the Congregation of Israel, a collective body which obediently extends its neck into the yoke of Torah and commandments. The emphasis placed by the Talmudic culture on the observance of the commandments has no parallel in the Biblical culture. The latter knew that one was enjoined to observe and practise, but only the former turned the performance of a precept into the very essence and heart of its creed, thereby turning Judaism into a religion of observances. The Talmudic culture certainly did not ignore the importance of faith and homiletics, of Torah-study and exegesis. But the new emphasis was on acts, on the total immersion of body and soul in the performance of the precepts.[2]

The source of Biblical laws: the covenant

Let us now consider three aspects of the commandments in Israel's cultures: the source of the commandment, its nature, and the reason or justification given for its observance. What is the source of the commandment? In the Biblical culture the answer is relatively simple: the commandment is written in the law of Moses. This code contains accounts of deeds and events, instruction in ethics and faith, as well as specific statutes and laws. The Torah's laws, however, are clearly more than mere formulations of a legal code such as Hammurabi's; they are the words of the living God as enounced by His Prophet. We will not, I trust, be charged with nineteenth-century liberal-rationalist apologetics when we say that the essence of the Torah is not its political and social legislation, but rather the religious and ethical content that embodies an ideal constitution, a blueprint for God's kingdom. For this reason, incidentally, one finds that Biblical law, unlike legal systems based on a political-organizational conception, neglects at times to mention the penalty for an offence. Its purpose, it appears, was to guide the Israelites in the "path of righteousness." Many of the Bible's laws are actually ancient customs, accepted usages in the life of the tribes, desires and noble aspirations, instructions, admonitions, warnings, and intimations of future destinies. The Holy Scriptures are very broad in nature and do not even contain a political constitution in the form of a detailed kingship law. The Torah contains elements of state law, but it is not essentially a book of political statutes. Moreover, one surmises that what the Torah and other Biblical writings *do* contain by way of a political constitution was already outdated at the time the kingship was instituted in the kingdoms of Judaea and Ephraim.

The anchoring of all Biblical law in the idea of a covenant has been frequently pointed to in Scriptural research as the most unique feature of this law. Let us then briefly examine this extraordinary idea that nurtures all of Biblical law. Varying expressions, distinct in coloration and in depth of tone, are given in the Bible to the nation's relationship with its God. The essence of the tie between the Almighty and His worshipers was expressed in a complex array of attributes, reflective of God's sway over the forces of creation and of nature, over the lives of men and states, and over the events of history: God is Israel's King, the Creator of the universe, the Judge of all the earth, a faithful Shepherd. Such epithets for the deity were not unique to Israel's tribes; other nations and faiths had, in larger or smaller measure, conceived similar appellations. But in addition to these concepts and to the experiences which had triggered them, Israel developed a concept uniquely its own; this was the idea of the covenant. The God who had brought Israel out of Egypt and had given His people the land of Canaan, was Israel's ally and covenantal partner. Perhaps the most remarkable thing about this covenant was the freedom in which it was undertaken. It sprang from a conscious act of volition and choice, a testimonial not so much to the lordship of God, as to the freedom of the nation that elected to enter into it. The bond between the two covenanted partners was by no means a normal, self-evident tie; neither was it weighted with a terror of nature and of nature's master; it was not, that is, a magical bond. It was, above all, a voluntary and freely undertaken engagement.

The covenant between God and people also determined the nature of the bond between people and land. Other ancient nations might experience a natural-magical adhesion to their lands. Israel's tie to its land was made conditional upon certain human choices and acts, upon the will to ethical commitment, upon the nobility of man's differentiation from his surroundings in an act of free will. In general, other nations clung to their lands with primordial instinct – strong, healthy, opaque to the transcendent. But for Israel, its dwelling in the land was by no means a self-evident and routine natural event that occasions no questioning or wonderment. The experience of the covenant taught Israel that the three constituent elements of its world – its existence as a nation, its inheritance of the land and its divine partner in the covenant – were inextricably interwoven by virtue of a volitional act it had undertaken for a certain purpose. It was as though without this tie, each of these elements were rendered meaningless.

The concept of the covenant was transplanted into the distant past and was counted in the historical experiences of all past generations, until eventually the unfolding of the entire Jewish history from the earliest beginnings came to be viewed in its light, as though Abraham's covenant were periodically renewed. In any event, the ancient Hebrews had the option at Sinai of *not* entering into the covenant, yet they accepted it in freedom. It was a covenant contracted not over matters of ritual, but over concerns of law and justice (see Jer. 34).

The covenant and the laws

It is important for our understanding of the commandments in the Torah to bear in mind that the covenant was a form of mutual obligation; there is little evidence in the Bible of mutual obligations in private affairs which do *not* take the form of covenants. Yeḥezkel Kaufmann asserts that faith in the covenant was the base for that "peculiar Israelite mixture of law, morality and cult."[3] The Bible was not, of course, immune to influences from the surrounding dominant civilization (any more than were subsequent Jewish cultures in their milieux). Scholars who have compared Biblical law to other legal systems of the ancient Near East, especially to Mesopotamian jurisprudence, have pointed to many similarities between the laws of the Bible and the code of Hammurabi (*c.* 1700 BCE). An entire literature has arisen around this comparison which need not be elaborated here.

It is the dissimilarity between the two legal systems that is more interesting than the points of similarity. In the ancient Near Eastern states the king alone was the source of authority and the wielder of power, both lawgiver and judge. The laws of Babylonia are inscribed on memorial tablets celebrating the justice and integrity of the deceased monarch, proclaiming his greatness of spirit to all future generations. An infraction of Babylonian law was considered an offense against the king's authority and honor. In contrast, the laws of the Torah symbolize the tie between God and His people, and an infraction of the law is an offense against God, rather than against the king. The law stands above the arbitrariness of mortal rulers, who are themselves subject to it. Moreover, the law of the Torah contains no special laws for each class in society; one law obtains for all Israel and even for the alien residing in its midst.

These obvious differences stem from a culture which derived the authority for all injunctions and interdictions from the idea of a covenant between people and God, a sort of contract aimed at uniting the nation and transferring governance from the state to the plane of the divine contact. The covenant binds all of Israel's tribes into a single national unit and does not distinguish between religious and secular law (*ius* and *fas*), between criminal or social law and ritual commandments. All three codes of laws in the Pentateuch (the Covenant Code, Exod. 20.22–3, 33; the Priestly Code, Lev. 17–26; and the Law of Deuteronomy, Deut. 12–26) begin with ritual commandments and move on to social and criminal legislation. These laws are not imposed from without by a king or a charismatic leader, but are accepted by a people after hearing the words of the covenant.

True, other cultures also had gods who handed down laws to men. Shemesh, lord of the heavens, gave Hammurabi his code. He and Sin, the moon god, maintain the order of the world so that day and night, summer and winter may not cease. In the western Semitic world there was a god named Zedek (Justice), as we learn from Scripture: "Melchizedek King of Salem", "Adonizedek King of Jerusalem" (Gen. 14.18; Ps. 110.4; Josh. 10.3). The promise held in the name did not, however, bind the god himself to act in justice. The god of the ancient Hebrew was from the outset not only an omnific ruler of the world, but also a just judge of all the earth. The demand to be just was incumbent upon God himself: "Shall not the judge of all the earth do what is just?" (Gen. 18.25). God's essential quality is seen as ethical and redeeming.

The Torah contains laws in three separate codes which differ in style, in order of presentation, and in content, and much has been written on this subject and needs no repeating. There are few laws which appear in identical form in each of the three sources. What all three codes have in common, as Kaufmann pointed out, is that peculiarly Israelitic phenomenon of a "tradition [that] knows no secular legislative authority. Ideally, only the prophet, as the spokesman of YHWH, can legislate."[4] Elders and monarchs could act as judges; they could not make laws.

What is most important to us here is that all three legal codes in the Pentateuch are anchored in the idea that God contracted a covenant with Israel regarding the laws He gave them. The great differences between each of the codes and within each code testify that there existed in ancient Israel a well-developed legal-ethical literature, and that the law was not a political constitution formulated by the king's scribes, but the law of God as given to priests, Prophets, and a succession of spiritual men.

The commandments and the covenant in the Talmudic culture

The idea that the commandments stemmed from the Biblical covenant was retained by the Talmudic Sages. There are scholars who believe that, during the Second Temple and in subsequent Mishnah and Talmud times, the concept of the Biblical covenant was transformed into a notion of public consent, and that this became the basis of the Oral Law. As proof they cite the Talmudic dictum, "We should not impose upon the community unless the majority of the community will be able to stand it" (*Bab. K.* 79b and elsewhere). Ḥaim Tchernowitz, for example, claimed that according to the Talmud, the Torah's authority rested on the concept of the covenant and on the community's consent, and that this consent embodied the idea of a Rousseau-style social contract, wherein the law's authority is seen as emanating from the general will and the mutual consent of the nation.[5] But this is a very dubious theory. According to the Sages, the law does not exist merely because the community desires it; of course, a commandment which most of the community cannot tolerate is ineffective and must be abolished, but nowhere does the Talmud speak of a ruling which should be abolished merely because people do not want it.

Scholars like Tchernowitz attempted to confer upon the Talmudic concept of the commandments an ethical and rational autonomy; the acceptance of heaven's yoke was made dependent upon the community's consent. E.E. Urbach rightfully comments that thinkers of this liberal school (Tchernowitz, Moritz Lazarus, and earlier precursors), who sought in the

Oral Law an autonomous, human ethic emanating from the demands of man's reason, were voicing their own wishful thoughts, not the intention of the Sages.[6] Numerous interpretations have been rendered by such scholars in this faulty manner, especially when dealing with Talmudic dicta that if this or that *mitzvah* had not been commanded in the Torah, by right it should have been commanded, i.e. that there were commandments the rationale and sense of which were simply self-evident, mandated by human reason. None of these sayings, however, change the plain fact that in the eyes of the Talmudic Sages the law was theonomic and not autonomous: God alone was the Giver of the commandments.

Clearly, the idea of the covenant underwent a very fundamental change during the Talmudic culture. The aspect of free choice did not perhaps entirely disappear, but it was transposed to a distant past, to the time of the giving of the Torah. No longer do we see before us a party engaged in a present, live covenant; instead we have a tradition of a covenant. Whosoever desires to cleave to God, must take upon himself the yoke of *mitzvot*. The notion "yoke" was brought to bear upon the fulfillment of all the practical commandments. There was a yoke of Torah, a yoke of matrimony, a yoke of one's profession – all were incumbent obligations one had to fulfill by specified deeds.

Commandments lacking sufficiently clear reasons, or the meanings of which were not self-evident to human reason, were called by the Sages "covenants." Some of these had a foundation in the covenant contracted in the Torah, such as circumcision or the Sabbath (often referred to in the Bible as "a sign" and "a covenant"). The Sages, however, expanded the concept "covenant" to include, for example, the prohibition of mixing milk and meat. Rabbi Simeon says: " 'Thou shalt not seethe a kid in its mother's milk.' Why is this law stated in three places? To correspond to the three covenants which the Holy One, blessed be He, made with Israel: One at Horeb, one in the plains of Moab, and one at Mount Gerizim and Mount Ebal."[7] This saying has a number of versions. Elsewhere, Rabbi Simeon makes the even bolder claim that the covenant was made not only over the prohibition of mixing meat and milk, but over *all* other commandments.

The Sages also deemed it a singular privilege to fulfill the commandments under conditions of peril and persecution, which call for suffering and sacrifice. There are many sayings on the merit of suffering and its connection with the covenant, such as: "Precious are chastisements, for just as a covenant was established concerning the land, so also a covenant is established by means of chastisement. For it is said: 'The Lord thy God chastiseth thee' [Deut. 8.5]. And it is also written: 'For the Lord thy God bringeth thee into a good land' [Deut. 8.7]."[8] We learn, therefore, that he who is in the yoke, is in the covenant. The dramatic events that first brought about the contracting of the covenant between God and the Patriarchs, and later between the lord of the Prophets and all of Israel are submerged in the Talmudic culture in myriad *halachic* commandments. The Sages expounded, "I will bring a sword upon you, that shall execute the vengeance of the covenant [Lev. 26.25]; now 'covenant' means nothing else but the Torah" (*Sab.* 33a), whereby they referred both to the commandments of the Torah and to its study. I believe we may rightly conclude that the concept of the covenant was essentially changed. It was transposed to a happening in the distant past, to a non-recurring event which was no longer subject to modification, and which the nation was commanded to accept as the Sages interpreted it.

Coercion and free choice

The Rabbis surely regarded the community's consent to the commandments as desirable and important at any period, although, as we have said, it was not a precondition for the covenant's force. Rabbi Abdimi ben Ḥama's famous *derash* that the verse, "And they stood *under* the mount" (Exod. 19.17), "teaches that the Holy One, blessed be He, overturned the mountain upon them like an (inverted) cask, and said to them, 'If ye accept the Torah, 'tis well; if not, there shall be your burial'" (*Sab.* 88a) was an exceptional view. The Rabbis generally did not share the opinion that the Torah had been forced upon the nation from above, like an overturned cask. They did not believe in coercion. A man must accept the Torah willingly. However, as there is no mention of free consent between covenanting parties who conclude a conditional agreement with eath other, the only freedom that remains of that Biblical concept is the Rabbis' freedom to interpret the Torah.

The Sages differed in their opinions about this matter of coercion and choice; they agreed generally with Rabba's opinion that if a man desires the Torah, he makes it his own:

One should always study that part of the Torah which is his heart's desire, as it is said: "But whose desire is in the law of the Lord." Raba also said: At the beginning (of this verse) the Torah is assigned to the Holy One, blessed be He, but at the end it is assigned to him (who studies it), for it is said: "Whose desire is in the Law of the Lord and in his (own) Law doth he meditate day and night" (*Ab. Zar.* 19a).

The commandments are obligatory, but it is also obligatory to love them, and to fulfill them, not only out of fear or hope for reward, but out of love. These are, of course, the classical arguments and cravings of all dominant cultures: first to have their authority accepted in subservience and fear, later to see it loved and accepted for its own sake. Moreover, many, if not all, of the champions of the Talmudic culture saw in the commandments and in the warnings about their detailed observance the very essence of Scripture.

They queried: "Why were the Ten Commandments not said at the beginning of the Torah?"[9] Underlying this question is the assumption that the commandments are the quintessence of the Torah, and that Israel was elected to receive the Torah for the exclusive purpose of their fulfillment.

Three Talmudic ideas regarding legitimation

The issue of the commandments was far from simple for the Talmudic Sages. The Bible explicitly forbade any additions or detractions from the written word. The Sages had to vindicate the innovations entailed in their legislation, both to themselves and against the attacks of Sadducees and various sects. In order to effect this legitimation, the Rabbis advanced three propositions, by virtue of which they could clear their way to innovating *halachot* in the light of their own ontology.

The first proposition maintained that the statutes and ordinances contained in all the books of Holy Scriptures require interpretation, and that only the interpretation of the Sages accurately renders their true meaning. The second idea was that the Torah was given to Moses at Sinai complete with all its subsequent interpretations and nuances. The third thesis argued that not only Moses and the Prophets had received their authority from Sinai, but that upon each Sage in every generation authority devolved from that same source.

Let us examine these three central Talmudic propositions, which later cultures of faith likewise adopted as the solid foundation for the validity of innovated commandments. Each culture, of course, interpreted these propositions in the light of its own ontology, but no full-fledged Jewish culture during the ages of faith was ever antinomian, i.e. favoring abolition of the Torah's commandments as previously interpreted by the Talmudic Sages. To be sure, one could always find individuals and minorities who rejected, in lesser or greater degree, the third proposition. The debate over the authority of the Sages reappeared in one form or another in each culture.

The purpose of the commandments

Post-Talmudic cultures diverged considerably when it came to understanding the nature of the commandments. What was the commandments' purpose? How do they alleviate a Jew's distress, i.e. what is their soteriological value for the salvation of the individual soul and for the redemption of Israel? The precepts of the Torah, we have said, were viewed as incumbent upon Israel regardless of whether or not their underlying reasons were clearly understood; they were the essence of the covenant between God and His people. In fact, the Torah rarely elaborates on the reasons for the commandments. Isaak Heinemann pointed out in his detailed study on this subject[10] that, in the Torah's view, the precepts are enjoined because they reflect both the Creator's will and man's ethical conscience. Even "irrational" commandments, i.e. commandments the motives of which elude man's comprehension, never contradict the universal human ethic. The assumption is that from the legislator's point of view they are, in fact, entirely rational.

Where the Torah does provide reasons for specific commandments, Heinemann classified them as follows: God's authority, as an expression of a commandment's value ("I am the Lord," or "You shall fear the Lord your God"); ethical reasons, such as the requirement to leave a portion of the harvest to the poor; historical reasons, for example, commandments connected with Passover, and remembrance of the covenant (laws regarding fringes and phylacteries); emotional reasons, aimed at arousing feelings of sympathy, pity, and love (for the alien, the slave, the needy); various logical and utilitarian reasons. The Torah stresses: "It is a thing very near to you, upon your lips and in your heart ready to be kept" (Deut. 30.11), i.e. it is not beyond your understanding, although, as we have said, neither is it conditional upon your understanding; it emanates from a superior legislating authority.

The Sages laid great stress on the need to accept the yoke of the commandments even against one's own inclination or reason. They exhorted man to practise them with a whole and willing heart. They did not, of course, view this yoke as necessarily vexatious and oppressive; rather, being God's will, it was viewed more as a voluntary commitment. But the minority opinion of Rabbi Ḥanina could also be entertained: "He who is commanded and fulfills (the command) is greater than he who fulfills it though not commanded" (Kid. 31a).

The Sages emphasized that the commandments were useful to man, that God, in imposing the mitzvot, had wanted to "grant merit" upon Israel, to "refine" them; after all, He Himself had no need to be worshiped. They distinguished between "rational" commandments and commandments which were based not on reason but rather on Revelation (Mitzvot shim'iyot, to borrow a later expression). Counted among the rational commandments was the ruling midah keneged midah ("measure for measure"), as well as precepts whose reasons were symbolic, such as the four species on the Festival of Sukkot, precepts that had a pedagogical value (to remind or to teach a lesson), and all the social-ethical commandments. Heinemann notes[11] the curious fact that when we survey the reasons given by the Sages for the commandments, the ethical motives appear relatively infrequently. It never occurred to them, as later philosophers would claim, that circumcision or the prohibition of certain foods were useful, rational measures for the curbing of one's passions. It was only later philosophers who, in order to distill the sharp heteronomy of a precept ordained from above, felt they had to find for the observance of commandments persuasive reasons. The Sages, more ingenuous perhaps in their faith and tradition than the philosophers, had greater confidence that a just and merciful God, their Father in heaven, would not ordain rules which were not for the benefit and edification of His children; they did not probe for the meaning of the commandments. Probes, questions, and doubts were the fit occupation of a more critical consciousness than theirs was. It was generally accepted in the Talmudic culture that the reasons for the commandments were: to reward those who practise them; to "refine" or "discipline" people (letzaref bahen et haberiot); and to add holiness. It was said, for example, about the Sabbath: "'For it is holy unto you.' This tells that the Sabbath adds holiness to Israel."[12] There were some Sages, especially among the Amora'im, who ruled that one should not attempt to discover the motives for the commandments at all, for what if the motives remain hidden, or, if revealed, are found unsatisfactory, tending rather to promote discord and heresy? Commandments which had no clear purpose (e.g. the red heifer, or the laws of ritual cleanness) were known as ḥukim (statutes) and had to be kept simply because they were so ordained by God. This is the meaning of Rabbi Yoḥanan ben Zakkai's famous instruction to his disciples: "By your life! Neither the dead person defiles nor does the water purify; only this is the decree of the Holy One, blessed be He. The Holy One, blessed be He, hath said: I have ordained a statute, I have issued an edict, and thou hast no right to transgress mine edict."[13]

Talmudic scholars in our generation have established that the notion of the "joy of mitzvah" was doubtlessly a polemical concept directed at those who sought to fulfill precepts on account of the reasons underlying them. The commandments had to be fulfilled for no other reason than that they had been ordained by God. The Talmud says: "'That delighteth greatly in His commandment' (Ps. 112.1): In his commandments, but not in the reward of His commandments" (Ab.Zar. 19a). A Jew must rejoice at the very observance of the commandment, not at the resultant material or spiritual reward. The Sages allowed that by first engaging in the commandments not "for their own sake," a man will eventually keep them "for their own sake," for pure and disinterested motives. Generally, however, they held that it was not a requirement for the commandments to be performed with intentness, except, of course, for prayer.

Subsequent Jewish cultures generally accepted this idea that commandments were given in order to bestow rewards upon their practitioners, or to refine their intentions and deeds, or to increase holiness, but opinions differed as to the nature of the reward, the refinement, and the holiness. No one seriously questioned the above-stated basic three tenets regarding the importance of the newly introduced Talmudic commandments: "Halachot are the body of the Torah," announced the Sages.[14] And even: "Not a day passes in which the Holy One, blessed be He, does not teach a new law in the heavenly Court."[15] They acknowledged that Halachah was difficult and oppressive, as we learn from the Tanna debe Eliyahu: "In order to study the words of the Torah one must cultivate in oneself the (habit of) the ox for bearing a yoke and of the ass for carrying burdens" (Ab.Zar. 5b). Yet it had to be fulfilled. The emphasis was always on the importance of the deed, the practice. "Is study greater, or practice?" the Sages asked. Even Rabbi Akiba, for whom study was of the utmost importance, gave due tribute to practice: "Study is greater for it leads to practice" (Kid. 40b). Rabbi Simeon ben Gamliel, however, said outright: "Study is not the most important thing, but deed" (Avot 1.17). The dispute among the Sages was mainly about the origin of certain commandments, and especially about the status of the Ten Commandments.

The status of the Ten Commandments

The status accorded to the Ten Commandments is of particular importance in evaluating the mitzvot in relation to the first and second Talmudic propositions we have mentioned, i.e. that the mitzvot required the Sages' interpretation and that this interpretation originated at Sinai. Despite the Sages' insistence that divine revelation in all generations and to all the Prophets was focused in that non-recurring event at Sinai (or perhaps precisely because of this insistence), they could not assign special merit to the Ten Commandments. They could grant no pre-eminent status to certain commandments over others. This is the inescapable paradox resulting from their assumption that the Torah – Written and Oral – was all given at Sinai, that it rested upon the Ten Commandments, yet was not entirely encompassed in them.[16] As Rabbi Levi ben Hama said in the name of Rabbi Simeon ben Lakish:

What is the meaning of the verse: "And I will give thee the tables of stone, and the law and the commandment, which I have written that thou mayest teach them?" [Exod. 24.12] "Tables of stone": these are the Ten Commandments; "the law": this is the Pentateuch; "the commandment": this is the Mishna; "which I have written": these are the Prophets and the Hagiographia; "that thou mayest teach them": this is the Gemara. It teaches (us) that all these things were given to Moses on Sinai (Ber. 5a).

The Sages did not share Philo's view that the Ten Commandments merited a more honored status than other precepts; that idea, as scholars have rightfully pointed out, appears only in midrashim of the late Geʾonic period. Rashi cites Rabbi Saʿadiah Gaʾon's work on this question in his commentary on Exod. 24.12:

"The tablets of stone, and the law and the commandment which I have written to teach them" – all the six hundred and thirteen commandments are implicitly contained in the Ten Commandments and may therefore be regarded as having been written on the tablets. Rabbi Saadia specified in the *Azharot* which he has composed those commandments which may be associated with each of the Ten Commandments.[17]

The Sages did not believe that the Ten Commandments contained every law, or that they alone were given to Moses at Sinai, but they did, apparently, believe that in and between each of the Ten Commandments its own commentaries and refinements were already contained: "Between every two commandments were written the sections and the minutiae of the Torah."[18]

We summarize here by saying that in dealing with the question whether all commandments were actually contained in the Ten Commandments, or whether to each of the Ten were appended commentaries, refinements, and eductions (using the hermeneutic principles with which the Torah was to be interpreted), the Sages were anxious not to overstate the importance of the Ten Commandments. They were thus in a better position to refute the claim that the Ten Commandments alone were given at Sinai.

Legitimation and polemics in the Talmudic culture

The third and most polemical proposition that the Sages advanced for the legitimation of their need to innovate, namely, that their authority was bestowed upon them on the occasion of that first giving of the Torah at Sinai, was widely discussed in the Talmudic culture. Rabbi Akiba's contention that the Torah had been given with all its refinements and minutiae by Moses at Sinai was an attempt to eliminate the distinction between the two Laws – Written and Oral – thereby legitimizing the Sages' authority to interpret the Torah and to expand its meaning with all manner of new precepts. This was done, of course, in the belief that they were not actually engaged in independent innovation, but were simply taking the implicit and general meanings of the Torah and moving them, via the newly innovated details, into the realm of the explicit. And Akiba was not talking here of the discretionary innovation permitted to a man desiring to go beyond the strict "letter of the law" (*lifnim mi-shurat ha-din*), to do more than is the minimal justice required of him, an activity which, though voluntary, is extremely important (as we learn from Rabbi Yoḥanan: "Jerusalem was destroyed only because . . . they based their judgments (strictly) upon Biblical law and did not go beyond the requirements of the law" (*Bab.M.*, 30b). No, Akiba was thinking of innovation in matters pertaining precisely to the strict letter of the law.

This polemic in the Talmud concludes with the triumphant declaration that Sages do indeed have the authority to change and innovate. With sovereign consciousness the Sages embrace the great rule: "There is authority in the hands of the Sages." With great self-assertion they advise: "Be more careful in (the observance of) the words of the Scribes than in the words of the Torah" (*Erub.* 21b). They believed that a Sage was superior to a prophet, that there was no need to "pay attention to the Bath Kol [the heavenly voice]" (*Ber.* 52a and elsewhere). It was sufficient for Sages to discuss and to conclude, their decision was law.

Innovations of the Talmudic culture – a summary

As we listen to these clamors for legitimation we cannot help sensing that the molders of the Talmudic culture were fully aware they had created a system of meanings very new and quite different from the Biblical framework. Gedaliahu Alon justly observed[19] that the early Sages did not necessarily seek validation for their authority in the Written Torah; the Oral Torah, although anchored in the Written Torah, had, they believed, its own validity. Hillel the Sage, for example, in attempting to convince a proselyte who declared himself prepared to accept the Written but not the Oral Torah, did not seek in Scripture support for his argument. He said rather: "As you accepted the Written Torah on faith, so accept the Oral Torah on faith" (*Sab.* 31a). Alon concluded from this that the Sages viewed both laws as equally valid; one did not require the other for validation of its truth. This view seems to find further support in the formulation given by the Sages for Israel's chosenness: God "chose them and their words" as he had chosen Moses and the Prophets and their words. Alon cites a *baraita* attributed to Rabbi Akiba: "Blessed is the Lord, God of Israel, who chose the words of Torah and the words of the Sages, for the words of the Torah and the words of the Sages abide forever."[20]

Let us add here one more important distinction that separates the Talmudic culture from the Biblical. The Biblical constitution evolved from the early traditions of the tribes and from all that the legislator, in obedience to God's word, put before the nation. It contained not only matters of religious ritual, but all the manifestations of Israel's tradition throughout the ages. The Talmudic constitution on the other hand undertook a monumental task of regulating and disciplining all aspects of life to the Written Law and its interpretations. The canonization of Torah, Prophets, and Hagiographia subordinated the nation to the strict discipline of the Torah's laws as they were interpreted by the new class of Bible interpreters, first the Scribes, later the Tanna᾿im. The Torah was henceforth conceived as a book in which God's will had been revealed, its laws were His commandments, and every Jew was personally responsible for their observance. The notions of personal reward and punishment express this change. Moreover, the Torah was elevated beyond the accidents of time and place and was identified with the divine wisdom that antedated the world's creation. It was no longer given to change, except through its authorized interpreters who, however, insist that they themselves have not changed, added, or detracted at all.

The practical precepts of the Torah, such as the sanctity of the Sabbath and the Holy Days, circumcision, marriage laws, dietary laws, mourning and burial laws, all were expanded in the Talmudic culture to an intricate web of rules: detailed laws of *kashrut*, which entirely forbade certain foods or the manner of their preparation, the strict prohibition on eating milk with meat or meat with milk products, the prohibition of eating bread if a portion of its dough had not been set aside (*hallah*), the interdiction to consume fruits within three years of their planting (*ʿorlah*), the prohibition on libation wine (*nesech*), or wine which had been processed by Gentiles. The Rabbis defined thirty-nine main classes of work ("fathers of work," *ʾavot melachah*) forbidden on the Sabbath and various other activities derived from these main classes ("offspring," *toladot*); every aspect of a Jew's life, his dress, manners, conduct, and deeds, was placed in a web of laws and ordinances – a strict codification by the promulgators of Halachah.

Alon's view cited above is not a lone opinion, but its conclusions, as regards both the perspectivistic examination of Israel's cultures and the changed values manifested in the different ontologies, have not yet become sufficiently clear to scholars. Indeed, to many they appear puzzling, even unsubstantiated. Professor Yeshaʿayahu Leibowitz, for example, clearly realizes that the Talmudic conception of the commandments is quite dissimilar to that of the Bible, but this realization seems to have no bearing on his acceptance of the "yoke" of Torah and commandments as construed by the Sages. The religion of Israel, the world of the Halachah, of the Oral Law, Leibowitz states sharply, was not created by Holy Scriptures; rather, the Holy Scriptures are one of the institutions of the religion of Israel. From a religious and a causal-logical viewpoint, the Oral Law, being the world of the Halachah, antecedes the Written Law, which is the world of faith and values.[21] Leibowitz concedes that the creators of the Talmudic culture felt they possessed supreme authority to interpret the stories of the Bible and its laws according to their own conception, i.e. he realizes that the Sages defined the meanings of the Biblical culture as they saw fit (as Alon maintained), or as he puts it: "The Halachah of the Oral Law, which is a human creation, draws its authority from the words of the living God in the Bible, but it is the former that determines the content and meaning of the Written Torah." Nonetheless, Leibowitz cleaves to the Talmudic culture, or rather to the later Rabbinic culture, as if this were the only system of meanings which so treated its predecessors, and as if it were the only one of the seven Jewish cultures to possess real legitimacy.

Let us now look at how the commandments were perceived in two other

Jewish cultures: the Poetic-Philosophic and the Mystical. It will become evident that each of these cultures deals sovereignly with its predecessors, no less with the Bible than with the Talmud, and each one indeed "determines the content and the meaning of the Written Torah." We begin with Rabbi Sa adiah Ga'on and his method of rationalizing the commandments.

Rational and revelational commandments in the Poetic-Philosophic culture

Rabbi Saʿadiah Ga'on (892–942 CE) sought to base the commandments on a conception of religious rationalism. As explained in his *Book of Doctrines and Beliefs*, the religion of Israel was founded upon "the necessary science" and withstood its rigorous tests. As one of the founders and early molders of the Poetic-Philosophic culture, Saʿadiah argues sharply with those who maintain that decisions based on reason and logic lead to heresy: this is the vulgar opinion of fools, who turn darkness into light and light into darkness. To those who argue that the great Sages of Israel, Talmudic and others, had explicitly warned against esoteric speculation (*maʿaseh bereshit* and *maʿaseh merkavah* mysticism, i.e. the mysteries of Creation and the mysteries of the Godhead), the Ga'on replies: "It cannot be thought that the Sages should have wished to prohibit us from rational inquiry seeing that our Creator has commanded us to engage in such inquiry in addition to accepting the reliable Tradition. Thus He said, 'Know ye not? Hear ye not? . . . Have ye not understood the foundations of the earth?' [Isa. 40.21]"[22] Our Sages only wanted to deliver the masses from error. But in fact any Jew capable of meditation, thought, and study may engage in these, and for two reasons: "(1) In order that we may find out for ourselves what we know in the way of imparted knowledge from the Prophets of God; (2) in order that we may be able to refute those who attack us on matters connected with our religion."[23] The "reliable Tradition" bids us engage in philosophical contemplation – this is a basic assumption in the Poetic-Philosophic culture and one that legitimates this opening of gates to a whole new conception. The Ga'on stressed this point on numerous occasions, presaging Maimonides' statement in the *Guide for the Perplexed*:

It was not the object of the Prophets and our Sages . . . to close the gate of investigation entirely, and to prevent the mind from comprehending what is within its reach, as is imagined by simple and idle people, whom it suits better to put forth their ignorance and incapacity as wisdom and perfection, and to regard the distinction and wisdom of others as irreligion and imperfection.[24]

The third chapter of the *Book of Doctrines and Beliefs*, which discusses the origin and nature of the commandments, states that God bestowed upon man two great acts of kindness:

The first of His acts of kindness towards His creatures was the gift of existence, i.e. His act of calling them into existence after they had been non-existent . . . Thereafter He offered them a gift by means of which they are able to obtain complete happiness and perfect bliss . . . This gift consists of the commandments and prohibitions which He gave them.[25]

The fulfillment of the law is a greater reward than bliss received by God's grace alone, for "one who obtains some good in return for work which he has accomplished enjoys a double portion of happiness in comparison with one who has not done any work and receives what he receives as a gift of grace." This is so clearly a judgment of reason that it is impossible for God Himself to ignore it. Therefore He commanded that He should be adored and thanked for His Creation and for the Torah.

All commandments can be classified in two categories, perhaps along the lines of the above-mentioned two acts of God's kindness. The first category is "confirmed by speculation" and contains commandments to learn to know God and worship Him in sincerity, as well as admonitions against returning His bounty with ingratitude. For example, one is prohibited from vilifying or treating Him with contempt. This set of laws consists of commandments and prohibitions which allow for civil behavior among people, such as prohibitions against killing, cheating, or lying: "He did not permit us to trespass upon one another's rights nor to defraud one another."[26] This first set of laws is called "Laws of Reason" (mitzvot sichliot).

The Second Class of Law consists of matters regarding which Reason passes no judgment in the way either of approval or disapproval so far as their essence is concerned. But our Lord has given us an abundance of such commandments and prohibitions in order to increase our reward and happiness through them.[27]

These laws, instances of which are the "Sabbath and Festivals; the selection of certain individuals to be Prophets and Leaders; the prohibition to eat certain foodstuffs; the avoidance of sexual intercourse with certain people," etc., are called "Laws of Revelation" (mitzvot shimʿiyot), because they were revealed to Israel at Sinai. Of course, it is impossible for the Revelational Laws to be entirely bereft of motive or sense, or, as the Gaʾon puts it: "One cannot fail, upon closer examination, to find in it some slender moral benefits and rational basis."[28] Although God's wisdom is far above human understanding, there is in the Revelational Laws some "rational basis" compatible with human understanding. The mission of the Prophets, for example, though revelational by definition, is also important for the rational laws, whose practice

cannot be complete unless the prophets show us how to perform them. Thus, for instance, Reason commands gratitude towards God for the blessings received from Him, but does not specify the form, time, and posture appropriate to the expression of such gratitude. So we are in need of prophets. They gave it a form which is called "Prayer"; they fixed its times . . ., etc.[29]

Saʿadiah Gaʾon energetically argues against the contentions of Christians and Karaites that the Torah and the commandments are likely to change or to be abrogated, or that they have already been abrogated by God. The Gaʾon states categorically that in every sphere of activity there is a "reliable tradition" and there are truthful conveyors of that tradition. A ruler's command, for example, is accepted by his people even when it is conveyed through emissaries. Not in every instance can we rely solely on our senses. People generally accept a "true report":

And unless there was a true tradition in this world, a man would not be able to know that a certain property was owned by his father, and that this is an inheritance from his grandfather, nor would a man be able to know that he is the son of his mother, let alone that he is the son of his father.[30]

The Gaʾon declares: "Reliable tradition is as true as the things perceived by sight." And the proof: numerous instances where Scripture states that the Torah is "a covenant for ever" and "for your generations." In each such instance the reference is to both Laws, the Written and the Oral. In this context we read the famous lines:

Moreover, our people, the Children of Israel, are a people only by virtue of our Laws [i.e. by virtue of both Laws – the Written and the Oral], and since the Creator has declared that our people should exist as long as heaven and earth exist, it necessarily follows that our laws should continue to exist as long as heaven and earth are in being, and this is what he says, "Thus saith the Lord . . . If these ordinances depart from before Me . . . then the seed of Israel also shall cease from being a nation before Me for ever".[31]

The Gaʾon believed that everything that was not explicitly stated in the Written Torah was to be found in the Oral Torah, and anything that was not explicitly stated in the latter was to be determined by reason. This opinion too is very important for the legitimation of the new culture. Scriptures, claims one of the chief proponents of this culture, is not the only source of our religion. It has two additional sources: one that precedes it – the fountain of reason, and one that follows it – the source of tradition.

What is the purpose of all the commandments? Saʿadiah explains:[32] the purpose of all Creation is man. Despite a small and puny body, man's soul is wider than heaven and earth, for his knowledge encompasses all that they contain. Man must mount the steps of wisdom until he attains knowledge of that which is beyond them, i.e. of the exalted Creator. The purpose of all the commandments is this – comprehension of the divine wisdom and its realization.

Maimonides on the purpose of the commandments

Maimonides' system presents, I find, four new formulations of the reasons for the commandments, though these ideas are basic also to the entire Poetic-Philosophic culture. These are:

1   The commandments' chief aim is to bestow perfection of the soul, derived from the acquisition of intellectual knowledge and adhesion unto the Primal Cause.

2   The commandments are, in the main, a pedagogical tool; they are meant to guide men's conduct and opinions and enable the attainment of the true end. This is why these directives evince an element of God's "cunning" and "ruse."

3   The perfection of the individual and the body politic in the paths of righteousness and justice is a prerequisite for the advancement of the soul in true wisdom. The commandments seek to straighten man's character and conduct by guiding him along the middle path, the golden mean.

4   The principles of the Jewish faith are imposed in the form of commandments, i.e. knowledge of his faith is encumbent upon the Jew as an order from above.

In the interest of brevity, only the first two of these innovations will be discussed here.

Maimonides distinguished in the Torah meanings that were manifest and plain, and meanings that were hidden and figurative. The plain, he thought, was but preparation for the hidden, comparing to the latter as silver does to gold. The verse, "a word fitly spoken is like apples of gold in vessels of silver" (Prov. 25.11), was brought to bear upon the relation between the manifest and the hidden in the Torah: "It shows that in every word which has a double sense, a literal one and a figurative one, the plain meaning must be as valuable as silver, and the hidden meaning still more precious."[33] The entire language of symbols and metaphors employed by the Torah requires study, thus anyone who construes the Torah's words literally is himself misguided and misguides others. The word *mashal* (metaphor, parable) appears in the introduction to the *Guide for the Perplexed* no less than fifty-seven times. It is the nature of a metaphor to serve as a tool of explanation and understanding, like that "taper worth only one *issar*," mentioned by the Sages, with which a man who has misplaced a valuable coin can illuminate and search his house. This, says Maimonides, is the key to our understanding of the Prophets and the Sages.

Indeed one may see in the *Book of Knowledge* section of the *Mishneh Torah* and in the *Guide for the Perplexed* an extended polemic against the literalists. Already in the first chapter of the *Guide*, wherein the concept *tzelem ʾelohim* ("the image of God") is explained, we learn that Israel's Torah is "intellectual perception, in the exercise of which [one] does not employ his senses".[34] Hence the Torah's disapprobation of God's incorporification, its belief that He is not a physical body and that there exists no likeness between Him and His creatures: "'Let us make a man in our zelem' [Gen. 1.26], the term signifies . . . [man's] intellectual perception, and does not refer to his 'figure' or 'shape.'"[35] In the same sense man's purpose in life is explained in the book's final chapter as the attainment of "the true perfection of man."[36] The purpose is to acquire – as far as this is possible for man – the knowledge of God, the knowledge of His Providence, and of the manner in which it influences His creatures . . . Having acquired this knowledge he will then be determined always to seek loving-kindness, judgment, and righteousness, and thus to imitate the ways of God."[37] No wonder, then, that in an earlier chapter, in the parable of the king's palace, Maimonides rebuked the innocent mass of believers who study the Talmud without intellectual apperception:

Those who desire to arrive at the palace, and to enter it, but have never yet seen it, are the mass of religious people; the multitude that observe the divine command-ments, but are ignorant. Those who arrive at the palace, but go round about it, are those who devote themselves exclusively to the study of the practical law; they believe traditionally in true principles of faith, and learn the practical worship of God, but are not trained in philosophical treatment of the principles of the Law, and do not endeavour to establish the truth of their faith by proof.[38]

In these and numerous other instances Maimonides seems to be minimizing the importance of practical commandments. Witness his confident declara-tion in *Mishneh Torah*:

One only loves God with the knowledge with which one knows Him. According to the knowledge will be the love. If the former be little or much, so will the latter be little or much. A person ought therefore to devote himself to the understanding and comprehension of those sciences and studies which will inform him concerning his Master, as far as it is in human faculties to understand and comprehend – as indeed we have explained in the Laws of the Foundation of the Torah.[39]

Similar declarations can be found throughout his writings and their intent is clear. The truth demonstrated by the philosophers is not only authenticated by the Torah and Prophets, but also by the homiletics of the Sages. The Sages, too, were actually philosophers, according to the lights of their own views, but because they addressed the masses of ignorant people, their literal interpretations appear to us far removed from reason. These must be translated into the philosophical language of conceptual thought so that their true light may shine forth.

We might add here that Maimonides also leveled his polemics against the Karaites, and that this debate is apparent at a very substrative level of all

those ideas which, by imposing the commandments as a duty of faith, seek
to strengthen philosophy's tie with Scriptures and Talmud. The Karaites, we
know, viewed the Talmud as a new Torah unto itself. Maimonides' effort
was, therefore, directed at reuniting the two Laws, Oral and Written, into
one single Torah based on true knowledge. Bible and Talmud are united in a
world-view validated by philosophy. Simple believers and Talmudists
absorbed solely in the practical-*halachic* aspect of Torah have almost entirely
ignored this ontology and have thereby let the Karaites undermine the faith.

And what is the precise nature of the commandments? They are the
manifestation of God's wisdom and His will to guide Israel in the paths of His
wisdom. Against those who see the commandments as arbitrary decrees,
dictated by God's whim, Maimonides has this to say: "All commandments
and prohibitions are dictated by His wisdom and serve a certain aim . . .
There is a reason for every precept, although there are commandments the
reason of which is unknown to us."[40] We must believe that there is indeed a
reasonable motive for each commandment but that our limited understanding is not always capable of apprehending it. The purpose of the entire body
of commandments is the perfection of man's soul and body, it seeks to instill
true knowledge, in keeping with the intellectual capacity of each individual,
in the minds of the masses, and to remove evil from their hearts "by teaching
every one of us such good morals as must produce a good social state."[41]

God's cunning and stratagem

We have explained that Maimonides held the purpose of human life to be the
contemplation of God, the adhesion of man's intellect to the divine intellect.
This contemplation, however, is not a mere theoretical or abstract activity.
It has a soteriological function too: as long as man cleaves to God with his
intellect, the power of evil can gain no hold upon him, and the more he
cleaves, the more God's providence extends over him. Contemplation of God
liberates man from the randomness and contingency of this world.
Knowledge thus becomes a shelter and a refuge: the path of ceaseless
contemplation of God, as described at the end of the *Guide for the Perplexed*,
protects man from the accidental by enveloping him in the beneficent
influence of divine providence.

Providence depends upon the strength, the immediacy, and the intensity
of the link that unites the human intellect with God. When a man neglects
contemplation of the Primal Cause, he lays himself open to harm:

Hence it appears to me that it is only in times of such neglect that some of the
ordinary evils befall a prophet or a perfect and pious man; and the intensity of the evil
is proportional to the duration of those moments, or to the character of the things
that thus occupy their mind.[42]

The constancy of God's nearness is not to be counted upon. It wavers, it has its highs and lows. To obtain God's protection, a man must "know Him" and "love Him," in the spirit of Psalm 91, as Maimonides expounds it: "When a man's love is so intense that his thought is exclusively engaged with the object of his love."[43]

The idea of divine providence and the love of God leads Maimonides to the idea of God's artifice and cunning. The commandments are but a method, an instrument that enables man to cleave to God; the key to their understanding is to be sought in the cunning, as it were, which the divine Teacher–Pedagogue employs as a device for Israel's instruction. This concept is referred to in the *Guide* as: "God's cunning and stratagem" (ᶜormat ha-Shem ve-tahbulato), "His wisdom and stratagem" (*hochmato ve-tahbulato*), and, more explicitly, "this divine cunning" (ha-ᶜorma ha-ᵓelohit).[44]

Maimonides knows that this is difficult for a believer to accept. Must a Jew observe the commandments knowing that they do not mean what they purport to mean, that there is a hidden ruse behind them?

I know that you will at first thought reject this idea and find it strange; you will put the following question to me in your heart: How can we suppose that Divine commandments, prohibitions, and important acts, which are fully explained, and for which certain seasons are fixed, should not have been commanded for their own sake, but only for the sake of some other thing; as if they were only the means which He employed for His primary object? What prevented Him from making His primary object a direct commandment to us, and to give us the capacity of obeying it?[45]

A question so skeptical of divine wisdom could be dismissed as a "disease." Maimonides attempts to allay these doubts by explaining that it is difficult for human beings to achieve the "original object" of the commandments, which is "to spread a knowledge of Him (among the people), and to cause them to reject idolatry."[46] Most mortals cannot easily cleave to God by intellectual contemplation. Therefore the Torah must, as it were, insinuate itself into their consciousness by "divine wisdom, according to which people are allowed to continue the kind of worship to which they have been accustomed, in order that they might acquire the true faith, which is the chief object of God's commandments."[47] And why is this stratagem necessary? Because human nature is but an amalgam of matter and form, feeble flesh and blood, doomed to sin, and ever needy of guidance. This nature is not given to change: "The nature of man is never changed by God by way of miracle."[48] Miracles may change the natural properties of a particular individual being, but they do not set out to change human nature as a whole. God could, of course, change man's nature; this is not impossible for Him, but He does not wish it, for He has no desire to deny man the freedom of choice. If man were not made of clay, if he were not subject to human frailties as well as being master of his own free will, there would have been no need for the Prophets or for the commandments. God has no choice, then, but to devise stratagems with which to instill His knowledge in men's hearts. God's cunning in the use of the commandments is a pedagogical program whose devices are meant to guide Israel on the hard road to truth. Sacrifices, prayers, fringes, *mezuzah*, phylacteries, "and similar kinds of worship," are all aimed at inculcating the true faith, the spread of which will excise from mankind the evils of injustice and corruption.

The source of the commandments, the purpose and the means

The creators of the Poetic-Philosophic culture stressed that the object of science was to determine the causes of phenomena, especially the Primal Cause, in order to understand phenomena's origin and purpose. The same scientific approach, they thought, could explain the Torah and the commandments.

We heard earlier that the distinction between "rational" and "revelation-al" commandments became prevalent in Saʿadiah's time. The Gaʾon traced the term revelational (*shimʿiyot*) to the sense of hearing (*shemʿa*), but earlier Islamic scholars had used this term in the sense of discipline (*mishmaʿat*) and it appears the Gaʾon adopted the term and its meaning from them.

A sociological observation is in order here: the Poetic-Philosophic culture developed within a feudal aristocratic society which chose to circumscribe its conduct with intricate ceremonies and rituals, with rules of knightliness, homage to nobles, and obedience to kings. It is important to bear this factor in mind when we consider that the Torah's commandments too were viewed as an obligatory discipline emanating from a source entirely distinct from, and external to, man himself, i.e. from a transcendent and heteronomous source. The culture of the Islamic courts where these formalities of etiquette were cultivated became a model for Jews employed in the service of Arab kings and nobles. Beautiful form, perfect structure, a highly stylized mode of life, rigidly defined standards of conduct for those who would partake of life's sweet rewards – these ideals of the Arab élite in its heyday were embraced by the poets and philosophers of the Judaeo-Spanish "golden age." Such social differentiation meant separation from the life-styles, opinions, and images of "the masses" via numerous distinguishing commandments, a sort of prefiguration of the Emancipation culture's *salons*.

This phenomenon is evident in Spanish Hebrew poetry, as also in all other branches of Jewish intellectual creativity of the time. The representatives and spokesmen of the new vision, Jewish patrons of the arts, labored with tireless enthusiasm on its realization. It was an effort to endow Jewish life with the splendor and glory of forms and rules of etiquette, of pleasing harmony and symmetry, in the classical manner then spreading in the Islamic courts: civilized conversation, the wit and playfulness of rhymes and riddles, poetry, thought, and song. The object of poetry was to beautify and elevate reality through good taste, with a delightfully complex artistry of measure and rhythm, and a multitude of clever inventions, all rendered, of course, in the culture's agreeable forms, beautifully shaped and impeccably formulated. The earlier gushing expressiveness of Eliᶜezer ha-Kalir and the unpolished *midrashic* poets was found entirely unacceptable, as we learn from complaints by Abraham Ibn Ezra. This is the beginning of a host of new "revelational commandments" in matters of language and style and the imposition of strict discipline and self-control.

The courtly culture of the Jewish élite in Spain, and later in Egypt, doubtlessly influenced Maimonides. His style and thought evince a meticulous attention to the rules of symmetry and harmony. The Greek ideal of sophrosyne (moderation, observance of proper measure and balance), seems to have been embraced by the courtly Arab culture in which Maimonides moved. Indeed, it was his life's blood: the golden mean was for him "the way of the wise."[49] This measure has many names in Maimonides' works. In *Mishneh Torah*, it is called "the way of good people" and the "right way." In describing this quality he uses verbs like evaluate, adjust, measure. Initially, it may very well have been Aristotle's theory of the *Nicomachean Ethics* which gave Maimonides the tools for explaining the sophrosyne, that measure of restraint that characterizes the "way of the wise," but, in the main, his endeavors to organize life, opinions, and beliefs according to the rational classical model, and to give the force of commandment to beautiful ceremonies and rituals were determined by the culture of his environment and his own social standing.

Horror of the extremes is never far from men's consciousness in the Poetic-Philosophic culture. They fear the immoderate: "The right way is the mean in each group of dispositions common to humanity; namely, that disposition which is equally distant from the two extremes in its class, not being nearer to the one than to the other."[50] Only saints do sometimes abandon the "equal distance" from "the exact mean towards the extremes," but they do so by way of supererogation.

All commandments aimed at realizing the mean – the "way of the wise" – are "revelational" in the broad sense, because they do not emanate autonomously from human reason, but are incumbent upon the individual as an obligation, regardless of the intelligibility of their reasons.

Maimonides made an interesting and bold distinction between laws that contained a truth "which is itself the only object of that law, as, for example, the truth of the Unity, Eternity, and Incorporeality of God," that is, "true ideas" in themselves, and laws which, though indispensable, were not necessarily based on truth, laws that were

only the means of securing the removal of injustice, or the acquisition of good
morals; such is the belief that God is angry with those who oppress their fellow men,
as it is said "Mine anger will be kindled, and I will slay" etc. (Exod. 22.23); or the
belief that God hears the crying of the oppressed and vexed, to deliver them out of the
hands of the oppressor and tyrant, as it is written, "And it shall come to pass, when
he will cry unto me, that I will hear, for I am gracious" (Exod. 22.25).[51]

As early an exegete of the *Guide* as Shem Tov Ibn Falaquera (*c.* 1225–90)
already pointed out:

As it is commanded to believe that the Lord's anger will be kindled at those who
transgress His Will, and this belief is not true, because He is not moved and His Anger
is not kindled, as it is written "I am the Lord, unchanging" (Mal. 3.6), so it is
necessary that the common man be moved and that he believe this, for even though
it is a lie, it is necessary for the preservation of the state; therefore these
commandments were called necessary beliefs, not true ones.[52]

In other words, most, if not all, of the commandments are based on Torah-
statements which are untrue, on beliefs which are necessary, but not true.
The paradoxical nature of Maimonides' method exemplifies the tension
underlying the religious rationalism of the Poetic-Philosophic culture, and
much has been written on it. Opponents of Maimonides, from his own
contemporaries all the way down to Jacob Emden and Samuel David
Luzzatto in the eighteenth and nineteenth centuries, have taken this as a
convenient point of departure for their attacks, on the grounds that in
abrogating the commandments' absolute validity, he jeopardized their very
observance.

There were some differences of opinion among medieval scholars on
reasons for the commandments, but in general all agreed that the essence of
the Torah's commandments was the conferral of intellectual and moral
perfection upon man. Even Judah ha-Levi, who accorded to the irrational a
much larger scope in his philosophy than did Maimonides, recognized the
important status of reason. It is the intellect, he said, that rules our will and
our instincts and thus "the first place . . . is very appropriately given to the
prayer for intelligence and enlightenment" through which man is "brought
near to his Master."[53] The creators of the Poetic-Philosophic culture were
no longer content with heteronomous, or divinely ordained, reasons for the
commandments; they did not appreciate reasons from which human
intellect was excluded and were prepared to do battle with those who, in Ibn
Paquda's plaint, "place[d] tradition before speculation."

The commandments in the Mystical culture

As in the two preceding cultures, in the Mystical culture, too, a distinction
was made between the manifest, or the literal, in the Torah, and the hidden,

or figurative, but manifest and hidden now took on new meanings. Indeed, the distinction between the manifest and the hidden became the most characteristic methodological tool used by the Mystical ontology in its interpretation of Scriptures. This allowed for polemical discussion with the preceding cultures, but was not in itself the most important feature that distinguished this culture from the Poetic-Philosophic culture. The main difference was in the new meanings the Mystical culture attributed to concepts like God and commandments, or to the manifest and the hidden Torah.

Gerschom Scholem, his disciples, and his colleagues have studied at length how the Torah and the commandments were conceived in the literature of the Kabbalah. We shall, therefore, single out here only one thesis that emerges from these studies: in the Mystical culture the observance of commandments is assigned a divine-cosmic rationale. The commandments are not simply acts, not even parables for abstract concepts, nor pedagogical devices for the inculcation of good character and true knowledge of God. Their purpose is man's adhesion to the supernal lights and a decisive restoration of harmony (*tikkun*) in the order of the world and in the secret of the deity itself.

In this culture, too, the rule obtained that nothing in the Torah lacked a purpose, and that everything it contained was given to interpretation. As Naḥmanides bluntly put it: when the Torah is read only for its literal meaning, it is "vacant and empty." God's Torah could be considered whole (*temima*) only when it was completed and perfected through the understanding of the secrets it contained. The unveiling of these secrets is the wisdom to which Kabbalah alone is privy. Each of the preceding cultures was subjected to the Mystics' polemics. Let us examine some of these expressions.

We have already cited earlier (chapter 1, p. 28) the Mystical exegesis on the word *bereshit* ("in the beginning"), to the effect that without the revivifying waters of Mysticism the Bible was an "arid place." Similar polemics were leveled at the Talmudic Sages. The Kabbalists said of the Talmud, the Mishnah, and the Baraita that they were but the handmaidens of Kabbalah: "The Mishnah is its [the Shechinah's] handmaiden."[54] They went so far as to suggest that it was the Mishnah which was responsible for Moses' death and burial outside the Holy Land: like a servant-maid who has usurped the power of the lawful mistress of the house, so the Mishnah has overpowered the tradition of Moses.[55] The Mishnah has overwhelmed Mystical knowledge and has thereby strangled Moses and his Torah. This, according to the *Zohar*, is the meaning of the verse; "If a handmaiden inherits her mistress" (Prov. 30.23), a clear reference to the Mishnah's displacement of the true Torah. Talmudic teachings of *halachah* and commandments are very often deemed inimical to Mystic knowledge. Thus does the Zohar, by a clever anagram, ridicule the Sages of the Mishnah, the Tannaʾim: אירתנים = תנאים (ʾetanim, strong ones) – these Sages are so "strong" with their tongue that the revered Moses, a man of impeded tongue, had better beware. Similar criticism is leveled at the Talmudic Sages, the ʾAmoraʾim, whose disputations increase discord between the Shechinah and her Spouse.[56]

Nor is the philosophers' conception of the manifest and the hidden any more satisfying. The Kabbalists themselves often had divergent opinions on the nature of the Torah's secrets, but all agreed that it contained no intellectual knowledge, and that its wisdom was divine and superior to all human wisdoms and sciences. The Bible's verses were viewed as sparks of spiritual, divine, and angelic essences, and intimations of the relationships between these spheres and man. Its verses are, to be precise, expressions of God's names. The Bible may, therefore, be read by those who possess the requisite knowledge in this secret wisdom as the numerous combinations of the divine names. A Kabbalist studying the Torah is illumined by sparks from those supernal lights, ensconced in, and symbolized by, God's names. A world in grace, the divine cosmos in all its expanses and divisions is unveiled before him. Such divisions are the limbs and joints of the *adam kadmon*, the primeval man, the mystical anthropos, which, in turn, is one manifestation of the deity, or the ʾen-sof (the Infinite). What is the nature and status of the commandments in this teaching?

Two Mystical ideas regarding the commandments

Two leading ideas in the Mystical concept of the commandments are of particular interest to the modern reader. Both have been adequately explained by Scholem and are briefly presented here. They are, I believe, at the foundation of the entire Mystical culture as it was typically expressed throughout most of its development. The first idea explains the source of the commandments; the second idea presents the enormous responsibility that observance of the commandments places upon the individual.

The book *Raʿayah mehemnah* (part of the *Zohar*) explains that the commandments given to Israel originate from the Tree of Knowledge (also called the Tree of Death, since its fruit proved fatal to man). It was in the secret of the Tree of Knowledge that good was distinguished from evil, the sacred from the profane, the permitted from the forbidden. It was in order to restrain the powers of evil, destruction, and death, that the laws of the Torah were given. Prior to man's original sin, however, the world-order derived from the Tree of Life, which symbolizes the full emanation of holiness without the admixture of the "shells" of sins and death. At the end of days, in the Messianic aeon, the original order of the world, the order rooted in the Tree of Life, will be reinstated, and the need for the commandments as practised today will cease to exist. The divine essence will again flow into all the worlds without hindrance, and the yoke of commandments and prohibitions will be lifted forever.

Certain hints regarding changes that will affect Halachah in the Messianic age can be found in the Talmudic culture too, but only in the *Zohar* does redemption appear primarily as a manifestation of profound spirituality, a spiritual revolution destined to unveil the Mystical (and deemed to be the literal) content and meaning of the Torah.[57] In a world-order rooted in the Tree of Knowledge the divine Torah has been distorted; on the day of redemption it will regain its original form. Today we know that this Mystical idea was destined to exercise great influence on the Sabbatean movement, when it was invoked as a license for release from traditional prohibitions and even as an argument that a *mitzvah* could actually be accomplished via a transgression.

The second guiding idea in the Mystics' concept of the commandments is that of the practitioner's personal responsibility for the entire world, even for the world's Creator, in the elemental battle between good and evil. By observing the Torah's commandments, a man abrogates the exile of the deity and vanquishes the powers of evil. Every deed he performs in the true spirit of the commandment is capable of tipping the scales on the side of merit, while every sin plunges him into the dark, foul embrace of the evil powers. From this battle there is no escape. The observance of commandments thus takes on a divine-cosmic dimension, and bestows merit not only on the individual, but on the collectivity, on the entire world, and on God Himself.

Clearly, observance of the commandment is seen here not as a simple fulfillment of a law. Rather, the commandment is a visible symbol hinting at the internal, secret, and hidden life of the deity, and a means that allows the Jew to approach the root of this secret. "The supernal Torah is hidden and concealed," wrote the Kabbalist Isaiah Horowitz ("the Holy Shela," 1565?–1630), author of *Shnei luḥot ha-berit* ("The Two Tablets of the Covenant"). And because it is hidden and concealed, it is necessary for the Oral Torah to elucidate its secrets and bring to light its mysteries.[58]

Scattered Talmudic statements intimating that observance of commandments increased the supernal powers and added strength, as it were, to God became in the Kabbalah a complex lore on the "higher need" of the commandments. By performing commandments, man influences the deity and all the spheres, as though God had need of these acts; thus the commandments served a "higher need" than the individual's private benefit or pleasure.

Already in the book *Bahir* (compiled in twelfth-century Provence), the commandments were explained in relation to the activities of the divine spheres, a conception which spread at the end of the thirteenth century and more so after the expulsion from Spain. Interpreters of Naḥmanides explained his meaning in expounding on the verse, "Israel in whom I will be glorified" (Isa. 49.3), that when Israel performed commandments, the Shechinah was glorified. Similarly, it was explained that through the commandments all the worlds were joined and bound together, thereby enabling the Shechinah to join the Infinte One, the ʾen-sof. It is thus in the power of pious and saintly men to pronounce decrees that both "higher" and "lower" beings must obey, to cancel divine decrees, and even to subjugate the natural order to the will of their pure souls, for their will stands above the natural order and is, in fact, the will of God Himself. In short, by observing the commandments man can wield tremendous power over the world.

In this respect practical Kabbalah is closely bound up with theoretical Kabbalah. A Kabbalist who knows the meaning of the holy names and their "combinations" is like a man entrusted with "the keys to every single thing that man needs for every aspect and matter in the world." Thus declared Joseph Gikatila (1248–1305),[59] author of a key to the rules of Kabbalistic wisdom and to the holy names in the ten spheres, a composition offered to his readers for "practical" purposes.

Hence we conclude: he who fulfills the laws of the Torah takes upon himself responsibility not only for his own soul, but for the life of the nation, for the secret of maʿaseh bereshit (Creation mysticism) and maʿaseh merkavah (mysticism of the Godhead), i.e. for the preservation of the world and the completeness of the hidden life of the Infinite One. In Lurianic Kabbalah we learn that with the "breaking of the divine vessels," sparks of holy light fell within the ambit of the evil forces; the fulfillment of commandments, however, can bring about the restoration or mending of Creation after this breaking.

We see, then, that the Mystical culture did not reject the Halachah previously introduced by the Talmudic culture, but vested it with a new religious-cosmic dimension. By fulfilling precepts man can actually bring about the unification of Being according to its hidden orders, while transgressions violate this unity and endanger all of Creation. The ʾen-sof, the hiding God (so unlike the living God of the Bible who boldly reveals Himself in the natural order and in the history of nations), is very susceptible to the deeds of men upon whom His entire fate, as it were, depends. The commandments are not merely laws that Israel is enjoined to observe, but the hidden constitution of the whole of Creation. The purpose of their observance is to hasten the day of the "anarchic utopia" (in Scholem's phrase), when man will be freed from all prohibitions, and the Torah in all its spirituality will be revealed in the secret of the Tree of Life.

The difference between the Mystical and the Talmudic cultures as regards the commandments can now be summarized. Clearly, the Mystics did not propound a simple, innocent doctrine on the observance of *mitzvot* and the discharge of good deeds, but an entire theory of divine-cosmic harmonization. The secret of this harmonization, or the secret of the necessary link between man and God, has been revealed to certain initiated men. These men know that the fulfillment of a precept, such as prayer, is the Mystical means that bends the deity to man's will as by the force of magic.

If there is substance in the assumptions and conclusions of this study, one can only marvel at the astonishing belief of past generations in the authority and efficacy of the Halachah. In spite of fundamental differences of opinion regarding its source and value, the Halachah acquired in the consciousness of those generations an extraordinary and, to a modern observer, most baffling "depth structure". Even in times of great anguish those believers knew that the commandment was a lamp, the Torah, a light (Prov. 6.23), that the Holy One had blessed them with Torah and commandments in order to grant them merit, and that Judaism's ultimate message was "Fear God and obey his commands; there is no more to man than this" (Eccles. 12.13).

5

THE THREEFOLD TENSION
IN JEWISH HISTORY

Tensions in Israel's history

Three distinct tensions characterize the dynamics of creative forces in each one of Israel's cultures. By tension we mean here a contest, sometimes open, at times subterraneous, between conflicting tendencies that alternately battle and accommodate one another, until they are resolved in a generally acceptable equilibrium which, once attained, determines the character of the culture. An equilibrium is not necessarily peaceful; it is, however, a viable coexistence which turns conflicts into a dominant and endurable normalcy. The nature of these tensions in each culture and the history of their eventual equilibration constitute, in my view, the essence of Israel's history.

The first tension pits "universalism" against "particularism," if the use of these abstract and somewhat hackneyed terms may still be permitted. The essence of this tension is the enduring struggle between the ethnic-national and religious body, with its law and ethics, language, beliefs and customs, style and self-image, as they have been fashioned and molded by the specific, exclusive memories and hopes that have crystallized in the process of its historical individuation, and contrary ideas and visions that break through this ethnic barrier to embrace humanity at large. The need for national separation and exclusiveness confronts the desire for an openness and an expansion that allow spiritual latitude for the insights of all nations.

The second tension characterizing all Jewish cultures sets the desires of the individual Jew against the national collective will. This tension is evinced in the individual's struggle for his private rights and benefits against the control of the collectivity and the demands of its institutions. The measure of individualism and collectivism operating in each one of Israel's cultures has direct bearing on the creative personality and on the esteem in which it is held. Thus, it is important to examine who in Israel is empowered to decree or to change rules of conduct, what is the nature of the leadership – who rises to power and who is deprived of influence – what is the status of dissident sects in a culture and how they are treated. The measure of freedom an individual is granted in order to develop his creativity also expresses the relation between the universal human account and the national Jewish score, between humanity in Judaism and Judaism in humanity.

The third tension we find in our study of Jewish history is between the various constituent elements of the culture itself. How did race, language, land, religion, economy, social class, army, government, social law, national and religious symbols all fuse into one cultural unit? How does a culture achieve integration, if only a relative and temporary one at times, of its constituent elements? In the course of time many changes occur in the relative strength and importance of a culture's components, and it is important for us to understand what in a culture is a means to an end, and what, in fact, is an end unto itself. A question that raised animated controversy in this century, for example, was whether the Jewish religion was the decisive factor determining the fate of the Jewish people, or whether religion was merely a means that enabled Jews to preserve their nationhood, a sort of "instrument of exile" (*kli golah*), to use a famous phrase, provided by Israel's hidden Guardian to insure that the people would not perish when the national soil slipped from under its feet. Was the heavy yoke of Torah and commandments imposed in order to shield it from assimilation among the nations of the world? What are the elements of a culture that preserve and protect a nation: is it the contents of its faith, or practical precepts or perhaps external factors like land and language? The third tension is illustrated by the manner in which each culture related to its inheritance, for example, to the Land of Israel or to the Hebrew language. In this regard the goal of the Messianic vision can be defined as the desire to alter the existing relationships between a culture's different constituent elements.

Our study points, then, to three great tensions in all Jewish cultures:

1 Between nationalism and universalism;
2 Between the Jewish individual and his collectivity;
3 Between the elements constituting a culture: land, language, religion, state, present conditions, and visions of the future.

Every person lives between the opposing poles that characterize his culture. But in the course of a lifetime the tensions that govern one's world may undergo some change. There were periods in Jewish history of both negation and affirmation, twilight zones between cultures, when a Jew experienced a shifting in the equilibrium between these tensions. We have stressed the inadequacy of theories that see in Israel's history a single, uninterrupted and integrated national-universal vision. Nor can it be alleged that this history is founded on harmony between universalism and particularism, i.e. on the perfect equilibrium between the opposing tendencies to redeem the nation and to save the world. Jewish historians have too long ignored the internal contradictions within each culture between visionary aspirations and actual dispositions; they have especially ignored the shifts in emphases and the intentional omissions employed by cultures in their struggles with one another and with the outside world. They have further neglected the study of the resultant changes. Having failed to make the distinction between different cultures, many scholars have inevitably failed to notice such changes. We should beware the lure of that seductive theoretical-sentimental abstraction known as "Jewish essence," for it has, as we try to prove in this study, no basis in the reality of Jewish history. It is, I believe, quite evident that each Jewish culture expresses different views on the universal Creator, who is a God of justice and righteousness to all nations, and a God of Israel, who elevated one nation alone to be His chosen people.

Israel and the nations

Let us examine this first tension and the equilibrium, or resolution, it achieves in the Biblical, Talmudic, and Poetic-Philosophic cultures. We preface this discussion with some general remarks about the dualistic framework of all human existence. The fundamental dualism of our life condemns us to perpetual oscillation between abstract humanism and historical-concrete nationalism, between intention and realization, between our elevated, unsullied ideals and the unseemly reality of our mortal existence. Human beings seek in these oscillations a measure of equilibrium and respite. The tension between reality and its "potential" is inescapable; no degree of moralizing, nothing, in fact, short of Messianic intervention, can resolve it. Neither is it possible to gloss over Jewish nationalism by resorting to "ecumenic" concepts: symptoms of Jewish particularity in no way contradict the universal spirit; on the contrary, absent the distinctive marks of Jewish particularity, the ecumenic spirit only leads to wholesale assimilation by obviating the entire problem upon which the tension depends. A rational ethic is by definition universalistic and the more ethical and rational, the more general it tends to be. The same holds true for the universal monotheism of an Israel purely "of the spirit," postulated as a rival to Christianity. Such an Israel is doomed to complete extinction.

However, there is no doubt that the coupling of the monotheistic idea with the notion of God's zeal for the national honor of His favored people, irritated the pride of other nations and roused resentment. We need not go so far as to accept the generalization proffered by Toynbee and others that Europe's nationalistic fanaticism originated from Jewish Scriptures and tradition, that Nazism, therefore, was a logical, if unholy, offspring of Judaism, and that the poison emitted by Hitler was of Jewish provenance, but there is no doubt that the absoluteness of God's unity, joined to the absoluteness of Israel's unity, provoked Gentile charges of Jewish separateness and xenophobia.

The tension, at any rate, existed also within: how to weld, without arousing resentment and strife, a universal religion addressed to all human creatures, with a national creed? The universalistic idea is not in itself inconsistent with the idea of power and dominion. After all, God's kingdom is also a dominion. In every confrontation between two opposing forces, an organizing and ordering power inevitably makes its authority felt. The results of such struggles are destructive whenever a temporary and partial realization is misconstrued for a complete and permanent fulfillment. On the other hand, in a reality where arbitrary might prevails, where there is no hope for the promise to be fulfilled, utopianism crops up, or worse still, cynicism. The tragic dualism of our existence is expressed in this inescapable tension – the existence of power devoid of meaning, and of meaning bereft of power. The object of divine providence is to unify these two, power and meaning. The kingdom of God – the ultimate purpose of human history – signifies the attainment of plenitude in all of life's undertakings; Israel's role is to be the instrument that expresses the Prophetic vision of God's deeds and might.

Besides the obvious dichotomy between an idea and its realization, the idea itself is subject to articulation in greater or lesser degrees of fidelity or "authenticity." The idea of a reality transcending national and geographical barriers toppled the local pagan deities and created an ecumenic world, but in fact it was difficult to eliminate national definitions and distinctions. "Every definition is a negation," said Spinoza – this rule is very much true in the life of nations.

Israel's national separateness, the cause of so much Gentile reproach, was, however, an absolutely necessary condition for the universalist idea. Without this individuation of the national image in a peculiar historical essence, no universalist idea could be nurtured. Israel understood that only national individuation insured existence in this world, and that every existence was necessarily limited, individuated. Leo Baeck's words are appropriate here:

Had monotheism not become the religion of Israel, had it not gained its firm security by becoming a national possession, or had not the national consciousness of being the chosen people given it the spiritual strength which carried it forward, it might, perhaps, have become the secret, mysterious doctrine of an esoteric sect, and in some old writing a record might have been left of it. But it would never have been able to resist the change of time, and so to become the religion of all time.[1]

The development of the universal ethical idea is an issue unto itself. Clearly, it was an idea that combatted both particularistic idolatry and philosophic paganism. The latter, incidentally, also achieved in its time a high degree of cosmopolitanism, especially in the Cynic and Stoic schools (the word "cosmopolitan" itself was coined by the Cynics).[2] It is also clear that the universalist idea was always more than merely another way of looking at existing reality; it was above all a desire and wish, a human ideal, the noble expression of a hidden intent seeking to be revealed in the fulness of real life. The instrument for this revelation was, as we have said, the "chosen people."

The idea of Israel's chosenness proclaimed that the Jewish people was destined for a special role in the soteriological process, which is the essence of man's history in this world. The idea of the election justified the national individuation required for the fulfillment of the ideal. The covenant between God and Israel expresses the mutual relation between universalism and particularism and all the problematics entailed therein. Israel is free to abandon God, to betray the covenant, and to indulge in the worst, idolatrous kind of particularism. But it is also privileged, and this has even been imposed upon it as a commandment, to be the instrument of divine universalism and to assume the special status of those who dare to be chosen and dare to give self-conscious expression to their chosenness. Fortified by the idea of its chosenness, Israel's faith in its lofty historical role could withstand conditions that belied all signs of outward success. The external results were not taken as any kind of decisive proof. On the contrary, to all appearances Israel was actually inferior to other nations – the few and the weak trying to make their way among the numerous and the strong, hardly a "success story." The idea of chosenness demanded, of course, a certain abstention from the ways of the nations, a separation for the purpose of sanctification: "You shall be holy to me, because I the Lord am holy. I have made a clear separation between you and the heathen, that you may belong to me" (Lev. 20.26).[3] Devotion to this exalted destiny imposed certain hardships. But the universalistic message anticipated in its visions a future where that which had been hidden would be revealed. Beyond the cloud veiling all nations a real force was at work, as yet imperceptible to the blindness of human eyes.

Clearly, there is a close connection between universal monotheism and the idea of one humanity acting on one historical stage. Religious cosmopolitanism grasped the whole world as a single unit transcending the barriers of nations and territories. But the basic dualism of human life does not permit beings of flesh and blood to see clearly the full revelation of God's will. In this full revelation all tensions are resolved, but no eye has yet seen this resolution, at any rate, no human eye.

The tension between a universal religion and a religion peculiar to one nation has many facets. Notwithstanding the widespread diffusion of its offshoot religions, Christianity and Islam, which, in their own ways, emphasized its universalism, the religion of Israel never succeeded in gaining acceptance among other nations and remained the lone legacy of "Abraham's seed." Christianity, we know, held that the two tendencies, the prophetic-universalistic and the Pharisean-nationalistic-particularistic, failed to achieve in the Torah and in the usages of the Jewish people any kind of satisfactory integration for the general humanistic mind, and therefore the Jewish faith could only spread among the nations after the impediments of its individuation, its "stubbornness," "ritualism," and "legalism" had been removed.

The chosen people and the universal God

Let us now examine how this tension was reflected in the cultures of Israel. The Jewish people lived and developed in the midst of the Mediterranean cultures, in a region where many nations and creeds met. Israel intermingled with them. Nowhere does the Bible commend Israel for cultivating a racial purity. Nonetheless the nation did develop an image of separateness, of "a people that dwells alone, that has not made itself one with the nations," in the words of the foreign prophet Balaʿam (Num. 23.9). Another classical formulation of the reason for hatred and persecution of Jews in the diasporas was given in Second Temple times by an outspoken and well-known foe: "There is a certain people, dispersed among the many peoples in all the provinces of [the] kingdom, who keep themselves apart. Their laws are different from those of every other people" (Esther 3.8).

The Bible presents the history of Israel as the individuation of a people through faith in one God and a covenanting of an alliance with Him, and as a series of rises and falls in the nation's self-image, an oscillation between a "holy nation" and an entity "like all other nations." The process of individuation was disrupted by idolatry, especially by the cults of Baʿal and Ashtoret, the deities of the land and its fertility. Scriptures emphasize that there is no natural bond between the people and the land: "because the land is Mine" (Lev. 25.23). The Land of Israel was given to the nation only by virtue of its covenant with God. Israel's Holy Days celebrated events connected with the exodus from Egypt, but no festival was ordered for marking the conquest of the land or for any other national-territorial triumph. The tremendous novelty of the Biblical culture in its rejection of idolatry was the idea that Israel's national God was not the God of only one nation and one land, but the lord of all nations and all lands. Israel's special tie to its land in no way limited the jurisdictional reach of its God.

The Biblical culture conceived the idea of a universal God and expressed this idea in many forms, two of which are key: the God of Israel is the God of the world, ruler over nature and over the history of all nations; his Torah, although given to Israel in a special covenant, is destined for *all men*. The

God of Israel is Lord and there is none other, and faith in Him and in His teaching must be accepted by all men. The two ideas are quite explicit: on the one hand, Biblical accounts testify that God Himself, as it were, consented to the idolatry of the nations and gave His true Torah only to Israel. He is God of a particular nation and a specific land. Banishment from the land, "the Lord's inheritance," is viewed by David as a threat to go and worship "other Gods" (I Sam. 26.19). Ruth the Moabitess in following Naomi to the land of Judaea hopes to "take refuge under the wings of the Lord God of Israel" (Ruth 2.12). But on the other hand, idolatry is looked upon as belief in falsehood, as worship of "wood and stone." The Prophets' vision expresses the desire to spread Israel's Torah among the nations, and the belief that at the end of days this Torah will be universally accepted. God's covenant with Israel will be kept forever, but the nations, like Israel, will all continue as separate entities. Every nation will keep its own distinctiveness, but all will rise together and come to tell the Lord's praise in Jerusalem, "when peoples are assembled together, peoples and kingdoms, to serve the Lord" (Ps. 102.22).

The Prophets' chastisement is prompted by their assessment of the state of the covenant: why does Israel not keep it? What if Israel persists in denying it? But the Prophets also know that, regardless of Israel's adherence to the covenant, the Lord of all the earth, the God of justice and righteousness, does not cease to be the God of His chosen people. God is destined to root out idolatry and establish universal justice and peace in the world. Sinful Israel is punished by Assyria, "the rod" of God's anger (Isa. 10.5–6) which is sent to devastate Israel, the "godless nation," and "trample them like mud in the streets." But the Assyrian too will not be spared. "Because you yourself have plundered mighty nations, all the rest of the world will plunder you" (Hab. 2.8). And the same justice is in store for other nations: the spilled blood and the land's iniquity will all be atoned for. At the end of days Israel will return to Zion from the far corners of its dispersion never to stray again from the path of righteousness, and the nations will imitate its ways. The vision, "for as the waters fill the sea, so shall the land be filled with the knowledge of the Lord" (Isa. 11.9), the final triumph of righteousness and peace in the world, is also the vision of Israel's redemption in Zion, when all will acknowledge that God alone is king over all the land.

Ideals clash with reality

Modern Biblical research has brought to light many of the direct and oblique influences which the narratives and beliefs of the Bible absorbed from the surrounding ancient Mediterranean cultures. It has long been established that the stories of Creation, Adam and Eve, the garden of Eden, the flood, all contain materials borrowed from other ancient cultures, but it is also clear, as such scholars of standing as Kaufmann, Cassuto, and others have shown, that the Bible breathed new life into these stories, in keeping with its own new faith of individuation.

Scholars have pointed out an interesting parallel: the idea of man created in God's image was one of the cornerstones of all Jewish cultures, though its interpretations differed from culture to culture. We know, for example, how vigorously Maimonides fought against any conception that suffered the incorporification of God's image and likeness. It has now been shown that in the Canaanite language, following a Babylonian model, the simile, *tzelem elohim* ("the image of God"), was in fact a corporeal simile, "in keeping with the anthropomorphic conception of the deity among the ancient near eastern peoples."[4] This is the reward for seeking enlightenment of Biblical meanings in the expressions of the neighboring cultures!

In a collection of letters addressed to the kings of Assyria in the eighth and seventh centuries BCE, we read: "The father of my lord king is Bel's image (*tzelem*), and my lord king is Bel's image (*tzelem*)." Scholars have established that it was customary in the language of the Assyrian court to compare the king to the image and likeness of a god. All other mortals are but the shadow of god, but the king himself is his god's very image and likeness. It is in this context that we can now appreciate the Biblical declaration that *every man* is created in God's image, that the title king belongs thus to every man. And this spiritual royalty is the lot of all human beings, not only of the Israelite, as Rabbi Akiba said: "Beloved is man in that he was created in the image (of God). (It is a mark of) superabundant love (that) it was made known to him that he had been created in the image (of God)" (*Avot.* 3.18).

Rabbi Akiba's dictum proclaims that Israel is beloved of God because they were called children of the All-Present. The ancient pagan nations viewed only their kings as sons of God. Hammurabi declared himself to have been sired by a god. In Psalm 2.7 we hear of another king who brags that God had said to him: "'You are my son . . . this day I become your father.'" In the Bible the expression is merely metaphorical and symbolic; moreover, in contradistinction to notions prevailing in the Assyrian and Babylonian courts, the Torah took the concepts of fatherhood and sonship out of their literal meaning and applied them to Israel as a whole by way of endearment, "You are the sons of the Lord your God" (Deut. 14.1), and it is on this that Rabbi Akiba based his dictum.[5]

Opposing this universalistic aspect of Scripture, the aspect which recognizes God's image in all men and commands, "love thy neighbor as thyself," there is always that other, particularistic dimension, which stresses the exclusivity of the covenant. This covenant commands that the nations of Canaan be destroyed, Amalek exterminated. It does not forbid to "press foreigners" (Deut. 15.3), and to "charge interest on a loan to a foreigner" (Deut. 23.20). Scripture countenances bloody deeds against non-Israelites committed by King David that were far out of keeping with the spirit of his son Solomon's prayer for "the foreigner . . . who does not belong to thy people Israel" (I Kgs. 8.41). Jeremiah's "Pour out thy fury on nations" (10.25) sounds antithetical to the Messianic vision that he himself, and indeed all the Prophets, proclaim elsewhere.

The reality that so collided with the vision was in fact the theme of the Prophets' chastisement, "There is blood on your hands" (Isa. 1.15), or "O my people! Your guides lead you astray" (Isa. 3.12). The tension was a daily, palpable anguish. Israel, the "chosen people," and man, the "image of God," did not behave in the anticipated and desired manner. Instead, they indulged in militant nationalism and jealousy, often led by those ideologues of particularism known in the Bible as "false prophets." Yeḥezkel Kaufmann has devoted many pages to the dissonance between laws and reality in First Temple times.[6] The laws did not reflect actual practice and it is difficult to learn from the writings of visionaries anything about the historical reality.

Moreover, you also find in the Biblical culture complaints that God, who does "whatever [He] pleases, in heaven and on earth" (Ps. 135.6), fails to exercise justice, "Why dost thou countenance . . . why keep silent?" cried Habakkuk (1.13). The tie between Israel's Holy One and a just God "who does no wrong" (Deut. 32.4) was to many members of the Biblical culture far from apparent. They saw the incongruity between His cruel deeds and His benign commandments. The terrible events following the incident of the Golden Calf are just one example: Moses "took his place at the gate of the camp and said: . . . 'These are the words of the Lord the God of Israel: "Arm yourselves, each of you, with his sword . . . Each of you kill his brother, his friend, his neighbour"'" (Exod. 32.26–7).

Within the Biblical culture itself one finds considerable discussion over God's ethical image. A great gap yawns between the dictate of Deut. 20.16, "In the cities of these nations whose land the Lord your God is giving you as a patrimony, you shall not leave any creature alive," followed, often to the embarrassment of modern readers, by "do not destroy its trees by taking the axe to them . . . the trees of the field are not men that you should besiege them," to the vision of universal justice and peace when the land will fill with the knowledge of God "as the waters fill the sea." It is difficult to point to any one of Israel's cultures for a smooth, intelligible, and sustained equilibration between the universalism of the Prophetic-Messianic vision and the individuated chosenness of its carriers.

From the Bible to the Talmud

Nineteenth-century Bible scholars tried to prove that the Prophets' faith in one God evolved in the course of a long process of intellectual development, a view still held by many scholars today. I tend to agree with Kaufmann that the creators of the Biblical culture conceived from the outset a universal God rather than a limited national deity, but I believe that Kaufmann exaggerated the purity of Israel's early monotheism. Biblical literature was intimately familiar with the pagan faith practised by Israel's neighbors, and the idols so vehemently execrated in the Bible were not regarded simply as insignificant local fetishes. Kaufmann's narrow concept of myth fails to take into account the numerous Biblical images and stories which closely resemble the myths of other nations. The nature of mythology as it is defined today by modern researchers, such as Eliade, would encompass a considerable amount of the Bible's mythical material, and it is difficult to deny that even Judaism's universal monotheism, with all its lofty abstraction, was not immune to the influence of a mythology that was pagan, particularistic, tribal, and national.

It is also clear, however, that it was widely believed in the Biblical culture that the universal God revealed His name and His will to Israel alone, that this was His nation, whereas to other peoples He did not thus reveal Himself; to the latter, the Leader of the world and the Judge of all the earth remains a "hiding God." The Torah relates the creation of man and the spread of his progeny on the face of the earth with no mention of Israel, its land, or its temple. Idol-worship and the separation into tribes and nations came later, after the revolt against the universal God. The history of the nations, like the history of Israel, unfolds the rises and falls in the level of acceptance or rejection of the universal God.

The account of the world's beginning and the vision of its end illustrate the Bible's view that the end of days will witness the triumph of the national God, for He is from the outset the God of all the world. This Jewish idea became progressively more pronounced and eventually spread among the nations, but not in its distinctly Jewish garb. Through Christianity, Israel in time exercised a tremendous spiritual influence over the nations of the world, but this occurred only after the collapse of the Jewish common-wealth. Jews had always considered themselves God's favored children and now they were banished from their Father's hearth. Judging at least by the outward appearance of historical events, their history gave little proof of divine predilection.

The universalistic dimension in the Talmudic culture was expressed in a number of fundamental opinions and certain new ordinances and institutions. One of the more important opinions was that the Holy One had wanted to give the Torah to various nations, but they refused to accept it: "The Holy One, blessed be He, offered the Torah to every nation and every tongue, but none accepted it" (*Ab. Zar.* 2b). The nations of the world could have obtained the Torah and all its benefits, but they rejected the restrictions on bloodshed and adultery and the many commandments against which their instincts rebelled. The Torah was by nature a general-human law, but it was in the nature of the other nations to reject it. In the terminology of our study we would say that other cultures were nurtured by superordinating concepts and by archetypal collective experiences which did not enable them to accept the principles of Israel's culture.

Researchers have pointed out that in ethical-religious matters the Talmudic culture introduced many emendations to Biblical statements that were difficult for the Sages to accept literally. These emendations were usually initiated with the intent of defending the honor of the nation, the Patriarchs, kings or saintly men, and especially in order to preserve the loftiness of the Bible's ethic and an unsullied concept of God, which a literal reading of the Bible might undermine. "Moralizing," is the term coined by Leon Roth for this Talmudic tendency. Isaak Heinemann likewise gave numerous examples of this tendency and enlarged upon the practice of taking texts out of their literal meanings.[7] Literal meanings were often rejected because they seemed to imply polytheism or an incorporification of God, for example, "'And He rested on the seventh day.' And is He subject to such a thing as weariness?"[8] But, more importantly, these revisions reflect the Sages' new moral understanding. The struggle within the Talmudic culture between the expansive universalistic pole and contractive nationalistic pole was marked by opinions such as the following.

The universalistic aspect of Pentateuch, Prophets, and Hagiographa – man created in God's image, the commandment, "Love thy neighbor as thyself," statements like "God has told you what is good; and what is it that the Lord asks of you? Only to act justly, to love loyalty, to walk wisely before your god" (Mic. 6.8) – appeared in the Talmudic culture in a theory about seven basic universal commandments given to Noah's sons, and in such sayings as, "The righteous of the nations have a share in the world to come," and even, "a gentile who occupies himself with the study of the Torah equals (in status) the High Priest" (Bab.K. 38a). A number of non-Jews are referred to in the Talmud as sages and saints and even entire nations, such as the Medes and the Persians, were recognized for certain noble qualities. The Edomites, for example, supposed descendants of Esau, were given credit for the honor exhibited by their progenitor toward his father Isaac. Moreover, famous converts, saints, and sages had issued from the seed of terribly wicked men. The entire history of the world proved the merits of certain foreign nations and the sinfulness of Israel. On no lesser an occasion than Yom Kippur, when the book of Jonah is read in the synagogue, the inhabitants of Nineveh, a foreign city, are hailed as models of repentance. The annihilation of Amalek recounted in I Sam. 15.2 ("This is the very word of the Lord of Hosts . . . Go now and fall upon the Amalekites and destroy them, and put their property under ban. Spare no one; put them all to death, men and women, children and babes in arms") elicited from the

Sages these provocative questions: "And if human beings sinned, what has the cattle committed; and if the adults have sinned, what have the little ones done?" (*Yoma* 22b). Here the Rabbis question how this kind of indiscriminate killing accords with the rule: "A man shall be put to death only for his own sin" (Deut. 24.16). These questions indicate a large measure of individualism in the valuation of human deeds. But there were also many questions that were stifled, with the help of the verse, "Do not be over-righteous" (Eccles. 7.16). There were limits to the "moralizing."

The nations' antagonism to Israel and its Torah, and the savagery and licentiousness of the Hellenistic-Roman environment did little, however, to endear to the members of the Talmudic culture even idolators of such pacifist universalism as the Stoics. The Sages frequently refer to the nations of the world as wicked, both in the sense of wicked behavior and in the sense of their hostility to Israel. In contrast, they extol Israel above all nations and loudly tout its praises.

The tension in the Talmudic culture is exemplified in the variance between two versions of a famous *mishnah*: "If any man saves alive a single soul, Scripture imputes it to him as though he had saved a whole world" (*San.* 4.5 in Danby's translation).[9] There are some who claim (e.g. J.N. Epstein) that this is the correct version of the *mishnah*, but there are others who maintain that the *mishnah* speaks not of one soul, but of "one soul in Israel." This is the version that appears in Ḥanoch Albeck's edition[10] and we need hardly comment on the significance of this variance.[11]

In keeping with their universalistic bent, the Sages taught that a non-Jew who converts becomes an Israelite in all things. The verse, "Ye shall therefore keep My statutes and My ordinances which, if a man do, he shall live by them" (Ezek. 20.11), they expounded as follows: "It does not say 'If a priest, Levite, or Israelite do, he shall live by them,' but 'a man'" (*Ab.Zar.* 3a, also *San.* 59a). We should note the new Talmudic institution of conversion: no longer was residence and absorption of a foreigner in the Land of Israel, a geographical-cultural adhesion, considered sufficient for conversion; admission into Abraham's covenant was effected through a special ceremony. This concept of conversion as a religious institution was inaugurated during the time of the Second Temple. This new form of conversion brought foreigners under "the wings of the Shechinah" by allowing them to enter in full awareness and intent into the covenant that God had contracted with His people.

Indeed, in one respect, it can be said that Isaiah's Messianic vision of "the foreigner who has given his allegiance to the Lord" (Isa. 56.3) became a reality during the Second Temple. This vision had been temporarily suspended by Ezra and Neḥemiah whose experience of the acute demographic decimation following the first destruction prompted them to reject converts as a threat to the nation's racial purity and its spiritual existence.

But some generations later Sages again accepted the foreigner who embraced the Torah as an Israelite in all things. The Halachah was essentially egalitarian, more accommodating and accepting, in fact, than the Aggadah, which often reminisced fondly on the "seed of Abraham," i.e. on Israel's racial excellence.

Between the two poles

But what happened in reality? On the one hand, the Sages taught that the Torah was given in the wilderness, in no-man's-land, and in seventy languages, so that it would be available to all nations: "The Holy One, blessed be He, did not exile Israel among the nations save in order that proselytes might join them" (*Pes.* 87b). But it was also said: "Proselytes are as hard for Israel (to endure) as a sore" (*Yeb.* 47b). The Shechinah accompanied Israel into exile, shared its sorrow in all the diasporas, and upheld its faith that only through the Torah would humanity attain eternal salvation. But when the adversities multiplied, and salvation delayed in coming, Judaism shrunk within the four walls of its Torah, there to find whatever solace remained after the loss of the commonwealth and the destruction of the Temple. The Prophets had promised that the nation would not perish, that at least a remnant would survive. But they had also warned that God would abandon His people if they failed to obey Him. The transgressors of the covenant would not escape punishment: "They grow rich and grand, bloated and rancorous; their thoughts are all of evil, and they refuse to do justice, the claims of the orphan they do not put right nor do they grant justice to the poor. Shall I not punish them for this? says the Lord; shall I not take vengeance on such a people?" (Jer. 5.28–9).

The belief that, by giving the Torah, God had implanted in His people eternal, indestructible life gathered strength in the Talmudic culture, but the tension did not ease. There was an expansion of Judaism's universalistic reach as a result of the newly introduced concepts of conversion and "the righteous of the nations," who have a share in the world to come. But working against this expansion was the opposite tendency to shrink within Israel's own four walls. This was expressed, for example, in a series of derogatory sayings that begin with "the best of Gentiles . . ." and in a number of ordinances regarding idolatry and ritual uncleanness.

Israel's particularistic, separate, and individuated aspect did not diminish. Immediately upon the destruction of the Temple the Gentiles brought forth the argument that a people lacking political power, bereft of independence, smitten and dispersed among the nations was not a chosen people, but a despised and inferior nation. The Christians now made the claim that they were the true Israel, heirs of Israel's chosenness and primacy. The tension is particularly acute in the Talmudic culture because of the patent incongruity between the belief in the election and the anguished reality of the destruction. Only in the Messianic belief could the two conflicting elements, the universalistic and the particularistic, be welded together. Only in the ultimate vision of a universal covenant and an all-embracing knowledge of God could the concern for the preservation of the nation's uniqueness be allayed. The gates of nationhood were never thrown wide open to admit anyone who chose to enter. Although I do not see here a fundamental opposition between a "static morality" and a "dynamic morality" (in Bergson's definition), there was a ceaseless tension between the inclination toward national individuation according to the Torah, and the universalist vision of that same Torah, between life's actual practices and the hoped-for practices, for both Israel and the nations, in a future life.

Conflicts with the Gentiles in ancient Israel

From a *halachic* point of view, hostility between Jews and Gentiles was by no means inevitable. The Halachah established certain fundamental differences between Israel and idol-worshipers. Israel had been harnessed into the "yoke of *mitzvot*," whereas the Gentiles only had to keep the seven Noachian commandments; any who did so could be considered "righteous of the nations." These seven commandments were akin to the "laws of nature," which the Greek philosophers perceived as necessary conditions for all individual and collective existence, consisting essentially of prohibitions against bloodshed and incest and the adherence to a recognized rule of law.

But when, toward the end of the Second Temple period, the Talmudic culture had solidified and spread, a wall of contention and rivalry arose between Jews and Gentiles in the Land of Israel. Three main reasons, political, religious, and social-economic, accounted for this development. Politically, the Jews never resigned to Roman rule. The foreign government was viewed as the rule of evil and throughout the predestruction period, and even more so afterwards, Jews continued to challenge the cruel plunder, the compulsory labor (*anagria*), and the corruption which Roman rule brought upon their land.

In reality the Jewish attitude toward the Gentiles during the Tanna'itic period was dictated largely by a strong desire to set as great a separation as possible between Judaism and idolatry. The Sages' prohibitions, Maimonides said, were decreed "in order to keep people away from heathens, so that Israelites might not mingle with them, lest such commingling should lead to intermarriage." For this reason they forbade "drinking with heathens, even in circumstances where no apprehension need be felt for libation wine; and eating their bread or cooked food, even where no concern need be had for heathen cooking utensils."[12] The decree establishing the ritual uncleanness of Gentiles certainly helped to limit contact between Gentiles and Jews. Some scholars believe that this decree applied originally only to worship at the Temple, while others think that it pertained from the start also to non-religious spheres of activity.[13]

The history of the Halachah also testifies to the bitter struggles of the Jewish community against the settlement of foreigners in the Land of Israel. The fear that foreigners would take possession of Jewish lands and homes prompted various prohibitions against sale and lease of land to foreigners. "Nor be gracious unto them" (Deut. 7.2) is rendered as, "nor allow them to settle on the soil" (Ab.Zar. 20a). The idea was to prevent foreigners from gaining a foothold in the Land of Israel and to insure that Jews would not be dislodged from it. We speak here of the Land of Israel in the boundaries specified by the *halachah* for the observance of commandments related to the land (such as tithes), and not of its Biblical political or historical boundaries. The boundaries we speak of – "every place that had been in the possession of the Babylonian returnees"[14] – were in fact the real boundaries of the Jewish settlement during the early Tannaʾitic period. Without going into the details of the map, we know that Israel included Greek cities outside the boundaries prescribed by the *halachah*, and mixed cities within those boundaries. There were instances of both peaceful and hostile relations between Jewish and Gentile neighbors, depending on the circumstances and the times. For example, the Hasmonean Kings, convinced of the legitimacy of Jewish rights to the entire Land of Israel, embarked upon a policy of destruction of Gentile settlements throughout Israel. Thus did Simeon the Hasmonean reply to King Antiochus VII's demand for the return of cities captured by him: "We have not occupied other people's land or taken other people's property, but only the inheritance of our ancestors, unjustly seized for a time by our enemies. We have grasped our opportunity and have claimed our patrimony."[15] This spread of the Jewish population came to an end with the Roman conquest, but the struggle did not cease. The Jews who regarded the entire land as their patrimony tried to dislodge the foreigners, by war, banishments, or by use of economic pressures, and the foreigners continued to oppose these attempts. They condemned the Jews' desire for separateness and accused them of arrogance, contempt of other nations and religions, and general misanthropy.

The two conflicting Tannaʾitic tendencies are both reflected in the history of the Halachah: befriending the Gentiles and welcoming them through conversion, but also insulating Israel from their influence by harsh prohibitions. The Halachah, however, always required that the Gentiles be treated peaceably: one visited the Gentiles' sick, one eulogized and buried their dead, and one consoled their mourners, all "for the sake of peace."

The Tannaʾitic expressions "for the sake of peace," or "for fear of profanation of God's name," or the expression "for fear of ill feeling" more common in the language of the Amora'im, denote clearly the limits of decent, permissible aloofness from the Gentiles, commensurate with the interests of practicality and utility; not too much familiarity, but no hostility, friendliness without closeness. Just as the Sages forbade any act that might shame the name of Israel, so they forbade any abstention from an act that could exalt the name of Israel's God. Rabban Gamliel of Yavneh forbade theft from a Gentile, because it constituted "profanation of God's name." The profanation of God's name was a transgression of such serious nature that even repentance and Yom Kippur did not atone for more than one-third of it, suffering atoned for another third, and only death cleansed entirely.

The mixed communities in the Land of Israel were rife with Jewish-Gentile conflicts. The large city of Caesarea, founded by King Herod as a city of Gentiles, is a case in point. Judging by Herod's advocacy of Gentile interests in Caesarea, the Jews feared he planned to base his rule on the land's foreign population. He was, according to Josephus Flavius, "King over Jews and Greeks." The Gentiles of Caesarea ferociously attacked the city's Jews whenever opportunity arose, until finally, in the war of destruction (70 CE), they exterminated the town's entire Jewish population. The same state of ceaseless tension existed in Ashkelon, Acre, Tyre, Susita, Gader, and other locations. In fact, the bloody conflicts and unrest continued during the Tanna'itic period in those towns which had a Gentile majority and a Jewish minority (as in the coastal towns and in the communities east of the Jordan), and in cities where there was a Jewish majority and a Gentile minority.[16] The tensions between Jews and Gentiles in ancient Israel left upon the Halachah an indelible mark for all future generations. One may say that the Jew's attitude toward the Gentile crystallized in the final days of the Second Temple and thereafter changed very little throughout the generations of faith. Subsequent Jewish leaders may be more benign and receptive toward Gentiles, others may be more strict or hostile, but the Halachah itself remained unchanged. The events that had stirred the turmoil in the streets of ancient Caesarea and Jaffa continued to be experienced in their original traumatic acuteness for generations to come.

A better understanding of some of the conflicts that pitted Jews against Gentiles in ancient Israel, and a critical examination of how these conflicts eventually came to be reflected in the Halachah, enable us perhaps to respond more easily to the question: what was it that really prevented the spread of Judaism among the masses of idol-worshipers at that point of the Hellenistic period when the tremendous conversion movement first got under way? It should, at least, be easier now for us to understand the question itself. The scholars, we know, hold divergent views on this question. Christian scholars believed, of course, that it was Jewish "ritualism" and "legalism" that impeded the spread of the Jewish faith. The national need to separate from other people raised a tall barrier between

Israel and the nations, they thought. Jewish scholars maintained that strict practices and rituals were also adopted by Christianity and Islam, with no ill effect on their ability to expand. Kaufmann thought that it was only the ignominy of national defeat – the destruction of the Temple, the exile from the homeland, and subsequent catastrophes – that brought the conversion movement to an abrupt end. The Jews themselves felt that God's success in Jewish history was necessary for the spread of their faith. Israel's political success or failure determined the extent to which its faith would be accepted or rejected. Religion, after all, is not a private sphere of personal opinions and emotions; it is upheld – in practices, institutions, and rituals – by a group or a nation. When a group or a nation succumbs in political defeat, its religion too is seen in the eyes of its adherents, and even more so, of course, in the eyes of outsiders, to have failed. Israel's faith promised glory and greatness, a return to ancient honor, but a reality of poverty and oppression perpetually plagued the nation's religious consciousness: "How long, O God, will thy enemy taunt thee?" cries the Psalmist (74.10). "Why should the nations ask, 'Where is their God?'" (79.10). Foreign sources also attest to this attitude toward the Jewish religion, as, for example, Cicero's derisive comment: "How dear [is this nation] to the immortal gods is shown by the fact that it has been conquered, let out for taxes, made a slave."[17]

After the destruction of the Temple and especially after the failure of Bar Kochba's revolt (135 CE), the Sages had to defend Israel's religion both against the pagan argument that a vanquished people could not be a chosen people, and against Christianity's claim to the inheritance of the chosenness precisely on the grounds that it was an Israel of the spirit and not of the flesh, i.e. that it was indeed a church of all nations. Against this background the Talmudic debates about proselytes and the righteous of the nations, whether they were beloved by God, or whether they were a curse, become more understandable. The tension was clear cut: the God of all flesh chose Israel to spread the faith among the nations of the world. An increase in proselytes was an added testimonial to the veracity of Israel's faith. But, as we saw earlier, when times grew worse and catastrophes multiplied, the Sages came to question both the possibility and the necessity of effecting true conversions. Nonetheless, throughout the Amora'itic period efforts continued to bring non-Jews "under the wings of the Shechinah," until the Christian church prohibited this activity entirely.

Throughout the ages Christian theologians reproached Judaism for its national particularism, in which they saw the chief obstacle to its development into the universal faith envisioned by the Prophets. I tend to agree with the scholars who maintain that the disastrous political defeat was a far more likely cause for the nation's failure to propagate its faith. But the main cause of the failure is rooted, as we have said, in the cultures of the pagan nations themselves, in their inability to accept a religion devoid of the kind of mythological elements they had been accustomed to. The Jewish conception of God, world, and man had to assume first a Christian mantle, and later a Muslim garb, in order to become the heritage of many different nations.

The tension in the Poetic-Philosophic culture

The tension that juxtaposes the two polar conceptions regarding the nature of the Jewish people – universalism versus particularism, expansion versus contraction, the loftiness of faith and morality versus the conceit and confinement of narrow boundaries – that tension which characterizes all of Israel's cultures, is also very much apparent in the Poetic-Philosophic culture of the Middle Ages. Like all our other cultures, accommodation was sought between the yearning for the brotherhood of mankind in one faith and the opposing need for a chosen people's national individuation.

The creators of the Poetic-Philosophic culture were well aware that the belief in the common origin of mankind was as binding as a principle of faith. They believed that the Biblical story about the origin of mankind exemplified the religious-ethical conception that the oneness of the human race originated from the same source as the oneness of God. Monohumanity and monotheism were one idea: faith in the common origin of the human race equalled, as it were, the idea of *creatio ex nihilo* by one God.

In this culture, too, the outstanding expression for the oneness of the human race was to be found in the concept of man created in the image of God and endowed with intellect and the power of speech, a reflection of God the Creator. In the world of beings man stands, as it were, on one plane with God and is only "little less than a god" (Ps. 8.5).[18] Faith in the oneness of the human race enjoins brotherhood and friendship. To love one's fellow human beings becomes a supreme ethical command, and the worth of each individual created in the image of God is magnified.

I believe it can safely be said that the Poetic-Philosophic culture generally strove toward expansion rather than contraction, toward religious universalism over tribal or national particularism. Henri Bergson, as mentioned earlier, spoke of "two sources of morality and religion," one of which creates a "static" morality and religion, while the other creates a "dynamic" one.[19] Regarding the "static" morality and religion, Bergson said that these served the needs of a closed society, a society imprisoned in its past and its heritage, engaged primarily in strengthening the group's internal cohesion and in excluding outsiders. On the other hand, the "dynamic" morality and religion ignore ethnic boundaries and extend a loving affirmation to all human beings. In this sense one may say that in the Poetic-Philosophic culture the "dynamic" aspect prevailed. Bergson held these two sources of morality and religion to be "not of the same essence," i.e so unlike one another as to allow for no gradual transition between them. In Israel's cultures, however, the contrast between these two concepts is not, I believe, quite so radical; it resembles rather a ceaseless tension between the two elements.

The Poetic-Philosophic culture sees in Judaism no substantive dichotomy between national individuation and the oneness of the human race. Chosenness expresses a religious-moral dynamics, a major forward thrust in the history of mankind toward the opening of new wellsprings of human love and respect. In this Israel carved out for itself a unique path in the history of the world. It was, however, a path replete with obstacles and suffering that led to heights of spiritual devotion, but also exacted tremendous sacrifices, and at times engendered strange distortions bred of crude popular arrogance.

The tension in the Poetic-Philosophic culture between universalism and particularism is illustrated in the differing opinions of Judah ha-Levi and Maimonides on the nature of Israel's superiority and the ensuing opinions on the status of proselytes. According to ha-Levi, Israel is endowed with a special position among the nations of the earth by virtue of the "divine influence" that elevates it above all other nations. Proselytes cannot be considered equal to Israelites. "If this be so," says the King of the Khazars, "then your belief is confined to yourselves?" The Sage replies:

Yes, but any Gentile who joins us unconditionally shares our good fortune, without, however, being quite equal to us. If the law were binding on us only because God created us, the white and the black man would be equal, since He created them all. But the Law was given to us because he led us out of Egypt, and remained attached to us, because we are the pick of mankind.[20]

Ha-Levi goes on to prove that not only is Israel "the pick of mankind," but every single Jew is in fact "visibly distinguished from the ordinary degree of mankind." Of course, ha-Levi does not advocate a modern naturalistic racism. Israel's nature is a spiritual essence and it is the "divine influence" which distinguishes it from other nations.[21] Nonetheless, it is the nature of only one people.

In contrast to this opinion, which was surely not a lone position, Maimonides, in direct contradiction to the Mishnah's ruling in tractate *Bikkurim*, permits the convert to utter in prayer the words "God of our fathers." In his famous responsum to Obadiah the Proselyte, Maimonides states:

You should therefore pray, "Our God and God of our fathers," for Abraham is also your father. In no respect is there a difference between us and you. And certainly you should say, "Who has given unto us the Torah," because the Torah was given to us and the proselytes alike . . . Do not think little of your origin: we are descended from Abraham, Isaac, and Jacob, but your descent is from the Creator.[22]

What we see here are not simply two different approaches to the acceptance of proselytes, something analogous perhaps to the difference between the strict criteria of Shammai versus the leniency of Hillel, which the Talmud so picturesquely illustrates in the famous stories about Gentiles who came to these Sages for conversion. No, the reasons for the disagreement between these medieval scholars are deeper than mere approaches or points of strategy. Maimonides differed from ha-Levi in the matter of the proselytes because he could not agree with him on the fundamental issue of Israel's chosenness.

Both thinkers try to find a proper balance between the two ideas – national individuation versus the oneness of humanity. Ha-Levi, as we have explained, endows Israel with a natural superiority over other nations, which he sees as a sort of natural-racial (albeit spiritual) quality, while Maimonides attributes Israel's chosenness to God's will and the decree of His wisdom: "He willed it so; . . . His wisdom decided so."[23] To Maimonides there is no natural difference between Israel and the nations. Ha-Levi thinks that Israel's unique quality is manifested by the gift of Prophecy; the "divine influence" clings to Israel alone and only Israel is worthy of Prophecy. All other mortals, proselytes included, who cleave to Israel's religion, may "become pious and learned, but never prophets." "Those . . . who become Jews do not take equal rank with born Israelites, who are specially privileged to attain to prophecy."[24] In contrast, Maimonides stresses that it is possible for a Prophet to arise from among the Gentiles and, "if [he] urges and encourages people to follow the religion of Moses without adding thereto or diminishing therefrom, like Isaiah, Jeremiah and the others, we demand a miracle from him. If he can perform it we recognize him and bestow upon him the honor due to a prophet."[25]

We can say, then, in summary that these two medieval creators of the Poetic-Philosophic culture saw the religion of Israel as universal in two respects. First, Israel's God was the God of all nations, and, secondly, His Torah was worthy of acceptance by all people, because it was a law of righteousness and justice for every being created in the image of God. Of course, Israel was a chosen people and endowed with particular holiness, but all people were enjoined to walk in its path, to follow the "light unto the nations." In their Messianic vision both thinkers saw the nations of the world accepting the Jewish faith and "then they will revere the origin which they formerly despised."[26] But in matters of religion Maimonides saw no difference whatsoever between a born Jew and a proselyte.

This is not to say that the national-religious element was absent in Maimonides' thinking; the Talmudic commandments regarding separation from the nations receive renewed validation in *Mishneh Torah*:

We should not follow the customs of the Gentiles, nor imitate them in dress or in their way of trimming the hair, as it is said, "And ye shall not walk in the customs of the nation (which I cast out before you)" (Lev. 20.23); "neither shall ye walk in their statutes" (Lev. 18.3); "Take heed to thyself that thou be not ensnared to follow them" (Deut. 12.30). These texts all refer to one theme and warn against imitating them. The Israelite shall, on the contrary, be distinguished from them and recognisable by the way he dresses and in his other activities, just as he is distinguished from them by his knowledge and his principles.[27]

The "knowledge" referred to here is a Jew's faith, as explained in the 'Book of Knowledge,' the opening section of *Mishneh Torah*. Maimonides' strictness draws from the sayings of Tannaʾim and Palestinian Amoraʾim regarding the Gentiles. This passage on the issue of temporary residence of aliens in Palestine, clearly an echo of the suspicion and hostility prevailing during the Second Temple between Jews and Gentiles, is illustrative:

When Israel is predominant over the nations of the world, we are forbidden to permit a Gentile who is an idolator to dwell among us. He must not enter our land, even as a temporary resident, or even as a traveller journeying with merchandise from place to place, till he has undertaken to keep the seven precepts which the Noachides were commanded to observe; as it is said: "They shall not dwell in thy land" (Exod. 23.33) even for a time. If he undertakes to observe these seven precepts, he becomes a denizen proselyte.[28]

In general, however, Maimonides tended toward moderation, to a softening of the tensions, going as far as the written *halachah* permitted, and sometimes even beyond, as we have seen in the matter of the proselytes: "God charged [us] concerning the love of the stranger, even as He charged us concerning love of Himself, as it is said: 'Thou shalt love the Lord thy God' (Deut. 6.5). The Holy One, blessed be He, loves strangers, as it is said: 'And He loveth the stranger' (Deut. 10.18)."[29]

So much for the first tension. We have learnt from our long experience, validated by research in the last generations, that it is no easy task for a consciousness of chosenness to accommodate an all-embracing love of others. It is difficult for nations imbued with a sense of their own election to live at peace with one another. There is, in fact, no nation that does not believe in its own chosenness, either in the realm of spiritual or material assets, or in its destiny to wield power, or both. We allude to a complex social-spiritual and psychological phenomenon that takes intricate and, at times, dangerous turns. Nations reaped tremendous benefits from their consciousness of destiny, but also paid a heavy price for it. Chosenness is but one side of the coin; its other face is constriction within the narrow limits of nationalism. Belief in one's election may easily turn into a complex of superiority which, in turn, may be covering a sense of inferiority. Vulgar distortion lies in ambush for every noble idea.

Israel's history has been characterized by the great disparity between mighty visions and the reality of daily existence. This was true in ancient times, when the nation still dwelt in its land, as also later in the diasporas. Of course, there is a vast difference between a weak and exiled nation, imbued with a universal vocation it cannot fulfill because of its weakness, and a powerful nation or religion which sees itself destined to bring salvation to the world according to its lights. How power is maintained and used – that is the test of a people's chosenness, if we may borrow this theological concept for a non-metaphysical context. It is only with the establishment of the State of Israel that the Jewish people has acquired the right to mediocrity, that basic right of every nation to exist without having to justify its existence by the "contributions" it makes to other nations, and without lofty goals of enriching "civilization" in general. But this right, which does not stand in the way of an adventurous spiritual voyage toward greatness, and all that it entails in the State of Israel is a chapter unto itself.[30]

Integration of the elements

This framework of meanings which encompasses goods and values, literary and artistic creations, public institutions and interpersonal relations, temple and king, religion and army, and many other components, this framework known as culture – what is the nature and measure of its unity? Thousands of events and deeds, a chaotic amalgam of tools and opinions must coalesce into a framework of orderly meaning, into a cultural life whose constituent elements possess a certain commonality. All efforts are geared toward the creation of order from chaos, toward the structuring of the accidental and contingent into purpose, the harmonizing of contradictory phenomena into a whole world structure.

Anthropologists, sociologists, and philosophers have assumed that culture is not merely a collection of building blocks, but an entire organic edifice, a coherent unit of meanings, a unified configuration, or a functional unit, but few have elaborated on the nature of this unity.[31] Clearly, mere geographical contiguity or chronological proximity, or both, do not constitute a unified entity, either separately or together. An assemblage of particles (congeries) is not a unit. It is possible for two or even three cultures to develop within a single geographical location. Even in the tiny Palestine of the Hasmoneans one could find remnants of the waning Biblical culture, buds of the newly developing Talmudic culture, and side by side with these two Jewish cultures the Graeco-Roman culture was spreading. Jerusalem in the days of Herod was a city of many contradictions, and perhaps only a minority of its population was Pharisean. Neither is chronological sequence, generally delimited by political turning-points, such as the destruction of the Temple or the French Revolution, decisive in defining a culture in this sense. There is much of the accidental and the haphazard in geographical contiguity and chronological sequence.

Most scholars tend to emphasize the integration of a culture's elements from a functional-causal or organological aspect. They speak of culture as an operative-functional unit, or as a living body, and employ technological or organological metaphors accordingly; a culture's elements are compared to physical limbs or to interconnecting parts of a machine. Marx and his disciples examined society from both these angles and determined that the means of production were the decisive factor in establishing the super-structures of law and order, government and administration, literature and art. This decisive factor wields an overwhelming influence over all other elements, and when it is removed, the latter undergo change or vanish. It is, in fact, so critical an element in organizing a society, and so much of a condition to a proper understanding of its functioning, that the entire development of the culture can be accurately foretold and explained given a correct understanding of the means of production. Max Weber elucidated the influence of religious concepts and fervor on the work ethic and on the rationalization of all spheres of life. The concept of functional unity enables us to determine the overall relationship between the changing elements of culture and sheds light on many areas hitherto shrouded in darkness. This conception serves as the basis for modern studies on such issues as the relation between an economic crisis and birth or divorce rates, between urbanization and crime, between loneliness and suicide rates. If you can demonstrate that variable A is indeed the cause, or at least the antecedent, of variable B, you have established a universal rule; uniform order emerges out of that which previously seemed a mere aggregation of unrelated occurrences, thus enabling an intelligent prediction and a prescient orientation.

Other scholars have claimed to detect at the root of every culture a single, central grand design, an overall spiritual direction, a psychological source from which all details originate and which, in turn, all details must validate. In this view the nature of a culture's cohesion is not determined by spatial or chronological occurrences, nor by a causal relation, whereby one element is responsible for bringing about the creation of other elements. Rather, it is the pattern of one overriding psychological-spiritual design which exists *a priori* in all constituent elements of the culture, just as an individual's life-style can be recognized in all spheres of his activity. The Gothic cathedral, the works of St. Thomas Aquinas and the feudal hierarchy all belong to the same thirteenth-century style, just as compulsory education, technological inventions, and general elections are unmistakable hallmarks of our century. It is utterly impossible for a materialistic, industrial, and consumer society to embrace the values of, say, Rabbi Bachya Ibn Pakuda or Rabbi Isaac Luria, the "Holy Ari." The two are entirely different essences which simply do not go together. This model of cultural cohesion, then, largely ignores the causality factor in favor of a common internal essence.

This explanation, like the functional theory mentioned earlier, does, in fact, shed great light on widely different spheres of endeavor within a culture. Guided by the integral design, or the inner intention, of a certain culture, one is more readily able to grasp the relation between its cosmology and architecture, as Spengler explained, or between philosophy (a culture's measure of rationalism) and music, as Max Weber argued, or between achievements in the plastic arts and religious institutions, and many similar phenomena, which "belong" with each other in the overall large pattern. This third explanation can be found in the writings of a number of philosophers of history, including Buber.[32]

All such theories on the nature of a culture's integration must be viewed with great reservation. Geographical location and chronology, periodization according to primarily political turning-points – none of these creates a culture or makes a culture cohere, in our sense of the concept. A culture can stretch over a number of periods: the Talmudic culture began to unfold in the days of the Second Temple and reigned long after its destruction. In pre-expulsion Spain three cultures – the Poetic-Philosophic, the Mystical, and the Rabbinic – simultaneously vied with each other for dominion. The quest for a single design that animates the whole culture and is, as it were, its very breath and soul, its fundamental essence, is a very difficult undertaking, and really, an endless one. It readily outgrows the bounds of scientific inquiry to the point where it sees the will of a metaphysical power operating beyond the intentions of the culture's creators.

The perspectivistic pluralism advocated here seeks to take fully into account the intentions of individual creators, which alternately collided, compromised, and sought accommodations with each other. When these intentions merge into a single dominant tendency, a new culture takes over from its predecessor. It is in this sense we have spoken here of tensions and their equilibrations in Israel's cultures.

Halachah relating to the Land of Israel

Earlier in this chapter we described the third tension as one in which different elements of the same culture conflict with one another and strive for an equilibrium that will be found acceptable and enduring. How did relations crystallize between language and religious faith, race and temple, army and economy, social classes and government? We conclude this chapter with a brief look into the tension that existed between law and land – what happened when commandments whose fulfillment presupposed habitation of Eretz Israel, the Land of Israel, were dissociated from the land as a result of exile and changed circumstances?

During the seventy years of the Babylonian exile, living in the diaspora became a new mode of life for Jews, a communal life without sovereignty, land, or temple. Israel's far-flung dispersions were made up of exiles by choice, who had emigrated from the Land of Israel long before the destruction, even before the exile of the ten tribes, as attested by the Prophets Amos (9.14–15), Hosea (11.11), Isaiah (11.11), and Jeremiah (23.7–8), and of involuntary exiles. Together these two groups grew into a large Jewish community living outside the boundaries of its land. Notwithstanding the miraculous return to Zion (517 BCE), an unprecedented feat in the history of exiles, the decisive fact remained that a large Israelite diaspora which had arisen in Babylonia chose not to return to its homeland. This diaspora first presented the problematics of Jewish extraterritorial existence: a large Jewish community living outside its country of origin, which prays indeed for the "ingathering of the exiles," but which, in reality, experiences this prayer as a somewhat distant aspiration, as a vision of full redemption in a Messianic future.

The Land of Israel was elevated in the Talmudic culture to the highest level of sanctity, yet despite this tribute to the ancestral land, Talmudic Jews settled comfortably on foreign soils. Was it not justifiably argued over the centuries by both adherents and opponents of the Talmudic culture, by way of praise and censure, respectively, that it had made it possible for Jews to strike root in any land of exile? The Talmudic culture assumed that the Israelite nation was itself holy, thus wherever it wandered in exile, holiness – the Shechinah – followed it. Israel's holiness was incapable, of course, of hallowing foreign soil, and the waters of Babylon or the rivers of Europe and America did not match the majesty of the Jordan, but observance of the Torah no longer required habitation of the land. The Torah's authority had universal validity, not merely for an hour, and not only in the Land of Israel. Moreover, the Sages justified this dissociation between law and land by pointing out that the Torah had not been given in the Land of Israel, but in the wilderness.[33] Moses had only yearned to enter the land so that he could fulfill the "many precepts commanded to Israel which can only be fulfilled in the land of Israel" (*Sot.* 14a).

Most of the 613 commandments (in Maimonides' count, for example) hinge to some extent upon habitation of the land, and the existence of the Temple and the priesthood. Thus most of the original commandments depended on values and assets which were later abandoned. The Talmudic culture's great undertaking was to draw a distinction between the validity of universally applicable commandments, and commandments that drew their validity from the land and the Temple, and which were suspended with the destruction of the Temple and the exile from the land. The ordinances of Rabbi Yoḥanan ben Zakkai were an attempt to give the commandments autonomy so that they could be separated from Temple service and from habitation of Eretz Israel. Certain items were suspended even before the destruction of the Temple, such as the remission of debts on the seventh year. Hillel instituted his famous *prosbul* ordinance to counteract the practice whereby needy borrowers were denied credit as the seventh year, the year of debt remission, approached. Hillel's *prosbul* separated between the prohibition on collecting a debt extending into the seventh year, and the Bible's express command not to shut the door before needy borrowers. It was an example of the sort of "ruse" (*ʿormah*) we mentioned earlier in our discussion on the Halachah (chapter 4). This was also the case with capital punishment, i.e. with the penal code laid down in the Bible, which was abolished forty years before the destruction of the Temple. The Sages may still have believed that the "law of the four modes of execution was not abolished. He who is worthy of stoning either falls from the roof, or is trampled to death by a wild beast; he who merits burning either falls into the fire or is bitten by a serpent," and so forth (*San.* 37b). They might still say, "Since the day of the destruction of the Temple, although the Sanhedrin ceased [and capital punishment could no longer be decreed by Jewish courts], the four forms of capital punishment have not ceased" (*Ket.* 30a), but, in reality, they instituted a new penal code. Jewish courts throughout the ages ruled according to a Halachah distinctly autonomous of Temple and land.

Christian-Jewish debate centered precisely on this separation. The Christian claim was that the destruction of the Temple had, in fact, voided most of the commandments, and this was quite correct, as we have explained. The Sages responded to this argument by insisting that the destruction had no bearing on the Torah's validity. In the dispute between the second-century Christian apologist Justin Martyr and the Jew Tryphon, the former seems to have an edge when he contends: "Let us consider . . . whether one may now observe all the Mosaic institutions."[34] He refers to the observance of commandments after the destruction. And Tryphon (who is not the same person as Rabbi Tarfon, as some scholars have suggested) is forced to acknowledge that sacrificial offerings can no longer be presented. This argument strengthens Justin's claim that the *raison d'être* for all Torah commandments no longer exists. It was an argument sounded repeatedly in the course of medieval disputations between Christians and Jews. It reappears in a changed form in Spinoza's contention that Judaism is the religion of a particular state and that its commandments hinge upon habitation of its land. Once Jews ceased to live on their land, the validity of their Torah also ended.

Alert to the danger entailed in such arguments, the Sages gave every commandment an autonomous validity, as if every commandment was *ipso facto* valid and binding in every place where Scriptures did not specifically condition its observance upon some other commandment. For example, one may bring a burnt-offering without the *ʿomer*, and one may bring the *ʿomer* without the burnt-offering, although in the past, when the Temple still stood, the two had to be brought together. Or, "The [absence of the] blue [in the fringes] does not invalidate the white, neither does the [absence of the] white invalidate the blue" (*Men.* 38a).

The intention of endowing every commandment with a reality of its own is particularly evident in the desire to dissociate the commandments whenever possible from their dependence on the Land of Israel and on the Temple.[35] In this the Sages were aided by Scriptures, which designated certain commandments as being valid "for ever," "for all time," "from generation to generation." Such commandments include the sanctification of Yom Kippur and the Holy Days, even though these days are always mentioned in the Bible in connection with ritual sacrifices. Similarly, the eating of *matzah* and bitter herbs on Passover is no longer tied to the offering of the Paschal lamb.

In the same tendacious Talmudic spirit, large bodies of commandments became atomized into individual precepts each one of which preserved its own nature. They adopted a rule that everything that had to be abandoned as a result of the destruction of the Temple and the exile was considered suspended, while that which could be observed regardless of physical location, was made an autonomous precept. It is interesting to note that whenever possible the Sages tried to salvage even such commandments as were dependent on the existence of the Temple. Rabbi Akiba, for example, still wished to preserve the dedication of the firstlings, a distinctly Temple-bound practice (*Tem.* 21a). The Sages also ruled that the commandment regarding the Sabbatical year (*shemitah*) remained in effect in the Land of Israel with or without the Temple, as did the prohibition on eating fruits during the first three years of their growth (ʿ*orlah*) and the requirement to dedicate the fruits of the fourth year in Jerusalem (*kerem revai*).

The Babylonian exile, therefore, had laid the foundations for a Jewish life without Eretz Israel and without a Temple. The Talmudic culture erected a system of commandments which allowed exiles to dwell in foreign lands and still maintain their faith – an example of the equilibration of a tension.

We should perhaps briefly consider here how the relation between the Jewish people and its historic homeland was viewed by the two most recent Jewish cultures. The phenomenon of a Torah freed from dependence on the land, as illustrated by the Talmudic attitude to the Land of Israel, aroused great interest in members of the Emancipation and the National-Israeli cultures. This was, after all, the view of Abraham Geiger (1810–74) and his colleagues in the Reform movement, that Israel's Torah was a faith and a system of precepts that required no physical land. But it is interesting to note that even votaries of the nationalist school, like Dubnov, Aḥad ha-ʿam, and Bialik, expressed similar views, though for a different purpose. Let us examine one indicative paragraph by Bialik.

Bialik repeatedly argued in his lectures that the nation had retained for its guidance only dessicated Rabbinic laws, an entirely abstract Judaism. The nation had torn its culture away from its early roots, from the soil and nature of the Land of Israel, and had transformed all its concrete holdings into abstract, spiritual, easily mobile possessions, in keeping with the requirements of its errant, vicissitudinous life.[36] Bialik then proceeds to describe a situation which most aptly characterizes the culture of the Emancipation: thanks to his cerebral, *pilpulistic* weapons, the Jew survived all the heavy battles in his self-preservation. With this mobile mental baggage he was also able to insinuate himself into all the nations and cultures of the world. Tangible, bulky assets were unfit for hasty, clandestine movement, but brains and ideas could easily penetrate all barriers. The Hebrew people thus infiltrated every country in the world and poured its energies into these cultures for its own benefit and for that of humanity at large. Echoes of Jost, Zunz, and Heine on the "itinerant homeland" together with ideas from Graetz, Dubnov, and Aḥad ha-ʿam on the "instrument of exile" combine in Bialik's description of the spiritualiza-tion process which characterized the Talmudic, the Rabbinic, and the Emancipation cultures, based on their attitude to tangible possessions, and especially to the tangible Eretz Israel.

The National-Israeli attitude to the Land of Israel will be discussed at greater length in chapter 8. Here we merely wished to point out the problem of integrating a culture's components and the difficulties of integration in Jewish history. Since we have rejected three explanations for the formation of integration in a culture, i.e. geographical proximity and chronological continuity, one cause or a system of causes (economic or religious), and a culture's central grand design, it becomes clear that full integration is achieved by live men and women, and especially by their leaders, who, in each culture, struggle for the equilibration of the tensions we have described.

6

HISTORICAL KNOWLEDGE
IN THE SERVICE OF FAITH

Historical awareness then and now

Throughout the ages of traditional faith, from the Talmudic culture down to the Emancipation, historical awareness tended to underscore the permanent rather than the passing; tradition, rather than novelty and change, was venerated. Even momentous changes in the nation's life were apprehended via existing long-established emotional, intellectual, and theological models, and the historical uniqueness of events was obscured, often entirely eclipsed, by the dimension of permanence. In this respect Jews did not differ from Gentile traditional believers: historical happenings were viewed less as indications of change than as confirmations of accepted ideas and beliefs that were, to all appearances, immune to change. In periods of traditional faith Jewish awareness, i.e. the apprehension and understanding of internal and external occurrences in specific times and locations, was not "historical" in our modern sense of the word: it saw neither the concrete and specific uniqueness in the flow of individual or collective history, nor the distinctions individuating people and events, and the resultant sectarian, ideological, tribal, or social divisions.

Such a conception is, in fact, relatively new both in world history, and particularly in Jewish history; it is, therefore, important to note the vast difference in historical awareness of past generations and that of our own era. This difference is evident both in the high regard we accord the scientific (or physical-mathematical) method, and in our approach to historical thinking. These two attitudes quintessentially characterize our world view, and although the first conception largely overshadows the second, it cannot entirely eclipse it. Clearly, the successful adoption of the scientific method in both academic study and in efficient technological application – that entire array of phenomenal scientific and technological achievements which have been the unmistakable hallmark of modern human endeavor and creativity (without yet clearly revealing, however, where the adherence to this method as a basic model and guide might lead us), has unquestionably become a firm foundation for our vision of the world. At the same time, the second conception has also gained momentum: reality is increasingly being viewed in the context of its historical flow, as though there were no such thing as permanence in the world, except for the certainty of change itself, and as if only the relative were truly absolute in the ceaseless flux of the tides of time.

It seems, then, that the scientific method and the necessity of thinking historically are indeed the two main elements of our conception of the world. This is not to say, of course, that there are no other elements in a conception encompassing so many different manifestations. The inspired pioneers who heralded our modern world were not free of influences that were ahistorical and anti-historical, logical, and mythological. Allegiance to a Platonic immutability has not disappeared, and strong yearnings for a supertemporary reality are exhibited in the ahistorical concepts of psychology, sociology, philosophy, and even in the exact sciences themselves. Indeed, until only a few generations ago scientific methodology and historical research were antithetical. Descartes, who labored over the scientific method, did not yet recognize the importance of historical evidence, while the creator of the critical method in historical investigation, Giambattista Vico, opposed the tyranny of Descartes' scientific philosophy when the latter came to be viewed as an inevitable intellectual model and the definitive word on the nature of reality.[1]

The detailed relationship between these two approaches requires special study, particularly if we wish to understand the sense of time and the awareness of change in the various Jewish cultures. We must, however, immediately point out that a critical philosophy can accept no single approach as the final verdict on the nature of reality. The historical-critical approach itself, for example, negates the belief in the ability of historical perception to grasp the "absolute truth" of interpersonal reality. It is precisely the perspectivistic perception acquired as a result of the humanistic-historical approach which no longer allows us to indulge in absolutes. No vision of the world appears to us as self-evident, "natural," "necessary," in the sense of an absolute way of thinking for all men at all times.

Our modern sensitivity to changes affecting us in the present and our desire to mold the future are readily transferred to evaluations of the past and to assessments of the changes that have occurred in our history. The two are, in fact, closely related: sensitivity to changes in the present sharpens our awareness of past changes and of past attitudes to these changes. We are perhaps even more "historistic" today than were our nineteenth-century precursors who first introduced modern historical science and developed both epistemology and the rationale for historical perspectivism. An interesting paradox emerges: time and its varieties have become a self-evident dimension for contemporary thinking; we find it today most natural to inquire when and how an event occurred, what were its causes, how it was imprinted by its times and circumstances and whether this imprint is still valid today, where are its antecedents and what are its outcomes. These questions, so very new, appear obvious, as though they were natural tools of human comprehension at all times. This, however, was not the case, and our ancestors in the ages of faith certainly did not think as we do. It is this lingering attachment to absolutes which has tended to cloud the judgment of prominent historians even in our own times.

This chapter deals with problems of historical knowledge and awareness. It discusses briefly the special nature of Jewish historical awareness, as it was reflected in ancient Biblical and Talmudic historiography, and in religious rationalism. The chapter attempts to substantiate the thesis that Jewish history exemplifies the dramatic dynamics of seven distinct cultures, each the product of innovation and renaissance. The theory on the nature of history and historical research should elucidate the brief remarks offered in the first chapter and elsewhere regarding historical perspectivism. And finally, our debate with certain modern historians, notably the so-called Jerusalem school of history, will bring to the fore in chapter 8 the importance of the theory of cultures as a Jewish historical conception which is harnessed neither to the uses of a theological premise, nor to a national apologia.

Primarily, this chapter, together with chapters 7 and 8, attempts to illuminate the course of Jewish historical awareness, its evolvement in the cultures of traditional faith in the Talmuds and the *midrashim*, in chronicles, and in the historical writings of the Emancipation culture (Jost and Graetz in chapter 7) and of the National-Israeli culture (Klausner, Dinur, and Baer in chapter 8). We are interested especially in shedding some light on the manner in which the nature of the Jewish people and its history was grasped, on attitudes toward time and its varieties, on the value attached by historiographers to their own profession, and on the value their occupation presented to others. What is the nature and measure of historical awareness within the dimension of permanence of Jewish "statics" during and after the generations of faith?

Selectivity and dearth of historical knowledge

I believe we have by now established that each one of Israel's cultures envisaged a certain mental image of the Jewish people and its history, as these had been revealed in the people's relation to God, the Torah, and to other nations. This mental picture embedded in each culture is, of course, not necessarily a "true" image verifiable by historical research. Jewish awareness was primarily theological and highly selective, constantly sorting and sifting, minimizing and emphasizing, according to its needs. Its purpose was to demonstrate the Prophetic claim that the history of all nations, and Israel's above all, was God's work rather than an accidental flux of events devoid of eternal meaning and supreme purpose. Jewish Biblical and post-Biblical historiography is a prime example of this selectivity. Historiographic talent and artistry sought out the foci of interest, and in the recollections crowding the nation's spiritual world, truth and imagination mingled in strange, and, to the modern taste, even exceedingly bizarre, confusion. But we have already said that Jewish historiography in the ages of faith had a quite different purpose from that of modern research endeavors. Traditional historiography was saddled with the task of demonstrating that the recounted events in fact confirmed and validated one's faith in the God of justice, thereby bracing the nation to endure present ordeals and inspiring it with hope of a better world in the future. Whatever failed to serve as confirmation of this faith was considered "idle talk" which, in Maimonides' words, "has no benefit in it to man for his soul – purporting neither to transgression nor to rebelliousness, such as most of the discussions of the multitude regarding what has happened and what was".[2] No benefit can be derived from preoccupation with the past unless it is geared toward the strengthening of one's faith. Traditional Jewish historiography cultivated and propagated the belief that no fundamental changes had ever occurred in the nation's history: the superordinating concepts and the collective archetypal experiences appeared to endure firmly as girds uniting all generations in the "statics" of a historical continuity of shared destiny.

Indeed Jewish cultures in the ages of faith knew but little about their predecessors. Knowledge of history – the explanation of facts, the unfolding of processes – failed to gain currency in Judaism, and for a number of reasons. The Talmudic culture saw the events and deeds of the Bible through its own peculiar prism, without attempting to illuminate the past from even a minimally objective standpoint. Due to a lack of historical perspective and a confounding of separate domains, each culture imagined that its predecessors had spoken in the same language of concepts and experiences and had intended the very same meanings that were in fact exclusively its own. This problem of a dearth of historical knowledge in Judaism requires serious study. We may, however, safely assume that the inattention, the lack of interest, and the short memory were not accidental. These belong to the nature of the culture itself as one of its endemic qualities, and even as one of its most important characteristics. In other words, the extent of a culture's knowledge of, and interest in, the past are part of each culture's ontology, i.e. its apprehension of reality, as it had experienced it.

Our study of historical knowledge would be served by first clarifying a number of meanings in the concept "history." When referring to history we can be speaking of (a) a historical happening, i.e. the deeds and events ("the events of Assa's reign, from first to last," "the other acts and events of

Ahab's reign, . . . all the cities he built," "Jehoshaphat's reign, his exploits and his wars") or (b) historiography, i.e. the recording of those deeds and events ("recorded in the annals of the kings of Judah"³), or (c) the meaning of history, its nature, and its value. Historical happenings themselves are known as *res gestae*; the reciting of events is the *historia rerum gestarum*, and the third aspect is a theology or a philosophy of history. Of course, in addition to these three aspects of knowledge of the past there is the theoretical-critical aspect, which has spread among historians and thinkers in our times. Among the latter we find some whose thinking partakes of the third aspect and others who shun it: some painstakingly study the details and seek their significance in context, without promoting such significance to the level of a comprehensive or an absolute meaning of all deeds and events, while others embrace a theology of history in the guise of advanced critical research.

History, by its very nature, is subject to time's varieties, and as we have already heard in chapter 1, to various categories of evils that wreak havoc within time's domain. History unfolds within a sphere plagued by all the afflictions entailed in man's mortality, a host of evils, foremost of which is the Angel of Death. Man journeys toward his end, to a place of worms and decay: all the benefits history brings with it are outweighed by the great calamity of man's subjection to contingency and extinction. This category of afflictions is accompanied by the second category in our listing in chapter 1: evils rooted in the discords dividing individuals and nations, from petty quarrels to global war, all those divisions stemming from jealousy, hatred, and greed, which banish peace from men and nations. Each culture's soteriology offers relief from the four evils afflicting the human condition, and this, in addition to its specific benefits and consolations, is the essence of history. No culture can relinquish the soteriological dimension in the ontology it attempts to represent and inculcate. Indeed one could say that the key to the understanding of a culture's ideas and acts in the individual and public domains should be sought in its attitude toward time – how a culture deals with time and with its effects upon men and nations as they seek refuge and solace from its afflictions.

The soteriological dimension is understandably, therefore, the pre-eminent domain of religious faith. It is difficult to grasp the principles of religious faith and the modes of worshiping God (or idols), difficult to understand the Torah, the rituals, the observance of commandments, without viewing these as an attempt to mitigate the evil of human temporality. It is not surprising that quite disparate religions often pose very similar questions: what deeds and beliefs must a man embrace in order to escape mortality and discord and attain eternity and peace? The religions of Babylonians and Egyptians, Indians and Chinese, Christians and Muslims, all formed their opinions on history based on their attitude to time and to

war and peace. The various observances and rites were stratagems devised
to bring time to a standstill, or restore the believer to the past, or, by virtue of
a momentous cataclysmic event, such as the giving of the Torah (or the
Pauline conception of the resurrection and divinity of Jesus), to raise man
out of the past into a supertemporal sphere. In Indian and Persian religions
time itself became a deity characterized by creative or destructive changes: a
builder and a destroyer, lord of being and non-being. Various Gnostic
theories conceived God, the demiurge, as the originator of evil and
destruction.

Although the ontologies of the various cultures conceive of time in
different forms, a number of images keep recurring: time is a straight line
heading up or down; it is a revolving wheel guaranteeing that what has
always been will continue to be, and that which has been done in the past,
will be done again; it is a tempestuous river, forded by religion, its bridge; like
a living being, it experiences birth, growth, and death; like a tree, it grows
and withers; its ways are convoluted, with no clear lawfulness, subject to
the accidental and the occasional; it is guided by providence, all is
preordained, and there is judgment and judge; there is a perception of
novelty, and there is a weary sense of *déjà vu*. There is also a time beyond
time, a time of ecstasy and obliviousness to the world. Other similar images
abound.[4]

Historical knowledge in the Talmudic culture

It is from this angle, as attempts to overcome the accidents of time, to avoid
them, or to rise above them through Torah and good deeds, that the
Talmudic culture's attitude to history should be viewed. This was the
general attitude to historical knowledge, and we shall return to it shortly. As
to knowledge of the past in its details, we have already hinted that past
generations had scanty and exceedingly selective knowledge of historical
occurrences. The Talmudic culture has left us no historical writings. Its
creators made little effort to describe acts and events, certainly in no
comparison to the detailed narratives and the magnificent story-telling of
the Torah and the Former Prophets. One surmises that the Talmudic culture
had at least a semblance of historiographic literature, fragments of which
have been preserved, such as *Megillat ta'anit* ("The Scroll of Fasts") and
Seder 'olam ("The Order of the World"). The Talmud and *midrashim* allude to
Megillat yuhasin ("Genealogical Scroll") and *Megillat setarim* ("Concealed
Scroll"), and vaguely hint at the nature and contents of these works. For
example, Simeon ben Azzai (a Tanna of the second century CE) relates that
in *Megillat yuhasin*, it was written "so-and-so is a *mamzer* [i.e. a bastard]
from a married woman" or "[King] Manasse slew [the Prophet] Isaiah"
(*Yeb.* 49b).[5] But I would venture to guess that even had these scrolls come
down to us in their entirety, they would have shed little light on historical

events. Scanty information about the past and inattention to its preservation for future generations does not mean, however, that the Sages had no
conception of the past's nature and meaning, i.e. of that third aspect in our
classification of knowledge of the past.

Shaken by the vagaries of time and its abuse of even the most preciously
held beliefs, the Sages either diverted their attention from time, or revised
the past. Much has been written on their methods of recounting Biblical
stories of Patriarchs, Prophets, and kings by way of "revision," "addition,"
"suppression," and allegoric and metaphoric "transposition," to use
Benzion Dinur's terminology,[6] and we have already referred in our
discussion of the Halachah (chapter 4) to these methods. The Talmudic
culture turned King David into a symbol of the charismatic ruler and leader,
a model for kings of all times, with the Biblical story amended to conform to
changing opinions on the image of the desirable king. Thus, superlative
qualities were gladly conferred upon David, while aspects considered
unseemly for an exemplary figure were deleted and obscured. The same is
true for all other Biblical heroes. By the system of "suppression" and
"transposition," historical figures (or certain qualities of such figures) were
suppressed or obliterated, and their merits were transferred to a generalized
body. For example, the names of the Hasmonean brothers, Judah and
Jonathan, were not explicitly mentioned, but their exploits were credited to
the "beth din of the Hasmoneans" (*San.* 82a) or the "Hasmonean house"
(*Bab. K.* 82b and elsewhere). Similarly, the Sages ascribed to Biblical figures
conduct or opinions of individuals and sects that postdated the entire
Biblical culture. The sins of Sodom became the iniquities of wicked Rome,
and the homilies about Jacob and Esau, Koraḥ and his assembly, Do'eg,
Aḥitofel, etc., expressed opinions that were current much later, in the period
of the Mishnah and the Talmud.

We need, therefore, hardly demonstrate again that vast numbers of
historical memories were vested in Talmudic and Midrashic literature.
Scholars of the past five generations (beginning with Leopold Zunz's first
work *Etwas über die rabbinische Literatur,* 1818) have been studying the
impact ascribed to historical events and situations in the Aggadah and the
Halachah. The great landmarks of the Talmudic culture over a period of
approximately 600 years, such as the subjugation to Rome, the Great
Revolt and the destruction of the Temple, Bar Kochba's revolt and various
polemics, the exiles and persecutions, the active opposition to the Roman
oppressor and the *de facto* recognition of his rule in times of tranquility, all
these are clearly reflected in the Talmudic and Midrashic literature.
However, they were not recorded as historical accounts or explanations,
merely alluded to indirectly, in the course of *halachic* deliberations or
homiletic exegesis. Indeed many *halachic* discussions preserve allusions to
distinct events experienced by contemporaries.[7] An example for this was the

attitude to the governing ruler and to the Gentiles oppressing Israel. We already spoke elsewhere of the changes that occurred in the attitude toward Gentiles, and of Shmuel's ruling, *dina de-malchuta dina* ("the law of the kingdom is law," i.e. it takes precedence over Jewish law).[8] This ruling crystallized as a result of the development of certain conducive political conditions. One or two generations after Bar Kochba's revolt the status of Jews, and of the Palestinian Presidency in particular, improved. We surmise this from evidence in the *baraita* cited in *Megillah* 11a, "'I have not rejected them' [Lev. 26.44] – in the days of the Chaldeans . . . 'to break my covenant with them' – in the days of the [Romans] when I raised up for them the members of the house of Rabbi and the Sages of the various generations," a hint of improved political status. We hear also that Rabbi Yehudah ha-Nassi (Judah the Prince, 135–219 CE, redactor of the Mishnah) used to "travel to the Government [of Rome],"[9] and that he leased land from "Antoninus Caesar."

The improved status may further be deduced from the fact that Rabbi Yehudah ha-Nassi wished to abolish certain public fast days, such as that of the seventeenth of Tammuz, and according to one tradition, even the fast of the ninth of Ab, commemorating the destruction of the Temple. We learn this from the following *halachic* discussion: "Rabbi planted a shoot on Purim and bathed in the [bathhouse of the] market place of Sepphoris on the seventeenth of Tammuz and sought to abolish the fast of the ninth of Ab, but his colleagues would not consent" (*Meg.* 5a–b). Rome continued to be regarded as the wicked kingdom, but the Sages in the days of Rabbi Yehudah no longer harbored thoughts of armed resistance and tended to accept Roman authority, except, of course, when it decreed against tenets of the Jewish religion. In this period we hear statements that God had "adjured Israel that they shall not rebel against the nations of the world," and that He also "adjured the idolators that they shall not oppress Israel too much" (*Ket.* 111a). We hear Rabbi Yannai saying: "Fear of the dominant power should ever be before you" (*Men.* 98a). The Sages found support for this attitude in Moses himself, who treated Pharaoh with respect. Gedaliahu Alon remarked on this change in the attitude toward the ruler as highly significant: "No similar view had ever been embraced by Sages, from earliest times down to the war of Bar Kochba."[10]

The conclusions to be drawn from this view were manifested in the attitude toward government taxation: in contrast to the tax evasion prevalent in previous generations, there was now a prohibition against such evasion. Even more emphatically, a *baraita* in tractate *Semahot* declares that whosoever steals past customs and past the *herem* "is as if he shed blood – and not only shed blood, but also worshiped idols, committed acts of unchastity, and profaned the Sabbath."[11]

But again, all these historical indications are provided apropos entirely different matters, which the Sages deemed more important and worthy of detailed discussion. It is extraordinary that a major convulsion in the ancient world, such as the anarchy fracturing the Roman Empire in the third century, and the Persian conquests under the new Sassanian dynasty, is alluded to only indirectly and sporadically. These fifty years of anarchy (235–84 CE) between the reign of Severus Alexander and the rise of Diocletian Caesar have been recognized by historians as having abounded in events of decisive impact on the fate of the Roman Empire, a period which ended with the emergence of a regulated bureaucratic Christian Byzantine kingdom – a very different entity from the antecedent secular Graeco-Roman Empire. Most historians consider the disintegration of the ancient world as having begun in this period of anarchy, in which all the causes of the eventual collapse were already in evidence.

At this period, too, the Parthian kingdom was destroyed and a new Persian kingdom established, a kingdom which shook the Roman Empire to its foundations. The Sassanian rule hoped to renew the glory of the ancient Persian dynasty of Cyrus and Darius, and laid claim to all eastern lands formerly ruled by these kings. They revoked the autonomy of the feudal lords and minor kings and imposed a unified sovereignty upon all. The Persian rule renewed a national church based on the Zoroastrian religion, which began to persecute fanatically members of other creeds. The new Persians, beginning with King Ardashir I (230 CE), conquered Roman territories containing large concentrations of Jews, as in Syria and Cappadocia. Large cities were set on fire and their populace taken captive. The Talmud mentions the slaughter in the city of Caesarea-Mazaca ("When they told Shmuel that King Shapur had slain twelve thousand Jews at Caesarea-Mazaca," M.K. 26a). This slaughter is mentioned in a discussion on laws of mourning. Of the slaughter and the taking of captives in Nehardea, Shmuel's own city, we learn from a story about his father, who placed guards over female captives of that city. Likewise we learn, in the context of a discussion on the law regarding captives – whether or not they are "clean" – that Shmuel's own daughters were captured, and that their captors sent them to the Land of Israel (Ket. 23b).

This period of change and turmoil in the Roman Empire (and its Jewish communities) coincides with the activity of Rab and Shmuel. Rab had been in contact, according to Talmudic tradition, with King Artaban or Ardaban, whom the Persian King Ardashir had toppled. Artaban is reported to have sent Rab a precious pearl (Jerusalem Talmud, Pes. 1). Moreover, "Artaban attended on Rab. When . . . Artaban died, Rab exclaimed: 'The bond is snapped'" (Ab.Zar. 10b–11a). But Rab tells us nothing about his royal friend and of his defeat by Ardashir. He was engaged in his own occupations – studying halachah, formulating maxims on the righteous way of life, composing prayers.

And Shmuel? He died in 254 CE, after the short-lived Persian conquest of Syria, and before the captivity of Emperor Valerian. "Samuel (used to juggle) before King Shapur with eight glasses of wine (without spilling their contents)" (Suk. 53a), and used to interpret his dreams and inform him what he would dream the following night.[12] We infer a certain intimacy between the learned Rabbi and the Persian monarch, but the Talmud's spare statements give no clue to Shmuel's activity in Shapur's court beyond that of court-jester and interpreter of dreams.

Indeed one may find in Talmudic and Midrashic literature hundreds of references to contemporary events, but accuracy and detail are conspicuously absent. The Sages' *knowledge* of the past may be uneven, lacking, and neglected. Not so their *understanding* of the past. Its principles are quite clear, although these, too, are not set forth in a systematic and easily intelligible fashion. Accidental acts and events were considered of no consequence. Time, with its convulsions and uncertainties, was terrifying; the important thing was to derive a moral lesson and to educe allusions to the redemption, i.e. to concentrate on those pragmatic and soteriological dimensions of culture we described in chapter 1. Like Biblical historiographers before them, the Talmudic Sages contemplated contemporary and past events in order to "recount the Lord's acts of unfailing love . . . to the house Israel" (Isa. 63.7), or to "recall to mind [His] deeds" (Ps. 77.12), and, in particular, in order to "call to mind His covenant from long ago" (I Chron. 16.15).[13] Which historical deeds and events reveal the wonders God has performed for His people and teach the path of righteousness? This was the kind of thinking directed at history, and it tipped the scales in favor of historical theology and against historical knowledge based on tested evidence, rigorous selection, and objectivity. Hermann Cohen termed this thinking "idealization." In his view, the religious standpoint requires that history be viewed with "idealization," that is, with an emphasis on values, although not without insistence on proper testimony and evidence. What is most important are the "eternal ideas," not the outer shells of fleeting occurrences. This, thought Cohen, is how the Sages treated history. They practised a "symbolic" and a "realistic-pragmatic" idealization. The Bible and the Talmudic literature employed the same method. One could not, of course, compare the richness and vigor of Biblical historiography to the paucity of historical knowledge in the Talmudic culture, but the tendency, Cohen stressed, was the same.[14]

Clearly, we are witnessing here not a lack of talent to grasp historical reality in detail, but an unwillingness to do so, as well as a preference for the kind of knowledge which has no interest in contemplating events and acts objectively, as recommended early by Thucydides and as is generally practised today.[15] The Sages' ontology was an organic tissue in which a Jew was an individual within a community, and the modern "I" had not yet been awakened to self-awareness, with all its attendant joys and pains. The creators of this culture are almost anonymous, even though they are mentioned by name; Biblical figures too were transformed by the Sages into general types. The Sages sought to rise above history by cleaving to elevated examples, to models of good deeds and exemplary figures, in short, to build their world on the permanent foundations of unchanging principles.

What, in the view of the Talmudic culture, is the meaning of Jewish history? When the question traditionally directed at an individual, "By virtue of what have you deserved a long life?" is addressed to the Jewish people as a whole, the Sages' answer is unequivocal: everything depends on one's own deeds and on God's grace to His people. That is the entire secret of Jewish endurance through the vicissitudes of time. The basic presuppositions for historical knowledge are as follows.

The Jewish nation is one entity in all ages and in every dispersion. The Sages never doubted, for example, their direct descent from Abraham. "Happy art thou, O Abraham our father, that Rabbi Elʿazar ben Arach hath come forth from thy loins" (*Ḥag.* 14b), is how Rabbi Yoḥanan ben Zakkai lauds one of his disciples. Abraham was the "father of nations," a propagandist for the religion of one God through his personal example of hospitality and loving kindness. He would also have been the first martyr – Nimrod threw him into the furnace for having smashed the idols – had not the Holy One, blessed be He, come to his rescue. Abraham is the believer who has been put to the most trying of all human tests: the sacrifice of his son. From this aspect of a supreme individual, Abraham is a leader for the entire world, the helmsman of humanity at all times and in all places. The Sages applied the same method to all other Patriarchs, Prophets, and kings, a method of "idealization" in H. Cohen's phrase, of emphasis on the archetypical, on values. All these figures were conceived simply as direct reflections of the Talmudic culture; all were occupied with the observance and innovation of *halachot*. The ancient Patriarchs and heroes had all had foreknowledge of the Bible and were busy interpreting it. The Sages do not recoil from the most bizarre anachronisms: Isaac quotes the Ten Commandments, Jacob cites from the Torah, the Prophets, and Psalms, Moses recalls Hosea and David.

The Jewish nation is one unit, past, present, and future, in its ancestral land and in the dispersals of exile. It is emphatically not an accidental aggregate of random Jewish populations, living in different historical frameworks, and lacking a common tongue; rather, it is a people that shares one Torah, a system of beliefs and ideas, laws, customs, and manners, in a continuity of symbols, images, and concepts, a continuum of consistency, a unified ontology for all generations. In keeping with these basic assumptions the Sages constructed their knowledge of Jewish history. They took possession of the entire past, through ceaseless occupation with the give-

and-take of Torah and Halachah, until the past's flow was arrested and frozen in an eternal present.

Moreover, the Torah is not a fixed heritage – one's personal attitude toward it is of the utmost importance. It is a "tree of life," but only to "them that grasp it." It is also compared to thread and flax given by a king to his servants, not for storage and safekeeping, but so that they may use these materials to make clothes for their needs. Repentance, prayer, and righteousness deliver from death.[16]

In the battle against the vicissitudes and afflictions of time, the Talmudic Sages sought shelter and strength first of all in the performance of good deeds. To the question, "Why was the Temple destroyed?" they answered, "Because of groundless hatred," which is weighted as heavily as idolatry, harlotry, and murder. The breaking of the Sinaitic covenant is the cause of all destructions and defeats. "There is no difference between this world and the days of the Messiah except [that they will be free of the] servitude to the [foreign] kingdoms" (San. 98a), said Shmuel, the same Shmuel who also taught, dina de-malchuta dina ("the law of the kingdom is law"). The one hinges upon the other. This dependence had already been pointed to by Rabbi Yohanan ben Zakkai at the time of the Temple's destruction when he claimed that refusal to submit to heaven resulted in submission to the Gentiles.[17] The implication is clear: submission to heaven automatically ends all thralldom to the harsh rule of the Gentiles.

Since it was impossible to influence the course of political events, which was entirely in the hands of the Gentiles, the Sages withdrew introspectively to cultivate, as far as possible, personal and communal piety and righteousness via wise laws and good practices. It is not that the creators of the Talmudic culture were not eager to know where history was headed and what its meaning might be in their own time. The history of the Gentile kingdoms, however, held no intrinsic interest and there was no value in the details of the events or in their recording for future generations. The important thing was to know how redemption was to be attained, and this, as we are tirelessly reminded, could only be effected by the observance of commandments. The worshipers of God, not the worshipers of mortal kings, are saved or are likely to be saved soon. Laws that promote the "maintenance of the world" and the welfare of the community are the answer to the workings of history and a refuge from its catastrophes. If this is forgetfulness, it is a forgetfulness laden with age-old memories and yearnings for redemption. This inattention is in fact a turning of attention to the essence, which may be momentarily absent, but is likely to be fulfilled in the future.

The Talmudic culture's ontology became the most powerful and sweeping force to mold the Jewish people, shaping its beliefs, opinions, and conduct in all spheres of private and public life. Countless generations were

reared upon it. The Rabbinic culture accepted it unreservedly, with
profound awe. Even the Poetic-Philosophic and Mystical cultures, innovative and critical in nature though they were, did not challenge the *halachot*
established by the Talmudic culture and the many beliefs it injected in its
notion of Torah. The Talmudic conception took possession not only of the
past, but also molded in its own image a Judaism of Torah, which appeared
to be remote from contemporary conditions and severed from the changing
times; it was directed toward eternal life. The extreme impression created by
this phenomenon was ironically expressed by a profound Hebrew thinker,
M.H. Amishai (Maisels): "Pharisaic Judaism has no history, no structure,
more precisely – from Pumbedita [Babylonian Academy of the third century
CE] to Volozhin [Rabbinic academy founded 1803] it has been one single
long day. The nations "do" history unto us . . . from within we sat and
busied ourselves with matters of Torah." And in the same vein, "After the
destruction of the Temple there is history only in rebellions against exile,
and these rebellions are essentially a revolt against Pharisaic Judaism,"[18]
i.e. against what we have called the ontology of the Talmudic culture. These
rebellions found expression in Messianic movements, in the Karaitic
movement (during a period of two to three generations every fourth Jew
and, according to some, every third Jew was a Karaite rather than a
"Rabbinic" Jew), and wherever Jews sought to cast off the yoke of Torah and
the incessant occupation with its laws. Many disagreed with the Talmudic
culture and believed that its Sages had created a new Torah of their own and
were being needlessly strict. Yet this culture became the standard for many
generations, and no other Jewish culture ever attained a comparable force
and scope.

It is, of course, impossible in these few pages to do justice to the complexity
of as variegated a subject as that of historical awareness in the Tanna'itic
and Amora'itic literature. We have not even touched upon the role the
nations of the world were destined to play in Israel's history and in the
world's larger historical drama, nor can we discuss here the Messianic idea
or the interesting Talmudic notion that humanity is in a process of
progressive diminution: "If the earlier [scholars] were sons of angels, we are
sons of men, and if the earlier [scholars] were sons of men, we are like asses"
(*Sab.* 112b), i.e. time is viewed as a falling, rather than as an ascending line.
Like the great Roman historians, Sallust, Tacitus, and Livy, the Sages
complained of the age's decline.[19] God no longer spoke to His Prophets, His
voice was heard but faintly, until it was reduced to a dim echo (a *bat kol*)
from heaven. God's former revelations to His messengers and servants in full
public theophanies have become private revelations of the Shechinah. This
sense of decline became especially dolorous after the destruction of the
Temple. Tractate *Tamid* describes vividly and in considerable detail the
priestly ritual in the Temple, as though it were taking place before our very

eyes in the great Temple hall, before the altar. The tractate concludes, however, with an entirely unexpected hint of deep mourning and on a note of profound, moving, sadness: "This was the order of the regular daily sacrifice for the service of the house of our God. May it be God's will that it be rebuilt in our day, amen."[20]

Medieval Jewish chronography

Let us now take a closer look at Jewish chronography and its objectives in post-Talmudic times. The main intent manifested by the Talmudic culture was carried on in the Poetic-Philosophic culture; in fact, as the writings of Maimonides attest, the Greek rationalism of the Aristotelian philosophy of history merely served to reinforce it. A historian attempting to reconstrue medieval Jewish life based on extant records will seek in vain a clear picture, a comprehensive vision, an exposition of events, or of the nation's reactions to events impacting on its spiritual life. The records seem to flicker feebly and leave much in darkness, dishearteningly ephemeral and fleeting. Jewish historical awareness provides little insight into a rich and eventful world.

Traditional Jewish historiography, from the Talmudic culture down to the nineteenth century, was a hodgepodge of dates commemorating catastrophic decrees and lengthy homiletical accounts. These compositions may have filled certain emotional and intellectual needs, but they obscured distinctions between periods and cultures, even when precise dates were provided. The very obliteration of distinctions was one of these needs. Jews saw no need to benefit their own contemporaries or future generations with an orderly exposition of the important events that had befallen them, or deeds they themselves had performed, except haltingly and inconsistently, and only in response to specific requirements. A Jew in these cultures who ventured to question his elders about earlier generations would most likely have heard a series of unconnected facts, details which failed to add up to a comprehensive picture, with no hint of the broader background of events or intelligible explanations for their occurrence. Mostly, he would have heard historic *midrashim*, which, being expressive of the basic postulates of his culture, he would probably have found quite satisfying. The Biblical figures all had a familiar visage: Shem and Eber were learning Torah in the *beit midrash*; the Patriarchs were similarly occupied with innovating prayers and *halachot*; King David was busy with fine points of law, and the commander of David's army, the valiant Joab ben Zeruya, became the pious head of a *yeshivah*.

Scholars have labored in vain to uncover some regular pattern for the birth and spread of Jewish chronicles. It is difficult to find a general rule that would adequately account for their timing and motivation. True, one cannot escape the impression that periods of convulsive turbulence spurred the chroniclers to record what their generation had witnessed, but even here it is difficult to establish any kind of general rule. Ḥaim Ben-Sasson classified the chronicles in three groups corresponding to three periods of turbulence and crisis.[21] The first period (tenth century) produced the book *Josippon* in southern Italy (*c*. 950 CE), the writings of Nathan ha-Bavli on the autonomous institutions of Babylonia, and Sherira Ga᾽on's well-known epistle (986 CE) on the chain of tradition. To Ben-Sasson's survey I would add the writings of the Karaites: Jacob Kirkisani, in his composition *The Book of Lights and Towers* (in Arabic, *c*. 937 CE), gave a historical account of the growth of the Karaite sect. He and some of his cosectarians, such as Daniel al-Kumisi, a preacher and exegete, Salmon ben Yeruḥim, and Sahl ben Mazliaḥ, polemicized against the historical conception of the Talmudic Sages and developed an explicit theory on the role and destiny of their sect, whose origin they traced to the split between the erring majority (back in the days of Jeroboam ben Nebat, the first leader of the sinful majority) and the unblemished and upright minority. The Karaites ascribed to themselves all Biblical allusions to the righteous few, or to the undefiled remnant of Israel, or to the "wise leaders" mentioned by Daniel that "shall shine like the bright vault of heaven" (Dan. 12.3). To the Sages, the Ge᾽onim and all the "Rabbinic" Jews, they attributed the faults and failings of all past generations.[22]

The first period was thus heavily polemical: Karaites versus "Rabbinic" Jews, but also Exilarchs versus Ge᾽onim, Saʿadiah Ga᾽on pitched against David ben Zakkai, the center at Sura against the Academy of Pumbedita. Perhaps these polemics, and the ongoing debate with Christianity (as in the *Josippon*), stimulated the production of Jewish chronography.

The second chronographic period is the twelfth century. Abraham bar Ḥiyya of Barcelona (Savasorda) composes *Megillat ha-megalleh* ("Scroll of the Revealer"), Abraham ben David ha-Levi (Ibn Daud, known as the first Rabad) produces the *Sefer ha-kabbalah* or *Seder ha-kabbalah* ("The Book of Tradition," or "The Order of Tradition" *c*. 1160 CE) and other historical compositions. At this period Rabbi Solomon ben Shimshon and others wrote about acts of Jewish martyrdom during the first crusade.[23] There is a great difference between the chroniclers of Ashkenaz (Germany) and their counterparts in Spain: the former are overwhelmingly preoccupied with Jewish martyrdom at the hands of fanatic priests and incited Christian mobs, while the latter deal with a wide range of subjects. Ibn Daud is an example of the historical awareness characteristic of the Poetic-Philosophic culture. In contrast to the Jewish chroniclers in France and Germany, he expresses much greater trust of the Gentiles, and of the human-divine world generally, in his description of a successful Jewish leadership in the courts of benevolent kings. Jewish ministers appear to have been elected by divine providence to lead the nation. No less important, in his view, than the heritage of the Torah's transmitted chain of tradition are the high birth and the honor of Jewish ministers-courtiers, whose qualities "attest to their descent from the seed of royalty and from the ancient high nobility."[24] The service of kings is an honorable pursuit and the kings' servants deserve to be honored, for reasons not the least of which is the origin of their families; they are *zera hamissrah* ("the seed of authority," or "the noble descent") – an expression at once strange yet so typical. In similar fashion, Moses Ibn Ezra boasted that in Cordoba and Granada, in Seville and Toledo "there are people unparalleled in generosity, capable and highly born." Alas, none of this self-confidence helped Rabbi Abraham Ibn Daud in his hour of need and he died a martyr's death in 1180, just like his brethren in Germany and France, before and after him.

The third period of chronicles, in the sixteenth century, yielded compositions by Abraham Zacut, Solomon Ibn Verga, Elijah Kapshali, Gedaliah Ibn Yaḥia, Joseph ha-Cohen (*The Vale of Tears*, 1558), Samuel Usque (*Consolation for the Tribulations of Israel*, 1553). Most of the writers were exiles from Spain and Portugal who wrote of the bitter persecutions and expulsions they had experienced.

Maimonides on history

Before enlarging on the intentions of Jewish chronography, let us clarify briefly the historical awareness of the Poetic-Philosophic culture. Maimonides' conception of the past is illustrative of his culture's approach to the past and to knowledge of the past.

Maimonides, we know, did not acknowledge the Sages' authority in matters of science: "Mathematics," he said, "were not fully developed in those days; and their [the Sages'] statements were not based on the authority of the Prophets."[25] The Sages' opinions are hence entirely invalid for Maimonides in that large area of ontology that deals with science and knowledge of the world. In order to bring the Sages' views into closer alignment with the true opinions of his day, Maimonides attempted to interpret them in the spirit of science and philosophy. But in his essay on the resurrection of the dead he sharply assails all those "who take literally many homilies," especially in the matter of God's incorporification; such people might deem themselves true Sages of Israel, but in fact "they are mankind's greatest fools."[26] Maimonides likewise rejected the imagination, sentiment, and poetic license of Talmudic homiletic interpretations. The *derash* about the four species of trees used in the observance of the Sukkot festival, for example, whereby each species represented a different human quality, was entirely unworthy of being taken seriously by an educated person, because it had never been the Sages' intent to pass this as truth. In a number of instances in the *Guide for the Perplexed*, and also in the introduction to the section Ḥelek (in his commentary to the Mishnah, *Sanhedrin* 10), Maimonides dismisses the opinions of naïve believers, who accept the Sages' stories literally. He also tries to give historic-anthropological and geographic reasons for the commandments, as we saw in chapter 4. The Messianic eon and the advent of the Messiah are described in a historic "realistic" manner while prophecies and Talmudic *derash* on the subject are dismissed as metaphors, which have no basis in human reality.

But while the learned Rabbi investigated the reasons for the commandments, whether they were in keeping with the Creator's will and wisdom, nowhere did he allow for the possibility that they might also be, in part at least, the result of a historical, moral development of certain cultures and their varieties. In his historical account of the transmission of faith among the nations and in Israel he generally followed Talmudic homiletics. Enoch, Metuselaḥ, Noaḥ, Eber, all knew the Creator. Finally, Abraham appears on the historic scene: "After he was weaned, while still an infant, his mind began to reflect . . . When the people flocked to him and questioned him regarding his assertions, he would instruct each one according to his capacity till he had brought him to the way of truth . . . He implanted in their hearts this great doctrine, composed books on it, and taught it to Isaac, his son."[27] Yes, even books, especially about God's unity and His absolute incorporeality. Scholars have had no difficulty in tracing this opinion too to Talmudic sources. It is therefore with some astonishment that one observes philosophers who intrepidly scrutinize heaven and earth, whose purview sweeps the horizons from high to low, heedlessly disregard the "before" and the "after." Maimonides analyzes philosophical ideas with acuity and depth, but fails to examine the sequence and likelihood of historical events and deeds, as if this in no way concerned him.

Two examples, chosen from many others, will suffice here. In the introduction to the order *Zeraʿim* in his commentary to the Mishnah, Maimonides expresses the belief that Rabbi Dossa ben Hyrcanus was a contemporary of Simeon the Just, an assertion which extends Simeon's life down to Rabbi Akiba's generation and renders him approximately 400 years old. No less strange is Maimonides' echoing of a Talmudic homily (in the introduction to his *Mishneh Torah*) where, in a discussion of the chain of tradition, he mentions that the Prophet Aḥia the Shilonite lived from the time of Moses until after David and Solomon. No wonder that Abraham ben David (Ibn Daud, *c.* 1120–98, known as the third Rabad, or the Rabad of Posquières) disputes his judgment here. Maimonides' arguments are based on an idiosyncratic saying in the Talmud (*Bab.B.* 121b) which he had no need to cite, least of all as a historical and valid piece of evidence.

It is interesting that Maimonides paid little attention to Arabic historiography. Admittedly, most such writing was composed in order to exalt and vindicate particular rulers, while court anecdotes, gossip, and stories of love and dalliance certainly held no interest for Maimonides. But there were also important historians like al-Mas'udi and his disciple Mutahdar al-Muqaddasi, author of *The Book of Creation and of History* (966 CE). Salo Baron in his essay on Maimonides' historical outlook cites a number of important historical works which Maimonides could have consulted yet failed to do, perhaps, surmises Baron, because they contained things specific to the Islamic faith and unacceptable to Jews.[28] Their predilection for astrology probably also repelled him.

Maimonides went to considerable pains to arrange events chronologically, and on a number of occasions he discusses the chronology of personalities and events. Chronology was also important for the reckoning of the generations since Adam and for the accuracy of the Jewish calendar. But he knew no details and relied heavily on Talmudic stories and on his personal judgment, aided by hints in the Talmudic literature. Thus he counted forty generations from Moses to the fourth-century CE Amora, Rav Ashi – an unbroken chain of tradition.

Maimonides' conception of the past is better understood when we view his philosophy as a combination of the Talmudic world view and the conception of classical rationalism. Throughout its existence, from Aristotle to Descartes and Kant, classical rationalism preferred the fixed and immutable superhistorical content over the mutable occurrence. In this it did not differ from the Talmudic ontology. Poetry, Aristotle thought, was "something more philosophic and of greater import than history." The truth it contained rose above accidental and erratic events. Hence, even when we know that certain events are established facts, what purpose do they serve? They are extraneous, transitory, and trivial, whereas poetry ("its statements are of the nature rather of universals") and the mind's achievements are of greatest significance.[29] Vico's quarrel with Descartes and with this kind of thinking has already been mentioned. Kant, like Aristotle and Descartes, believed that historical awareness in itself, without a governing theoretical principle, was of no interest, a view shared also by Hermann Cohen, as we heard earlier. Maimonides' conception is, therefore, no more puzzling than that of other rationalist philosophers. He sees no benefit in occupation with the past unless it serves to strengthen faith. Indeed, if we properly knew the history of ancient nations, "we should be able to see plainly the reason for most of the things mentioned in the Pentateuch."[30] That is the sole utility of history; all the rest is idle talk. This was also the contention of many before and after him, like the Ga'on of Vilna and Jacob Emden, whom we shall have occasion to cite shortly.

One may say that traditional Jewish chronography and philosophers-theologians of history strove to inculcate the belief that no fundamental changes had transpired in the nation's history because the superordinating concepts and the archetypal collective experiences, as they conceived these, stood fixed and immutable in unifying girds, in a "statics" of historical continuity and shared destiny. It is, therefore, not surprising that, when measured by what today we call knowledge, the cultures of faith knew but little about each other, and the horizon of their entire historical knowledge was severely circumscribed. Maimonides was unfamiliar with Saʿadiah Gaʾon's *Book of Doctrines and Beliefs* or with the latter's interpretations of the Torah (although some scholars, notably Jacob Guttmann, believe that it is to Saʿadiah that he refers when he alludes to the words of "the latest Geʾonim").[31] It took 100 years for the Spanish scholars to hear about Rashi. And conversely, German Sages apparently knew nothing of events in Spain during the terrible persecutions of 1391 and thereafter.[32] Admittedly, the German Sages had troubles of their own, yet they had time for precepts, customs, and ordinances relating to matters of prayer and synagogue worship, Torah scrolls and fringes, matters of the forbidden and the permitted, issues of Rabbinic authority, etc. They did not turn, however, to the wide horizons of history; even of their own misfortunes they spoke but little, and this, too, only intermittently and sketchily.

Five objectives of traditional historians

Five main objectives, or preoccupations, or cognitive applications of the knowledge of the past, characterize Jewish historiography in the cultures of faith, accounting for the selectivity and the sifting, the oblivion and the obliteration, and clarifying the criteria used in the manipulation of events and deeds. A culture's ontology, the sanctum of its faith in personal and national redemption, is unmistakably expressed in these objectives.

1   Faced with calamitous exiles and persecutions, the first objective was to uncover the workings of divine providence in the world via God's miracles in behalf of His favored people. The chroniclers, in fact, seized upon the calamities for the opportunity thus afforded them to educe useful lessons from the happenings in the "vale of tears." The preface to Gedaliah Ibn Yahya's *Shalshelet ha-kabbalah* ("Chain of Tradition," 1586), for example, explains the benefits to be derived from learning Jewish history. One of the chief benefits, in the author's opinion, is to "proclaim the matter of the wonders, which the blessed Lord daily performs for Israel." There is justice and a just Judge, and Jewish history is the product of a wondrous divine providence. Therefore an author who undertakes to describe the times must not fail to mention the wonders which the Holy One has worked for Israel before, during, and after the misfortunes depicted in his chronicle. The story of these calamities should awaken in the reader a desire to emulate his forefathers, "to inspire the reader's desire to sanctify Heaven's name with all his heart and all his soul and all his might."

The truth is that the problem of theodicy, the vindication of divine justice in the face of evil, was an acutely distressing issue all through the exile. There was never a shortage of skeptics who cast doubt upon one of the principal elements in Israel's self-image, namely the idea of the election and redemption reserved for the Chosen People. The polemics with Gentile opponents centered exactly upon this sore point of Israel's lowly status. It was, therefore, imperative "to show God's wonders to our holy nation." The chroniclers and scroll-writers sought to prove that even in exile Jews were not rejected or abandoned by Israel's Guardian; His eyes were ever watchful over His people.

Jacob Emden (the "Yavetz," 1697–1770) discusses at length the prohibition promulgated by Joseph Caro, composer of the *Shulḥan ʿaruch*, regarding the reading of historical matters and the permission extended by Moses Isserles, author of the *Mappah* ("Tablecloth") to the *Shulḥan ʿaruch*, to read such material not only on the Sabbath, but even on weekdays. Emden proceeds to draw a distinction between history books that relate "God's wonders to our holy nation, which is persecuted since its very beginnings" – these may be read even on the Sabbath – and books that make mention of various wonders performed for our ancestors, which one is permitted to read only on weekdays. Other books, such as the chronicle of Gentile kings by Joseph ha-Cohen, and portions of David Gans' *Zemaḥ David* ("Offspring of David," 1592), and Abraham Zacut's *Sefer ha-yuḥasin* ("Book of Genealogies," 1566), there is no need to know at all, and their perusal is permanently forbidden.

The first objective, then, of religious chroniclers was to demonstrate God's wonders. The notion of God was, for this purpose, conceived as fixed and unchanged in all generations ("I am the Lord unchanging"), and this guaranteed the enduring existence of the sons of Jacob. This conception indicates, as we have said, that history is not an accretion of haphazard accidents, nor is it an ordered row of events governed by inflexible causes and effects, by inviolable law; rather, history is the revelation of God's wisdom as a response to man's actions, and in accordance with man's actions. It is a divine plan which may be confounded by human and natural calamities. History often appears as the exact antithesis of the future kingdom of heaven, ever a poor reality, incomplete, unredeemed. As long as Israel remains in exile, history is a cry of anguish and protest. The concept of exile (*galut*) is essentially a religious concept, unlike the concepts of diaspora or dispersal. It clamors for its consummation in the concept of redemption. The reality of exile attests to the incompleteness of human history.

According to the concept of Jewish history expressed in this first objective, the accidental and transitory require an answer derived from a Jew's freedom of action. This is accomplished by the fulfillment of commandments, which transforms fate into destiny, exile into redemption. One might add that the chroniclers of the ancient peoples saw history reflected in the eternal immutable cycles of natural phenomena. Gentile soothsayers, such as the oracle of Delphi, revealed and announced events, but usually did not attempt to chastise sinners or change their moral conduct. The inscription on Titus' Arch in Rome celebrating the destruction of the Temple in Jerusalem, establishes a fact, depicts a historical event via the symbol of triumph over an enemy, whereas the lamentations on the ninth of Ab, commemorating that same event, impose an obligation, require acts of repentance and charity, in order to accelerate the advent of the kingdom of heaven and its many wonders.

2 The second objective was of another sort. The polemics regarding Israel's election entailed contests over the authority of the Oral Torah. Christians argued that the covenant between Israel and a redeeming God had been abrogated when "Israel of the flesh" rejected the new gospel. Internally, too, there were many challengers to the authority of the Oral Law. The early sectarians may have passed from the world at the time of the destruction of the Temple, but their views were preserved in similar, or only slightly altered, forms. The antiquity of the Oral Law was doubted, and it was necessary to prove that it was indeed a legitimate link in the chain of original tradition, a continuous transmission from Sage to Sage, all the way back to Moses at Sinai, and that Israel was a nation thanks to its "two Laws" in Saᶜadiah's famous phrase mentioned in chapter 4, p. 99.

The chronicle *Seder ᶜolam rabbah*, for example, was written primarily in order to settle contradictions existing between Scriptures and the Talmud on historical points and on the tradition of transmission. Ibn Daud's *Sefer ha-kabbalah* was meant as a weapon in the debate with the Karaites. As in his philosophic work *Emunah ramah*, the purpose of the historical work was

to provide students with the evidence that all the teachings of our rabbis of blessed memory, namely, the sages of the Mishna and the Talmud, have been transmitted: each great sage and righteous man having received them from a great sage and a righteous man, each head of an academy and his school having received them from the head of an academy and his school, as far back as the men of the Great Assembly, who received them from the prophets, of blessed memory all. Never did the sages of the Talmud, and certainly not the sages of the Mishna, teach anything, however trivial, of their own invention, except for the enactments which were made by universal agreement in order to make a hedge about the Torah. Now should anyone infected with heresy attempt to mislead you, saying: "It is because the rabbis differed on a number of issues that I doubt their words," you should retort bluntly and inform him that he is a "rebel against the decision of the court."[33]

These introductory statements make the book's purpose abundantly clear. It is interesting that, contrary to known facts, Ibn Daud claimed that the Karaite sect had not attained a wide spread, and that it had failed to produce a single noteworthy Sage or poet. According to this "historian," the

Karaites were all "mute dogs, they cannot bark." Nonetheless he gave himself great pains to silence them.

3   The third objective, which derived from the second and was closely related to it, was the need to defend those in positions of legal, religious, and social authority, and to vindicate their right to interpret and promulgate laws and lead the community. This was the reason for the genealogical scrolls and the records of chains of transmission – legitimation of the establishment and vindication of its right to persecute heretics. This category includes the "Scroll of Evyatar" (a reverential listing of the "Ga'on son of the Ga'on," "grandson of Ga'on," etc.), the genealogical scroll of Aḥima'atz ben Paltiel (*Megillat yuḥasin*, "The Scroll of Descent," 1054 CE) and to some degree also the "Epistle of Rav Sherira Ga'on" (986 CE). The latter, a chronology of the Rabbinic authorities, in as much as it deals with matters relating to the Oral Law and practical precepts, is actually more concerned with the second objective. The same is true for Maimonides' introduction to the *Mishneh Torah*, where both objectives are intertwined. Books like Ḥaim Joseph David Azulai's *Shem ha-gedolim* (1774) clearly emphasize the third objective. The genealogical tracing of a family's noble ancestry strengthens the pillars of authority, the prestige of Rabbis and *parnassim*, which *halachic* tradition has established in positions of supreme authority. It is necessary to prove that the Rabbis received their authority rightfully, either in a chain of transmission, or by virtue of their erudition in Torah.

4   The fourth objective is implied by the word *seder* (order) which figures so prominently in the titles of many historical compositions, such as *Seder 'olam rabbah* or *Seder 'olam zuta* or *Seder Tanna'im va-Amora'im* – an implication of cosmic permanence and unity. These books titled *Seder*[34] expound the chain of transmission, influenced perhaps by the Latin expression *secundum ordinem* ("according to the order"), one after the other, according to their progression. No dynamics of change operate in the order of the generations, and the chronology of events becomes a sort of immutable order of the world, a cosmic divine permanence, over which time appears to have no sway, and which is entirely subject to the rule of its providential Creator.

The only difference between this theological history, or historical metaphysics, and philosophies from Plato and Aristotle down to Descartes regarding the insignificance of history in comparison to knowledge of nature's laws, I find illustrated in the Messianic idea, in the possibility of redemption. True, in Judaism too, as in Greek philosophy and later also in Christian theology, the wisdom encapsulated in historical events and deeds is a sort of pre-existing given which man is capable of discovering by the exercise of his attention and reason. There is an order implanted in the substance of events and deeds and in their relation to each other, and any philosopher, intelligent thinker, or a believer in providence may uncover it. In Israel's cultures of faith, too, this kind of "objectivism" was very powerful, although it took the guise of a transcendent absolutism. Nonetheless, the yearning for the future, for full salvation, never ceased to animate these cultures. This fourth objective in Jewish historical knowledge is indeed the fascinating and inspiring aspect of Jewish theodicy: the direction toward the future, in which God's glory will appear in a new redeemed world. Righteousness combines with power without that radical rift between the two, so tragically characteristic of the period prior to salvation. Even in exile, hope is not entirely paralyzed by afflictions. Despite sufferings, Israel does not turn its back on inspiring visions by clinging to a shattered and distressing past. Instead, every culture creates its own vision of the Messianic eon.

5   The fifth objective requires more extensive explanation, in order to clarify some of the points previously mentioned in passing regarding the great importance attached to the past and the present's strife with, and even defeat of, the past. We have mentioned two models for the conception of time provided throughout the ages by philosophies of history: the cyclical model, and the progressive model of a path leading to redemption. The first is a pagan prototype, exemplified in the writings of Greek and Roman philosophers. The latter was unique to Judaism, and was subsequently adopted by Christianity and Islam. But, in reality, the matter is not quite so simple and there are a number of snags in this neat division. Greek and Roman philosophers and historians also sought a non-cyclical model and they too had ideas about historical progress, about a step-by-step ascending line. Hesiod already used Prometheus as a symbol of triumph over ignorance and backwardness, and Lucretius explicitly stated that humanity progressed from barbarism to civilization "step by step" ("*pedetentim progredientis*").[35] The organological metaphor which directs the mind towards a cyclical conception did not exclude a conception of ascension and progress. In Judaism, Louis Ginzberg attests, the metaphor of a revolving wheel was probably an alien import, for in the Rabbinic literature it was merely a figure of speech, whereas in Indian philosophy it was a basic tenet.[36] The organic recurrence of growth and decay, birth, development and death was not autonomous in Judaism, and although Israel was frequently compared, especially in Mystical lore, to a body, there was always free will, and there was a Creator and a Guardian over the universe.

Nonetheless, you find in the Talmudic culture the idea of a prefiguration of both present and future in the past, illustrated by the saying: "The deeds of the fathers are indicative of the sons," or in the notion that the ancient kingdom of Edom is a reference to the Roman Empire; Esau, Nimrod, Pharaoh, Jeroboam son of Nebat – all the ancient personalities and acts return to the historical framework of the present. Esau becomes the progenitor of Rome, David becomes the father of the Messiah, the Patriarchs observe the Torah and the festivals and compose prayers. The past that is behind us now lies ahead of us, advancing toward us out of the future. If the past exists, it is bound to return. Restoration and renaissance are possible because things have already existed at an earlier time and were forgotten or neglected, and now they await to be rediscovered. Adam and Eve in the garden of Eden prior to original sin, the exodus from Egypt, all these are prefigurations of the final redemption.

In other words, the vision of final redemption was cast in the mold of the exodus from Egypt, the symbol of liberation from slavery. There were some who went to extremes, especially in Mysticism, and sought to revert the world to its original state, to the days of first man in the garden of Eden, prior to original sin and the defilement inflicted on the human race by the serpent. In the future all things are destined to return to wholeness, to their original unblemished state; in the Messianic age the world will be renewed in a sort of restoration and renaissance of lost perfection. The verse "Whatever is has been already, and whatever is to come has been already" (Eccles. 3.15) referred to the future resurrection of the dead, which had already occurred in the past "through Elijah, through Elisha and through Ezekiel."[37] And thus said Rav Aḥa: "All that the Holy One, blessed be He, intends to perform or to make afresh in His world in the Time to Come, He has already partly performed in anticipation in this world through the instrumentality of His righteous prophets."[38] The same is true for the troubles of the present. The exile was decreed, on account of the sins that precipitated it, many generations before it actually took place. The first exile was due to the sin of the Golden Calf, and there was no subsequent catastrophe which did not in some measure mete punishment for that most grievous sin committed immediately following the giving of the Torah and God's astounding revelation. The Sages taught that Jacob, in his dream of the heaven-scaling ladder, foresaw all future historical events. The present was weighted with the past. Rabbi Ḥiyya said that already at the first creation of the world "the Holy One, blessed be He, foresaw a temple erected, destroyed, and erected."[39] The nation's historical peregrinations are all foreseen, and exile and redemption are links in the chain of events of the world as it was, is, and ever shall be.

Does this mean that the cultures of faith were captives of the past, incapable of departing from its constructs? The idea of free will and the phenomenon of Messianic visions and movements argue against this interpretation. But the meanings ascribed to deeds, personalities, and events of the past, endowed as they were with a supertemporal authority, exercised considerable influence over the conception of the present. In the struggle between historical events in their time-bound flow and the concretions of meanings and their authority, the latter emerged supreme. For this must be said: every historical conception establishes meanings, connects events to their causes, personalities to particular happenings, in short, ties the timing of events to their meanings, or as N. Rotenstreich put it, associates temporariness and meaningfulness; a happening devoid of meaning is inconceivable in the realm of interpersonal relations and it certainly is not history. Meaningfulness endows history not only with a continuity of sequence (i.e. that the events duly follow one another), but also a continuity of relationships, such as causes and reasons. Rotenstreich maintains that a physical sequence does not become a historical sequence except when contemplated from the standpoint of meaning. Similarly, meaningful relations are not grasped as historical relations until they are given temporal sequence, for example, a historical sequence of progression and perfection or a sequence of decline and extinction.[40] Historical conceptions differ from one another in two things: in the relations between "temporariness" and "meaning," and in the nature of the meanings themselves. Viewed thus, it is clear that only with the Emancipation culture do we begin to find an emphasis on the "temporariness" of events, whereas in the cultures of faith the stress was on their meaning. Every historical conception provides – in narrative, description, and thought – a certain construct for the occurrence, and creates agglomerations of meanings and modes of comprehending concepts, as also of impersonal processes and institutions.

What, then, was the relation between the past and the present in Israel's cultures of faith, this relation which is the fifth objective of Jewish historiography? What did one generation transmit to another? We have already seen, especially in the examples drawn from the Talmudic culture, that meaning was ascribed to the past, but from the perspective and with the metaphors of the present. As in every revelational religion, here, too, authority, wherein ultimate meaning resides, anticipated the transitoriness of temporal events and crystallized these around its own pivot: before the giving of the Torah and after the giving of the Torah. The present was required to accept the authority that had been revealed and to emulate the past which had previously accepted this same authority. Each one of Israel's cultures saw the past reflected in the present as its prefiguration. One may say, in the language of Isaak Heinemann, that it was the intention of every culture to "render palpable and thereby to activate the eternal forces that are the undercurrents of Israel's history."[41] The past's special status, which was nurtured by the strength of the "eternal" authority with which it was endowed, and by the strength of images and desires of the present, acquired extraordinary power in Jewish history, extending even into the future, through the conception of the Messianic age and the world to come.

Temporariness is cancelled at the end of days, but even then, in the days of the Messiah, Israel's eternal Torah would continue to be studied. In the cultures of faith one preferred "meanings" or constructs over "temporariness," and there was a distinct tendency to dissociate the meanings from time. Meanings became generalized and typical, "covering" many events and deeds, and obscuring, or even entirely suppressing, the unique features of personalities and events, as if to submerge "temporariness" in the frames of the constructed "meanings." Echoing Pitirim Sorokin, we can speak of an "eternalistic" versus a "temporalistic" tendency. In the annals and chronicles describing the relations between the permanent and the temporary, between being and becoming, between eternity and the moment, the former reign supreme. The superior position of the "eternalistic" meanings is manifest in all the objectives of historical knowledge down to our very own generation. The cultures of faith differed from one another only in defining and evaluating the nature of these meanings.

One may summarize the fifth objective by saying that in spite of the chroniclers' intention to spread one single mantle over all historical occurrences, they, in fact, unfold before us a vivid landscape of different conceptions. But in each culture there is movement to and fro: forward and backward, future and past, a vision of the end of days and a vision of the early beginnings, each nurturing the other and together all are sustained by the supertemporal meaning of the supreme authority, which alone holds sway over kingdoms and nations, and over their histories.

Jewish cultures of faith were neither sentimentally lachrymose about the past, nor lightly credulous in the inevitability of progress. As long as Jews believed in divine providence, in judgment and Judge, it was impossible for the evident malfunctions of the grand historical design to drive them to complete despair, or to the cynicism and frustration typical of "heretics," for the simple reason that it was inconceivable that the negative forces of destruction and profanation could triumph in the long run. True, the confidence in the supreme purpose of the overall historical process was not borne out by the details of the process. Due to the inescapable dualism underlying human life, sin lies in wait at the doorstep of every deed and event, but although everything is foreseen in heaven in its minutest detail, here below man is ignorant of what may happen from day to day. The specifics of the events, no less than their grand purpose, are God's design and His secret, a matter for a handful of "calculators of the End," or for Kabbalists. But man is endowed with power to try to avert or mitigate the force of calamities. All Jewish cultures pitted the idea of divine providence against the demonic ("unclean") forces of contrariety; they were not, however, caught up by the Emancipatory optimism regarding the purposefulness of the world or by the progressivism of the last two centuries. J.B. Bury justly remarked that belief in progress spread only after the idea of providence had been rejected.[42] In truth, the two cannot coexist in harmony, but not for the reason Bury suggested. Bury, a student of faith in progress, believed that such faith contradicted the idea of divine providence because of its emphasis on the power of human creativity to mend the world through human deeds, and its faculty for discovery and invention. But this is only partially true.[43] The idea of progress differs from the idea of providence in that the latter gives full attention to evil in this world, to the forces of contrariety and destruction, as described in chapter 1. The belief in providence always took full cognizance of the power of destructive forces. In the Mystical culture their potency was exaggerated, in the Poetic-Philosophic culture it was minimized, but not denied. Each Jewish culture peered into the depths and waged its battle against the negative forces, guided by its overall ontology. By no means could a Jewish culture of faith treat lightly or ignore their tremendous power. Precisely because there was free will, there was also the demonic freedom to destroy.

In the final reckoning, so it was believed, history attested to a dynamics of elevation, a supreme purpose of complete restoration. But this purpose could not be attained before the world had undergone great suffering, the suffering associated with the "birth pangs of the Messiah," the raging of the evil forces. Every age is open to the duality of the tribulations attendant on the "birth pangs of the Messiah" and the serenity of his actual advent. The negative forces cannot prevent the establishment of the kingdom of heaven in which reality – history and everything in it – and supreme purpose are joined together in a triumphant wholeness.

7

HISTORICAL CONSCIOUSNESS IN THE EMANCIPATION CULTURE

What is the Emancipation culture?

The culture of Jewish Emancipation as it developed in Europe, in the United States, and in other countries expresses the achievements and predicaments, the joys and the sorrows of those generations of Jews who struggled for equal civic rights, obtained them, lost them again, and finally regained them: it is the culture of Jews who enjoyed these rights before the Holocaust and who enjoy them, in greater or lesser measure, in some countries of the diaspora today. The change of attitude began internally, in Holland and Italy in the seventeenth century, gained momentum in the eighteenth century and peaked in western Europe in the nineteenth century. The stronghold of the Emancipation culture today is the Jewish community in the United States. This culture came about as a result of profound changes in social, economic and political conditions in the world and it attests to the dynamics of the modern era. At first, Jews strove merely to improve their socio-economic lot concomitantly with the development of their host countries, and to diversify the range of their professions; in the end they achieved economic integration. This struggle produced moments of great triumph, but also disastrous failures. The eighteenth century, for example, witnessed some remarkable successes: opportunities opened up for German Jews to enter trade, and the development of capitalism broadened the economic base of many professions. Jews were integrated in trade, banking, industry, and various other urban professions and occupations. The old-time "Court Jews" – and of the myriad German principalities there was not one that did not have its Court Jews to finance its activities and provision its army – these Jews, their children, and grandchildren were transformed into industrialists, bankers, and big businessmen. A new social stratification emerged, based on new classes and professions. These processes were repeated in other countries and were at the foundation of the Emancipation culture.

A number of noteworthy features distinguish this from preceding cultures, features which are directed with polemical trenchancy against these predecessors. Essentially, this is a Jewish culture whose material and spiritual endeavors seek to accommodate secular needs. It is a culture of secularization, analogous to its European counterparts for whom the process of secularization had begun some 200 years earlier. Baruch Spinoza (1632–77) was an important early conceptualizer of this culture and a theoretician of its principles. Earlier we pointed out that it is difficult to substantiate the widely held view that the events occurring outside the ghetto walls caught western European Jewry by surprise and left it bare and vulnerable to the intrusion of a changed and unfamiliar world. The fact is that external factors merely accelerated the internal revolution already under way. Judaism's surrender of its tradition stemmed from a desire to join the common material and spiritual accommodations of other nations, and was largely the result of inner developments and choices. The Jewish transformation was not substantially different from that which other nations were experiencing.

A ferment of revolt against the established order of Jewish tradition had existed ever since the expulsion from Spain. Former Marranos, in particular, were eager to achieve integration in their host countries; the desire to negate the exile prompted a corollary desire to wipe out the entire exilic tradition. Messianic movements, notably Sabbateanism, invoked the nation to radical reformation. Fueled by Mystical yearnings and driven by the despair of oppression, these movements wished to tear down the barriers separating Israel from other nations. The radical Sabbatean drive to "dissolve the commandments"[1] ordained by Talmud and tradition left a profound impression on Jewish consciousness. Gerschom Scholem and his students have adequately mapped out the nature and course of this movement and we need not enlarge upon it here. The move toward worldliness, toward abolition of the Rabbinic stranglehold, became even stronger after Sabbatai Zvi failed to vanquish Satan with his esoteric wisdom.[2]

The following features, I believe, may be said to characterize the Emancipation culture:

1   First and foremost it is a culture animated by *the desire to end the exile and the mentality associated with exile*. It no longer cherishes the age-old Messianic hope of return to the Holy Land; it resigns itself to the reality of dispersal among the Gentiles and hopes instead to see a Jew's country of birth and residence become a homeland where he will enjoy freedom and equal rights with other natives.

"Native settlers" must become "citizens of the state," declared Moses Mendelssohn in his introduction to the German edition of Manasseh ben Israel's *Teshuʿat Israel*. In order to gain acceptance, western Jews were prepared to "mount the barricades" even to the point of denying their coreligionists in eastern Europe. French Jews, for example, disavowed their

Ashkenazi brethren in Alsace-Lorraine, as we learn from the writer Pinto in his famous letter to Voltaire, or from studies on the Jewish community of Bordeaux. This community, descended from the Marranos of Spain and Portugal, had become fully integrated by the eighteenth century. One of its members, the well-known banker and *parnas* (community leader) Abraham Portado, had been appointed by Napoleon to head the Parisian Assembly of the Notables (forerunner of Napoleon's Great Sanhedrin), and had authored most of the documents produced by that assembly. Notwithstanding this social and economic eminence, the Jews of Bordeaux viewed themselves as members of the élite Spanish dispersion, unconcerned with the larger issues of the Jewish problem in France, let alone in other parts of the world. Their ambition was limited to securing their own civic rights and seeing that these were scrupulously honored. The distinction between Sephardi and Ashkenazi loomed as large in their eyes as a chasm separating two nations. To be sure, this was only the beginning. In due course the Jews of the Emancipation created magnificent all-Jewish institutions. Zvi Locker, whose study on the Jews of Bordeaux is cited here,[3] concludes his article with the remark that the Bordeaux community survived until the twentieth century, its scions spearheaded the drive for emancipation, and although at first they set themselves apart and sought civic rights for themselves alone, their struggle paved the way for the eventual enfranchisement of all French Jews.

Such disavowals of the Jewish fraternity, and what these implied in terms of the weakening faith in the oneness of the Jewish people, will be enlarged upon below. For the moment we merely wish to point out that in the early stages of their struggle for civic rights western Sephardi Jews were indeed prepared to relinquish old ties with their coreligionists of Ashkenazi, Asian, or African descent and to sever the traditional allegiance to the ancestral land, in order to covenant with France for a new homeland. They were not prepared, however, to surrender their religious distinctness. Here they drew the line.

2 *The belief in Messianic redemption through miracles is shunted beyond the bounds of expectation, and is even derided.* A return to Zion resulting from political change is still deemed within the realm of possibility and desirability, but it ceases to be a matter of focal interest. The members of this culture are not eager to "press for the End." In their view, the desirable "End" is naturalization in their home countries.

Moses Mendelssohn's attitude toward the traditional Messianic aspiration is a characteristic case in point. Only on extremely rare occasions, when compelled by some external pressures, did Mendelssohn proffer any statements about the Messianic idea. His feebly worded statements on the subject raise more questions than they resolve. Yet, it appears that Mendelssohn valued the pragmatic-political aspect of the Messianic vision:

the ingathering of the exiles in the Land of Israel and the nation's liberty in its sovereign state. Echoing Maimonides' formulation of the Thirteen Principles of Faith, Mendelssohn expressed his faith in the Messiah as follows:

I acknowledge as true and certain that the children of Abraham, Isaac and Jacob will not always be exiled from the Promised Land and scattered among the nations, but that the Lord will raise, at a time known to Him alone, a Messiah of the house of David, who will render to this nation its ancient freedom and will rule over it in the land of the Patriarchs.[4]

But these words are spoken as a ritual cliché or an abstract formula, about an end which need not be "pressed." When a certain plan for the return to Zion was submitted to Mendelssohn in the winter of 1769–70, it left him unconvinced. He had scant faith in the nation's ability to redeem itself. The nation, he thought, "has not been sufficiently prepared to undertake the realization of any great project."[5] The oppression of centuries had eroded its boldness and vigor. The desire for national liberty could not activate a nation inured to suffering and accustomed to accept oppression in submission and meekness: "The natural desire for freedom has lost its force to activate us." Besides, the nation was widely dispersed and divided in its opinions; it could hardly be hoped that such a nation would have the spirit to unite in a great enterprise, especially in one that required a great deal of money. Lack of funds can chill most enthusiasms. It was difficult to see where sufficient funds for such an undertaking could be found, since the nation's wealth was not vested in real property, but primarily in credit, which could not be realized at will. Moreover, the plan would only be feasible at a time when the great sovereign states of Europe were so at odds with one another that each would be entirely absorbed in its own affairs, because in times of tranquility one of the jealous states would surely attempt to abort the enterprise, thereby subjecting the world to the danger of a new crusade, similar to the medieval crusades which "caused so many catastrophes." Towards the end of his life Mendelssohn replied in unequivocal terms to the argument that the dream of return to Zion stood in the way of full enfranchisement; the Sages, he said, strictly forbade us to contemplate a forcible re-establishment of our state in Zion. Happy is he who waits, said Mendelssohn, for it is in the nature of man, provided he be no "enthusiast," to love the soil where he feels happy and where he is tolerated: "At any rate the hope for the return to Zion has no influence whatsoever on our daily civic life."[6]

Not only Israel's redemption found itself shortchanged in Mendelssohn's vision of the future: he could not believe that humanity would ever be united in the gird of one purified faith. Even at the end of days nations and religions would not be of one heart. In fact, this unity, even if it were possible, was not really desirable: the pious hope of uniting all nations under the wings of one faith threatened the idea of tolerance, and with it Israel's existence, and the freedom of all nations; Mendelssohn thought it would inevitably culminate in "general hypocrisy." The multiplicity of faces and forms, the variety in opinions and beliefs, precisely these were, in his view, "the plan of divine providence and its ultimate goal."[7] Judaism would fulfill its divinely ordained mission by pursuing amidst the nations its course toward enlightenment and emancipation, toward worldly and spiritual redemption. Judaism's mission was "to be the only authorized teacher and guide of the eternal truth," not by proselytizing and soul-fishing, but by observing the commandments and leading a life of modesty and morality. Mendelssohn's vision of the future is a most striking antithesis to the Messianic vision of, say, Abravanel.

What little was left of the Messianic vision evaporated entirely with Mendelssohn's colleagues and disciples. A drastically diminished Messianic belief emerges from Herz Homberg's text book *Bnei Zion*, which the Austrian authorities instituted as a primer on Jewish religion for Jewish youngsters throughout its domains, and as required examination material for men and women applying for a marriage license: "We believe that God will send an annointed head, who will teach Israel to see God's light, will give it courage and strength to overcome evil impulses, will awaken it to brotherhood and unity and general love of mankind, and will rebuild a temple in which all nations will acknowledge God's name."[8] These statements have the ring of hollow lip-service to the requirements of traditional Jewish learning. In reality, the yearnings for redemption turned toward the present, toward the countries of birth, to the rulers and their magnanimity.

To be sure, the Messianic idea itself had changed, taking the form of a widely growing faith in progress. The hierarchical conception of dichotomous spiritual and material, higher and lower orders, was replaced by the idea that all men were born equal, hence, essentially free – this was the emancipatory Bill of Rights. This ideal was never fully realized in Europe and was, in fact, subject to many reversals, yet it served as the foundation of all the achievements of Emancipation Judaism. Eyes were fervently lifted toward progress, toward the future. Jews, ever eager to hasten the redeeming end, were prepared to suffer the tribulations associated with the new modes of "Messianic" advent.

Most of the early champions of the Emancipation culture who first embarked on a limited-scale private struggle for their own personal civic rights, found themselves wrestling willy-nilly for what eventually emerged as an agonized, overpowering, and inspiring drama for the enthusiasts of many nations. The hopes and yearnings of an Emancipation Jew thus echoed the "spirit of the time." In the history of Christian Europe this was perhaps the first time that the spirit of the time coincided with relief and benefit for the Jew.

3   *Loyalty to the state and to its laws now required surrender of the judicial and political autonomy* which Jews in feudal regimes had enjoyed in their status of a "state within a state." State law henceforth applied to all non-ritual matters and the complex world of traditional Judaism was reduced to private religious practices. Rabbis were no longer entitled to their traditional role as judges and definitive interpreters of Halachah, but functioned merely as preachers, teachers, and *dayanim* in ritual matters. The great *yeshivot* of the West began to disappear, Torah-knowledge declined, the Rabbinic ban of excommunication (*herem*) lost is efficacy and soon disappeared entirely. Economic changes promoted the rise of new social strata: traders, bankers, doctors, and lawyers. The old order of life founded upon all-encompassing traditional, theoretical, and practical precepts was irrevocably undermined. Many Jews changed their dress, their language, and even their names.

The controversy between Rabbi Jacob Emden and Rabbi Jonathan Eibeschütz, which convulsed European communities from Prague to Brody and from Hamburg to Constantinople for more than five years (beginning in 1750), was a dramatic landmark for the end of a period. It vividly signaled the changing of the guard in western European Jewish leadership and produced an impact on Jewish life that could be compared with only slight exaggeration to that of the French Revolution on other nations. This dispute, in a nutshell, focused on Kabbalah, Messianism, Sabbatean amulets, and the personalities of the protagonists who contended for the position of Hamburg's Chief Rabbi. It divided the Rabbinic world into adversary camps which fought each other with extraordinary zeal by means of endless mutual bans and anathemas, acrimonious polemics, and bitter abuse. The sound of the *shofar* announcing the ban was heard again and again throughout the Jewish diasporas, spreading divisiveness everywhere. "The rabbinate had placed itself in the pillory, and undermined its own authority" (Graetz).[9] The foundations of Judaism were being shaken from within at the very moment it was thrust into a difficult confrontation with the outside world.

A mere generation later, when the Rabbi of Altona menacingly pointed to the *shofar* that was to sound the ban on his adversary Salomon Maimon, and asked: "Do you know what this is?", the latter replied coolly: "A he-goat's horn." Discontented individuals began to venture into foreign pastures, many who looked for a new leadership found mentors in Mendelssohn, Wessely, Friedländer, and other Maskilim. Prior to the Emden–Eibeschütz controversy the Jewish world had still been largely unified and whole – the communities of Metz and Brody, Cracow and Altona, Prague and London, kept up close contact, the Council of the Four Lands commanded respect in all Ashkenazi communities; now, however, it began to disintegrate and the rift between the old and the new became irreparable.

4   The Emancipation culture believed in the individual's right to freedom. It held that *the state was founded upon a social contract between individuals for their security, well-being and happiness.* The individual who chooses to realize his right to be free, fulfills the purpose of Creation. The theories on natural rights and on the sanctity of private property justified the right to freedom and indicated its scope. The state's sole purpose was to safeguard the individual's natural rights, his person, his opinions, his attainments, and everything which he had acquired through work and enterprise. "New" and "nature" became the most popular pair of concepts in a culture which sought to remake the "natural" (i.e. the rational) conditions of personal and societal life. The old regime, weighted with historical irrationality, could no longer contend with the demands of natural reason and the exigencies of social morality. Man's reason was free to legislate laws for the state, and reason's first undertaking was the abolition of the positivistic-historical law which bestowed privileges and special benefits upon certain classes and groups and decreed subjugation, persecution, and misfortune for others. Liberation from the yoke of exile was connate with the notion of liberation from the yoke of Torah and Jewish communal unity. The Jewish individual awoke to this new spirit later than his Gentile counterpart, but perhaps because of this tardy awakening, he embraced it with added vigor. Hence the call for tolerance in matters of religion, for separation between church and state, and authority for minimal organized religion. Members of this culture witnessed an explosion of new Jewish individualism in a plethora of extraordinary and variegated talents deployed in all fields of endeavor newly reopened to Jews; the outburst of Jewish creativity in a brief period of one or two generations was truly amazing.

5   *The secularization of life* stemmed from the view that Holy Scriptures were no longer the human–divine encounter wherein solace, guidance, and eternal salvation were to be sought. The Enlightenment marks the beginning of textual criticism, and the end of faith in divine non-recurring revelation, in miracles, providence, and traditional reward and punishment. The new rationalism is pragmatic and utilitarian. An effort is made, however, to salvage remnants of the ancestral heritage, in which grandeur and value, wisdom and glory are found. Neglected and forgotten cultural treasures with which to restore confidence in the value of Jewish existence, past and present, are unearthed. The Science of Judaism in Germany grew out of the belief that by uncovering the treasures of the past, Jewish prestige and status among the Gentiles would be enhanced. Finally, the belief crystallized that Judaism's "true essence" was fundamentally in harmony with the modern spirit of reason and freedom. This same belief, however, also led to escapism, or to complete repudiation, wherever it failed to

produce results. We shall elaborate later in this chapter on the hope and danger presented by the Science of Judaism and on its controversial appraisal.

6   *The Emancipation culture challenged its two still very influential antecedent cultures*, the Rabbinic and Mystic cultures, as well as Ḥassidism, Mysticism's offshoot. Its adherents sought liberation from the Torah's yoke, from the entire legal and spiritual "particularism" of the ghetto. The Talmud was cast aside and the Prophets and the Psalms came into great favor. The community's jurisdiction was equated with that of a sectarian church, consequently unfit to administer the authority that was the rightful charge of secular government. The suppression of that autonomous individuation, which the Rabbinic culture had so cherished, would effect the free and happy spiritual unveiling of the Jews' singular qualities and would dramatize their religious and ethical mission. The Emancipation culture reverberates with caustic polemics against Rabbis and Kabbalists immersed in a world of visions, miracles, and idle superstition. The shift in opinions and in life-styles was swift and radical indeed. A collective and historic religion to which one was born and in which one died, became a matter for individual choice.

In his book *Ritualgesetze der Juden*, Mendelssohn advocated that the Jewish "colony" in Prussia adhere to its constitution but that its jurisdiction be limited to monetary matters.[10] At the same time Mendelssohn also suggested that Jews could bring their suits before non-Jewish courts, provided such courts were familiar with Jewish law. This suggestion, together with the abolition of excommunication by ban, forced the first crack in the community's autonomy, a crack that widened as time went on. Faith became a matter for the heart, and the authority of the organized Jewish community was abrogated. Many preferred the "religion of the heart," private worship, or the "natural truths," ethics based on reason, over the observance of practical precepts and community laws. They attacked the community's leadership and power structure. In vain the Rabbis protested that the Torah forbade innovation. The Maskilim echoed the widespread eighteenth-century accusations against the corruption of venal priests who rob the poor and squander their possessions. Even the Rabbinic homiletic literature of the time depicted Rabbis with unprecedented harshness: as rapacious and dishonest, toadying to the rich, and immersed in vanities. The Maskilim were eager to cast off the yoke of clerics and clerical doctrine. Incapable of nurturing deep spiritual needs, tradition withered and crumbled from within. Not many years would elapse before Heine expressed the harsh truth in his wonted biting sarcasm: "We no longer have the strength to wear a beard, to fast, to hate, and out of hate to be forgiving."[11] Judaism, many felt, was trapped in a dark impasse, while "Europe" was a spacious and luminous world.

7 *The survival of the Jews as a separate nation was called into question.* There was wonder over the enigma of the Jewish past, its miraculous surmounting of numerous and bitter foes, its durability, and, especially, the meaning of its election. This wonder prompted an increased interest in Jewish history, and in the uses it might hold for the present. The Emancipation culture began to evaluate Judaism in comparison with other nations: what was its nature and what was the nature of religion in general? Was religion a private matter between man and God? Like all Jewish cultures, the Emancipation culture stood in the shadow of the threefold tension we described in chapter 5, but being itself so radical a departure from all previous cultures, it experienced these tensions with particular acuteness. Its most keenly felt pain was the tension between "universalism" and "particularism," and its greatest effort was directed at finding a counterbalance for Judaism's "particularistic" pole. The yearning for equal rights and for internal democratization and liberalization brought it into conflict not only with the outside world, but also with the established communal order and its traditional leadership, thus exacerbating the second tension, the one between the individual and the organized community. The tension between different elements of a culture, the third in our count, also heightened progressively, as witnessed by the growing indifference to the Land of Israel and the Hebrew language. At first Hebrew was still used in scholarship and in poetry, and initially it appeared that writers of this culture, like their successors in modern Hebrew literature, might feel the urgency of developing a Hebrew culture in all spheres of creativity, rather than drawing exclusively upon non-Jewish sources, be they as powerful as Shakespeare, or as sublime as Goethe and Schiller, so deeply revered by German Jews. But after a generation or two these writers ceased to develop artistic creativity in Hebrew and the language was reduced to a "sacral" tongue, a fact which undoubtedly contributed to the weakening of this culture. We can summarize, then, by saying that not only did the tensions become more acute as their equilibration was more radically disturbed, but, as we saw above in connection with the Jews of Bordeaux, and as we shall see again in the following pages, the very existence of the Jewish people as a unified and historically continuous entity was seriously questioned.

The Emancipation culture was a shaken and bewildered culture pondering its course in perplexity. Confused and restless, anxious and hopeful, young Jews swung from fanatic orthodoxy to radical heresy. Jewish liberal rationalism of the eighteenth and nineteenth centuries by no means resembled the religious rationalism of the Middle Ages, which contemplated the wonders of the world and the secret of divine providence. Liberal rationalism critically questioned the reasons for the commandments, and viewed the state as an expediter of the new "Messianic" world-order. Thus viewed, it was not unreasonable for the Second Rabbinical Assembly in Frankfurt to permit Jewish civil servants to work on the Sabbath, and even to endow this work with the aura of a *mitzvah*. Judaism's practical precepts (the "ritus") were increasingly discarded in favor of its moral code (the "ethos").[12] The ramparts protecting traditional Judaism were dismantled, because the "essence of Judaism" was henceforward defined on the basis of different assumptions than those guiding previous Jewish cultures. This essence, too, was subject to conflicting valuations, and its authority to discipline individuals and unify the community was much reduced.

8   *Conditions conducive to assimilation were thus created*, assimilation being, as we have suggested, an ideological transformation in opinions and beliefs, in symbols and concepts, in desires and feelings, encapsulating the individual's experiences in his interpersonal and intercommunal relationships. The first transformation was the adoption of an ideology that censured and discredited Judaism while glorifyng non-Jewish cultures, attributing inferiority to the former and superiority to the latter with a host of biological, ethical, religious, or political arguments. The second change drew upon the individual's own experiences, on his personal, real preferences, rather than on any general and abstract preference – a live certainty that "based on *my* experiences" with Gentiles and Jews, the former are superior. These changes were both conditioned and rationalized by Jewish inferiority, which deepened during the Emancipation culture; they were also the source of an entirely new kind of self-deprecating Jewish humor that poked fun at the Jew who apes the Gentiles, yet knows in his heart that he equals and perhaps surpasses them.

The inevitable innovations resulting from historical processes did not content the Maskilim; they consciously and deliberately strove for a radical regeneration and remolding of the nation. Haskalah literature talks endlessly of the need for total reform, in conduct and usages, in manners and opinions; it preaches a return to "productive" labor and artisanry, and occasionally luxuriates in feelings of inferiority and self-abasement *vis-à-vis* the Christian world. It finds little value in the Rabbinic culture; the new age must now rectify what countless Jewish generations have corrupted and neglected in the "three centuries of darkness" since the Spanish expulsion. Utilitarian values are favored over piety; a "practical philosophy" for the attainment of a pleasant life and a knowledge of reality is prized more than "idle" contemplation of the supernatural. Adoption of Gentile culture is deemed a requisite condition for improvement in civic status and life in general.

Lazarus Bendavid's (1762–1832) modestly titled book *Etwas Zur Charakteristik der Juden* is typical of his generation's stinging indictment of traditional Judaism. The main question he poses is: "What must Jews do in order to prepare themselves for civic reform?" The reply to this question is entailed in a comprehensive discussion of two other questions: "What are the fundamental defects of the Jewish nation? How did they occur and how are they peculiar to this nation?"[13] Although Jews in our times, the author explains, are radically different in character from their ancestors in the Land of Israel, so much so that you might even think they were an entirely different people, the root of their defects can be traced to the ancient Hebraic constitution. The renewal of learning in the mid-eighteenth century signals to the author the first hint of improvement in the situation. The prestige attained by Mendelssohn among Christians and Jews clearly demonstrated that it was possible for Judaism to accommodate science and that it was an added grace, and a useful one at that, for a Jew to earn the esteem of Christians. Above all, the author abhors Jewish separateness, "Jewish particularism" and believes, like so many other Maskilim, that equal rights will liberate Jews from the strictures of their spiritual ghetto. It should be noted, however, that many of Bendavid's contemporary Jewish intellectuals who shared his vision of full acculturation, did not embrace the two tenets of assimilation described above, and rejected some of Bendavid's assumptions as too radical.

The Emancipation culture today

In time the sense of inferiority abated and even assimilation did not invariably lead to complete secession from Judaism. The tensions were balanced. We need hardly repeat that the "Judaism" that so antagonized the Emancipation culture was not of the Biblical or Poetic-Philosophic variety (of these, on the contrary, the Maskilim were most proud) but Talmudism and Rabbinism, Kabbalah and Hassidism. It should, however, be noted that opinions on the Talmud itself were not uniformly critical: Jost, for example, found many faults with the Talmud, whereas Graetz wrote about it in glowing terms. Both condemned the Rabbinic rule and reviled Kabbalah and Hassidism. As time went on tolerance increased. In the beginning, of course, a wide chasm separated the Orthodox and Liberals. But eventually the Emancipation culture penetrated the Orthodox camp, while among Liberals faith in Israel's unique destiny never quite disappeared. At the end of the Emancipation period in Europe, shortly before the Holocaust, Jewish thinkers like Hermann Cohen, Leo Baeck, Franz Rosenzweig, and Martin Buber were attempting to prove that Judaism alone was an absolutely true faith. Thus, the Emancipation culture which had feebly started its course in subversion, abrogation, and self-deprecation, ended in pre-Holocaust Europe in a mighty rush of creative and preservationary endeavors. It also changed its attitude toward the establishment of a national home in the Land of Israel.

We summarize here by emphasizing that the Emancipation culture marks a change in Jewish attitudes in the eight features we have listed, namely in respect of the country of residence and the Land of Israel, the Messianic expectation, Jewish self-governance, the rights of the individual in the community, the authority of Torah and its precepts, religious leadership, Jewish destiny, and, lastly, non-Jews. This culture, so briefly characterized and illustrated here, extends over wide expanses of space and time. It encompasses today that large, influential, and unprecedentedly successful American diaspora, where the age-old yearning of past generations for Jewish pride, freedom, and prosperity, aided by the amazing advances of modern science and technology, finally brought forth this new, affluent culture. One may say that what Messianic, combative Judaism had sowed, the Jews of the Emancipation, American Jews in particular, have cultivated and reaped.[14] The dominance of this culture did not end with the Holocaust and with the creation of the National-Israeli culture. On the contrary, like the National-Israeli culture, in spite of the Holocaust and as its antidote, it has gained strength in the past generation.

In Jewish life today no single culture predominates; even though the diasporas have harnessed themselves to the Zionist endeavor, they belong to the Emancipation culture. This culture is a strong rival of the National-Israeli culture. Voluntary ʿaliyah to Israel from Emancipation countries is so difficult because it signifies much more than immigration from one country to another; it requires the substitution of one culture, both general and Jewish, for another. This substitution of cultures rendered the absorption of western European Jews in Eretz Israel difficult even in the days of the British Mandate. The complaints of the young National-Israeli culture about its older sister of the Emancipation, throw much light on the nature of the rivalry between the two cultures, on their development and interdependence.

The complaint about the Science of Judaism

An examination of how the Emancipation culture was evaluated by the National-Israeli culture provides an illuminating example of typical misunderstandings between Jewish cultures. In the system I have advanced here each culture relates to other cultures, especially to its immediate predecessor, both by identification and conflict, with respect, even devotion, and in outspoken opposition. The following example illustrates the polemical confrontation between the generation of the "national renaissance," the creators of the National-Israeli culture, and the founders of the Science of Judaism, and the obvious disregard, I believe, of the former for the true intentions of the latter.

The Emancipation and Reform movements were associated with the movement for the advancement of the Science of Judaism, or Jewish Science, a scientific discipline that undertook to research Judaism's nature and history. In 1819 a number of young men of great scientific talents founded the Society for the Culture and the Science of the Jews (Verein für Kultur und Wissenschaft der Juden). Its president was Eduard Gans, who later acquired fame as a great jurist, and its members counted Yom-Tov Lippmann (Leopold) Zunz, Isaak Markus Jost, Lazarus Bendavid, and the young Heine. The time was one of renewed oppressions and even pogroms in Germany after the brief Napoleonic interlude of Jewish liberation; these fresh insults aggravated the desolation within. Jewish youths felt trapped in a great quandary, many surrendered to despair. The Society's founders set out to cultivate a new generation of Jewish talent, whose labors would rejuvenate Judaism and thereby enhance the civic status of Jews. Armed with newly acquired research methods, these young intellectuals endeavored to illuminate and justify Israel's past on rational grounds, in line with the sensibilities of the present, to unveil its splendor to the educated of all nations, and, above all, to prove that Judaism had not ossified over the ages but, on the contrary, that it had retained vitality both to produce and to absorb, to draw renewed vigor from its own sources and to benefit from the spiritual movements of the new era. Another goal of the Society was to develop historical consciousness, an understanding of the flow of time which traditional Judaism, so long confined within itself and rotating on the axis of its own immutable values, had always appeared to defy. Its program spoke also of a structural change in Jewish professions, of educating the youth to undertake labor and agriculture.

The Society was short-lived. It disbanded in 1824 with meager accomplishments to its credit: some verbal pronouncements and three issues of an annual journal edited by Zunz. Gans himself turned apostate, as did a number of other members, Heine among them. Yet the Society had mapped out a course for the future. Its members had introduced Judaism to the spirit of scientific criticism, and had demonstrated both its great intrinsic merits and its contributions to European culture. For some of these young men smitten by the dazzle of European culture, there seemed to be little that the Science of Judaism could offer to help them persevere in their tenuous Judaism. Some despaired of the possibility of national survival in exile and abandoned the covenant entirely. In thus doing they clearly demonstrated that a science stripped of affinity to a living and life-desirous peoplehood could not by itself keep Judaism alive. With insight and talent, these young scholars plunged into Israel's past, but, in the end, with no more than a tepid desire for a Jewish future, they succumbed. However, they are not to be taken as typical of the majority of their contemporaries who adhered to the guiding ideas proclaimed by the initiators of the Science of Judaism.

The ideology of west European Jewish Science aroused harsh criticism in the twentieth century, mainly on the grounds that it was fundamentally destructive, that its aim was to ravish and scuttle the living nation. Jost,

Zunz, Geiger, Steinschneider, and others were accused of being deliberate "embalmers and undertakers." It was argued that the scholars of Jewish Science, in the guise of scientific objectivity, of historiography for its own sake, of a "pure" science of Judaism that could take its place among other academic disciplines, and be equally subject to methodical investigation, strove to relegate the entire material and spiritual Jewish heritage to the exclusive realm of the past, with no view to the future. These scholars, it was claimed, merely wished to prove that traditional Judaism had nothing to offer to serious seekers of spiritual life, no message that could nurture the present and the future. Aḥad ha-ʿam energetically articulated this charge:

> "Jewish Science" owes its being not to any nationalist impulse . . ., but to other impulses . . . which were calculated for the most part to sever the national bond not merely between past and present, but even as between the scattered groups into which the nation is divided today . . . "Jewish Science" became nothing more than a memorial tablet to our dead spiritual activity. But as regards our own hearts, our need for an internal revivifying national ideal – how much of this could the Science of Judaism fulfil?[15]

Were these complaints about the Science of Judaism warranted? In truth, its founders had frequently claimed that the wellsprings of Jewish creativity had already been depleted in the Rabbinic tradition some generations earlier. It was now time, they said, for a serious appraisal of Judaism's cultural achievements throughout the ages. They felt that much in this summation was cause for pride, and that the ancient heritage of this glorious culture (prior to the depletion of its creative powers in the Rabbinic tradition) would serve contemporary Jews in their struggle for full emancipation; the Science of Judaism too would thereby find itself serving the needs of the living. Zunz expressed this slogan plainly: ethical and social equality for Jews would ensue from the equality won by the Science of Judaism in the scientific world.[16] It was, of course, a claim quite remote from any historical realism, but at least it demonstrates that the creators of the Science of Judaism were by no means wizened undertakers, bent on rolling the stone over Judaism's grave.

Two tendencies were intertwined in the Science of Judaism and were viewed as mutually interdependent: the idea of "pure" science (science "for its own sake"), and the furtherance of the social-political struggle. Perhaps the movement's early scholars inclined to overemphasize the need for a pure scientific method in the study of Judaism's treasures. Their works leave no doubt, however, that they also believed wholeheartedly that science was not necessarily detached from the requirements of life. German historicism in its first mighty awakening (Romanticism) similarly advocated science for its own sake, yet served nonetheless a variety of German national needs.

Jewish scholars were judged with severity for this same offense. Even in our era they have been accused of making use of their science for extra-scientific ends, hence of hypocrisy, deliberate deception, and at best, unintentional contradictions. That they might in their own way, honestly and without internal inconsistencies, have embraced the twin purpose of summing up the past while preparing for the future, seemed suspect. Scholem detected in the Science of Judaism from its very beginning "a peculiar dialectical relationship," but failed to realize that this tension was present in each of Israel's cultures, as we have explained. I shall return later to Scholem's argument.

It is illuminating to examine here for a moment a remarkable document from the early period of the Science of Judaism. In 1822 Immanuel Wolf opened the *Zeitschrift für die Wissenschaft des Judentums*, edited by Zunz, with a programmatic essay on the need for studying "the idea of Judaism" in human history. Wolf was undoubtedly influenced by the German idealist philosophers – Kant, Fichte, and Hegel. His ideas are noteworthy for their lucid conception of Jewish Science as a scientific-public movement for the rejuvenation of Judaism. For Wolf "the idea of Judaism," i.e. the chief contribution of Jewish civilization to humanity's spiritual treasurehouse, was not an abstract principle, but a comprehensive world view, upon which Jews could build a new life in keeping with the spirit of the times and the changed social conditions in Europe. What precisely is this idea, according to the founders? "It is the idea of unlimited unity in the all. It is contained in the one word YHVH which signifies indeed the living unity of all being in eternity, the absolute being outside defined time and place. This concept was revealed to the Jewish people,"[17] whose historical role it is to preserve and refine this great idea. So important a factor in man's spiritual development is worthy of scientific investigation, and it is this study of Judaism's manifestations which the Science of Judaism sets out to do in an independent scientific discipline. Judaism as it had been hitherto studied by Christian scholars was merely an auxiliary branch of Christian theology. It need hardly be said that Christian studies had done little to enhance Jewish prestige and thereby to expedite Jewish emancipation. The nation would automatically rise in the esteem of the world when the glory of its culture was revealed in all its magnificence. The emphasis on pure science contained a sting directed at anti-Semitic Christian theology, but it was also aimed at the Rabbinic tradition.

Why did these and similar statements arouse in our Zionist and activist contemporaries, members of the new National-Israeli culture, the impression of deliberate deception, unintentional inconsistencies or a dubious "peculiar dialectical relationship?" Why did Bialik accuse the founders of the Science of Judaism of being "possessed by a frenzy of rights" and of chasing "after those miserable rights."[18] Those rights, in truth, were by no means so paltry; they were, on the contrary, an important requisite in the eyes of all those who fought for emancipation. A student of our theory of cultures will find this polemic illustrative of how a culture relates to its predecessor in the dialectics of destruction and creation; frequently, as we have seen, it relates in incomprehension and disaffection.

It is by no means my intention entirely to vindicate all the objectives and deeds of nineteenth-century west European Science of Judaism. I wish only to point out that the defects its critics faulted it with were in principle present in each one of the preceding cultures. There is no denying that the movement's apologetic stance often tended to exaggeration. But here, too, I believe it is unfair to charge these scholars with fraud or deceptive inconsistency; certainly, they ought not to be held to stricter standards than those we apply to ourselves. What harm was there in looking to science for support of a community's struggle for equal civic rights, provided this science did not willfully seek to distort records and treasured testimonies of the past, or pervert opinions and meanings of historical situations? A pragmatic approach is not necessarily condemned by the theory of consciousness in modern historical science. It is today far more reflective and skeptical than were those early proponents of total objectivity, the champions of facts "as they were." We recognize that personal inclination, economic dependence, socio-political role and status, the entire social stratification, are all influences which find reflection in the opinions of scholars. Dubnov, for example, rightly reproaches Jost, one of the early and bold forces in Jewish historical research, for his "prejudices": "Jost wrote the general history of Jews on the basis of old sources . . . and he himself lacked the necessary critical sense. In line with the ideas of his time – a moderate assimilationist and reformist, a mediocre publicist and apologist – he inserted these ideas into his historical works."[19] The result of Jost's rationalist tendencies was a condemnation of the Judaean Zealots' revolt against Rome and the "process of isolation during the era of the Talmud;" Aggadah and Midrash he considered as "trivial yarns," and "he tries to extenuate the persecutions of Jews and their martyrdom, and praises 'wise and gracious monarchs' for the slightest alleviation of the Jews' plight." Dubnov's complaints of Jost are all close to the truth and are by no means exhaustive. "Prejudices," personal inclinations and every sort of deliberate or unintentional "bias" can easily be found in all those who engaged in the Science of Judaism. But today our knowledge of the social sciences and of conditions of consciousness informs us that in this the Science of Judaism was not unique. Dubnov himself was not free of "biases" and "prejudices." Personal perspective does not except the greatest of the great, even when they honestly believe that they merely decipher the times according to events as they "really happened." On the contrary, the more the naïvety of the historian is inclined to withhold his intentions, the more manifest is his ideology. Even the most sophisticated historians betray their ideology between their lines. Meticulous, complete, and impartial accuracy is a worthy goal for every researcher. Yet all scientific knowledge is animated by a living purpose, and not always does the latter necessarily shortchange the former.

In a melancholy essay on the Science of Judaism in the nineteenth century and during the first generation of the Hebrew University, Scholem charges these scholars with "very provoking" sins:[20] they excised from Judaism its irrational sting and demonic ardor; Jewish history, a force so potent and vital, they minimized and dwarfed.[21] They buried the essential, emphasized the immaterial, and trapped themselves in three fundamental contradictions. By theologizing and spiritualizing history they falsified the past and obscured Judaism's schismatic and mutinous elements. They dissociated Jewish history from its real foundations and indulged in much sentimental lamentation (a charge reminiscent of Baron's complaint on the "lachrymose" historiography propounded by the founders of the Science of Judaism). Self-justification with an apologetic eye to what the Gentiles might think has distorted our history and disfigured its glory. In brief, these nineteenth-century scholars created a "bourgeois" image of Jewish history, in line with corollary prejudices of liberal historiography at the time. They were, says Scholem, "giants in learning and dwarfs in thought, and apparently this is what the generation wanted."

It is difficult to determine what a generation wants, but it is easy to see that the Romantic in Scholem is displeased by Biedermeier bourgeois "dwarfs." With considerable emotionalism and no small measure of arrogance he heaps reproach on these scholars, belittling their achievements and presenting them as contemptible mediocrities. Scholem yearns no doubt for towering geniuses, for bold adventurers whose turbulent hearts seethe with the dialectic tension between the will to destroy and the will to preserve. In fact, the author's position in this matter is essentially one of confusion, because disapprobation warps a considered historical assessment, which ought to know that value-judgments are a trap. It is, however, this very historian, who in his own area of investigation, Mysticism and its offshoots, neared the truth when he recognized that Jewish history was a drama of conflicts and affiliations between individuated cultures. Scholem argued that the Mystics sought new inner meanings for outdated and jejune concepts, a new understanding of Judaism into which they could introduce their own religious world. In my opinion, this was precisely the aim of each one of Israel's cultures. The Science of Judaism embodied the spirit of one of these cultures according to its special conditions and in the language of its own symbols.

Was the Science of Judaism merely retrospective?

Let us resume our investigation of the Science of Judaism as it reflected the tendencies characterizing the Emancipation culture. Scholem's sad musings deplored not only the Science of Judaism in Germany but also, as he put it, the "truncating of the dream" envisioned by those young scholars who later took part in creating the National-Israeli culture, the dream of a truly original, bold and totally different Science of Judaism. This disappointment led Scholem to inquire into the origins of the Science of Judaism wherein he thought to discover a sort of original sin, a fault so grievous that to this day it continues to taint Jewish scholarship. This sin consists of those three contradictions alluded to earlier in the dialectic tension, namely between declarations about an objective, pure science and the undeniably political role this science played in reality; between Romantics in program and Maskilim, captives of a dry and sober rationalism, in practice, i.e. men supposedly committed to the glorification of the splendorous past[22] but, in fact, quite alien to it; and, thirdly, between the preservatory and demolitionary impulses. Due to the impersonal and sober nature of objective investigation, Scholem maintains, the destructive role of science could become constructive and liberating by discovering and unleashing forces of reality, or values, thereby unintentionally transforming remnants of the past, for example, mystical trends, into symbols of extraordinary vigor in Jewish life. Unfortunately, in the case of Jewish Science the historical consciousness of its scholars obstructed the positive utilization implied in their system, and their Romantic science appears rather like a ghastly funereal rite.[23] To this day, complains Scholem, the Science of Judaism has failed to extricate itself from these contradictions.

A number of these charges were made in the same year (1945) by Nathan Rotenstreich. Couched in philosophical terminology, and without Scholem's admonition and elegy, Rotenstreich's critique likewise draws attention to the contradiction between a desire for scientific objectivity and a science with extra-scientific objectives, as, for example, the goal of laying the groundwork for Jewish emancipation. In essence Rotenstreich too claims that the Science of Judaism severed the living tie to the Judaism of the past, relegating the latter to reflective contemplation. This movement was not an endeavor to "interpret the past" creatively, but to "understand" it.[24] Rotenstreich, it seems to me, repeated Scholem's error in his assessment of nineteenth-century Science of Judaism and its later practitioners. Classical Science of Judaism was by no means merely a reflective discipline engaged in contemplating the past with no thought of its future. It had, of course, no desire to continue the tradition of the *immediate* past, i.e. the Rabbinic responsa literature in the style of Moses Sofer (the Ḥatam Sofer, 1762–1839). It adopted an "attitude of detachment" toward the Rabbinic heritage and, like every scientific inquiry, wished to consider the past without naïve and intuitive empathy, as befits an attitude implanted in critical-scientific consciousness itself. But there is no denying that these scholars drew on the Biblical and the Poetic-Philosophic cultures, which they greatly admired, and even on the Talmudic culture. Not one of these scholars seriously doubted that the "eternal" ideas of Jewish history were capable of fructifying the present. The detachment from "Jewish creativity," if by this Rotenstreich means the Rabbinic or Mystical cultures, was for the purpose of change and rejuvenation.

In fact, the Science of Judaism dealt both with the nation's historical existence and with its ideas and doctrines. While it can perhaps be contended that its horizons in the nineteenth century were still narrowly limited, and that its accomplishments did not match its expectations, there is no denying that it constituted a major thrust toward the expansion of Judaism's vision and, aided by the new historical awareness, the creation of an entire Jewish culture. How can one label as "undertakers of the past" scholars who, like Zunz, could declare with so much emotion:

Every preacher, rabbi, instructor or orator will know how to find the word of God in the Bible or the Haggadah and will understand how to extract good gold from old and new deeds, to discover in the present the true destiny . . . Then will God's spirit return to dwell in your academies, O daughter of Zion, and His voice will again be heard in living speech, calling to action, full of enthusiasm, to establish foundations in Israel.[25]

Indeed, "to extract good gold" and to "establish foundations in Israel," that was the goal. In the book's introduction Zunz deplored the social and political discrimination of Jews and largely attributed it to Gentile ignorance of Judaism. Gentiles were still gleaning their knowledge of Jews from books by seventeenth-century authorities like the anti-Semite Eisenmenger, or Schudt and Buxtorf, and from sources of even lesser credibility. Melioration of the Jewish condition, said Zunz, depended in no small measure upon the dissemination of accurate information about the Jewish people. Do statements of such commitment and ardor justly merit the spleen of Aḥad ha-ʿam and his successors?

Inspired by the impetus animating the movement's pioneers, many young scholars began to delve into Jewish literature and history. The Science of Judaism branched into sub-disciplines, each producing its own experts. Important critical works began to appear on the Bible, the Midrashim, the Talmud, on poetry, ethics, doctrine, and history. Scholars roamed the world in quest of books and manuscripts; in the course of this endeavor many important records were rescued from oblivion. The Jewish people seemed driven to make up in a short time for all that it had neglected for hundreds of years. The horizons widened and the appraisal of the past changed.

The generation of founders, Yom-Tov Lippmann (Leopold) Zunz (1794–

1886), Salomon Judah Rapoport (1794–1867), Zacharias Frankel (1801–75), Abraham Geiger (1810–74), Isaak Markus Jost (1793–1860), Samuel David Luzzatto (1800–65), and Naḥman Krochmal (1785–1840), whose writings have been recognized as seminal and classic works, was succeeded by a host of fine scholars each of whom broke new ground in his chosen discipline. In history it was Heinrich Graetz, Moses Güdemann, and David Kaufmann; in the history of Jewish thought, Salomon Munk, Jacob Guttmann, the latter's son Julius Isaak Guttmann, and Manuel Joel. In Talmudic literature, Israel Lewy wrote on the redactorship of the Mishnah and the Talmud, Arye Schwarz on Talmudic logic (the thirteen hermeneutic rules of interpretations we mentioned in chapter 2), Wilhelm Bacher on Talmudic and Midrashic ʾaggadah. Alexander Kohut gained fame for his *Aruch ha-shalem*, a major contribution to Talmudic lexicography; Moses S. Zuckermandel wrote on the *Tosefta*, Zvi Hirsch Chajes on the Oral Law, Saul Horowitz on the Midrash. Important contributions were made by Yeḥiel Michael ha-Cohen Guttmann, A. Buechler, S. Krauss, A. Marmorstein, and others. Many researched the Bible and the *targumim*, the Hebrew language, and Hellenistic literature. The Science of Judaism numbered so many scholars in varying locations and times that we should not be surprised at a considerable diversity in their views. They moved in different directions and currents.[26]

Samson Raphael Hirsch (1808–88) introduced the neo-Orthodox current not only into German Jewish communities but also to the Science of Judaism. For a long time the Rabbinical Seminary in Breslau (the pioneer of the Historical School) founded by Zacharias Frankel was the sole institution for training Rabbis in Germany. In time an important research center arose at the Reform-oriented Higher Institute for Jewish Science in Berlin, and later a neo-Orthodox Rabbinic Seminary was founded by Rabbi E. Hildesheimer. Some of these scholars undeniably had an "archeological" or, in Nietzsche's phrase, an "antiquarian" penchant, a tendency to reduce the Science of Judaism to a "science of antiquities" disassociated from the Jewish people of the present and from its aspirations for the future. But this direction could be found not only in western Europe. When Isaac Baer Levinsohn (the Ribal, 1788–1860), today considered the first and foremost Haskalah writer in eastern Europe, remonstrated that the Science of Judaism ignored the Hebrew language despite the importance of language as the paramount characteristic of a nation, he too had no intention of transforming Hebrew into a spoken language; he merely wished that more scholars would devote their attention to its historical foundations, styles, and grammar.[27] The truth is that Scholem's plaint had already been voiced with nearly identical arguments in the previous century by the Orthodox and neo-Orthodox schools. The preacher and scholar Michael Sachs (1808–64), for example, charged that the Science of Judaism, whose pretense it was to represent the spirit of the present, had, in reality, banished from the present all spirit.

There was, then, no single ideological stream within the Science of Judaism in western Europe which attained sufficient dominance to reduce the movement to a science of the past bereft of relevance to the aspirations of the living. The Science of Judaism may have imitated other scientific disciplines in vaunting the autonomy of scientific rigor, its meticulous exactitude, its freedom from bias and from digression into issues that lay outside the ambit of its study. Hence the appearance of detachment from the roots. Steinschneider, upon whom Scholem heaped his harsh critique, wished to remove the study of Judaism from Rabbinical seminaries, because he believed that the study of Israel's culture should not be a profession restricted to Jewish schools but an integral part of the humanities and the social sciences, like the Graeco-Roman culture, a discipline for university scholars, not the occupation of "Jewish theologians." For this reason he accepted no teaching position in any of the Rabbinical seminaries. He believed that national continuity and commonality, being a factor beyond the subject-matter directly under study, should be disregarded when researching the past. It is intriguing to note that Aḥad ha-ʿam invited this "destroyer" and "undertaker" to publish in his journal Ha-shiloaḥ.[28] Even Aḥad ha-ʿam occasionally had to resort to the Science of Judaism in order to dispel prevalent anti-Jewish prejudices. For similar reasons certain scholars wished to eliminate from the Science of Judaism the discussion on the essence or value of Judaism and to pare it to strict study of the past, or, as Jost said: "The time has arrived to cease the discussion on Judaism's value and commence the study of its body, its inception, and its development."

The originality of the Science of Judaism was indeed the idea that the religious orientation, as Rotenstreich explained, was no longer dissociated from the historical process and no longer independent of it. Admittedly, religion was no longer "independent" of the historical process, but only in a very restricted sense. This dissociation was the license arrogated by the Scientists of Judaism, led by Jost, Zunz, and Geiger, to build a new culture on the foundations of the old. However, the Science of Judaism never entered into the philosophic question regarding the relation between the verity of the idea itself and the process (the sum of functions and manifestations of that same idea), i.e. whether the historical process was merely a means of realizing the eternal (revealed) idea, or whether it was much more than this: the origin of the idea itself.

The foundations of historical awareness in the Emancipation culture: the quest for objectivity

The clarification of the problem of historical knowledge, its conditions and limits, touches on the very foundations of historical awareness in the Emancipation and National-Israeli cultures: in what way does the historical awareness of these two cultures differ from that of the cultures of traditional faith? This comparison requires a closer study of the historians of the Emancipation – the undertaking of this chapter – and of the National-Israeli cultures, in the following chapter. According to my conception, Simon Dubnov and Salo Baron are representative historians of the Emancipation culture. Dubnov advocated the naturalization of Jews in their countries of residence coupled with a measure of national autonomy. He viewed the Land of Israel as one of the possible, but not necessarily the most sizable, future centers for the Jewish people. Despite his prominent role in the national movement of east European Jewry, his entire ontology was both expressive and supportive of the Emancipation culture. This is all the more true of Salo Baron, whose basic approach to Judaism resembled Jost's, the pioneer of modern Jewish historiography, with the advantage that superior talent, modern investigative tools and nearly 100 years of added knowledge can provide. We shall speak more of Baron when we examine how he, and the entire Emancipation culture, were evaluated by Yitzhak Baer. If we may judge by the main trends emerging from Baron's collective scientific work, it appears that what Jost initiated in his generation, Baron has completed in ours.

What happened in the modern age to the five main preoccupations of traditional writers of history? How do modern historians deal with the workings of divine providence through miracles and wonders, the unity of the Jewish people and the Torah, the defense of those in positions of legal, religious, and social authority (legitimation of the so-called "chain of tradition"), the Messianic idea and the eschatological vision, and, finally, with that prefiguration, or preformation, of Jewish history through eternal ideas or spiritual forces inborn and branded in the Hebrew nation and in its history? What shape did these themes, so predominant in the previous cultures of traditional faith, assume in the writings of modern historians? Our answer must be brief, for an elaboration would require an entire book on the nature of modern Jewish historiography. We are dealing here only with a minuscule portion of its volume, and our main purposes here are to point out its novelty in comparison with antecedent cultures, to show the differences between the Emancipation and the National-Israeli cultures, and to draw attention to the grave errors that occur when the past is evaluated without a historical perspective, such as that offered by the theory of cultures. We shall examine to what degree modern historians identified with the five preoccupations of traditional Jewish historical awareness.

How did the Science of Judaism deal with God's wonders in the history of His chosen people? These modern historians doubtlessly sought to explain Jewish history with no recourse to miracles, wonders, and divine providence, but rather as the outcome of natural causes. They attempted to put historical science on the same footing as the "objective" physical sciences, so that each occurrence could be examined in the light of independent laws and forces by which it was governed: one law obtained for the history of Israel and the history of the world, as enjoined by objectivity. German historiographers like Niebuhr, Neander, and later Leopold von Ranke, who influenced the Science of Judaism, were themselves pious Christians (the first two were even very orthodox in their faith, Neander having abandoned Judaism for Protestantism when he was seventeen years old), yet they sought to base their investigations on "objective truth," not on religious tenets. All Jewish scholars followed suit in adopting this principle, as even a casual reading of their works will show, although, upon closer examination, considerable differences emerge in the extent of their faith in the workings of divine providence. Their primary conscious intention, however, was to discover in history the objective truth – the past as it was and the events as they had occurred. Deliberately or in ignorance, they disregarded the great quandary that preoccupied contemporary philosophy as to the possibilities and limitations of cognition, a dilemma which raised innumerable doubts and misgivings: was objective truth, free of interference from individual or collective prejudice, possible at all? What was the nature of objective cognition and what were its possibilities? Kant had proposed a solution to this complicated problem, but, for reasons that are beyond the scope of this discussion, his critical method was deflected to speculative uses which robbed its main thrust of vitality. Ignoring Kant's system, these historians maintained quite simply that history could be disclosed "as it was" and that objective truth could in fact be ascertained, provided reliable research tools were meticulously employed.

The assumptions underlying this theory are quite clear, and indeed for many generations before Kant's "Copernican revolution," they were considered self-evident. It was posited that the past and all that it entails exist independently as objects of cognition confronting the historian's consciousness. The events and deeds of the past are separate and distinct from the consciousness of their beholder. The investigation of records and witnesses enables the historian to know these objects as they existed. Moreover, for the purpose of the study, the historian is able to remove himself from all religious, political, social, and economic biases and can examine these objects without involvement of any kind, as though they were indeed outside or beyond him, enabling him to reflect them in his writing as in a burnished mirror.

A second important assumption insured that the multitudinous and diverse events of the past were linked to one another in a certain system of relationships, such as causality: events are by their very nature arranged in a certain order and form which the historian must and can uncover and describe accurately. Admittedly, history should be viewed as a system of human events and deeds operating in accordance with the laws of the natural and human order, but this internal structure, even if it is not the work of a divine providence, but rather entirely immanent, greatly aids the historian in executing his task faithfully. Thus, it is possible, according to these assumptions, for human wisdom and accumulated knowledge to uncover the objective truth ensconced in historical reality.

Today there can be no doubt that this theory and all its assumptions were in fact a dogmatic belief (in Kant's sense of the term dogmatism), a sort of naïve realism in the theory of cognition carried over into the domain of historical research. It is not difficult to understand how this theory came about, and why it gained such wide currency, in the nineteenth century. It challenged the traditional religious belief in divine intervention in history, but also railed against the latter's reincarnations in the philosophy of absolute idealism. Hegel's philosophy of history had interpreted historical phenomena as manifestations of an absolute spirit, a sort of mighty philosophical deity acting upon the nations, their leaders and their creations for a "higher purpose." For this reason, apparently, this naïve historical realism or historicism (in the general sense) set out to banish every theology or speculative philosophy from the realm of history. It sought to limit itself within the boundaries of human reason and experience. It was rationalist, empiricist, or positivist, according to the researcher's bent. Needless to say, this naïve historical realism, notwithstanding its vehement rejection of philosophical speculation, was itself impressed with the unmistakable stamp of a philosophy of history.[29]

One who was instrumental in disseminating this realistic theory, and exercised strong influence on Graetz and other Jewish historians was Leopold von Ranke, who aimed at the reconstruction of the past as it was and pretended to do so in his books, in explicit contradiction to Hegel and his idealistic philosophy, though not entirely free of his influence. Ranke averred that human history was a "revelation of the Deity," but in practice he treated this belief with the utmost caution. Nor did he believe that God's ways were as clearly perceptible to man as historical facts. In the history of human acts and institutions only the "finger of God" is revealed, a hint of God's workings, "a sacred hieroglyph." In the spirit of both Protestant piety and pantheistic philosophy, Ranke declared that history disclosed God's workings in the world, but that in fact these workings were a mystery, and that not more than their tip could be discovered by the historian, and this only through an objectivity sufficiently rigorous to satisfy believers and non-believers alike.[30]

Naïve realism, then, rashly announced that it was possible to know history "as it really was," and Jewish scholars paid no more heed than their German contemporaries to the intricacies of historical awareness and thinking. It was impossible for them not to have noticed at least some difficulties, since there was not one among them who had not been repeatedly charged with lack of objectivity in one matter or another.

Isaak Markus Jost, for example, considered his historical conception as "critical-scientific." Emulating the great French *philosophes*, Jost, a typical product of eighteenth-century enlightenment, sought to demolish with intellectual critique the strongholds of traditional faith. Personally, he may have believed in divine providence, but in his books providence is only glimpsed from afar; it does not intervene even in the most decisive historical events. Natural causes, such as geography, climate, and events in neighboring countries, are called upon to explain Jewish history, not miracles. Divine leadership made itself manifest in the laws of nature and the acts of men, not in direct teleological design. Jost, like later skeptical Maskilim, attempted to interpret Prophecy and Mystical visions in a rational or allegoric manner. He did not think the luminaries of Israel's past were God's emissaries, or, as Hegel imagined, emissaries of the spirit. It was not the individuals of an age who fired his imagination, but the culture of the entire group as it was reflected in its daily life and institutions. In the interest of objectivity Jost tried to limit value-judgments, and to provide facts as he found them in the sources, merely to describe and to recount. Geiger faulted him for this and regarded "the entire man with all his reservations and assertions about lack of tendency and principles, as merely foolish."[31] Graetz complained of Jost that he had removed Judaism's crown of glory and had treated it with the dullness of a petty bourgeois. And Dubnov, as we heard earlier, reproached Jost with a lack of critical sense and with favoring the assimilationists despite his avowed espousal of impartial research.[32]

Heinrich Graetz (1817–91) also wished to write history based on "general historical" laws, a "history freed of theology," as he announced in the introduction to volume 1 of his *magnum opus*. Yet he was still a strong adherent of the traditional belief in personal and general providence: there is reward in store for individual men, and there is judgment over nations. Transgressor nations are punished and doomed to extinction. Indeed history is the world's tribunal, as Hegel said. Not all of God's deeds are manifest, the meting of reward and punishment is not always self-evident, but there can be no doubt that the supreme Judge does not abandon the world to anarchy and mere accident. Graetz described the events of the Damascus blood libel (1840) as having begun in anguish and ended in salvation. Due punishment overtook the perpetrators and protagonists of that abominable libel.[33] A concise summary of this conception may be found in a letter to the Hebrew translator of his book, Saul Pinhas Rabinowitz (1845–1910): "I myself am convinced that God's hand has ordered the course of Jewish history, 'the hand of God has done all these'. But this hand must not always be presented as manifest, rather the historian should no more than refer to it allusively as the finger of God, just as the author of the Book of Esther presented the wonderful rescue without divine intervention."[34] Even when there is complete assurance that God's hand performed these deeds, one must not overemphasize this faith, because there are many skeptics and heretics who would take issue with it.

One of the latter was Simon Dubnov (1860–1941). By training, spiritual development, and environment he belonged to the group that fought for liberation from the "chains of tradition": the science of history must treat its subject – man, his acts, and his experiences – with objectivity, i.e. with rationality and universality. The Jewish people is indeed distinct in that it is more "historical" than other nations, for it had greater impact on human development, both in terms of its temporal duration and in terms of the geographic span within which it evolved and acted. It is "a people of the world" (am ʿolam). But it is not an "eternal" people in the popular sense of "the eternality of Israel," which is a theological and metaphysical concept. Dubnov summarized his overall conception thus: "This entity known as Judaism is nothing but the outcome of the nation's growth in its adjustment to conditions of life, which are indeed quite unique, but which are not beyond the bounds of general laws of history."[35]

Unity and continuity, sectarians and established authority

What happened to the idea of the oneness of the Jewish people and eternal validity of its Torah in the face of this sectarian secession from the chain of tradition, and how did the new historians approach the legitimation of Jewish leadership and the entire institutional establishment? The discussion that follows combines these two issues, the second and third in our count of five chief historiographic themes of the cultures of traditional faith.

Jost rejected the idea that the subject of all Jewish history was the oneness of the Jewish people or the continuity of its history and Torah. He believed that the Jewish people had changed over the ages, that modern Jewry was not ethnically identical with ancient Jewry. Secondly, during most of its history the Jewish people had not been an active subject but rather a passive object, absorbing the actions of the more powerful nations upon whom its fate depended and reacting to them. Thirdly, he argued, continuity could be claimed for Jewish history only if we think of it in terms of a religious church, because in the realm of religious-spiritual creativity it was less contingent upon external events and was largely confined to its own orbit. Jewish history as a whole, however, did not attest to continuity.

But even Jost was moved to marvel at the extraordinary longevity of Jewish existence and admitted on occasion that the miracle of this prolonged existence was an indication of special divine providence. His book *Allgemeine Geschichte des Israelitischen Volkes* (1832) opens with some enthusiastic remarks:

We view the Israelite people as historically unique. It grew from a family into a people, achieved statehood, succumbed to the change in its lot like all states, and its mighty structure finally collapsed, but it arose again from its ruins with renewed strength. It was not reduced to being a component of other peoples; although no longer playing a role in world events, it remained a vibrant image of times gone by. It saw states established, blossom and wither; it saw national constitutions change, heard nations called by new names; it accompanied people on their migrations from one part of the world to another and exchanged language and mode of thought with them . . . scattered in all directions, and yet, though dispersed everywhere, it always coalesced in times of tranquility, striving toward a primordial form which constitutes its inner essence.[36]

We shall return to this "inner essence" later, when we discuss the fifth issue in our count of Jewish historiographic themes. But here we must draw attention to the novelty of Jost's approach. He believes that following the destruction of the First Temple, a different nation came into being, the nation of the Jews. Jost continues to call them Israel, or Israelites, simply because a certain odium has clung to the term "Jews." Upon the return from the Babylonian exile this nation split in two: those who returned and settled in Jerusalem and Judaea, and the large remainder who did not respond to the Edict of Cyrus and preferred their new countries of abode in exile to their ancestral homeland. The latter supported the returnees with money and provisions, says Jost, but they themselves favored their new places of residence over the land of milk and honey.[37] The interlude of national sovereignty during the Hasmonean kingdom was a passing episode. The entire subsequent course of Jewish history invariably depended on the history of the nations with whom Jews came in contact. Wherever Jews were well received, they reciprocated by doing everything in their power to bolster the strength of the benevolent state. Jost made this fact a principle: "Where independent activity has ceased, there too history has ceased."[38] Jewish creative activity is evident only in the religious sphere, therefore Jewish history is the history of Judaism and its sects. Jost writes in a subdued, sober spirit, in a show of superb "objectivity": even in the days of the First Temple, he argues, the Jews were not a special people endowed with unique ideal qualities, but a people no different from its neighbors. The people did not adhere to the law of Moses, and when it set a king at its head it became a nation like all others. The destiny of chosenness envisioned by the Torah remained an intimation for the future. This is not to say, of course, that Jost was indifferent to the nation's sorrows and triumphs. Like many other Maskilim, he too was moved by the scandal of the Damascus blood libel to view the Jewish people in all its diasporas as one "community of fate." One should also keep in mind that he wrote in Hebrew, was in fact a champion of the Hebrew language, and for one year (1841) published a scholarly Hebrew monthly called *Zion*.

Jost believed that the Talmud, the Rabbinic culture, the writings of the Kabbalah and Ḥassidism had all imposed upon the Jewish people a rule of laws that separated it from the nations of the world. The Talmudic Sages and the Rabbis who "invented" laws were motivated by a lust for power. "Rabbinism" had brought Judaism untold suffering. However, Jost also had praise for the Mishnah: the purpose of its redactor, Rabbi Yehudah ha-Nassi, was to present his people with "a new homeland" which would fully compensate them for the loss of their physical land. He compared the Mishnah to a "fortified rampart," a fortress within whose walls the Jews of all the world could take cover and which they defended with money and life.[39] Heine, a poetic reader of the early publications of the new Jewish scholars, also spoke in this vein about the Torah as an "itinerant homeland" of the Jewish people. This idea of Jost's was reincarnated in the works of Graetz and Dubnov, and reappeared with Aḥad ha-ʿam in the form of "the instrument of exile": the instinct for national survival encased Israel in a religion which had evolved into an instrument of exile, a safeguard for the nation's survival once its natural political soil had slipped from under its feet.

Graetz viewed the Jewish people as one nation with an unbroken history. Israel's Torah is as one large river, a confluence of the streams of all the sciences and the arts. The history of the nation in the diasporas is the story of Sages and martyrs, creators, activists, and sufferers. This people has a double image:

One aspect would show humbled Judah with the wanderer's staff in his hand, the pilgrim's bundle on his back, his features grave, his glance turned heavenward; he is surrounded by the walls of a dungeon, the implements of martyrdom, and the red-hot branding iron. The other aspect is of the same figure, bearing the earnestness of the thinker upon his luminous brow, the mien of a scholar in the radiant features of his face; he is in a study filled with a huge library in all the languages of mankind and dealing with all branches of divine and human knowledge. The external history of this era is a *Leidengeschichte*, a history of suffering to a degree and over a length of time such as no other people has experienced. Its inner history is a comprehensive *Literaturgeschichte*, a literary history of religious knowledge, which yet remains open to all the currents of science, absorbing and assimilating them.[40]

Moreover, the Torah, the people of Israel, and the Holy Land are bound by a special magic-mystical tie. The people of Israel is the carrier of a pregnant seed for the future.

Opposed both to Graetz's spiritualization of Jewish history and to Jost's views, Simon Dubnov contended that despite the absence of land and sovereignty, Israel was an active agent in history, not only in the spiritual sphere, but also in the affairs of the nations with which it lived. Dubnov saw a substitute for statehood in Jewish autonomy, in the self-governance of communities in Jewish diasporas since the days of the Judaean kingdom, especially after the destruction.[41] Dubnov found the secret of this unified and continuous existence in the absolute injunction of early prophecy: "The sceptre shall not pass from Judah" (Gen. 49.10). During the ancient kingdom, this sceptre signified absolute power; in the diasporas it meant merely communal autonomy. Dubnov attempted to describe the "national entity, its origin, growth, and struggle for existence,"[42] and presented Israel's religion as the manifestation of its national life rather than as an independent historical force. According to the instrument of exile theory, Judaism's religious faith safeguarded the nation's existence and autonomy against enemies from within and from without.

It is interesting to note that in dealing with the issue of Jewish unity, both Graetz and Dubnov inclined to minimize the significance of dissident sects and currents in Israel's history. Graetz, who, like Yitzhak Baer later, contended that the entire history of Israel was a revelation of the idea of Judaism in different manifestations, believed that internal struggles and contradictions contributed to the refinement of the Jewish essence towards perpetual progress.

How so? Dissident sects and currents always stimulated opposition, but it was precisely the strength of the latter which drove Judaism to progressively refine itself from the dross which controverts and falsifies its essence. Sectarian dissensions stimulated spiritual progress: early Christianity, for example, forced Judaism to fight for its life, to bolster its foundations, thereby creating the Talmud wherein Judaism became incarnated in all the minutiae and details of practical precepts.[43] Thus the establishment of Christianity effected the renewal of Judaism.

Similarly, after the Talmudic culture had become ossified to the point where it neglected even the study of the Bible, the Karaite movement emerged and became a driving force in Jewish history. It injected a new spirit into Judaism and renewed interest in the Bible, but its hostility to the Talmud undermined its success. The currents which worked against ossification and paralysis brought Judaism to a refinement of its self-knowledge. Thus all those "subversives" (in Graetz's phrase) and heretics of the sixteenth and seventeenth centuries – Rabbi Yehudah Arieh of Modena, Joseph Solomon Delmedigo, and especially Uriel Acosta and Baruch Spinoza – had, through internal dialectics, influenced Judaism in a positive way. They were the leaven in the dough; the opposition they provoked increased Judaism's self-awareness of its true essence. One may even proudly claim Spinoza as a loyal Jew because his genius is representative of the great spirituality of the Jewish people, or the "Israelite race." His impact resembled a storm – destructive and uprooting, but also purifying and regenerating.

Dubnov viewed dissident sects and currents in Judaism as the expression of personal, emotional religiosity of souls thirsting for the living God, as opposed to the organized religion of the collective-national body. In the face of Christian and Karaite onslaughts on the nation's protective ramparts, the Jewish people could not permit itself the luxury of personal religiosity without collective religion. Like Graetz, Dubnov concedes that the Karaite movement had also been very beneficial to the Jewish people by introducing Biblical research and philosophy.[44] But in the final analysis Karaitism had to be rejected because it jeopardized the nation's existence. The same was true for the pioneers of the Haskalah movement in the sixteenth and seventeenth centuries (Graetz's "subversives") who championed the liberation of the individual from the chains of collective national discipline. They anticipated their time. The hour was not yet ripe for the full emancipation which they advocated and there was, therefore, a distinctly tragic aspect to the collision between the individual and his collective in the pre-Emancipation period. The yoke of laws and commandments was meant to preserve the nation; hence rebels against the precepts were justly banned and excommunicated for jeopardizing the nation's existence: "Three centuries had to elapse before the generation of secularized Jewry recognized the fact that it was possible to remain in the nation though one harbored complete religious freethinking."[45] The early rebels did not yet know that one could be a national Jew without necessarily adhering to the traditional religion. Dubnov for some reason believed that Jewish individualism and its resultant personal religiosity only became admissible after the Emancipation period, because only at that point in our history did it cease to threaten the nation's existence.

We shall not dwell here on how the reflection of the third theme in our count – vindication of the leadership – is reflected in modern historiography. It is not difficult to see that the historians' own choices and preferences in the controversial issues of their times, whether in favor of Reform, neo-Orthodoxy or the national movement, found expression in evaluations of Sadducees, Pharisees, or Karaites, in attitudes toward Talmudic Sages, philosophers, Mystics, Rabbis, the Council of the Four Lands, etc. Jost, for example, had a special predilection for the Sadducees and the Karaites. The latter movement, he thought, presented a certain analogy to the Protestant reaction to the Catholic establishment. The Karaites, in his view, were champions of progress in beliefs and opinions, haters of coercive authority and seekers of knowledge. Graetz, on the other hand, sang the praises of the Talmudic Sages, especially in the fourth volume of his book (the first volume to be published). He saw the Pharisees as a popular religious party, constituting the bulk of the nation, the marrow in the spine of its history. As for opponents to traditional authority, we have already heard earlier that they were viewed as having been themselves misled and as having led others astray, yet their existence too was not devoid of some merit. The matter of autonomous governance particularly occupied Dubnov. "The sceptre shall not pass from Judah" was symbolic: the nation owed its great capacity to resist the oppressive rod of foreign rule to the internal sceptre wielded by its leaders in administering Jewish communal autonomy, a kingdom of Israel, as it were, in the midst of the kingdoms of Gentiles. The leadership's authority was founded upon national feelings, discipline, a will to live, and a common constitution.

The idea of redemption and the eternal essence

How did these historians of the Emancipation conceive the Messianic hope? How did they imagine the nation's future and the future of humanity? The Emancipation culture's attitude toward the Messianic idea has been described earlier in its general outline. Jost, Graetz, Dubnov, and others believed that the spread of scientific knowledge and fraternity among nations, together with the political emancipation of Jews in the countries of their domicile, was the long-hoped-for end of days. Next to the universal significance of redemption they also emphasized the "renaissance of Israel" in one form or other. Graetz spoke of a "rejuvenation of the Jewish race," that race which was destined to be a light unto the nations.[46] After describing the evolution of the Messianic belief, Graetz expresses his opinion that the hope of Israel's sublime Prophets, visionaries, and great Sages could not simply be mere delusion, fated to remain forever a dream. The history of the world clearly signals to "a Messianic kingdom of peace, brotherhood among men and a purified knowledge of God."[47] Perhaps the founder of this Messianic peace will emerge from the bosom of Judaism, for Judaism has proven a mighty creative gift for advancing the happiness of humanity at large. Israel is a "Messianic people." Belief in the Messianic advent need not be enunciated as a principle of faith; a dogmatic formulation which would exclude from Israel's fold any who believed otherwise was not an authentically Jewish expression. The Messianic eon would be a time of brotherhood and mutual conciliation without the persecutionary zeal that stigmatized doubters with apostasy and heresy. However, Israel's hope for return to its homeland and re-establishment of its statehood is, in Graetz's historical interpretation, considerably dimmed.[48]

Dubnov was not much concerned with distant hopes. He believed that freedom in a friendly environment would produce a healthy national life, provided this freedom was accompanied by an internal awakening of the national will.[49] The Land of Israel was one center with others in Europe and America, and after the bloody events in Palestine in 1929 he commented "that the tragedy of wandering Israel did not come to an end at the threshold of this historic land, and that there was still another Diaspora – Israel among the hostile sons of Ishmael."[50] Zionism appeared to Dubnov as a defiance of the laws of history, aimed at effacing the nation's natural boundaries and vitiating its historical destiny.

How did the Emancipation scholarship reflect the prefiguration, or preformation, of the present in the past, i.e. what were their thoughts on the "ideas," or the forces, driving Jewish history? Jost had already spoken of the nation's "inner essence" to which it yearns to return from the far-flung wanderings decreed by the vagaries of its fate. He too spoke of "the nation's spirit," which creates a unique world of its own. This spirit, however, is only revealed in the course of the nation's history. While Jost was working on the second volume of his book (1821), the German statesman and philosopher Wilhelm von Humboldt published an essay, "Über die Aufgabe des Geschichtsschreibers," which had immediate impact on German historiography. Humboldt argued that it was incumbent upon the historian to identify in historical deeds and events certain ideas that forged these events into a single unit of meaning. With the intuition of an artist the historian must contemplate the ideas that shape the occurrence, and explain it accordingly. Without these ideas, the historical happening disintegrates into assemblages of details and minutiae. These ideas are history's principal creative forces:

The number of creative forces in history is by no means exhausted by those manifesting themselves immediately in the events. Even if historiography succeeds in unraveling them all, severally or in their combination, and ascertains the shape of, and transformation taking place in, the earth, the changes of climate, the intellectual capacity and character of nations, as well as the even more peculiar ones of individual personalities, the impact of arts and sciences, the deep imprint of social institutions, there will still remain an even more powerful principle to be detected. Although not immediately visible, this principle lends impetus to those forces and gives them direction. We are referring to *ideas* which, by their very nature, exist beyond the circle of finality, and yet they imbue and dominate world history in all its parts.[51]

Jost's writings only hinted at this theory of ideas, but with Zunz, and especially with Graetz, this theory became quite explicit. Once adopted by Ranke, it penetrated wide areas of scholarship in Germany and elsewhere. It also commingled with the Romantic theory of a national spirit and with the idealist systems of Fichte and Hegel. Like all the idealist systems which succeeded the religious-metaphysical faiths, this theory of ideas sought initially, and still more insistently in its subsequent extensions, the "essence," "core," "root" and "source": the art historian must have a clear understanding of the basic principles of aesthetics, such as beauty, unity, symmetry; the student of ethics must be able to distinguish good from evil and understand the imperatives of morality. In every sphere of reflection and science there are certain *a priori* concepts, intellectual pincers which enable us to grasp reality. The same is true for historiography. According to this theory, history is nothing but the reflection of ideas. There are basic essences which are not subject to the flux of historic occurrences, and only these essences, the fixed and unchanging forms, impart true knowledge. In the religious tradition this basic unchanging "essence" is revelation, as it has been transmitted by the givers of the Torah, the Prophets and the Sages. This essence may be corrupted and distorted by error and sin, it may not be properly understood and developed, but its original form endures forever. Modern idealist systems also regarded ideas as beginnings and sources, but tended to stress the development toward objectives, the drawing upon the sources, and how this process unfolds throughout the ages. A dynamic character was thus variously introduced into the immutable ideas. This immanent dynamics was also considered to have a psychological basis: ideas are imprinted on the individual's soul, and, especially, on the soul of a nation; their sum constitutes the "spirit of the nation," a sort of ideational-organic essence, a psychic-social unity, the history of which inevitably discloses its unique characteristic qualities.[52]

This theory is clearly illustrated by Graetz's opinion that Jewish history in all its periods seeks to realize but one idea, which is the spiritual essence of the Jewish people. This is the establishment on earth of the God-idea through the constitution of an organized people commanded to fulfill its moral destiny. Judaism was "born complete in its full stature," but in the course of its history it "continued to gather strength, to expand and develop and make itself serviceable to the needs of life. The ethical ideals were destined to be embodied to some measure in one people, and that people was destined to accept the mission and the martyrdom entailed therein."[53] The young historian opens his work "The Construction of Jewish History" (1846) with the query: "What is Judaism?" He was not satisfied with the answers of contemporary thinkers and scholars (although they too spoke of Judaism's "essence" and "idea"), until he had found that "it can be demonstrated that Jewish history in all its phases, even in its apparent aberrations and inconsistencies, exhibits a central idea and basic conception."[54] The idea, as we have said, is the "transmundane God-idea" which "sought concrete embodiment in the life of the people; an appropriate state constitution was the vital bearer of this idea which found expression in the customs of the people and in the attitudes of the individual."[55] This idea assumes new forms throughout history. The history of Israel is the changing forms of that one fixed idea or essence. Shmuel Ettinger justly commented that "this kind of view is basically unhistorical,"[56] and its gist apparently expresses the belief that just as this essence, the idea of the Jewish people, is eternal, so also is its existence. In chapter 8 I will be making a similar critique regarding the historians of the National-Israeli culture.

Dubnov advocated a "sociological and realistic approach," which would go beyond a mere literary or martyrological view of Jewish history. However, his assumptions drove him to conclude that the Jewish people were imprinted with a spiritual essence, albeit of a more formal type. In Dubnov's view, the Jewish people, like every other national-historical group, was a spiritual entity. Its spirituality was determined by the shared memories and hopes it held in common since its inception. Moreover, since the Jewish people was "more" historic than other nations, as we heard earlier, it was also more spiritual, indeed it was the ultimate prototype of a national-spiritual essence. Dubnov thought this idea was "a saving idea for a thinking Jewry."[57] The development of this national-historic entity known as the Jewish people progressed from the material and physical level toward the idea. Life's heavy trials and tribulations had stripped it of its physical trappings until it stood revealed in its national selfhood. Dispersed, divided, and bereft of a state and sovereign institutions, the nation preserved its selfhood intact in the face of all the powerful forces threatening its existence throughout the ages. The gist of this selfhood was the will to survive, to preserve the greatest measure of social and cultural individuality, and to strive toward a better future, an urge for inner development, for the perfecting and ennoblement of the soul. Like all national groups, Jews too wished to protect this person and their independence, to be autonomous whenever and wherever possible. The autonomy they exercised throughout the ages amid alien people was their most typical historic mode of life, whereas the existence of the Israelitic state was merely episodic. This autonomy was fundamentally national, not religious. Religious and metaphysical messages were merely husks encompassing the inner will to exist and to preserve national historic selfhood. Such messages are subject to change with time, but national selfhood endures forever; it is this essence which distinguishes one nation from another. The religious essence, i.e. the contents of the Jewish faith, is a significant part of the cultural consciousness upon which the nation is founded, one of its important strata, but it is national selfhood which dispenses life, creates values, including religious values, and modifies them in keeping with new needs. The religion of Israel was an "instrument of exile" assumed by the Jewish entity, or the national will to self-preservation, in order to sustain itself in the difficult conditions of its stateless dispersion, as explained above.

The novelty that sets apart modern secular Judaism from its traditional antecedent is that the former defines itself exclusively in terms of form, based on the national will and the consciousness of a historical-cultural unity, while the latter, like the Judaism of the Emancipation, defines itself in terms of contents: the world is destined to recognize the national society as a higher form of life than the state. Therefore, as long as Israel carries its special cultural-national idea, the dispersion is not to be viewed as its decline, but as an ascent. Geiger, Graetz, and other votaries of the Emancipation culture, strove diligently to uncover Judaism's perennial ideational essence, whereas Dubnov had reservations about an essence of contents; in secular spirit, both pragmatic and theoretical, he stressed instead the cardinal importance of the social-national life-form itself. It was an attempt to vindicate diaspora life and remonstrate against the coercive force known as a state by use of a comprehensive theory postulating human historical development from statehood to national societies, and all this, in his opinion, on the basis of critical-scientific investigation.[58]

Needless to say, we are not engaged here in a debate with Dubnov's theory. Our interest is in emphasizing the potency of that preformation and projection we spoke of in chapter 6 – from the events of the distant past to the struggles over national autonomy in Dubnov's own time. Dubnov did not share his predecessors' views about the importance of the religious essence – the contents of certain beliefs – as the dominant idea in Jewish history; instead, he discerned driving spiritual forces that activated Israel as a self-carrying organism struggling with other nations for its selfhood. These forces, however, he regarded as eternally fixed and immutable. Dinur rightly remarked that Dubnov

inclines to see the stability of things rather than their mutability, to see existence in its stabilized consolidation rather than in its unfolding, to describe the framework in its entirety rather than in the process of conjoining its links. Dubnov sees in all history the existent forces of life and the fight for self-preservation, life set within a framework, and the fight for that framework.[59]

This framework, the desire for maintaining individuality and independence, the adherence to the national-historical essence, are stamped in the spirit of Israel as powerful preformations, which develop and reveal themselves in the course of its history.

We have now examined the views of some of the great historians of the Emancipation culture regarding the five major themes of traditional historiography. These historians, we believe, represent in their philosophy of Jewish history the historical consciousness of this culture. We were primarily interested in the changes they introduced into those five basic themes. Of course, there were many innovations in the tools of research and its forms, in the amount of available material, and the methods used. We have found that the idea of objectivity exacted meticulous investigations of historical occurrences and a rejection of the miraculous workings of divine providence in the events of the world. Doubts arose regarding the historic and geographic oneness of the Jewish people and the continuity of its history. The attitude toward the old leadership and toward its dissidents was questioned. The "chain of tradition" and the former traditional leadership were generally vindicated, but for the present era and for the future a leadership endowed with new authority was sought. The Messianic idea was transposed to the universal arena (in the direction outlined by Maimonides, but far more radically), by passing in silence over the national dimension of return to Zion. As to the search for the eternal essence, the contents changed, but the substance of the belief in the preformation, or prefiguration, of the present in the distant past remained. The idea of an eternal essence imbued in all the manifestations of Jewish history down to today's National-Israeli culture is the subject of the next chapter. This metaphysical belief contradicts the theory of historical perspectivism which our study seeks to substantiate and validate. It disregards the finest accomplishments of modern philosophic and historic thought, perverts Jewish history, and warps the comprehension of contemporary reality. Why this belief still endures in National-Israeli historiography is a problem that requires special study. The answer apparently should be sought in the tradition of the previous cultures, including the Emancipation culture, and in the efforts of the new scholars to find shelter and comfort in this tradition.

8

THE STRUGGLE FOR SELF-AFFIRMATION

The National-Israeli culture and the new historiography

The National-Israeli culture came into being concomitantly with the Zionist movement and the new settlement in the Land of Israel, at a time of deepening crisis for its two immediate predecessors, the Emancipation and the Rabbinic cultures. It wished to replace these predecessors, but it continued to batten upon their riches, albeit polemically. The Zionist movement itself was initially founded upon the liberal and humanistic principles heralded by the revolutions of 1789 and 1848 and could be considered a late offshoot of the European Risorgimento; its creators followed the progressive European social thinking of the time. However, the difficulty encountered in achieving emancipation eventually banished liberal illusions and revived the age-old yearning for redemption in Zion. The National-Israeli culture was in no small measure the result of disappointment at the flounderings and regressions encountered in Europe in the course of the struggle for equality.

The Rabbinic world too had begun to disintegrate long before the Holocaust. It had been vested with tremendous national energies and profound historical experiences that had made Jewish communities into strong religious-political organizations, almost unrivaled in the world for the solidity of their unity and the courage of their endurance. But now Jews found they could no longer accept the ontology of the Rabbinic culture that had given birth to this difficult and extraordinary form of existence – a national-religious body within a foreign state. The National-Israeli culture stepped in to take possession of the benefits devolving upon it from earlier cultures, to salvage what it could of their material and spiritual holdings, but also to winnow and sift, reject, and suppress, in order to draw fully upon all of these antecedents, the Biblical one in particular, for the creation of a new life-sustaining framework for the generations to come.

National-Israeli scholarship clearly reflects this culture's presuppositions in terms of the three spheres – practical, intellectual, and redeeming knowledge – of its ontology. National scholars and historians actively participated in the immense culture-building efforts without which no new ontology can be translated into a way of life. The ontology they helped create did not originate solely in the "tent of Torah." It sprung from a Jewish activism, which ventured to confront in all spheres of activity and creativity the unprecedented disasters unleashed upon the nation in the modern era. The ontology underlying the National-Israeli culture emerged and crystallized in new modes of experience and thought, in a new life-style, in the major processes entailed in settling the land – resulting in the establishment of the State of Israel – and in all the changes and innovations engendered by the state to this day.[1]

Thinkers and historians of the new culture wished to provide a clear and unequivocal answer to the enigma of the nation's historical destiny among the peoples of the world, to explain the uniqueness of its character and past, and to comprehend the nature of its unbroken tie with its religion, so universal in aspiration, yet so exclusively confined to the Jewish people.

Yeḥezkel Kaufmann (1889–1963), a distinguished Biblical scholar and publicist of the last generation, thus formulated this critical question: "Why did Israel tread a unique historical path which no other nation or tongue in the world trod?" The question, clearly, is at once speculative and practical: "It inquires into the past, but its eyes are lifted to the present and to the future. Its beginnings are in historical and archeological study, but its end is a complex of agonizing and painful problems of life."[2]

Obviously, Kaufmann's question and its underlying assumption regarding the uniqueness of Jewish history, requires examination and study, in order to place this "unique historical path" in proper perspective.

Kaufmann's pivotal question was extended by others in the National-Israeli culture to include not only studies on the exile and on the nature of Zionist and Messianic redemption – on its proposed solution to "exile and alienness" (the title of Kaufmann's work) – but also studies on Judaism's essence and articulations, and on the causes of anti-Semitism. Modern Jewish scholarship devoted much attention to the relation between Judaism's ethnic and religious elements, and to relations between Judaism and other religions, especially Christianity. The extensions of Kaufmann's fundamental question thus gave rise to numerous important areas of new research.

The opinion that historiography applies itself to the past but directs its gaze to the present and the future, as Kaufmann put it, is not new. We have already explained that study of the past cannot be severed from the needs of the present, be they needs of a religious faith or of secular, national or social ideologies, and we have argued that this dependence poses no real threat to scientific objectivity, provided that the rigor of scientific method is upheld. Just as the Science of Judaism serviced the needs of the Emancipation, National-Israeli scholarship of the present draws its sustenance from both

SELF-AFFIRMATION 205

the new Israeli reality and its utopian dream of the future. The new scholars concede that there can be no scientific clarification of Jewish values or Jewish essence except through a study of the latter's development and crystallization. The pragmatic aspect – the wish to derive a lesson from the past about the events, desires, and obligations of the present – unites with the genetical aspect, with the inquiry into the beginnings, which, being free of "bias," may devote itself with the rigor of painstaking research to the achievement of scientific accuracy, in keeping with the standards set by modern historical science.

It must not therefore surprise us to see how modern Hebrew historiography harnessed itself with a sense of mission to the task of opening our eyes to the wealth of our past on the one hand, and to the creation of a new culture on the other hand. Behind this great endeavor beckoned the hope that the study of the past would disclose the nation's roots and ideal essence, to serve as a blueprint for its future. By re-establishing the "covenant" between the Jewish people and its land, these thinkers fused visionary ideas with painstaking research. Permeated with faith in the nation's rebirth in its ancestral land, in the renewal of its language and culture, in the return to the original national wellsprings, they sought to bestow upon their readers a knowledge of Jewish values, as these came to be reflected in the new National-Israeli culture. So large a group of thinkers was not, of course, without its share of individual differences, but there was general agreement that Jewish history was not merely the history of a religious sect, nor merely the history of a nation.

Basic assumptions of the new Israeli historiography

This new breed of thinkers and historians directed their arguments against the culture of Jewish Emancipation whose creators, striving to "liberate" the nation from dependence upon a political state and a national soil, had touted the benefits of dispersion among the Gentiles. In the programmatic essay titled, "Megamatenu" ("Our aim"), which prefaced the first issue of the revived Jewish historical journal *Zion*, the leaders of the new school announced their espousal of a theory on the independence and puissance of organic historical life, and their intention to carry on and emend the work of previous western European Jewish scholars: "We re-hoist the banner [of Science of Judaism] which dropped from their hands before they had pegged it in firm ground."

An early founder of the new historiography whose formulation of the essence of Judaism reverberates in the writings of most of his colleagues and disciples was Joseph Klausner (1874–1958), who wrote:

Judaism is not only a religion, nor merely an ethical code. Judaism is the sum of the nation's needs, all of which are anchored in a religious foundation. This is a national world view, which has a religious-ethical underpinning. For this reason, there are in the ethics of Judaism, as in life itself, high and low points, (the Book of Jonah with its deliverance of a foe, versus the Scroll of Esther with its cruel revenge upon a foe). Judaism is a national life, encircled, but not engulfed, by its national religion and by human ethics.[3]

This religious-ethical system bears the unique imprint which monotheism, Prophetic ethics, the Messianic idea, Halachah and Aggadah have stamped upon it and which is carried forth by one nation throughout its entire history.

National-Israeli historiography perpetuated certain notions handed down by the cultures of traditonal faith regarding the unity of the Jewish people and the continuity of its history. It attempted to explain the nation's history in the light of those forces and cognitive and emotional applications of national will which were thought to assist the nation in building its future. This historiography postulates that Israel is one nation (Herzl in the introduction to *The Jewish State*, 1896: "We are one *people, one* people" – two emphases: nationhood and unity), despite the disunity of the early tribes and later subdivisions in the diasporas. The Jewish people is seen as one national or religious-national entity throughout its history; by no means is it viewed as "Judaism," i.e. as a system of beliefs and customs characteristic of one specific, religious group. Similarly, the new historians assume an unbroken Jewish continuity, an "eternality of Israel." They are not, of course, unmindful of modern historical thinking, and they do pay heed to features of uniqueness in various events and deeds, but they continue to find in the heart of these historical processes the eternally unfolding development of the one nation. Changes, ruptures, and tears in the historical fabric are likewise explained by the dialectics of continuity. Another cardinal assumption of these historians is the existence of an unsevered tie between the Jewish people and the Land of Israel: for 2,000 years the nation longed for the return to Zion, praying for and, consonant with conditions and circumstances, striving toward its fulfillment.

Eminently responsible for crystallizing the ideology of National-Israeli historiography was Benzion Dinur (1884–1973), one of the most important founders of the Israeli historical school, a dynamic and influential scholar, who in the early 1950s also served as Israel's Minister for Education and Culture. We have mentioned him in this study more than once. The major goal Dinur set forth for National-Israeli historiography was to uncover the uniqueness of the Jewish people, and explain its continuity. This uniqueness, he thought, found its expression in six basic elements: ethnic, religious, social, geographic, linguistic, and political. These were "elements of permanence"[4] providing continuity and stability amidst the countless changes and transformations which acted upon the Jewish people and its historical fate. The detailed elaboration of the six elements is immaterial to our present discussion, but the relative weight assigned to each element is rather problematic. For example, with regard to the ethnic element, we know that mixed marriages were already common in Biblical times, very soon after the conquest of the land by the twelve tribes: "They took their daughters in marriage and gave their own daughters to their sons" (Judg. 3.6). After the downfall of the Israelite kingdom of Samaria, the country's foreign population and the rate of its mixing with the Jewish inhabitants increased significantly. The returnees from Babylonia likewise took foreign women, though they were later prohibited by Ezra from continuing this practice, as we heard in chapter 4. During the Second Temple there was a period of widespread conversion to Judaism. Dinur is well acquainted with all these facts. Yet he claims that "there is no doubt that throughout the generations and the ages Jews preserved the consciousness of their ethnic uniqueness."[5]

Surely, there is a great difference between purity of the ethnic origin and consciousness of ethnic individuation, which is a national-religious imperative to preserve separateness. In his discussion of religious individuation, Dinur mentions this factor as the common denominator in all the different currents, offshoots, systems, theories, sects, and groups known in Judaism. But here too he fails to distinguish between consciousness and reality, between the different conceptions of the religious element, or, in the terminology of our study, of the superordinating concepts and the archetypal collective experiences. Continuity in the last three elements listed by Dinur – the geographic, the linguistic, and the political – is perhaps even less self-evident, and we have seen earlier that these elements were in fact subject to considerable debate during the Emancipation culture. Here again we see the mixing, so characteristic of every ideology, between the ideal and the real. Dinur concedes:

Nonetheless, despite continuity in the six elements of Jewish historical individuation throughout the ages, it was only when Israel dwelt in its land that all the elements of individuation were extensively active and evident in the life of the individual and of the Jewish collective, even though their action and influence varied from period to period and from one historical era to another.[6]

Is it not precisely the intensity of this action and influence that determines continuity in the nation's individuation? We shall return shortly to Dinur's theory.

It must at any rate be noted that at least one of the leaders of Zionist historiography no longer indulged in naïve historic realism, and this was a novelty. Dinur recognized that knowledge of the past depended upon selection of "the facts," their generalization, and evaluation. Each generation, he readily admitted, had its own methods of selecting and grasping. Values which inspired early generations might subsequently be discarded, and replaced by new interests. The history of values, it has been said, is also the history of the neutralization of values. The imposition of certain emphases inevitably eradicates other emphases, although this always occurs within that horizon of interests in which the "spirit of the time" and the inner aspirations of the new culture are made manifest. Not all scholars in modern Jewish science recognized and acknowledged this, but there certainly were some who had abandoned naïve realism, at least in theory. The problem lies in the great gap extending between theory and practice, even in the works of so eminent a scholar as Dinur.

Modern Jewish historiography strongly emphasized the arbitrary nature of historical inquiry, the fact that it is based on valuation. Accordingly, it subjected the interpretations of Israel's history by non-Jewish historians and by the advocates of the nineteenth-century German Science of Judaism to a critical analysis. It attempted to "negate the negativity" of these scholars by exposing their "arbitrariness" and "prejudices." These scholars, it was argued, whether explicitly and consciously, or indirectly and unwittingly, had distorted Jewish history, belittling its great contributions to human culture, reducing the stature of the Jewish people, detracting from its accomplishments, or even entirely "destroying" its essence, until only a celebration of the nation's "funereal rites," as Gerschom Scholem had charged,[7] remained. In contradiction, modern Jewish historiography claimed to follow a more positive approach: to alter previous negative valuations, and replace them by an original independent vision of that somber yet brilliant history of the Jewish people. Thus what had appeared as a defect to non-Jewish historians and Jewish "detractors" was revealed as worthy of admiration; that which had been considered opaque and dark, warped and perverted, was transformed into something bright, fascinating, and powerful. Typical are the words of Professor J. Klausner:

History itself, the secular history of Israel during the Second Temple, like the history of the English, the French, the Germans, has not been written till this very day. The chapters relating to the Second Temple in the books of Renan, Schlatter, Wellhausen, Edward Mayer and others (of the most recent historians) are inadequately brief; neither do they correspond to historical truth, for they adopt a negative attitude toward Pharisaic Judaism, belittling its stature and contemning its value, in order to validate and maintain the prerogatives and primacy of its rival, Christianity.[8]

Aside from this tendency to correct what had been distorted, the new historians, such as Baer, also expressly emphasized the desire to reassess and re-evaluate historic judgments:

The knowledge of history is like a debate, a dialogue and a ceaseless contest between the knowledge and the desire of the present generation and the knowledge and desire of men of the past. He who studies history explores his entire being, his entire consciousness, because he absorbs the past yet remains a man of his own generation.

This polemical aspect is equally manifest in the works of Kaufmann and Dinur. Kaufmann introduces his *Religion of Israel* with the assertion of the antiquity and originality of Israelitic monotheism: that it is a creation absolutely distinct from anything the human spirit in the entire pagan world had ever produced, and that it constitutes a fundamental change in values. "This study," Kaufmann stated in the foreword to his *magnum opus*, "is a fundamental critique of classical criticism. It seeks to draw ultimate conclusions, to suggest a new position in place of the prevailing one."[9] Equally, Dinur strongly emphasizes that the past is not merely that which has transpired and passed; it is drawn from the commitments of the present, and is molded in our mind according to the facts we experience and the valuations we make: "In every nation each generation views differently its national past, in the light of its own experience. Phenomena which had previously been deemed insignificant or which had scarcely ever been noticed, now appear to be highly significant; that is the nature of historical issues."[10] Since Dinur's primary endeavor was the collection and explanation of sources, and as he could be charged with arbitrary selection of those sources, he attempted to explain that "the foundation of all historiography is a general picture revealed to the historian of the historical reality he has described and in light of which he also seeks out sources."[11] The sources may occasionally lead him to alter his view, but in the main "the problem of the sources is not decisive in drawing the basic outlines of history's general picture.[12]

Dinur and his colleagues knew that the occupations of the historian – description, narrative, explanation – were dependent upon his valuation, ministered by present needs or by his personal biases. They also realized that "facts" required interpretation, that they had no existence of their own, "as they were." Yet, it seems to me that they were still quite deficient in the kind of trifocal vision required by the new perspectivistic approach for examining the past, as we shall explain in a moment.

The theory of historical perspectivism

Three fundamental aspects in historical understanding

Modern historical awareness has learned to distinguish in the phenomena of the past three basic aspects: the aspect of uniqueness and distinctness; the dimension of change and transformation, and the dimension of chronological succession and continuity. An event can have no uniqueness without its separation and individuation from other phenomena, i.e. identity and distinctness are closely related, and one cannot determine the nature of a particular deed, event, or historical situation except by knowledge of other phenomena which are distinct and different from it. The kingdom of the Hasmonean Queen Salome Alexandra was unique: it did not resemble the kingdom of Elizabeth I or Elizabeth II, nor even the kingdom of Cleopatra. Differences emerging from the process of individuation become part of the lively arena of confrontations, contradictions, divisions, and battles between individuals, sects, parties, classes, and nations. Changes and transformations are the product of distinctness and often also its source. Transformation refers to a change that is comprehensive and profound, such as the transformation of a culture or the emergence of a new and distinct culture from the remnants of an older antecedent. Changes and transformations are the medium for the formation and crystallization of new meanings, which confer upon individual and group the ontology wherein their culture organizes itself. Chronological succession and continuity are the dynamics of change in actions and events in the flow of personal and collective time. This change process is not necessarily a direct chronological succession to the point of unbroken continuity. History is often characterized by leaps, spurts, and surprising new starts which derive from no continuity, as we have repeatedly argued in this study.[13]

A modern historian wishing to study the past "as it was" can no longer ignore these three aspects. The writings of Dilthey, Croce, Collingwood, and others have sufficiently demonstrated that there are no brute facts; rather, there are phenomena in the context of the three basic aspects we have listed above. It is impossible to describe and understand the single isolated phenomenon without its comparison and contrast with other phenomena and without due consideration to its evolvement, i.e. without distinctness and chronological succession. One need not be an excessive romantic in order to insist that the historian describe the historical phenomenon's uniqueness and that, aided by our emotions and reconstructive imagination, he guide us toward its comprehension. King Herod and his reign, Hillel the Elder, the pogroms of 1648–9, the U.N. resolution of November 29, 1947 on the partition of Palestine – the uniqueness of these phenomena is not grasped outside the context of distinctness and chronological succession. One may even enlarge this rule to encompass not only historical phenomena, but every existent thing in being, even a mountain or a river: each stands out in its unique presence and is thus distinct from its environment, neighbors, friends or foes, and it too is in the process of becoming and changing, i.e. it carries within itself a biography. This, of course, is even truer in the case of a human-historical phenomenon.

The problem of continuity

Of the three fundamental aspects in our understanding of the past, the second aspect, dealing with changes and transformations, and the third, concerning chronological succession and continuity, merit particular attention in our generation, especially when considering Jewish history and the nature of Judaism. To recall briefly a subject raised earlier (in chapter 1), the experience of the last generation has been primarily one of convulsive transformations, resulting from sudden disruptions and disasters, as well as from successful acts of cultivation and upbuilding. The sudden reversals experienced in the violent uprooting of foundations and the laying of new ones, all compressed within the short span of one lifetime, were truly confounding in their lack of continuity and order. An event did not ensue from an earlier occurrence, a situation did not logically proceed from an antecedent, and time did not progress in a tranquil flow. The large Jewish centers succumbed to a sudden and untimely death; neither did the establishment of the State of Israel result from organic, gradual growth, but from a tremendous abrupt leap – born of acts of courage and inspiration. The essence of our generation's experience has been convulsions and disruptions on the one hand, leaps and new beginnings on the other; catastrophes, sudden ruptures in the cycle of cause and effect, but also discontinuous lines which re-emerge and reascend from the depths. These experiences have inevitably altered the angle from which the modern historian now inspects the past. Continuity for the modern historian has clearly become problematic.

However, as a necessary general principle, continuity is left intact even by historic surprises and breaches. Continuity is a function of one's knowledge of the historical system as it unfolds; barring continuity, no perception of the breaches would be possible. This phenomenon hides a dialectic tension between continuity and breach. Each is conditional upon the other. The profound reason for this dialectic is that every continuous historical development requires an independent subject, so that the latter can be perceived in the process of its becoming. Every breach testifies to the existence of this independent subject, which stands, as it were, outside the frame of continuous development. On the other hand, this subject is only revealed in the process of its development, i.e. within the entire continuous framework, even when it deviates from this framework. Unlike a natural occurrence, the continuity of a historical event is characterized not only by the fact that it takes its place in a sequence of events, but also by its unique non-recurring qualities. It is fixed in a certain position in the sequence of events precisely because it leaps out, as it were, in its non-recurring uniqueness, from that line of successive events. In brief, continuity is nothing but a "postulate," as we have said, a task for knowledge in its examination of the sequence of historical events. This task seeks more than attachment to a continuum, but has difficulty in attaining its object.

The threefold viewing of history

Knowledge of the past, then, requires cognizance of the above three aspects: uniqueness and distinction, change and transformation, chronological succession and continuity. But in parallel to this cognizance, historical knowledge also demands a trifocal vision of the past that can take the following three considerations fully into account: how did the past itself actually evolve, how was it subsequently perceived and experienced and how is it synoptically viewed and evaluated today?

Let us begin by clarifying the first of these approaches to historical study. Aided by the reconstructive interpretation (described in chapter 2), each culture must first be studied for an understanding of its own uniqueness and distinction – what it sought to communicate, how it judged itself and its predecessors, what it regarded as its uniqueness *vis-à-vis* other cultures. The perspectivistic approach seeks first of all to situate past events in the context of their own past, as they were viewed and interpreted by those who experienced them. It thereby objectivizes past events and establishes certain hiatuses: the past was one thing, the present is something else. As in art, so in the study of history, perspective substantiates the external world and carefully observes it in its peculiar texture. On the other hand, it also extends the sphere of the examining "I." Perspective has posed an intellectual dilemma ever since it was introduced by Renaissance art: what use will the artist make of this dualistic method? Will he pursue subjective "illusionism," or will he embrace objective "realism"? Where will the artist position his own point of view and what measure of distance will he establish between himself and the things he beholds, and among the observed things themselves?[14]

The analogous problem faced by historical perspectivism may be resolved, we believe, by the suggested three-way viewing of history. The first way to view history is to attempt to grasp things "as they were," in accordance with the world view, the background, and the circumstances prevailing in the past. This area of research studies "facts" and combinations of facts as they "really" were, as well as their underlying psychological motives. The second viewing examines the dynamics of an occurrence. Each culture undergoes change when its sun begins to set. How did later cultures evaluate earlier ones in the larger historical topography? How have a culture's meanings changed in subsequent cultures from what they had been in their own time? Lastly, the dimension of long-range changes and transformations must also be duly considered: how is a past culture judged by our own culture, which is governed by the presuppositions underlying contemporary ontology? This dimension of context encompasses the aspect of continuity. The third view of history is essentially reflective; it is accompanied by critical cogitations on the circumstances surrounding its own efforts, and their limitations. It knows that its particular conception is restricted to one culture only, and that the establishment of continuity is an unending task.

Wherever I have spoken here of "facts as they are," the reservation implied in the use of quotation marks is directed against the assumptions of naïve historical realism regarding the existence of brute facts and data. Most contemporary thinkers agree that without interpretation, no historical facts and data are possible. Facts are what they mean, in their unique, as also in their general, context. They are interpreted in consonance with the conceptions held and the evidence considered by the investigating researchers, and verified according to the standard of research prevailing in their day.

That which once had been future is dead and gone, and all that remains of the past are testimonies and documents, agreements and disagreements as to its character, and methods for its reconstruction. We might even say that when we speak of "viewing the past" we are merely using a figure of speech. In reality we do not have before us any visual forms or other sensory experiences. Our knowledge of the past is founded upon our methods of historical investigation, within the confines of confirmed and verified knowledge at the level of science obtaining in our time.

Nevertheless, if these three aspects and three viewings are set aside, i.e. if all interpretations are stripped off so that an underlying foundation is finally reached, one does find a sort of primal matter of cut-and-dried facts. These facts are cut-and-dried precisely because they lie beyond the historical perspective, or below it, in a preperspectivistic or subperspectivistic sphere. This is a physical sphere anterior to interpretation, like primal matter waiting to take on form. What, then, remains of a fact when it has been stripped of all the points of view of different ages? What is that hard core of permanence which will neither alter nor ever again recur? Some say: nothing remains. From a strictly historic-scientific viewpoint, this may indeed be so. We, however, have argued that it is possible to believe in the survival and remainder of a certain physical something. This something is simply the primal matter for meanings. Consider, for example, the destruction of the Second Temple, an indubitable physical fact, as evidenced by one remaining western wall. There are many testimonials to the destruction of the Second Temple, but what is the historical nature of this event, i.e. what was its importance in the eyes of the generation that experienced it, what was its significance for the generations that followed it, and what is its meaning for us today? The original cut-and-dried fact must accommodate many meanings. Many in our history considered the Second

Temple of lesser importance than the First, and its destruction therefore a lesser disaster. In some Jewish centers, in Spain for example, Jews of the Second Temple period were deemed to have fallen far short of the influence and greatness destined for them by the Prophets, an opinion shared by many medieval Sages. "They were not as sublime in the Second Temple [period] as in the kingdom of David and Solomon," declares Don Isaac Abravanel.[15] To Abravanel the period following the Hasmonean kingdom seemed of mediocre and inferior quality, and in terms of national independence, was no better than if it had been "ruled by Ishmael, who rules over Jerusalem today."[16]

A classical example illustrating how a meaning of a fact is determined (and we have already established that there can be no fact without meaning), is Julius Caesar's crossing of the Rubicon between Italy and Cisalpine Gaul on the night of January 11, 49 BCE. This crossing is a cut-and-dried fact. But as a historical event it has undergone important developments and changes. Did Caesar wish to promote his own political position in Rome and betray the Republic, or did he, on the contrary, wish to bolster the Republic? A river-crossing is an act that can be subjected to measurement or photographic recording. But it remains no more than factual primal matter, the building block of a historical event, that sparse residue upon which naïve historical realism quite rightly relies. The historic event is a construct, not primal matter itself.[17]

Add to this the creative and formative dimension of language. Expressions, descriptions, and concepts cannot be viewed as mere reflections of reality, charged simply with giving reality verbal formulation; they participate in its very creation, more akin to painting or sculpting than to photography. Language fashions modes of comprehension and ways of conception and valuation. Even when it merely purports to report observations, to describe sensations and events "as they are," it selects, fashions and directs their dynamics. Thus, language largely determines how our entire perception of the world is organized.

This conception of language has led many contemporary thinkers, following Collingwood, to propose a theory of radical constructionism in their approach to history. In additon to the important role of language, they emphasize the power of the scientific method, which establishes facts, and accepts or rejects testimony. For constructionism, the methods whereby a fact is verified and confirmed are critical. Like Collingwood, these researchers draw a distinction between testimony and proof. Testimony is a matter of witnesses who saw an event, or who heard about it from other witnesses; the historian, however, must confirm testimony and documents and establish proof. What is decisive is not the testimony, but its verification. The historian examines each piece of evidence in the light of other available documents. Thus he may glean from these testimonies much more than they explicitly reveal, or he may disqualify some or all such testimonies and uncover facts which were not mentioned in the documents at all, but which may be derived by implication.

Historiography is thus an intellectual effort which examines the proof provided by the various sources of information, a methodical effort directed toward the obtainment of verified knowledge. This obtainment, however, is circumscribed by certain limitations. "I know the real event, as it is given to me to know it by means of the procedures available for knowing it," claims Leon Goldstein.[18] In his exposition of the constructionist system, all knowledge, including knowledge of the past, is irrevocably tied to a method of knowing, and the truth of the determination we make depends upon this method. Goldstein goes so far as to claim, and here he exposes the extremism of this thesis, that the "real past [is] irrelevant to the practice of history."[19] Everything we know about the past is based on the methods utilized by historical research; absent the research methods that prove the reality of past events, nothing can be truly known. Compelling brute facts do not exist. Thus, the methods of proof with which we attain knowledge of the facts are constructs of conception and conceptualization. The testimony of those who saw Julius Caesar cross the Rubicon is secondary and irrelevant to the procedure of the historian who determines the truth or falsity of their report.

Putting aside this issue of constructionism's exaggerated claims, I would uphold the great power inherent in the physical fact, that small residue which never quite disappears under layers of interpretations and perspectives. But one should add the following consideration to the problem of relativism and absolute truth in historical perspectivism: just as physical observation leaves intact at least a small residue of the fact beyond perspective and below it, so thought has limitless scope beyond perspective and above it. Human thought has always striven to scale the ladders of abstraction from corporeality to that infinity of perspectives converging in the one, absolute, super-human truth, as it is revealed to God in His heights. This tenacious metaphysical aspiration is, in Kant's opinion, quite legitimate, provided that the investigating thought does not presume to have attained its goal, and does not identify its own truth, with that absolute truth. God's eye watches and apprehends everything at one glance, without bias and error, oblivion or favor; this is a "regulative idea" which should guide the efforts of thinkers and scientists. Just as the primal matter revealed in the subperspective is the beginning of human consciousness, so this super-perspective is the supreme purpose of human consciousness. The first belongs to physics, the latter to metaphysics.

In other words, the quest for historical truth endeavors to approach the absolute purpose, but never attains it. By no means do I claim that historical truth is relative, but I do believe that the opinions of thinkers and historians and their achievements are relative. The full truth itself is many-faceted, not unequivocal and clear-cut for all generations. To borrow Spinoza's terminology: God has infinite attributes. The full truth is the task of knowledge, the obligation of inquiry, the quest for and the exertion toward it.

This quest has led thinkers and scholars from Leibniz to Karl Mannheim to propose methods for combining different perspectives into an inter-perspectival view, mainly by seeking out common and unifying elements. When one seeks common ground upon which contradictions may be maximally harmonized, and insofar as this act of harmonizing is successful, each position-valuation makes its contribution to the common treasury of knowledge. However, the nature and operation of this harmonizing art is itself quite problematic.

The perspectivistic view by no means relinquishes objectivity, but it does not imperiously presume to have successfully arrived at any absolutes, or to imagine that such success is even possible. The perspectivistic approach does not seek out one favored look-out point situated beyond history, an elevated position from which to survey the past. Perspectivism assumes that the multiplicity of viewing angles is not an indication of intellectual defeat, but on the contrary, proof of the spirit's triumph, of the mind's abundance and generosity, of the wealth inherent in the world of values. The aspiration to the loftiness of absolute norms extending beyond temporal horizons, is also imprinted with the stamp of historical time.

Regarding the ambition of ideology versus the unpretentiousness of perspectivism the following may be added: for many years two major conceptions exercised an almost unlimited sway over the study of the past. The traditional conception sought to uncover in history the manifestations of divine providence, or the hidden hand directing history's course. This conception was not confined to the religious world view, as attested by the secular forms it has assumed in various philosophies of history. The second conception, one which became widely prevalent in the nineteenth century, advocated the study of history's objective structure through the observation of events and actions as they organized and coalesced into a single unit of development "as it was." Both conceptions presupposed a stable order of a world fixed in its absolutes. As a historical conception, perspectivism's claims are more modest, and thus also in better harmony with the experiences and spiritual climate of our own lives. This congruity is the essence of the lesson derived from perspectivism, to wit – that each culture, whether consciously or not, judges the importance of acts and events in which it is interested, determines how these should be researched or whether to desist from researching them altogether. Each culture creates concepts and general frameworks for its hermeneutics. In forging its own "creative interpretation," it naturally tends to deal with the past rather heavy handedly. It is precisely this tendency which impels perspectivism to advocate caution and modesty. The past must be preserved from the onslaught of the pressing, domineering needs of the present. The misconception of the past due to distorted perspectives of nearness and distance, of similarity and distinctness, cloaks the generations of the past in the myths of the present.

This, then, is the reproach I direct at the National-Israeli historians mentioned earlier: their emphasis on the importance of the collective will imposes a view of the past dictated by the needs of the present. On the other hand, it seems to me that the thesis regarding the multiplicity of Jewish cultures enables us, empowered as we now are by an awareness of history's three dimensions, to move cautiously between the past, the present, and our expectation of the desired future.

Elements of the perspectivistic theory may be found today in systems propounded by a number of thinkers in history, the social sciences and the humanities. I have merely suggested here that these elements be merged into a single theoretical scheme, that the three aspects or dimensions and the threefold viewing of history be drawn together into one formulation which provides an adequate theoretical basis for the understanding of history in general, and for the examination of Jewish history and the methods applied to its study in particular.

Clearly, an historian or a thinker who offers us a historical conception based on the new National-Israeli ontology, must fully recognize the special position from which he observes his subject, must take into account his own wishful thoughts, and his personal presuppositions. He must recognize that scientific objectivity does not mean reservations, distance or the absence of deep interest in his subject, as the early adherents of scientific objectivity in nineteenth-century "empirical" positivism imagined. On the other hand, if he is to be true to himself, he must respect the "data." Admittedly, without interests (personal and collective "biases"), thought is rendered sterile and dull. The main question, however, is always to determine the nature of these interests and how they relate to a rigorous examination of the "facts" as they were, in their transformations and in their contexts. To ensure a well-reasoned answer, the historian must adopt the trifocal vision of history, as explained above.

National perspective – Benzion Dinur

The direction taken by the new generation of National-Israeli historians, the so-called Jerusalem school of history, received a most forceful expression in the works of Benzion Dinur. Dinur strongly stressed that aspect of valuation and judgment which, in his view, expresses not only the desire of an isolated individual, but the collective will of the Jewish public, "a will characterized

by moral transcendence." Earlier we heard of Scholem's disillusionment
with these colleagues: "From the frying pan to the fire," was his comment.
"After the hollowness of the assimilationist stance we now get the
hollowness of bombastic national posturing." And further on: "We have
cultivated in scholarship a national exegetical homily and a florid national
oratory in place of the exegetical homiletics and florid oratory of religion."[20]
To which of his colleagues was Scholem alluding? Did he mean Joseph
Klausner? Benzion Dinur? Even Dinur's disciple, Shmuel Ettinger, a
distinguished historian in his own right, described his teacher Dinur as an
"amalgam of a national ideologue and an eminent national historian."
Ettinger explains: "This is not a rare phenomenon in the history of nations;
great historians . . . especially of oppressed nations, have served as
ideologues of national movements, and their historic work was frequently
dedicated to the reinforcement of their nation's struggles."[21]

Dinur should indeed be viewed in this light, and with no sense of
disappointment. With great erudition and acuity this outstanding historian
investigated the development of Hassidism, the struggle for emancipation in
western Europe, the Zionist movement, the establishment of the State of
Israel and other events, movements, personalities, ideas, and institutions,
some of which he was the first to bring to light. He is owed a universal debt of
gratitude for the essence of his work, i.e. the attempt to encompass Jewish
history in one series of books, brought together under the comprehensive
title *Toldot Yisrael mesuparot ʿal yedei mekorot u-teʿudot mireshit Yisrael ve-ʿad
yameinu ʾeleh* ("History of Israel, Original Sources and Documents from the
Beginnings of Israel to Contemporary Times"). He commenced this large-
scale *oeuvre* in his youth and worked on it until the end of his life. Its volumes
titled *Yisrael ba-golah* ("Israel in the Diaspora") in the revised and expanded
edition, although uncompleted, are a monumental undertaking. Dinur
selected and edited the sources and documents according to subjects and
chronology and added explanations, notes, and bibliography. In these he
invested incalculable spiritual labor and a wealth of talent and knowledge,
which rightly earned him profound admiration and veneration.

How did Dinur relate to the three dimensions enjoined upon the historian,
and how did he fare with that trifocal viewing of history? Dinur, who
devoted greater attention to problems of methodology than his colleagues,
was to some extent a theoretician of perspectivism. In theory and in practice
his studies emphasized those subjects which singled out the dimension of
uniqueness in the historical phenomenon he chose to describe, clearly
establishing the differences between one phenomenon and other phenomena; he investigated changes and transformations and took great pains to
uncover Israel's historical continuity. In what way, then, was his
perspective lacking as a result of that "amalgam of national ideologue and
an eminent national historian"?

The concept "ideologue" requires some clarification, since I do not know what definition of "ideology," whether Marxist or other, Professor Ettinger had in mind when he thus characterized Dinur. I would define ideology as a mixture of ideas and interests representing individual and collective needs, of explanations *ad rem* based on scientific criteria, and a rationalization of beliefs and urgent needs that must service the collective struggle. Ideology, therefore, denotes an interwoven network of ideas, i.e. on the one hand, universal truths, tested opinions, and valuations based on the finest research and thought, and, on the other hand, of illusions, prejudices, untested beliefs, products of personal or collective biases. In ideology the interests – and these need not necessarily be limited to material interests – attach themselves to true opinions and transform these into myths. Ideologies diffract the rays of ideas with the thick wall of the collectivity's perceived needs. The consumer masses latch on to ideology. In the social and spiritual reality idea and ideology are dialectically interconnected, and it is impossible for a social idea to acquire any measure of force to effect change in the public sphere without this interconnection. It is the task of political philosophy to distinguish between idea and ideology, while the task of historical or sociological research is to examine why and how a certain idea developed and prevailed in a particular historical situation, what was its effect, how it developed into an ideology, and what were the latter's effects. The task of intelligible political will, which seeks to make determinations based on the soundest methods of socio-historical research and thought, is to find a way for the idea to direct and control ideology, and not *vice versa*. An ideologue is one who, depending on the degree of his ability, either himself creates an ideology, or clings to an existing one. The idea, however, is rather the province of the historian who views the past with the trifocal lens we have described above.

An ideology no doubt underlies the studies of the Jerusalem school of history and it is the purpose of the following sections to examine this ideology, especially as expressed in the writings of its two foremost representatives, Benzion Dinur and Yitzhak Baer. It is my contention that, to a large extent, Dinur imposed his own view upon earlier generations, a view rooted in Zionist ideology which he shared with other creators of the National-Israeli culture. To his credit it must be said that he examined and reconstructed the past in a superb investigation of testimonies and documents. He also faithfully reported what later generations had said about earlier acts and events, and he successfully evaluated the latter in the light of opinions held by the National-Israeli culture. But none of these perspectives was free, in my view, of "biases" that imposed extreme emphases on certain opinions and beliefs of past generations while uprooting other emphases, in order to highlight or to obscure the past in keeping with the priorities of the new culture. Thus we sense the elimination

of natural hiatuses between cultures, between an event and its consciousness in a particular generation, and in later generations.

Let us illustrate this by two examples, beginning with the problem of
periodization. We have already explained in chapter I its importance for
every researcher, since the concept "period" serves as a framework for the
organization and understanding of historical events and acts. The division
into periods draws the events and acts of a certain period into a distinct unit
of meanings. It also determines which decisive events distinguish between
one unit of meanings and other such units. We take as examples two events
which, in Dinur's opinion, initiate new periods. Israel's history in the
diaspora opens with the Arab conquest of Palestine (634–40 CE), which
brought about the final territorial dispossession of the Jews from their
holdings in ancient Palestine:

> In the phenomenon of "Israel in the Diaspora" (i.e. the existence of the Jews as a
> people without a country) two main factors must be distinguished: (1) the gradual
> disappearance of the specifically Jewish character of Palestine and the emergence of
> a different national majority in the country; (2) the survival of the Jewish nation and
> the preservation of its national character outside its own land, in periods when that
> land had ceased to be Jewish . . . It is only from the time when the nation was deprived
> of the soil on which it had developed its own specifically national form of life that the
> problem of the individual Jews' preservation of their national character in the
> Dispersion became particularly acute.[22]

I am reluctant to question historical findings advanced by so outstanding
a historian as Professor Dinur, yet, such a fundamental statement cannot be
accepted without closer examination, which quickly reveals that the
emigration from Palestine long predated the "exile." It is well known that a
sizable Jewish diaspora already existed in the first century BCE, after the
Greek port cities opened to Judaean trade and a great change in the
economic, social, and spiritual life of the nation began to take shape. In my
system of periodization, this is the period of the Talmudic culture's growth.
The contention that the Jewish dispersion resulted from deportations and
royal edicts alone has long ago been disproven. Admittedly, such acts drove
thousands of Jews out of their homeland, but in the Second Temple period it
appears to have been mainly the fertile commerce with foreign lands which
attracted Jews abroad. Jewish communities sprung up, as Philo testifies, not
only on the mainland, but also on the islands of the Mediterranean and
adjacent seas. Strabo, Herod's contemporary, informs us: "This people has
already made its way into every city, and it is not easy to find any place in the
habitable world which has not received this nation and in which it has not
made its power felt."[23] We know that Herod established a Jewish naval fleet
and steered his subjects toward intercontinental commerce. The Jewish fleet
even participated in Rome's campaign on the Bosphorus. Herod also

promoted Jewish trade with India by stringing a network of military outposts along the trade route to India. There is no doubt that these commercial relations assisted Jews in settling in foreign lands. Herod extended his protection, so it appears, over the political and economic rights of expatriate Jews, so that Jewish overseas outposts were considered daughter colonies of Jerusalem. This is how the Jewish centers in the diasporas first developed. Later disasters – the war with the Romans, the destruction of the Temple, Bar Kochba's failed revolt, the hostility of subsequent Judaean governments – naturally gave further impetus to the growth of these centers.

In the Christian-Byzantine period the authorities endeavored to assist Christians in striking root in Palestine. Jewish Babylonia therefore continued exercising its attraction for many Palestinian Jews, who felt impelled to leave a land where they were subjected to constant harassment. It is a fact that the Jewish community in Palestine dwindled in the Byzantine period, and although the Christians were short of an absolute majority, they already had a relative majority. Jews and Samaritans together numbered more than the Christians, but the country was still inhabited at the time by a large number of pagans. "If we assume that the Jews dropped to about one quarter of the total [population], we shall not be far from the truth," concludes G. Alon.[24]

Now, Dinur proposes the thesis that Israel's existence as a nation living in the diaspora can be considered to have properly begun only with the Arab conquest, while prior to that event there had been the "mere existence of scattered Jewish communities in foreign lands."[25] And whilst the existence of alien communities in foreign lands was not a phenomenon unique to Jews, the real exile began only when others came and settled in their land permanently, and their own soil slipped from under their feet. A different ethnic majority predominated in Palestine, and the Jews from then on struggled for their special form of existence in conditions of exile. But as we have indicated above, this proposition is factually doubtful. It is difficult to accept a physiocratic-national view that attributes the inauguration of a new historical era merely to the physical dispossession from land. The Arab conquest certainly opened a new era, and the period which in my system is called the Poetic-Philosophic culture can hardly be imagined without the social and spiritual ferment activating the Messianic and Karaitic movements, which spread throughout the Arab realms and ensued from events taking place within these realms. Influenced by the contiguity with Arab literature and philosophy, this culture developed and spread in the conditions of the relative affluence attained by Jews in the urban professions and in the courts of the rulers.

It is equally difficult to maintain that those generations themselves saw the Arab conquest of Palestine as a decisive turning-point in their history, such as the point marking the beginning of the exile era. What makes the eviction of a few thousand Jewish farmers from their land – the last survivors of Roman and Byzantine persecutions and confiscations – worthy of inaugurating a new era? For in truth this was not more than the final stage of the eviction process which had begun long before, most intensely following the Bar Kochba revolt. The increased urbanization of Palestine – the foundation of towns like Bet Govrin, Emmaus, Lod, and others in the third century CE – was also a factor in the dwindling of the Jewish agricultural population. Alon infers from a dispute in the Jerusalem Talmud on the *mishnah Demai* 2a that the Palestinian Sages at the end of the third century "were doubtful whether most of the lands of Eretz Israel were in Jewish hands."[26] In brief, neither usurpation of land nor the decrease of the Jewish population began with the Arab conquest.

A second example of Dinur's periodization method is the choice of the year 1700 – the year when a group of 1,000 followers of Rabbi Judah Hassid (the Pious)[27] arrived in the Land of Israel – as the beginning of the "modern era" in Jewish history. Dinur attributed important symbolic value to this organized immigration: it presented three main elements of increasingly ideological and practical import in Jewish life at the time, namely,

the raising of the nation's desire for redemption to the level of a primary and principal prerequisite for the latter's realization, the emphasis on the connection between the Jewish people and its land as an essential, vital and practical factor anchored in the nation's very being, and the marking of the awakening activism to settle the Land of Israel as a necessary means of preparing and expediting redemption.[28]

Unlike Graetz, who considered the spread of the Enlightenment in Germany in the mid-eighteenth century as the beginning of "modern times," or Dubnov, who chose the French Revolution and the granting of civic rights to Jews as the starting-point, two views which essentially agree upon the paramount importance of the Enlightenment movement and its consequences as a historical turning-point, Dinur explains that the arrival of Judah the Pious and his band of followers in the Land of Israel clearly marks "the beginning of a more realistic course of messianic activity,"[29] which paved the way for later migrations and eventually brought about the State of Israel. The establishment of the State of Israel marks the end of a period begun with the arrival of Judah the Pious.

What does this periodization teach us? Its guiding principle is the importance of the Land of Israel in the nation's history. According to Dinur, the clinging to the land by physical habitation, the migration to it, and the yearning for it, are notable characteristics of the nature and the course of all Jewish history. This is another innovation presented by Dinur's conception, and an important one in the National-Israeli culture.

The Holy Land's centrality in Jewish history was much disputed in the Emancipation culture. Dinur endeavors to prove that until the first crusade the land still contained a massive Jewish population. He points out that the call for a return to Zion was also part of the Karaitic platform, that later efforts to settle the land were made by Jewish masses in the exiles throughout the ages; that the land attracted "the most whole element in terms of its Jewish loyalty and tenacity." Therefore the Land of Israel is organically bound up with the history of the entire nation. It is the fulcrum of "tension" in Jewish history in its struggle for Jewish independence.[30]

We need hardly say that neither Jost, nor Graetz, nor Dubnov, shared this view regarding the centrality of the Land of Israel. Do the facts, when differently interpreted, prove that the land was indeed in all ages the center "which attracted all Jewish tension connected with the independence of Jewish being and its historical continuity?" Dinur himself concedes that all through the ages it was always "the strongest elements in Judaism" which flocked to the Land of Israel.[31] It was an undertaking destined for a chosen few. There is no denying the efforts of the majority to support Jewish settlement in the Land of Israel with money and moral encouragement, and there is no doubt that the Land of Israel had the vitality of an "idea" in the hearts of the masses. Dinur rightly emphasizes the historical continuity of the Jewish community in the land, which no persecutions ever completely severed.

But, again, how many Jews really dwelt in Eretz Israel? There certainly was a ceaseless effort, animated by great faith and yearnings for redemption, to preserve a small Jewish remnant in the land in the form of a few scattered communities. But does not the historian–ideologue transform mere yearnings and faith into a real fact? In order to extricate himself from this difficulty Dinur is obliged to distinguish between a "center of influence" and a "center of authority," i.e.

between a community connected with all the others by certain organizational ties and unquestioningly accepted by them as their authority in religious matters, and a community that, while not connected with the rest of the Diaspora by any such organizational ties, has, in consequence of certain historical circumstances, come to serve as a social and cultural model to all the other communities, which copy its example for a certain period of time. Such a center of authority was Palestinian Jewry.[32]

Such a distinction, however, is open to doubts. Dinur would be hard pressed to explain where we have ever found a "center of influence" that had no authority. Did he mean the centers in Babylonia, Spain, or Poland? If so, it is difficult to entertain this distinction. What additional authority is required of a center, which never ceased to be emulated, whose life's manifestations "serve as a social and cultural model to all the other communities"?

Dinur is well aware that the history of Israel begins with the Patriarchs, with Abraham and his tribe who "were imbued with a sense of their national individuation and their religious destiny before they ever entered the land."[33] The Patriarchs only sojourned in the land, while the Canaanites dwelt in it. The national memory has preserved throughout the ages the separation of the land and the people: the geographical and ethnic elements never merged into one whole, and this is why the Prophets perceived exile and separation from the land as a natural punishment. There is much validity in Dinur's opinion that precisely because of this separation, which characterizes the consciousness of the Jewish people and is alien to other nations, "no other nation had such permanent, strong intimate ties with its land. The land is destined for the nation since ancient times. God Himself chose it for His people, and indeed the people held faith with the land."[34] Dinur also remarks upon the nation's extraordinary ability to raise the land from time to time out of its devastation; when Israel comes to cling to its land, the soil responds to it as to no other possessor. But if the existence of the nation depends on an ongoing referendum, on a daily decision of will and valuation, perhaps one should not attribute to the Land of Israel so central a position in the nation's consciousness, at any rate not from the point of view of demographic and geographic reality. As we have seen, the exodus from the Land of Israel was already largely under way in the days of the Second Temple, and much more so, of course, after the destruction. Dinur himself cites Philo's famous words, written long before the destruction: "For so populous are the Jews that no one country can hold them, and therefore they settle in very many of the most prosperous countries in Europe and Asia both in the islands and on land."[35] No doubt, the Land of Israel continued to act as a spiritual center but not in all periods was it a center of authority or a center of influence, in Dinur's own terms. Here too the symbolic idealized reality of faith and expectation has replaced factual reality.

Obviously, Jews in all ages, with the sole exception of the Emancipation culture, knew that their countries of dwelling were not homelands, that they and the Shechinah in their midst, were consigned to exile, and that the Land of Israel was the object of desire and yearning; they never ceased to pray for the ingathering of the exiles, the return to Zion, and the rebuilding of the Temple. But this self-evident aspiration cannot be considered identical with the centrality of the land which Dinur's theory claimed.

So much for Dinur's philosophic-historic conception and its ideological limitations, as these have been revealed to us in his approach to periodization, in his emphasis on the centrality of the Land of Israel, and in the turning of formal and general elements into ideational "substance" and "essence."

Yitzhak Baer's philosophy of history

The needs of the present imposed upon the past by a social-religious will and a nationalist ideology warp proper historical perspective in the work of another eminent scholar, Yitzhak Baer, one of the greatest Jewish historians of all times, and for many years Dinur's colleague, both at the Hebrew University in Jerusalem and in the editorship of the journal *Zion*. He also trained many students who eventually formed the Jerusalem school of historiography, influential in Israel and abroad.

The principles of the philosophic-historic theory guiding Baer are readily discernible even when they are veiled in descriptions, narratives, analyses of documents, and citations from sources. What are the principles of this theory? Baer opens his book, *A History of the Jews in Christian Spain*, with this proposition: "Jewish history, from its earliest beginnings to our own day, constitutes an organic unit. Each successive stage in its development reveals more fully the nature of the unique force guiding it, a force whose initial vitality is universally recognized and whose future course arouses widespread interest. Let this observation be the key to our study."[36] According to this thesis, there is a special force working throughout Israel's history which ties all its episodes and events into one organic unit. This force had a beginning, "whose initial vitality is universally recognized." What is that force and what and where was the vitality of its beginning? We are immediately reminded that the yearning to return to the initial vitality, to the wondrous genesis, to the roots and the source, is a characteristic feature of every traditonal conception, which believes in the occurrence of a divine revelation (as the Sinaitic epiphany) in the community's early days. The humanist movement of the Renaissance similarly believed that it came to renew the initial vitality of classical Greece and Rome. Modern Hebrew historians were infected with this Renaissance faith in return to ancient sources and a revival of early beginnings. Those beginnings are imprinted upon our entire history, a sort of spiritual preformation, which must be revealed and developed. It is Israel's eternal fixed essence, constant through all the vicissitudes of time and integrating all historical episodes into one organic whole. Or, as Baer says at the end of *Yisrael ba-ʿamim* ("Israel among the Nations"):

Every episode in the long history of our nation contains the secret of all periods, both preceding and following. In the end there will remain of the ancients' metaphysical-historical structure a few large columns, which the early pietists sunk into the soil of the Land of Israel, and these are implanted in the heart of every man, and will mark in the future Israel's place among the nations.[37]

But what exactly is this "unique force" which distinguishes Jewish history from that of all other nations? In *A History of the Jews in Christian Spain*, Baer explained that this is the force of the common people's mystical faith, as opposed to the worldly rationalism of the wealthy courtiers and ministers (whom I have called the bearers of the Poetic-Philosophic culture). Jews in the twelfth and thirteenth centuries held important positions in the politics and administration of the Iberian peninsula, and some Jewish grandees did not refrain and were not hindered from preying upon the poor, both Jews and Christians. As for religion, this imperious élite tended to prefer allegorical and metaphorical to literal interpretations of the Torah. Many abandoned altogether the yoke of commandments. In the Jewish quarter in Saragossa and in Toledo, Jewish prostitutes could make a living. The educated stratum of these haughty worldly aristocrats accepted rationalism's acknowledgment of the Torah's ideational-symbolic content, but threw out the outer husk of the commandments. Some ended in total religious nihilism. Thus enfeebled from within, this circle lacked the strength to withstand the harsh trials later brought down upon Spanish Jewry by the Inquisition; its descendants betrayed their people and religion, or lost faith in all religion.

In contrast to these men of position and privilege, says Baer, the Jewish masses comprised petty traders, shopkeepers, and artisans, who fought a harsh battle for survival. The social antagonism between the two classes periodically erupted in bitter discords, and in periods of economic and social crisis in the Gentile world, such as the second half of the fourteenth century, also led a number of Jewish communities to open rebellion. The rifts were also evident among the Jewish agricultural population, especially in the villages of Andalusia, between rich landowners and their laborers and small leaseholders. The rich lived on interest and tax-collection and held positions in the fiscal administration of the church. The Mystical movement in Spain developed in the thirteenth century on the background of these social contrasts.[38] The Kabbalists were not visionaries solely absorbed in mystical thought; they wished to reform the religious and social life of their coreligionists and launched a vigorous attack against the dominant courtier class. In their moral social aspirations, they were strongly influenced by the Ashkenazi (German) Jews, the Ḥassidim (the Pietists), disciples of Rabbi Judah he-Ḥassid (the Pious, or the Saint), and Rabbi Elʿazar ha-Rokeaḥ, in whose school the famous *Sefer Ḥassidim* (twelfth century) apparently originated. In an article devoted to the socio-religious purpose of *Sefer Ḥassidim*, Baer endeavors to substantiate his opinion that the pietists of Germany created a unified and distinct philosophy, which was visibly influenced by Christian views transmitted through books of Christian theology or through sermons.[39] The Jews of Germany absorbed their new views from ideas emanating from the abbey of Cluny, from the school of St. Francis of Assisi, and from other Augustinian and Stoic theologians. But regarding the philosophy expressed in *Sefer Ḥassidim*, Baer says at the end of the article: "This philosophy is the very philosophy of life without which Jewish society cannot exist, and even though it is impregnated with Christian influences, it only reiterates that which the ancients had taught – that there is justice and a just Judge and that all the deeds of man are recorded in the Book."[40] If that is indeed the whole philosophy, what, one may ask, is its novelty? A philosophy of Jewish asceticism imprinted with twelfth- and thirteenth-century Christian monasticism? Nevertheless, the author testifies that this philosophy was all "Jewish contents" and "Jewish inwardness." These German pietists arrived in Spain with their new philosophy and were joined by Mystics from other circles. There they collided fanatically with the bearers of another culture.

The pietists and the Mystics were contemptuously regarded by members of the urban upper classes as "benighted and credulous fools," but "their preaching gained the sympathetic attention of the petty shopkeepers and artisans and the poorer classes residing in the towns and hamlets inside Spain." In a certain sense Kabbalist theory is the "sublimation" of social conflicts within Judaism and of political contrasts between Judaism and the nations of the world:

The whole current of mysticism, along with its individual eddies, had a single goal. The mystics – like the rabbis of the tannaitic period when faced with Hellenistic rationalism – sought to remove Judaism from mundane entanglements to the sheltered precincts of Halakha and Aggada and guide it toward a way of life, mytho-mystic in outlook and ascetic in practice. The attack against rationalism in the name of faith is typical of all the cabalistic works produced during this period.[41]

In my book *Don Isaac Abravanel ve-geirush Sefarad* (which I dedicated to Baer with deep appreciation upon his seventieth birthday), I pointed out this weakness and clarified its implications: precisely those elements in Spanish Jewish culture which were of Ashkenazi (German) provenance embodied for Baer the profound essence and outstanding merit of that community, while that which it had produced independently was, from the spiritual viewpoint of the "unique historical force" characterizing Jewish history, merely an appendage and a defect.[42] This tendency to "Ashkenize" Spanish Jewry denies the special qualities of the extraordinarily gifted community that had created the brilliant Poetic-Philosophic culture and its ontology. It seems to me that the valuations–preferences expressed by the erudite historian of Spanish Jewry illuminate some aspects of his subject in a strange, alien light, while other large areas are left in darkness.

I freely grant that every one of Israel's cultures wished to possess itself of the utmost authority in order to vindicate its beliefs and acts, and that it fought vigorously against preceding or rivaling holders of authority. Baer explicitly takes the liberty of playing arbiter in this polemic between the competing cultures at the end of the Spanish period. We can only wonder how he failed to read in the literature of the times the vitality and pre-eminence of the Poetic-Philosophic culture, a force that remained central in Spanish Jewry until the expulsion despite all the vigorous, often fanatic, exertions of Talmudists and Mystics. The carriers of this culture enriched Jewish literature with works in linguistics, philosophy, and the sciences, and with reinterpretations of the literary patrimony. One may further point out against their detractors that, by and large, they withstood the persecutions with no less courage than members of their rival cultures. After all, Talmudists and Mystics were also known to have abandoned Judaism in the face of savage coercion, and some even did so voluntarily – becoming willing, often even vindictive, apostates. For many Spanish Jews religious philosophy was a spiritual stronghold and a refuge. Joseph Albo's *Sefer ha-ʿikkarim* ("Book of Principles"), for example, seems to have had wide appeal. It was one of the first books to be printed (Soncino, 1486, only two years after the printing of the Talmud and even before the printing of the *Guide for the Perplexed*), and went through seven editions in about fifty years. Joseph Albo, it is true, sought to create a viable compromise between the cultures, but his method is grounded on philosophy and on its achievements. Isaac Hirsch Weiss rightly remarked on the incessant strident bickerings between the Talmudists and the philosophers, among the Talmudists themselves, and between the Mystics and all the others. In the shadow of the Inquisition and with the impending expulsion and final destruction looming on the horizon, the Spanish communities were being torn apart by acrid infighting.[43] Weiss for one does not place the blame on the philosophers, but rather on the Talmudists and especially on the Mystics. The antagonisms and disputes fractured the Spanish communities and sapped them of their vitality long before disaster befell them: "All had a share in the loss of their homeland, the common people as much as the sages, the Talmudists no less than the scholars and the Mystics . . . all are guilty . . . because they knew not how to live in peace with each other."[44] A sobering spectacle of disintegration – the result of polarization and lack of mutual tolerance.

The conflict between the bearers of the three cultures – the Poetic-Philosophic, the Rabbinic, and the Mystical – was keenly intensified during the last three generations of the Spanish community's existence. Thus, the final century in Spain, from the persecutions of 1391 to the expulsion of 1492, was a difficult period for Jews, not only because of external oppression from rulers and inquisitors in the twilight of the disintegrating feudal regime and the ascendance of the monarchy, but also because of the bitter internal divisions. So angry and bitter a struggle between the upholders of three co-existent cultures had never perhaps been witnessed. Each camp accused its rivals of heresy and blamed it for past and impending persecutions. Indeed, the calamities did not fail to come, and every camp believed it alone had foreseen the future with a call for repentance that had remained unheeded. This collision of cultures, a spectacle reminiscent of the atmosphere preluding the destruction of the Second Commonwealth, is a compelling example of what happens in Jewish history when the equilibrium is shaken and dissolved, and a regnant culture loses its power. Yitzhak Baer, however, intervenes in this collision to issue a verdict in favor of one culture over the others.

Critique of Baer's system and conclusion

In the interest of brevity we shall not dwell here on Baer's other major book *Yisrael ba-ᶜamim*, although I trust that most of these concluding comments will be found valid for that work as well. Baer claimed that the Jewish nation was "an organic being" possessing "an internal development": "Its destiny is anchored deep in its soul and the historian needs to understand organic life as it is in itself."[45] This short phrase reveals two fundamental traits in Baer's historical conception: organicism and historic realism. Everything – the physical and the spiritual – grows out of the nation's soil, from the depths of its inner soul. The internal forces encounter external events and are sometimes deflected by the latter from their course, "but they always seek to return to their essential tendency."[46]

 Baer assures us that the historian is given a "sure and reliable test with which to examine the history of our times, by uncovering layer by layer the unique forces of the entire historical development and by separating the accidental phenomena which have accreted in the course of time on the fundamental essence."[47] But it is difficult to say that Baer keeps his promise. By what tested method can one distinguish between essential and trivial, between substance and contingency? And how is it that when Baer applies himself to the investigation of a particular phenomenon in Judaism, it is rather the phenomenon's foreign sources that attract his attention? The Ashkenazi Ḥassidim borrowed asceticism and many items of lore from Christian theologians. Baer emphasizes that the "inner forces" of Ashkenazi Jewry were not impervious to external influences, perhaps less than Spanish Jewry, but claims these Ḥassidim were more adept in preserving Jewish tradition. Similarly, although the Tannaᵓitic Sages were influenced by Greek philosophers, especially by Plato and the Stoics, and although the Temple service evinced certain borrowings from pagan rites, both created and embodied original, universal values which served as an "ideal and a testament for generations." It is almost as though the monotheistic idea was sufficient to transform foreign influences into inner substance: Jews acquire beliefs and opinions from their neighbors, but then discover internal meaning in the spirit of monotheism. It seems, however, that Baer has introduced more than the magic wand of monotheism to turn outer husks into inner meanings, and contingencies into substance.

 Baer believes that his conception reveals the "substance," the "essence," the "internal contents" of Jewish history. Like his teacher E. Täubler,[48] he believes that there is one basic idea underlying all the activity and creativity of the Jewish people in its entire history. One emphatic passage summarizes the essence of his conception:

The battle against enlightenment, which begins in Spain with Judah ha-Levy and gathers momentum under the influence of the Kabbalah, and in the movement of German Pietism, is an anti-rationalist, anti-secular, anti-capitalist movement, similar to the movement of the Prophets, the Pharisees and the Tanna'im. It transforms the people into a religious proletariat.[49]

This, then, is the essence of Judaism, and the measure against which the forbidden and the permitted are defined. It is charged by Baer with the task of transforming external influence into inner meaning, contingency into substance, husk to core.

How does all this affect historical perspective? Baer believes that this single essence is the key to all Jewish existence. Jewish history has been an organic unity from the age of the Patriarchs down to our day, with every one of its chapters a direct sequel to whatever preceded it; thus it is an essence that confers upon each generation a measure of understanding. Baer has to concede that "this gigantic organic growth suffered from convolutions and predicaments resulting from its confrontations with other organic essences,"[50] but believes that by and large it remained intact – an "eternality of Israel." Only in our day has this growth been threatened, a fact which emphasizes all the more the historian's role of separating the wheat from the chaff and standing vigilant guard over the substance, essence, and contents. One cannot help wondering whether Baer did not mistake the transitory and the contingent in our history (asceticism, martyrdom imposed by external circumstances, pneumatism, etc., elements stressed in *Yisrael ba-ʿamim* as characterizing the Tanna'itic period) for the permanent and the essential?

Another question we must ask is if there really was any unity in these "inner forces"? There always were special forces in Jewish history which sought to carve out a path in the face of opposition from hostile forces, both internal and external, but there never was only one such operative force. One should be especially wary of imposing spiritual tendencies and specific characteristics revealed in one culture upon all other cultures. We noted earlier that Baer failed to recognize the greatness of the Poetic-Philosophic culture, and always viewed it as a symptom of decline, a foreign implant, the antithesis and adversary of the pietist trend. He believed that our life in the diaspora had to be examined and evaluated in keeping with criteria emanating directly from the ancestral spiritual wellsprings of the early pietists and the Sages of the Mishnah. Baer thus saw unity and continuity where, in fact, divisions and distinctions seem much more compelling. He tenaciously argued that in Jewish history all forces and tendencies infected by rationalism had led Jews to acculturate in their countries of exile and that these forces were the extreme antithesis of the ancient spiritual heritage handed down from the days of initial vitality: "All that we have done on foreign soil was to betray our essential spirit."[51]

Baer shares Dinur's views on the centrality of the Land of Israel in the nation's history, and cites the sentence put by the Sages in God's mouth: "I prefer a small sect in the Land of Israel to a large Sanhedrin abroad." Baer accepted Graetz's opinion that in Jewish history the idea of the transcendent God sought an embodiment in a "national substance" on earth in the shape of an organized society – Graetz speaks of a state – which observes the Halachah as an organized group in keeping with the divine constitution. Baer also shares Buber's view that the carriers of this God idea were the pietists and the Mystics, "pneumatic" personalities, who believed they had received revelations via the "holy spirit" or through visions of God, but unlike Buber, Baer emphasizes the importance of the Halachah as an instituition.[52]

In summary, Baer confirms the Zionist assumption in Jewish historiography in respect to the unity of the national body, the continuousness of historical occurrences despite changes and transformations, and the special intensive affinity to the Land of Israel. In these three points Baer does not differ from Dinur.

In his sharp critique of Salo Baron's *Social and Religious History of the Jews* (first edition), Baer argued against the Emancipation culture so eloquently articulated by Baron. The essence of his criticism was that Baron failed to discern in Jewish history the "true inner forces" confronting rationalism, secularism, optimism, and capitalism in an ongoing endeavor to transform the nation into a "religious proletariat." Baron did not grasp the "immanent theory of Jewish history,"[53] according to which the Prophets, the Sages of the Mishnah, and various schools of pietism sought to establish a utopian kingdom of heaven inspired by metaphysical models like Platonic ideas. Baer reproaches Baron with the optimism and rationalism that characterize "most historians today," who forget the hardships of oppression and the intensity of the exiled nation's yearnings for its homeland (a reference to Baron's complaint on the "lachrymosity" of Jewish history). Like Jewish Science scholars of the Emancipation, Baron glorifies the period of the nation's sovereignty on its historical soil but also finds merit in Israel's dispersion among the Gentiles. Baer further accuses Baron of propounding theses, "general statements which surely do not belong to the experimental sphere of history."

Indeed, Baron's theses are diametrically opposed to Baer's. Baron's approach to the causes shaping the course of Jewish history is pluralistic and not monistic. He sees in history antagonisms, tensions, and irreconcilable logical contradictions. Baron's conception is tolerant, embracing wide horizons, and refraining from imposing abstract theories upon Jewish history. It advocates a multiplicity of cultures in the life of the Jewish people today. In contrast to this conception, we have seen that for Baer, Judaism is not an optimistic but an ascetic, pneumatic, and martyrological religion, at any rate not a religion conducive to the enjoyment of this world. Baer sees Judaism's essence reflected in Rabbinic sayings by Sages like Rabbi Akiba, Rabbi Abbahu, and Rabbi Isaac as, for example: "Those who are insulted but do not insult, hear themselves reviled without answering, act through love and rejoice in suffering, of them the Writ saith 'But they who love Him are as the sun when he goeth forth in his might'" (Rabbi Akiba in *Sab.* 88b).[54] Rabbi Abbahu said: "A man should always strive to be rather of the persecuted than the persecutors as there is none among the birds more persecuted than doves, and yet Scripture made them [alone] eligible for the altar" (*Bab. K.* 93a). Rabbi Isaac said: "Woe to him who cries [for divine intervention] even more than to him against whom it is invoked!" (ibid.). Baer knows that Zionist ideology is not at home in this kind of mentality. Therefore he draws the Zealots, the national "freedom-fighters" of yore, into prominence, defends them against the criticism of Josephus, and makes Rabbi Yoḥanan ben Zakkai a prominent figure in their midst.

Baer certainly appreciated the soteriological element in Jewish history and rightly emphasized that Jews in all eras hoped and yearned for the coming of the Messiah. The yearning for redemption lends a special flavor to Jewish history. It is on the soteriological foundation, one might add (and not merely on the Sages' "utopian state," as described in *Yisrael ba-ʿamim*), that we find anchored all values-ideals whose fulfillment in the historical reality the human soul craves.

By now we know, of course, that every culture, whether Jewish or Gentile, possesses a soteriological dimension, though there are obvious differences in degrees and emphases, depending on the nation and the period, and on the manner redemption is conceived. But for Baer, the only theory of Jewish redemption that appears to operate through the ages is of the type envisaged by pietists and Mystics. Whereas Scholem emphasized the novelty of the Mystical culture, Baer stresses its importance in all Jewish history, as well as in our own times. One cannot help noting regretfully that Baer's world view presents too many unknowns: the nation's "soul" and "will," its "organic essence," the "utopian state," and all those "true inner forces" operating through history. Baer's affinity with dreamers of spiritual-mystical salvation ("pneumatics"), has turned this erudite historian of the National-Israeli culture into a trumpeter of salvation.

To summarize this critique: my evaluation of Baer's conception of Jewish history expresses both admiration for his ability as a researcher, and criticism of the speculative-metaphysical theses that guided him, or that were revealed to him, in his study of the source materials, as he understood them. My main contention is that in the final analysis even in Baer's own opinion, Jewish "essence," that special historic force, remains intact. Of course, this force, or these spiritual tendencies, are immersed in the flux of events, but in fact they have already occurred, and their continuity is the continuity of an idea, as in the systems of idealistic philosophy. Admittedly, modern historiography gave the idea a new form, but by and large it resembles, in terms of its continuity, the visage of the God-given Torah from Sinai, as perceived by the generations of traditional faith. We, however, have argued here that Jewish history must be viewed in a more complex, threefold perspective.

It is interesting to note that the historian who was ascribed a particularly strong nationalist, even nationalistic, ideology, Joseph Klausner, was the one who actually came closest to the truth of historical perspectivism: objectivity, he said, was a matter of research devoid of personal or collective "bias" based on the methodology of scientific criticism. Even the most objective scientist is but a mortal and an unconscious subject to the influences of notions current in his particular time and milieu:

The Roman and the Jew in ancient times could not hold a similar opinion of the Emperor Titus: for the former, Titus was the "delight of mankind," while for the latter he was "Titus the wicked." And the truth is this: what is evil for the one can be good for another, and vice versa, and this is after all the nature of every important historic personality, but an honest historian must see both sides of the commonly accepted historical coin.

Klausner also said: "every generation of historians revises the evaluation of its predecessors and thereby comes closer to the historical truth."[55]

9

CONCLUSIONS AND IMPLICATIONS

Toward a summary

Our study began with a definition of the concept "culture" and with preliminary explanations of the new method for understanding Judaism and Jewish history, and it has spanned a hitherto largely uncharted course, ending with the detailed examination of modern National-Israeli historiography. Certain ideas presented in this study have been methodically developed at relative length, while other important subjects were barely mentioned, or were alluded to only in passing. A number of important topics have not been addressed at all, such as distinctions between Judaism and Christianity, the significance of Jewish history in world history, transitions between cultures, and the concurrent interplay of rival cultures.[1] I have also omitted discussions on the polemics attending a culture's legitimation methods; of particular interest are the nature and strength of the Rabbinic culture, which looked to the Talmud for the validation of its authority as the Talmud had looked to the Bible, but without the boldness and vision that characterized the Sages' "creative interpretation," and how this culture came to dominate in central Europe and why it is still powerful – and even gaining strength – in the State of Israel today.[2] We must also leave aside later philosophical and theological debates on the "essence of Judaism," and how this essence actually related to the transformations affecting the nation in the Emancipation and the National-Israeli cultures.

An attempt has been made here to validate a number of fairly complex and abstract theories by use of more readily understandable concrete historical examples and proofs: theories on the nature and development of culture, and on the vitality of cultures as renaissances and renewals, on perspective in history and the problematics involved in explaining historical facts, methods of interpretation, and the hermeneutics of cultures, tensions and integration in a society, the *halachic* commandments and their meaning in different cultures, and more.

What can we explicitly derive from all of the above on Judaism, on the articulations of its ideas, and on the understanding of its history, and what conclusions can we draw from this new interpretation? The next few pages seek to summarize and clarify, to draw explicit conclusions and to add and re-emphasize certain points. These final pages take us back to the thesis presented in the introduction: the new approach may aid a modern Jew, both in Israel and in the diaspora, to resolve some of the confusion about his own identity and about the nature of Judaism. We wished to demonstrate that in the spacious and generous mansion that is Israel's history and its affirmations, there are many available spiritual treasures. We have signaled how he may take possession of the patrimony legated by his forebears of earlier generations and cultures, and how he might continue to enrich that patrimony for the benefit of his own successors. Our thesis is not an undemanding one for the modern Jew: the picture it paints is of a creative people initiating change and transformation prompted by the needs of its own salvation and the socio-religious "redemption" of the world. It is also a thesis that clearly demands certain ethical standards and certain forms of activity and creativity.

Jewish identity in a changing world

In seeking a modern view of Jewish identity and the nature of Judaism, it is useful to consider for a moment the history of Judaism's summarizations in the form of dogmatized creeds, or binding principles of faith ($^{c}ikkarim$). At least five fundamental attitudes have crystallized in the course of Judaism's dogmatization:

1   Scholars and community leaders appropriated unto themselves the authority to transform principles (beliefs and opinions which they considered quintessential to Judaism) into speculative abstractions, to be embraced as basic truths of the Jewish faith, the acknowledgment and observance of which was made incumbent upon every believer, while disbelief or denial forfeited a man's "portion in the world to come" and warranted social ostracism. This is what Maimonides did, for example, in his famous thirteen principles of faith.

2   Other scholars and leaders deflected the principles of creed in the direction of *halachic* observance, as in the case of Moses Mendelssohn who maintained (influenced perhaps by Spinoza) that the Torah had not commanded faith but rather observance of commandments, hence there were no binding principles of faith. We need hardly add that the observance of commandments was recognized by all Sages as a fundamental tenet of Judaism, with some Sages emphasizing more heavily than others the Talmudic view that certain types of transgressors could have no portion in the world to come.

3 Some scholars anchored Judaism's essence strictly on faith in God's existence: Adam's sin was essentially one of atheism; anyone who fulfills even a single commandment with complete faith is granted the grace of the Shechinah.

4 Others have selectively stressed certain beliefs, such as the coming of the Messiah. These latter two positions are, of course, clarifications and elaborations of the first position.

5 But there were also some Sages in Jewish history, notably Don Isaac Abravanel, who held that in Judaism no distinctions could be drawn between the essential and the seemingly inconsequential, there was no difference between a phrase like "the sons of Ham, Kush and Mitzraim" and the verse: "I am the Lord thy God." Everything is essence in the divinely given Torah, hence the whole attempt at formulating Judaism's principles was an undesirable consequence of "mixing with the Gentiles by learning their books and acquiring their sciences."[3]

Whether opinions leaned toward the speculative or the *halachic*, the sufficiency of one belief or the emphasis on certain selected beliefs, or whether an equal value was assigned to all Pentateuchal articulations, the question of Judaism's essence re-emerged in every period where loss of simple faith and unquestioned conviction was experienced. This generally resulted from external influences, as Abravanel had justly noted. But the preoccupation with Judaism's essence was also an internal necessity – to accomplish the internal reform envisaged by the thinker in question. Judaism's identity and essence became acutely pressing issues in periods of great perplexity in the wake of eroding faith. Dogmatic formulations did not, however, diminish disagreements and disputes, and no wonder: they were attempts to set boundaries and to fence in that which by its very nature was open, unfenced, and subject to change, to the same changes, in fact, taking place in the cultures' ontology. Solomon Schechter and others pointed out that the formulation of principles upon which Maimonides wished to base Judaism was to be viewed as a sort of temporary preventive measure; for example, seeing that the concept God was being dangerously anthropomorphized, he established the principle that God was incorporeal and was inapprehensible to the corporeal.[4] The Poetic-Philosophic culture championed by Maimonides could not acquiesce to incorporification. Similarly, reacting to the Muslims' extollment and magnification of their Prophet, he laid down the principle that Moses was the chief of all Prophets, both of those that preceded and of those that followed him. The enunciation of principles of faith was essentially a strategy in the battle to establish and reinforce the Poetic-Philosophic culture's ontology. It did little, however, for internal concord and harmony.

The five cultures of traditional faith are separated by a fundamental and very obvious difference from the last two secular cultures in the definition of Jewish essence and identity. Human history ceased to be experienced as a divine drama in which the Jewish people, God's portion and inheritance, was the leading protagonist, second only to the Creator Himself. The entire frame of reference, as the sociologists would say, and the entire ontology, have changed: the ontology of recent generations no longer permits the derivation of explanations for the ways of the world still less the derivation of consolations and hopes for redemption, in a simple and direct line from the sacred conceptions of religious systems of culture. An unmistakable sign of the novelty is the abrogation of *halachic* authority in daily life.

Indeed the change has been vast: in a world of tradition, of relative permanence both in society's institutions and modes of organization, and in its beliefs and values, the question of Jewish identity did not arise. The interrogation, "Who is this person?", was answered with, "This is so-and-so, son of so-and-so," and if there happened to be two of the same name in a town, one added the person's address, or his livelihood, or other such external signs. This is how Jews were identified as recently as two generations ago.

Today it is change which is deemed important and desirable. It is a superordinating concept in the self-conception of modern man. Social mobility, rapid changes in life-styles and in sources of livelihoods, migrations to unknown places, frequent exchanges of dwellings, intermixing of nations, weakening faith in the existence of God, in reward and punishment, in immortality – all of these changes loosen identity from its moorings. This is all the more true in the case of Jews who have stepped outside the restrictive spiritual boundaries of the *shtetl* to establish themselves in societies exposed to every waft of influence. Modern man holds multiple and quite diverse social roles, as dictated by the demands of his profession and the circles or groups within which he moves. This multiplicity of roles, which periodically mandates that he disclose a new and different facet of his identity, also compels him to work hard on cultivating that element of his identity which is to remain stable and unchanging.

Today the question regarding a man's identity is answered in the light of his various roles, his status, and his personal achievements. I am what I am by virtue of myself, by virtue of the experiences and achievements of my life. Modern man develops his identity from the ground up, at least so he believes, and this independence is the most characteristic feature of post-Renaissance European culture. Not tradition, not external or superior authority, but personal experiences are the source of his consciousness, the root of his conception of himself and the world. His partners are contemporaries who share the same life experiences, a partnership that sustains his private identity. Social reality, which assigns man to his specific place in the world and individuates his identity, is simply the mutual consent of these partners to a world of shared feelings and experiences, conceptions and symbols. From the social viewpoint, reality is merely that which is held to be real by those who have acquired importance in the eyes of their fellows. They confirm and support their reality, they prohibit and dispense, disqualify and approve, accept as real or reject as unreal. They create the identity and validate it. The difficulty arises when the "pillars of society" themselves lack a permanent identity. This condition is not uncommon today, especially for many diaspora Jews, who find that their Jewish identity, even when unwanted, is not easily eradicable. The European Holocaust was a reminder of this fact.[5]

The same is true when one addresses "the nature" of Judaism. Formerly when one queried, "What is Judaism?" one was referred to the Bible or the Talmud, to one's elders, to a learned Torah scholar. Judaism's nature, even though it in fact underwent vast changes, as we saw in the foregoing chapters, was viewed as having been indelibly imprinted with the mark of permanence. The Torah stood forever, unchanging and unalterable. Where they knew that corrections and changes had been made, Jews believed that these too had been the express design of Holy Writ, and were not really innovations, or at best that these were the innovations of a seasoned scholar guided by the spirit of the Writ. Even Hermann Cohen, a modern thinker with a Platonic-Kantian view on the essence of Judaism, explained in his book on the Jewish religion that while the Sages' homiletics did violence to the text's literal meanings, they left its contents intact; the entire purity of monotheism, Cohen thought, hinged on this.[6]

The truth is, as we have seen in this study, that in the ages of faith change was introduced via interpretations and reinterpretations; there was no clear realization of the nature of the change and its many dimensions, because history was apprehended through a hazy and unfocused lens. The slow pace of change in life-styles gave the impression that everything remained static, and was an inevitable sequel in the natural order of events. It was also customary to think, often in complete disregard of actual practice, that the Torah could not be adjusted to individual details, periods, and locations, adapted to each community in every age and country. As innovative a thinker as Maimonides did not depart from the belief commonly held in ages of traditional faith:

It follows that the laws cannot like medicine vary according to the different conditions of persons and times; whilst the cure of a person depends on his particular constitution at the particular time, the divine guidance contained in the Law must be certain and general, although it may be effective in some cases and ineffective in others. If the Law depended on the varying conditions of man, it would be imperfect in its totality, each precept being left indefinite. For this reason it would not be right to make the fundamental principles of the Law dependent on a certain time or a certain place; on the contrary, the statutes and the judgments must be definite, unconditional, and general.[7]

With the collapse of traditional faith in the Torah's sacredness, the gates were thrown wide open to acculturation in the diasporas, and the desire to confine Judaism within the bounds of a "religious church" grew; new attempts were initiated to formulate the essence of Judaism. Many adherents of secular nationalism, as, for example, Saul Israel ha-Levi of Horowitz (1862–1922), a radical opponent of attempts (such as Aḥad ha-ʿam's) to fence Judaism in narrow, rigid formulations, thought that Judaism was essentially whatever the Jewish heart chose to believe, yet such thinkers too were eager to cling to a spiritual essence, an eternal idea that would epitomize and represent Judaism's distilled, and glorious, nature.

The debate in the last century centered on the question of the attitude to historical development, i.e. the attitude to tradition and to the very possiblility of renewal and change. Jewish opinion, like opinion everywhere, was divided between staunch "guardians of the walls" engaged in stemming the tide of change, and the innovators. The influence of Herder, Hegel, and Wilhelm von Humboldt was much in evidence in the debate (which persists to this day) on ruling and guiding ideas, on a necessary essence. We pointed out earlier that those who wished to nail down a Jewish essence, or to define the Jewish faith in terms of specific dogmas, were acting with polemical intent. Such attempts to simplify the complex phenomenon of Israel's cultures have generated much error and confusion. Our introduction listed three such typical errors.

How, then, will reflection upon the nature of Judaism confront the modern era, subject and sensitive to so much change? What is the meaning of Jewish identity and Jewish essence? In an age of revolutionary transformation in modes of life and thought, when ontology bases itself on the soteriological efficacy of science, experimentation, and technology, it appears to many as though Israel's Torah, or the Jewish essence – a fixed ideational essence incumbent upon every Jew – has become an anachronism, a burden, a meaningless onus. The quintessence of our answer, if it needs restatement, is approximately this: Israel's Torah has no finite measure. It has never been a cut-and-dried dogma; on the contrary, it has always possessed many faces, and its opinions and beliefs can be interpreted in more than one sense. If we include in the concept Judaism all written and oral Jewish articulations of opinions and beliefs, as well as the Jewish people's movements through history and the inter-relationships between its various articulations and systems, surely one must concede that the question of Judaism's uniqueness and essence is not given to any categorical answer. If the Talmud, which is only one system of Jewish culture, can be likened to an "boundless sea," then surely the existence of six other systems of culture makes Judaism a wide and full ocean, incapable of being summarized and exhausted in a single definition. The commonality that unites the seven distinct cultural entities resides in the potency of the directing superordinating concepts, God, Israel, Torah, and all concepts derived from these with the compelling force of commandments. These cardinal constructs, although differently conceived in each culture, imposed obligations which distinguished the Jewish people from other nations. In the first five cultures this distinction lay in the practical precepts emanating from a "chosen people's" consciousness of election.

It is by no means my intention to deny all usefulness to the concept of essence and Jewish essence. When nonessentials and appendages of a matter are stripped off, one does arrive at the essence of a phenomenon. The phenomenological school went a long way toward clarifying the nature of many essences by removing nonessentials in what Husserl called "eidetic reduction": the eidos, the idea, the essence, is revealed when one "places between parentheses" that which is extraneous to the thing's essence. Removal from the tangible and the actual, which is from the eidetic viewpoint but a shell, allows us to focus on the necessary existent, which is the core. Many of the concepts employed in this study, such as culture, or ontology, are ideas in the sense of essences. But our study wished to emphasize the following two points: there is no single Jewish essence for all of Israel's cultures; at best one can speak of the essence of each individual culture. Secondly, essence is not a metaphysical substance or force which possesses sovereign existence in an "objective" reality, but a construct of thought that allows access to the heart of an issue. It is an ideational structure with which to open the gates of phenomena and peer beyond them.[8]

Spiritual needs in a secular culture

The debate over the nature of Judaism which arose at the end of the last century and continues to this day resulted from secularization in the modes of life and thought of many east European Jews. Large areas of Jewish life were emptied of religious sacrality and of its power to interpret reality and impose binding norms upon the individual and the group. The collapse was most keenly felt in the secularization of the legal and educational systems. Jews ceased to believe in miracles, in the power of Torah and prayer, in saints and intercessors and in the *zechut ʾavot* ("the merit of the Patriarchs") who shield and deliver in the hour of need. This crisis of values was destined to widen and deepen to the point where today in the State of Israel it has wrought spiritual havoc of alarming dimensions. The authority of public institutions has been undermined, structures of knowledge and foundations of beliefs have collapsed. Max Weber described the process of European secularization and ever-increasing rationalism as the dissipation of the world's magic ("die Entzauberung der Welt," Friedrich Schiller's phrase), i.e. the dissolution of the magic bonds, the strings of charm and enchantment in which the world was bound when it was guided by a personal providence and open daily to new wonders.

The extent to which elements of public order and conduct were undermined when faith as a directing and reassuring public institution disappeared became poignantly apparent. Lost was the savor of Sabbath, holy days, and festivals, gone was the joy of *mitzvah* and the sorrow of mourning over the destroyed Temple. The eventful Jewish calendar with its dramatic commemoration of the highs and lows of national life became a chronological plateau of monotonous, barely distinguishable days (at least in the public domain). The disappearance of divine providence also banished from the world the fear of hell and the delight of paradise, the joy of the resurrection of the dead and the world to come, the attributes of judgment and mercy. The lights which guided and controlled individual and communal actions were extinguished and the boundaries between the permissable and the forbidden blurred. All the commandments pertaining to human inter-relationships were given over to the heart, or were made subordinate to secular laws. To paraphrase, by a slight alteration in punctuation, the Sage's famous question in the *Ethics of the Fathers*: Which is the right course? That a man should choose for himself! (*Avot* 2.1). Jewish lawlessness was given wide latitude. Many historians and thinkers have described the reverberations from the shock of this great rupture in the public sphere, but only creators of Bialik's or Berdyczewski's stature succeeded in conveying the profound sorrow in the personal domain, over the separation from the world of faith, and the spiritual anguish resulting from the recent transformation.

But spiritual needs, and especially the soteriological need of seeking redemptive meaning, do not disappear for long. Even a materialistic and worldly culture seeks personal and collective redemption according to the lights of its ontology. The transcendent need is overwhelming: the ontology may wish to deny it, but it persists. After the "death of God" had been declared in the Christian world (and long before Nietzsche's "madman" in the *Gay Science*), ideological sects and currents seeking a substitute for the God of tradition had already made their appearance. Beliefs transmigrated from traditional formats to new versions of religiosity, which aspired to draw sustenance from the marrow of the old tradition and nurture the soul as the latter had done and even to exceed it. Scientific methods became the new redeeming message, religiosity without God was held up as true religion. Analagous phenomena were to be found within Judaism.

The thinkers whom I have faulted with the various types of errors in the definition of Jewish essence were all products of this crisis and their opinions express it, in greater or lesser conceptual and emotional power. They all witnessed what had happened to the Jew after the "breaking of the tablets." The sorrow of parting was profoundly and feelingly expressed by Michah Joseph Berdyczewski (Bin Gorion, 1865–1921): "When we defeat the past, it is we ourselves who are defeated . . . elixir and poison in one and the same substance."[9] And even more poignantly: "The Israelite who laid down his life for a single one of the minor commandments, his blood cries out to me from the earth; and whenever I transgress that commandment, the image of that martyr, broken, shattered, blurred, and crushed though it be, confronts me as reproof."[10]

But with all the obvious differences between the religious and the secular worlds, the need for a certain measure of continuity should not be minimized. Neither should we belittle the power that inheres in ideas to impose obligations. Our century has amply witnessed both the constructive and the destructive power of ideas. My point is simply that there is no one unique national idea which can be made binding upon all members of a secular or progressively secularizing culture.

A Jew carries within himself the sum total of Jewish antecedent and subsequent existence. No matter how far he progresses in the quest for new directions, he cannot desist from the effort of irradiating these with his understanding of the past (inasmuch as he identifies with this understanding), although, as we have suggested, old treasures too should be tapped only after a duly critical examination. There is no "giving of the Torah" without "acceptance of the Torah," according to the culture and personalities of the age. If in the cultures of faith observance of commandments symbolized the battle against evil in the world, it follows that the rationale for the commandments, indeed their very essence, changed with the changing conception of evil in each generation. Soteriological thought changes and with it the redeeming effort.

We are, therefore, led to make a basic assumption, namely, that although the ideological world of the Jewish religion differs in some principal features from the world of the modern secular Jew, certain of its basic creeds are animated by experiences and opinions which are abiding spiritual needs. These are not easily expressed in modern idiom. The "light of Judaism" is revealed precisely in the transposition of concepts from the language of preceding cultures to our own conceptual vocabulary. It is clear to me that those motives and impulses which formerly crowned the edifice of traditional Judaism in its first five cultures, a towering structure of Torah, commandments, customs, experiences, and thoughts culminating in a complete creative ontology (but also fenced with endless circumscriptions), are no less operative in the modern Jew who seeks his way in the world today. The renewal of the historic patrimony is therefore first of all a matter of uncovering these motives and impulses ("the quest for meaning," one would call it) and the symbols in which they have wrapped themselves, and examining how they may be made fecund in our own age. There are fertile kernels within the husks: the quest for God in earlier cultures was the quest for wholeness in its actualization of absolute meaning, in the kingdom of heaven. Faith in goodness, in happiness, in "true beatitude," has not become less of a necessity for modern man. And similarly, the opinion that man's well-informed conscience is a reliable and true judge, and that success is not necessarily achieved in wealth, honor, and domination, attests to the moral fiber of a nation and an individual. Man was created in the image of God and is enjoined to imitate His attributes: "As He is clement and merciful, so you be clement and merciful." Those who insisted upon the distinction between inner "core" and outer "husk" were right. All renewal movements in culture and religion acted in keeping with this fundamental distinction.

Toward a reinterpretation of chosenness

We are speaking of a new creative interpretation, of a critical hermeneutics of cultures. For example, the State of Israel has been viewed as the first step toward "redemption" (at³halta di-ge³lah). Its Messianic vision, if you will, is bound up in ostensibly prosaic matters, such as land resettlement, absorption of new immigrants, development of agriculture and industry, closing of educational and social gaps, and strengthening its capability for military deterrence. The pioneering spirit embodied in the great constructive endeavors, in the creative imagination and the transcendent intellect that frequently defy the narrow, balancing calculations of common sense, leads to redemption and to the uplifting of redemptees. It depends upon "miracles," which human beings perform in bold actions – testimonials to the educated will-power of individuals and nation to divagate from the grip of conformity and routine. The heritage of our culture and the conditions of our existence in the State of Israel impel us to extraordinary feats.

This secular rendition of concepts that are found in traditional faith perpetuates a strong religious, especially a soteriological, element. True, the observance of commandments as traditionally prescribed distinguishes between the secular and the religious Jew, a distinction that appears increasingly adversarial in contemporary Israel, but a wide meeting-ground still remains. Indeed, I believe that an utterly secular, "normal" Judaism, an entity "like all the nations" does not exist today, as it never existed in the past.

Paradoxically, the State of Israel has given Jews the right to mediocrity, that basic right of every nation to full existence without contributions to other nations and without exalted destinies to enrich human civilization at large. It is undoubtedly the only answer to Auschwitz and other political disasters. But unlike Jewish diaspora communities, Israelis seem to excel in, of all things, agricultural and military endeavors, and to lag behind in economic organization. The Israeli talent has failed to achieve optimal expression in the traditional Jewish professions: trade, industry, and banking. Qualities which had captivated Gentile imagination while Jews dwelt in their midst – the keen Jewish intellect, the scientific and artistic genius, all those pungent and penetrating ingredients which had spiced the cultures of the world seem in Israel to have diminished, at least temporarily.

The right to mediocrity, to the normalcy to which all nations are entitled, cures the Jewish soul of the ills of both inferiority and superiority which have clung to it over the ages, and perhaps psychologists are correct in believing that the superiority complex is but the counterface of inferiority and of its selfsame mettle. An ideology of superiority rationalizes inferiority and covers it up. A fault is easily transformed into an advantage that is henceforward seen as acting for the "sake of heaven," or for the mending of the world, or to the greater glory of human civilization. Jews effaced their own individuality in order to make weighty contributions to others, to be the "salt of the earth." The nation's talents, its very existence and security were sacrificed on the altar of self-effacement for the benefit of universally human, religious, ethical, and social causes. This was not a result of any failure or backwardness but, on the contrary, it sprung from an excess of progress, from too much alacrity and zeal, from running before the chariot of the redeemer. This was the stance adopted by most of Emancipation Jewry, a proclamation by the vulnerable: see how strong we are, a "light unto the nations," God has done us a veritable kindness by dispersing us among the nations.

Yet the self-depreciation of Emancipation Jews in western Europe contained one element that, despite various distortions and falsifications, is still important for us today. It is an element with which the literature of the Haskalah is surfeited and which has been the cause of much grief and controversy. I refer to the element of self-reform, that is, the self-criticism and self-correction undertaken by Jews in order to find grace and favor before the Gentiles, to be useful denizens to the resident community. Zionism and the State of Israel sought to redeem Jews from this "correction": Jewish life was not a right bestowed upon us by the nations, that we should be reformed according to their preconception and for their benefit; we are entitled to existence whether or not we find favor in the eyes of others. Concurrently, Zionism called for "moral transcendence." We must be reformed for our own sake, for our own good and benefit, we should be an exemplary community and exemplary human beings. We cannot be a light unto the nations before we see a great light in ourselves. This healthy core of the oft-falsified theory of destiny is certainly worth preserving in the State of Israel today.

Jews in Israel still experience a deeply felt spiritual need for ideas and achievements that transcend the mediocre, for an articulation and realization of "chosenness." Just as earlier generations were imbued with the conviction that God had of all nations chosen them for His own, so today Jews living in Israel sense in their existence as a nation, dwelling in its historical homeland, a transnational and transpolitical dimension of chosenness. Chosenness here is not some absolute essence that exists in its own right, but a self-imposed obligation and an expectation geared to the performance of great and good deeds. I am speaking here of so-called secular Jews. The novelty of the National-Israeli culture may be described in the older Rav Kook's phrase as a "holiness that destroys," whose benefit, the Rav said, unlike the benefit of "the holiness that builds," was not at first apparent, "because it destroys in order to build what is nobler than that which has been built already . . . From the holiness that destroys there emerge the great warriors who bring blessing to the world. They exemplify the virtue of Moses, the man of the mighty arm, who broke the tablets."[11] He went on to explain that "one who cannot tolerate spiritual destruction" has no "edifices he has built himself. He finds shelter in naturally formed structures, like rabbits who find protection in the rocks." Most Jews today are descendants of Jews who piously observed the *halachic* commandments as set forth by the Rabbinic culture. Although they no longer believe in a God who exacts observance of these laws, their Judaism is still animated by a sense of their own individuation and uniqueness, and they cannot, either as individuals or as a community, disavow this consciousness of belonging to a "chosen" people.[12]

The commandments remain, of course, the chief barrier between secular and Orthodox Jews, but secular Jews are free to interpret the commandments, perhaps in this vein: commandments were given in order to aid Israel, they are an educational process aimed at mending man and the world for a better future. The *halachic* law is essentially a symbol or, in the language of the Bible, a "sign" or a "memorial." Sanctification resides not in the commandments themselves but in their power as symbols-signs that actuate a Jew to good deeds. This is an idea frequently found in the Talmud and in the writings of the Poetic-Philosophic culture. As the Midrash puts it, "A man may wish to become a priest and yet he cannot; he may wish to become a Levite and yet he cannot. And why? Because his father was no priest, or no Levite. But if a man, Jew or gentile, wishes to be righteous, he can be this, because the righteous do not form a house . . . Of their own free will, they have come forward and loved the Holy One, blessed be He. And that is why He loves them."[13]

Hermann Cohen explained the nature of the commandments in this secular vein: the Jewish prayer book contains a distinction which may instruct us in the symbolic value of *halachic* laws. The wording of the formula opening the benedictions, "Blessed art thou, O Lord our God, King of the Universe, who has sanctified us by His commandments," might seem to suggest that it is through obedience to the commandments themselves that our sanctification is effected. If this were so, the commandments would lose their symbolic value and resemble the sacrificial offerings brought in the time of the Temple. However, the prayers also contain the formula: "Sanctify us by Your commandments and purify our heart." Here the symbolic character of the commandments is made unmistakably clear. The power of sanctification is not in the commandments themselves; instead, God is asked to further our sanctification through our fulfillment of His laws.[14] In this manner *halachic* laws become universal blueprints for conduct, geared toward spiritual salvation and national redemption, the ultimate object of the Torah and the commandments.

Moreover, the secular Jew who loves his people and who wishes to "refine" himself and mend the world, but is unable to accept the commandments in their Talmudic-Rabbinic format, may still wish to select a certain number of commandments and earnestly observe these, as Franz Rosenzweig suggested, and as many do today. After all, no Jew observes each and every one of the 613 commandments. A Jew who celebrates the Sabbath, lives honestly, abides by the law of the land, and performs deeds of righteousness and loving kindness in a world of rivaling demands and countless impulses and constraints bearing upon a scientific-technological society of vulgar mass consumption, can surely be said to be keeping faith with the Jewish sensibility of chosenness and rendering continued testimony to that chosenness.

In speaking of the transposition of bygone concepts and beliefs to the present and the desire of the National-Israeli culture to expand and magnify the wisdom of the past another important fact must be recognized. The Rabbinic culture chose to fence itself within the bounds of Halachah and the contraction of its horizons rendered it intolerant of philosophic speculation and scientific inquiry. Throughout its long reign it did not produce a single work of philosophy, and it had limited use for the works of Jewish philosophers of the Poetic-Philosophic culture. The be-all and the end-all for members of the Rabbinic culture was the study of the Talmud and the Halachah; study of "external wisdoms" was generally prohibited. An illuminating example of this lacuna is a discussion between Rabbi Solomon Luria (the Maharshal) and Rabbi Moses Isserles (the Rema), both architects of the Rabbinic culture in seventeenth-century Poland, on Aristotelian philosophy, with which neither of them was familiar except through echoes reaching him via Maimonides. Isserles excuses himself to Luria for never having read the works of Aristotle in these words:

What you have written, honored sir, that it follows from this that some students say the prayer of Aristotle . . . I would say: Heaven forbid that . . . I should behold such a thing without protest. All this [philosophizing] continues to be a fecund source of venom and wormwood, inherited from their forefathers who followed the philosophers and trod in their paths. But I myself have to this day never seen or heard [this philosophy].[15]

The Rabbis belittled the importance of Bible-study and disdained Hebrew grammar and stylistics. Philosophy and Judaism parted company. Jewish thinkers like Spinoza, Bergson, and many others, no longer emphasized, as Saʿadiah Gaʾon, Judah ha-Levi, or Maimonides had done, the universal importance of Israel's Torah and people. No effort was made again to reunite modern science and Torah; 300 years without any systematic philosophic endeavor to confront the problems of man and nation, faith and knowledge, life and its complexities, and without critique of the foundations of its own activity and creativity, are a calamity in the development of a nation. A Jewish philosophy which engages in open give-and-take with modern science and its innovations is an absolute necessity for a nation desirous of life. In the absence of philosophic thought, the concept of religion has shrunk and diminished, has even become corrupted, and we need hardly wonder that creative energies have turned to secular channels, to expedite redemption via science and technology or through modern Messianic movements, such as socialism and communism, to the detriment and neglect of the wealth of heritage.

Creative continuity or rupture?

What is the main practical function of a cultural policy in Israel today? In a word: the creation of conditions for mutual tolerance. Just as one must demand that Israeli Orthodox Rabbis interpret *halachic* laws pertaining to the state and to society in light of present-day conditions, so the secular public must be asked to encourage those elements in the religious camp who wish to adapt the Torah to reality, as Israel's Sages have done in the past. Religious tolerance is a *sine qua non* for a modern state. Everything our ancient sources contain in praise of tolerance should now be brought out into the full light of day to the attention of believers and non-believers alike. Our theory on the cultures, tensions, and transformations operating in Israel's history may serve as a suitable ideological foundation for a rectified cultural policy in modern Israel. This theory, it seems to me, develops and complements the tendencies espoused by many of those who championed the National-Israeli culture. Some of these champions, for example, Bialik and Buber, did not wish to strip the National-Israeli culture of all that had been lofty and noble in Jewish religion and Jewish life, but on the contrary, to add, interpret, and expand, in a sort of revolution of continuation, as each culture had done *vis-à-vis* its predecessors. Such revolutionary continuation transcends the collision that in the simplistic view hurtles rupture and continuum against each other.

These and like-minded writers believed that the heritage required reinterpretation, that our contemporaries could be led to rediscover the spiritual wellsprings which had calked in the conditions of exile, and that Jewish minds should now be opened to the gifts of life and the expanses of knowledge and creativity introduced into the world by the modern era. Each one of these inspiring builders expressed in his own way the historic and solemn feeling that there was a real need to undertake a reinterpretation of the cultures of traditional faith and to review its superordinating concepts – God, Torah, Israel – and its archetypal collective experiences as spiritual symbols, which the commandments had endowed with institutionalized force for Israel's preservation as a "nation in its two Torot," to use Saʿadiah Gaʾon's famous phrase. In these concepts and experiences one could detect hints of a spiritual signaling, a summons to seek the meaning of the nation's life in its ancestral homeland.[16]

However, other notes, calling for dissociation both from traditional Judaism and from Jewish diaspora communities, were also heard in Hebrew literature and thought in the last generation. Immediately following the establishment of the State of Israel the fear arose that with the ingathering of the exiles in a normal state, there would be increased division between the state and the diasporas. A nation dwelling in its own land, speaking its own language, constituting a majority, and living in independence has of necessity little in common with ethnic and religious minorities residing in foreign lands and speaking the languages of their host countries. Whether or not we agree with the demand and the aspiration that Israel in its land be a nation like all others, the fact of normalization is beyond the stage of both wishful or apprehensive thinking. Some fear a theocratic state in the Holy Land, while others fear a "Canaanite" entity. Many are alarmed that a new public-spiritual entity might arise in Israel unlike any which exists in the diasporas or which we have hitherto witnessed in Israel itself. Some contend that a people returning to its land has the right to sever all ties with its long history, especially with the history of its exile.

Positions favoring dissociation from the past have long been present in Hebrew literature, witness Judah Leib Gordon (Yalag), Berdyczewski, Tchernihovsky, Brenner, and contemporary authors. Such views were not alien to a portion of the young generation growing up in Mandatory Palestine. That generation was raised upon the tension between the goals of the Zionist movement, a movement of Jewish activism alert to the danger threatening the nation's mode of life in the diasporas and its very existence, and believing that it held the keys to salvation, and the Jewish masses immersed in all other movements, efforts, achievements, failures, and impotencies of the day. Schools in Eretz Israel educated students to the proud and erect posture of Hebrew citizenship in the state-to-come, or, at least – in what was to become the nation's new hegemonic center. And just as during the British Mandate youths were educated to a confrontational encounter with political reality, so were they imbued with a consciousness of their importance *vis-à-vis* diaspora Jews and diaspora history. To be sure, at times this consciousness degenerated into a sense of superiority and arrogance.

During World War II, in the midst of the Holocaust, a small but vocal young group calling itself the "Canaanites" began preaching the abrogation of Jewish historical continuity. It claimed that a new Hebrew nation had arisen in the Land of Israel where the ancient Hebraic people had dwelt before it became "Jewish." This new Hebraic-Canaanite nation, they claimed, had nothing in common with Jewish communities in the diasporas. It had more affinity with other ethnic groups of Canaan, a concept encompassing Lebanon, southern Syria, and Jordan. There was no relation whatsoever between the present and the recent past, or even with the more distant past. The teachings of the Prophets, their monotheistic faith and vision of a national and universal end in the world to come, were irrelevant. In their view, an affinity to the priests of Baʿal and Ashtoret was more helpful than adherence to Prophetic teachings in consolidating the sense of homeland and the formation of an open-minded community that was ready to absorb all human beings regardless of religion and race.

These young men negated entirely the national definition of the Jewish people throughout its history, and in particular the continuity of its culture, or cultures. The lineage of both Israel and the Canaanite was traced back to Teraḥ, Abraham's father, not to Abraham the breaker of graven images and sire of the Israelitic faith. The Canaanite theory obliterated the experience of Israel's common destiny and reduced its entire spiritual heritage to the Hebrew language and land. The Canaanites forgot, of course, that modern Hebrew was no longer the language of the Bible or of the early Canaanites, but the product of Jewish concepts and experiences evolved through the ages and that anyone speaking this language was willy-nilly resorting to an instrument heavily weighted with the cultures of many generations: Bible, Mishnah, Midrash, Halachah and Aggadah, poetry and philosophy, Kabbalah, Ḥassidism, and Haskalah.

This theory was a questionable mixture of provincial territorial fanaticism and a shallow and hazy cosmopolitanism. It was rejected by most Israelis, but there are still some young Israelis, as well as certain Hebrew authors, whose thinking runs approximately along these lines: our Judaism lies in the fact that we live in the State of Israel and speak and write Hebrew. Whatever happened in previous generations is only important inasmuch as it affects us directly and lives in us today. Since I was born and raised here, and since I write in the Hebrew language and this is my world, I am exempt from the problems of Judaism, in fact there is no problem of Judaism in Israel. The latter is only encountered when I travel abroad. In brief: I am what I am, a given fact, and therein lies my worth. The dilemma of every simplistic realism, of course, is that while it may wish to be just that – total realism – this can never be attained.

In the mean time a change has occurred in Israel: young Israelis are pursuing in the universities Jewish studies and philosophy; Yiddish, Ladino, and Judaeo-Arabic are *bona fide* subjects, and while most Israelis remain secular in their outlook, they are farther than ever from embracing the Canaanite outlook. Today it evokes only faint response. But the problem of continuity and rupture, the problem of renewal inherent in the establishment of the state and its attitude toward Jewish diasporas today and to previous Jewish cultures, remains relevant as ever and this was our reason for dwelling upon the Canaanite phenomenon which exemplified it so sharply. The National-Israeli culture is a new, surprising, and creative breakthrough, and announces a renewal of the heritage in the spirit of its innovative assumptions and unique ontology. The breach wrought by the establishment of the state was both more complete and more vigorous than any experienced in preceding Jewish cultures. For this reason it behooves us to devote our efforts to adjustment and harmonization, to transposition and creative interpretation, so that our new culture may enrich itself with the many insights and experiences legated by past generations.

We summarize, then, by listing four practical functions that the new pluralistic theory may fulfill. First, it wishes to restore to Jews who do not view themselves as Orthodox in their religion the full possession of their historical heritage, so that they cease to consider themselves inferior in their Judaism; rather, inasmuch as they gain acquaintance with one of the seven Jewish cultures, and, needless to say, if they become familiar with all seven cultures, the more fully Jewish, our theory claims, they will become. The secular Jew has hereby been alerted that the Jewish world was always susceptible to numerous conflicting currents and influences from within and from without. The new approach seeks to aid him in finding roots in the nation's vast and complex spiritual heritage both as an inheritor and as a legator.

Secondly, the new approach defies any despotic fanaticism which impoverishes the past by reducing Judaism to a single, fixed, and unified essence. Modern historical perspectivism knows that faith in absolutes is often not only aggressive and tyrannical in its ambition to invalidate and destroy opposing beliefs, but also that truth is generally not its hallmark. Against the fanatic imperialism of a single Jewish essence the pluralistic theory enjoins tolerance in matters of belief and opinion, and calls for increased tolerance in our midst.

Thirdly, this approach parades before our eyes the vast wealth that lies at the Jew's disposal, and invites the secular Jew to explore the transcendent dimension that is rapidly disappearing in this scientific-technological age. It renews the wonderment at the marvel of Jewish life and creativity in its multiple cultures. Judaism and Jewishness are altogether a cause for wonderment. True, wonders cannot be entirely rationalized as though they were scientific, lucidly formulated, soluble questions. But even wonders may be clarified by applying wisdom and the methods of reason. Only after we have clarified whatever is within intellectual reach does the remote appear more truly a wonder, and the imponderable becomes a mystery. For this reason it is important that we persevere in our efforts to grasp Jewish history and to understand its wonder: Israel's cultures are responses-reactions to the multiform wonder that is Judaism – to its existence in a hostile world, to its wisdom and lore, to the history and achievements of its participants.

Finally, the multiple faces of Jewish cultures informs us that unity and continuity are not self-evident in Jewish history (nor, of course, in the history of other nations). There are tears and ruptures, new beginnings, discontinuations and endings wrought by destiny and its contingencies, "the hand of God" or the acts of man, resulting from external disasters or from new awakenings, which may be called profound transformations, or revolutions. These are historical turning-points, foci of innovative acts and new valuations. True, the qualities which are unique to a particular culture distinguish it from other cultures, but until recently this uniqueness did not entail complete rupture. In our era, in the Emancipation and National-Israeli cultures, there is much concern for insured succession, for fruitful continuity. The new approach wishes to highlight the measure of responsibility for the preservation of the past that devolves upon us after the collapse of faith in the sacredness of tradition, in order that our past may not be divorced from the present. Our generation is not an entirely new and original being; it is fitting that it too be nurtured and sustained by the wealth of Israel's cultures. It is with us that the responsibility for Jewish identity in its continuity ultimately rests.

NOTES

I A wealth of cultures

1 The concept culture is based on certain theories regarding meanings and significance, social reality, the force of public imperatives, the nature and types of religious faith, etc. The constituent components of this concept in our study may be found in the writings of M. Weber, E. Durkheim, G. Simmel, T. Parsons, J. Needham, A. Toynbee, P. Sorokin, J. Feibelman, and the philosophers of language in our time. See the discussion on the concepts "culture" and "civilization" in James Feibelman, *The Theory of Human Culture*, New York, Duell, Sloan, and Pearce, 1946, and in V.F. Lenzen *et al.*, *Civilization*, Berkeley and Los Angeles, Univ. of California Press, 1959. Due to limitations of space, I mention here only two works dealing with the problem of reality: Burkhart Holzner, *Reality Construction in Society*, Cambridge, Mass., Schenkman Pub. Co., 1968, and Peter L. Berger and Thomas Luckman, *The Social Construction of Reality*, Garden City, Doubleday, 1966.

2 On knowledge interpreted not via language, see Michael Polanyi, *Personal Knowledge*, London, Routledge and Kegan Paul, 1958; and *The Tacit Dimension*, New York, Anchor Books, 1967.

3 See, for example, the discussion on historic forecasting which is so much a part of historical interpretation, in the writings of Karl Popper, *The Open Society and Its Enemies*, rev. edn, Princeton, NJ, Princeton Univ. Press, 1950, and *The Poverty of Historicism*, London, Routledge and Kegan Paul, 1957. See also R. Aron, W.H. Walsh, G. Florovskii, and younger scholars in R.H. Nash (ed.), *Ideas and History*, New York, E.P. Dutton, 1969, vol. II.

4 These and similar afflictions have been widely portrayed by existentialist philosophers like Jaspers, Heidegger, Tillich, Sartre, and Camus, who intensified our awareness of the "human condition." Their analyses inspired a literature of horror, caricature, and the absurd. The forces of free will which these thinkers had acclaimed as man's nostrum *vis-à-vis* the absurd are engulfed in darkness.

5 Sociologists and historians have frequently described the struggle for legitimation of authority. Two generations have now been drawing on Max Weber's theory of authority and power. T. Parsons, A. Shils, J. Eisenstadt, and others have extended his concepts to new contexts. The crises of our times have prompted scholars to examine the problems of legitimation in the past. See more recently Jürgen Habermas, *Legitimation Crisis*, trans. T. McCarthy, Boston, Beacon Press, 1973. The efforts invested by each culture to reject and winnow out were just as great as the energies expended in drawing hearts and minds into a new cohesion. Even the authority of the Prophets could be dismissed by the Sages when necessary: "'Many prophets arose for Israel,' – only the prophecy which contained a lesson for [lit., 'was required for'] future generations was written down, and that which did not contain such a lesson was not written" (*Meg.* 14a).

6 Of critical importance to the spread of each culture was the strength and number of its carriers and disseminators, i.e. the intelligentsia cultivating and guarding it against opponents. Can the spread of the Talmudic culture be imagined without the prolific responsa sent to the diaspora by the Babylonian Geʾonim over a period of 400 years? Every culture commanded: "Raise many disciples!" It was the strength of the professional intelligentsia upholding a culture which tipped the scales toward domination or defeat.

7 In *Sefer va-saif*, Jerusalem and New York, Yeshiva Univ. Press, 1967, p. xv, Moshe Carmeli-Weinberger distinguishes three main reasons for opposition to books: (a) Ideological opposition, such as the wars against philosophy, Kabbalah, the Sabbatean movement, or the Rabbinic culture's battles against Ḥassidism, Haskalah, and religious reform movements. (b) Opposition for *halachic* reasons, e.g. to objectionable books of *halachot*, to authors with whom fault had been found, to prayerbooks into which changes had been introduced, to books of erotica, frivolity, etc. The banning of books often had no other reason than competition between authors or publishers. (c) Opposition for political reasons, such as the struggle against the Emancipation or the Zionist movement. On the problem of heresy, see E. Shmueli, *Bein ʾemuna li-chfirah*, Tel Aviv, Massada, 1962.
8 Henri Bergson, *L'Enérgie spirituelle*, Genève, edns Albert Skira, p. 33.
9 Many valid points and interesting formulations on the revitalization of Scripture in the Talmudic culture are presented by Simon Rawidowicz in *Bavel vi-Yerushalaim*, London and Waltham, Mass., Ararat Publishing Society, 1952. It is a pity that this author, whose approach is not altogether alien to our own perspectivistic concept, distinguishes only between the spirit of the First and the Second Temple, or "House," and sees the entire subsequent Jewish history as a ceaseless struggle between the spirit of these two "Houses." An abridged version of this work can be found in Simon Rawidowicz, *Studies in Jewish Thought*, ed. Nahum N. Glatzer, trans. Lawrence V. Berman, Philadelphia, Jewish Publication Society of America, 1974, ch. 3, pp. 81–209.
10 Moses Maimonides, *Mishneh Torah*, ed. and trans. Moses Hyamson, Jerusalem, Boys Town Jerusalem Publishers, 1965, Book of Knowledge, Laws Concerning the Study of the Torah (*Hilchot talmud Torah*), ch. 3, 14, p. 59a.
11 Bachya Ibn Paquda, *Duties of the Heart*, trans. Moses Hyamson, Jerusalem, Feldheim Publishers, 1978, vol. I.
12 *Tikkunei ha-Zohar*, beginning of *Tikkun* 43, Lemberg, J.M. Stand, 1864, p. 151. The letters making up the word *peshat* ("פשט," literal meaning), instructs the *Zohar*, are also those of the word *tipesh* ("טפש," fool). Whoever learns only the *peshat* of Scriptures, removes the wisdom from the Bible.
13 As in the generations prior to the expulsion from Spain, between the massacres of 1391 and the decrees of 1492, or during the battle against the Sabbatean movement, for example, the bitter controversy (1750) between Jacob Emden and Jonathan Eibeschütz. The battle between the Karaites and the Geʾonim was far from an exercise in politeness. The same is true, as we shall see later, for the Mystical culture during the period of its growth and initial spread in the thirteenth century, when it leveled its polemics against the Poetic-Philosophic, the Talmudic, and the Rabbinic cultures.
14 It is this radical opinion, adhered to by Reish Lakish and other Amoraʾim and consonant, apparently, with Rabbi Akiba's system, which gained widespread acceptance: not only the commandments, but also all their refinements, commentaries, and eductions were given to Moses at Sinai, including the words of the Prophets, the Mishnah, and the Talmud. Witness Rabbi Simeon ben Lakish's commentary on Exod. 24.12:

"And I will give thee the tables of stone, and the law and the commandment, which I have written that thou mayest teach them." "Tables of stone": these are the ten commandments; "the law": that is the Pentateuch; "the commandments": this is the Mishnah; "which I have written": these are the Prophets and Hagiographia; "that thou mayest teach them": this is the Gemara. It teaches [us] that all these things were given to Moses on Sinai. (*Ber.* 5a, also *Meg.* 19b, *Taʿan.* 9a.)

This global extension of the concept "Torah from Sinai" or "from heaven" is essentially polemical, and was leveled at Sadducees, *minim*, Christians, and later at the Karaites and sundry adversaries of the Talmudic culture. According to *Megillat Taʿanit* ("The Scroll of Fasts"), an interpretation similar to that of Reish Lakish on the same verse was used earlier, during the Second Temple, in the dispute with the Sadducees. But it seems that in Rabbi Ishmael's school, this far-fetched method was not advocated; there it was, apparently, held that the *midot*, the hermeneutical rules, had indeed been revealed to Moses at Sinai, but not the substance of each subject. See Abraham J. Heschel, *Torah min ha-shamaim be-ʾaspaklariah shel ha-dorot*, London and New York, Soncino Press, 1965, vol. II, p. 230.

15 This is the fatigue evinced by the creator of one culture confronting creators of another culture. This confrontation poses an inescapable dialectic: on the one hand, the giving of the Torah at Sinai shuts the door, as it were, on a giving of a second Torah, which might cancel or subvert the first Torah. On the other hand, we hear that the Torah is not in the heavens, and that a Sage is superior to a Prophet. This imaginary encounter between creators of different cultures produces wonder, confusion, faintheartedness, but also a certain satisfaction that the principal of the great spiritual fund has not yet been depleted.

16 *Seder olam zuta*, Neubauer edn, part 1, p. 174.

17 E. Shmueli, *Massoret u-mahapecha*, New York, Sefarim, 1942, p. 296.

18 See Benzion Dinur, *Bemifneh ha-dorot*, Jerusalem, Bialik Institute Press, 1956, p. 22.

19 An entire literature dealing with differences among nations and religions has arisen in anthropology, history, comparative religions, etc. We should note here a relatively recent discipline known as ethnomethodology, which integrates a number of disciplines in order better to bring out that which distinguishes individuals and societies, to what extent they really "keep to themselves," and how they are "distinguished by their ways from all the other nations." See Harold Garfinkel, *Studies in Ethnomethodology*, Englewood Cliffs, NJ, Prentice-Hall, 1967, and Roy Turner (ed.), *Ethnomethodology*, Harmondsworth, Penguin Education, 1974.

20 Many similar expressions can be found in the Psalms, such as: "God is our shelter and our refuge, a timely help in trouble; so we are not afraid . . . God is in that city; she will not be overthrown, and he will help her at the break of day" (Ps. 46.1-5). There is, of course, also another direction: "My God, my God, why hast thou forsaken me . . . I cry in the day-time but thou dost not answer" (Ps. 22.1–2), and similar articulations of the feeling that God is distant, that He has abandoned the earth. Such feelings are the paramount theological subject-matter of every culture, and their intensity, the source of faith in redemption.

21 On the relation between theory and political action, see Nicholas Lobkowicz, *Theory and Practice: History of a Concept from Aristotle to Marx*, Notre Dame, Univ. of Indiana Press, 1967.

22 At least three scholars who studied this decree saw it as an accessory in implementing political goals of the Hasmonean kings. I.H. Weiss, *Dor dor ve-dorshav*, New York and Berlin, Plaut and Minkus Publishers, 1924, part 1, p. 105, believed that decreeing the lands of the Gentiles unclean was an attempt to counteract Jewish emigration from Palestine – Eretz Israel – following the persecutions of Antiochus. Rabbi Ḥaim Tchernowitz, Rav Tzaʿir, considers whether the Temple of Onias in Egypt was declared unclean by order of the first "pair" of Palestinian Tannaʾitic leaders. He explains that the Gentile lands declared unclean originally were not foreign lands, but sections of Eretz Israel itself that were inhabited by Gentiles. However, when the Hasmonean kings finally succeeded in banishing the Gentiles from their borders, the decree on uncleanness was automatically voided, not to be reinstituted until Gentiles again began settling in Eretz Israel, some eighty years prior to the destruction of the Second Temple. This decree then spread also to lands outside Eretz Israel in general, because it was believed that this was an ancient ruling of the first "pair." See "Ha-zugot u-mikdash Ḥonio" in *Louis Ginzberg Jubilee Volume*, Hebrew part (part 2), New York, Jewish Publication Society of America, 1946, pp. 233–47. But Louis Ginzberg himself was of the opinion that the uncleanness of Gentile lands extended to areas outside the borders of Eretz Israel already during the days of the Temple. See his *Al halachah va-ʾaggadah*, Tel Aviv, Dvir, 1960, p. 14.

23 The first Tannaʾitic pair of leaders decreed also against glass ware manufactured by Gentiles, and the reason, according to Louis Ginzberg, was that imported glass vessels created fierce competition to non-glass Israel-made products: many Jews preferred to use utensils that could not take on uncleanness (such as glass) to pottery and metal vessels made in Eretz Israel, which demanded more scrupulous observance (ibid., p. 15). For this reason, Rabbi Simeon ben Shetaḥ later decreed uncleanness upon glass utensils as well. Needless to say, I am not in a position to decide among these Talmudic experts. I merely point out that they all agree that the decrees on uncleanness had distinct political and economic dimensions. An in-depth study of the social, political, and economic implications of the Sages' opinions and acts during the Second Temple period can also be found in Yitzhak Baer, *Yisraʾel ba-ʿamim*, Jerusalem, Bialik Institute Press, 1955.

24 Harry Austryn Wolfson, *Philo*, Cambridge, Mass., Harvard Univ. Press, 1962, vol. II, and *The Philosophy of Spinoza*, New York, Schocken Books, 1969, vol. II.

25 Max Black, *Models and Metaphors*, Ithaca, NY, Cornell Univ. Press, 1962, p. 220.

26 E.E. Hutton, "The role of models in physics," *British Journal for the Philosophy of Science*, IV, 1953–4, p. 289.

27 Much has been written in the last generation on the value and shortcomings of the concept developed by Max Weber in *Wirtschaft und Gesellschaft*. See R. Benedict, T. Parsons, and many others, also in numerous introductions to Weber's writings. For a critique of the "ideal type" concept, see my monograph, "The 'Pariah people' and its 'charismatic leadership,' a re-evaluation of Max Weber's *Ancient Judaism*," *Proceedings of the American Academy of Jewish Research*, New York, 1968, vol. XXXVI, pp. 167–247.

28 Arnold Toynbee, *A Study of History*, London, Oxford Univ. Press, 1954; Erich Voeglin, *Order and History*, Baton Rouge, Louisiana State Univ. Press, 1956; Oswald Spengler, *The Decline of the West*, trans. Charles F. Atkinson, 2 vols., New York, Alfred Knopf, Inc.

29 On Toynbee's attitude to the Bible, and on the key concepts "challenge – response," see his article, "Indivisibility and unpredictability of human affairs" in Paul G. Kunitz (ed.), *The Concept of Order*, Seattle, 1968.

30 In his four-volume monumental work: Pitirim A. Sorokin, *Social and Cultural Dynamics*, New York, American Book Co., 1942–.

31 T.S. Eliot, *Notes Toward the Definition of Culture*, New York, 1944, pp. 13ff.

32 See B. Malinowski in the entry "Culture," *Encyclopaedia of Social Sciences*, New York, Macmillan 1933, vol. IV, pp. 621–45.

33 Edward B. Tylor's definition in the opening to his classical book on anthropology, *Primitive Culture*, New York, Harper, 1958, thus gained wide currency: "Culture is that complex whole which includes knowledge, belief, art, morals, law, custom and any other capabilities acquired by man as a member of society." See W.F. Ogburn and M.F. Nimkoff, *A Handbook of Sociology*, London, Paul, Trench, Trubner and Co., 1947, p. 15.

34 W.G. Sumner and A.G. Keller, *The Science of Society*, New Haven, Yale Univ. Press, 1932, vol. I.

2 Interpretation of Scripture in Israel's cultures

1 See Abraham Ibn Ezra commentaries to the Pentateuch, known also as *Sefer ha-yashar*, which appear in many editions of the Hebrew Bible, for example, in the *Mikra'ot gedolot* editions. The English excerpt cited here is found in Louis Jacobs (ed.), *Jewish Biblical Exegesis*, New York, Behrman House Inc., 1973, p. 9.

2 There is no need to list here the numerous books on hermeneutics, a rapidly developing discipline in the fields of philosophy of language, history, theology, and phenomenology. Suffice it to note here two volumes of Dilthey's complete works, which contain important chapters on interpretation in general and on comprehension and meaning. The introductions to these volumes by G. Misch and B. Groethuysen outline the history of the discipline up to their time. W. Dilthey, *Gesammelte Schriften*, Leipzig, B.G. Teubner, 1924, vol. V; 1927, vol. VII. Today the hermeneutics built upon the philosophy of M. Heidegger by R. Boltman, M. Dibelius, H.G. Gadamer, and P. Ricoeur is of greatest importance. For a good summary of hermeneutical efforts in our times, see Paul Ricoeur, *The Conflict of Interpretations, Essays in Hermeneutics*, ed. D. Ihde, Evanston, Northwestern Univ. Press, 1974. Needless to say, we make no attempt here to consider all the commentaries to the Bible throughout the ages, an impossible endeavor and one which would in no way serve our purpose. The emphasis is on the difference in the approach of each culture to the same Biblical text.

3 Isaak Heinemann, *Darchei ha-'aggadah*, Jerusalem, Magnes and Massada, 1960.

4 For a discussion of Ezra's place in Jewish history, see the introduction to Ezra and Neḥemiah by Mordechai Zer-Kavod, *Sifrei Ezra ve-Neḥemiah*, Jerusalem, R. Mass, 1948. The *aggadah*, Louis Ginzberg testifies, saw in Ezra a "Rabbi" figure, the first Rabbi and Sage, and the father of Rabbinic literature, who transmitted the Oral Law to the Sages in a "secret scroll," destined to be revealed only to the select few. This is how he is portrayed in the apocryphal Second Book of Esdras (known also as the Fourth Book of Ezra), written after the destruction of the Second Temple (70 CE), and in later Jewish tradition. See Louis Ginzberg,

Al halachah va-ʾaggadah, Tel Aviv, Dvir, 1960, p. 42, and *The Legends of the Jews*, Philadelphia, Jewish Publication Society, 1946, vol. VI (notes to vols. III and IV), pp. 135–7.

5 See Saul Lieberman, *Yevanim ve-yavnut be-Eretz Yisrael*, Jerusalem, Bialik Institute Press, 1962, pp. 135–213, wherein the author elaborates on the problem of Scriptural interpretation in *halachah* and *aggadah* and presents the views of various scholars. A. Schwarz did not detect the influence of Greek grammarians in the *midot* which the Sages applied to the interpretation of Scriptures. See the last of his six books on Talmudic interpretation, *Der hermeneutische Kontext in der talmudischen Literatur*, Vienna, 1921. See also his Hebrew book, *Midat kal va-ḥomer ba-sifrut-ha-talmudit*, Cracow, 1905.

6 Some Talmudic scholars today believe that the entire basis of the Talmudic structure in its relation to Scriptures is epitomized in the following dialogue: "Said Abaye to Rabbi Joseph: This, surely is Pentateuchal! – It is Pentateuchal, but the Rabbis have expounded it. All the Torah was expounded by the Rabbis! – But [the fact is that the prohibition is] Rabbinical, while the Scriptural text is [adduced as] a mere prop [*asmakta*]" (*Yeb.* 21a). The essence of this dialogue is that our Sages interpreted Scriptures freely, and that what is written in the Bible merely serves as evidence to the veracity of their interpretation. See Abraham Weiss, *Ha-Talmud ha-bavli be-hithavuto ha-sifrutit*, Warsaw, 1938–9, *Hithavut ha-Talmud bi-shlemuto*, New York, 1943, and *Le-ḥeker ha-Talmud*, New York, 1954. The above dialogue is presented in dramatic form in M.A. Tenenblatt, *Ha-Talmud ha-bavli be-hithavuto ha-historit*, Tel Aviv, 1973, p. 171.

7 Azariah dei Rossi, *Meʾor ʿeynaim*, Vilna, 1866, ch. 15.

8 Heinemann, *Darchei ha-ʾaggadah*, p. 96. An extensive bibliography on Biblical exegesis is provided there on p. 197.

9 Ibn Ezra's introduction to the commentary of the Pentateuch, in Jacobs, *Jewish Biblical Exegesis*, p. 16.

10 *Sifre* on Deut. 1.7. Published by the Gesellschaft zur Förderung der Wissenschaft des Judentums, Berlin, (n.d.); republished (Hebrew only) by the Jewish Theological Seminary of America, New York, 1969.

11 Ibn Ezra in Jacobs, *Jewish Biblical Exegesis*, p. 21.

12 Moses ben Naḥman (Naḥmanides), *Peirush ha-Torah*, Jerusalem, Mossad Harav Kook, 1969, in his commentary on the periodization of the verse, "When the Canaanite king of Arad who lived in the Negeb heard that the Israelites were coming" (Num. 21.1–3).

13 See his commentary on 1 Sam. 28.25 in *Mikraʾot gedolot*, Schocken, 1938.

14 Moses Maimonides, *Mishneh Torah*, trans. Abraham M. Hershman, New Haven, Yale Univ. Press, 1949, The Book of Judges, Laws Concerning Rebels (*Hilchot mamrim*), ch. 1, 3, p. 13a.

15 Moses Maimonides, *Mishneh Torah*, trans. Isaac Klein, New Haven and London, Yale Univ. Press, 1979, introduction to the Book of Agriculture (*Zeraʿim*).

16 *Midrash Exod. Rabbah*, 46.6, trans. S.M. Lehrman, London, Soncino Press, 1939, p. 475. This is derived from a word-play on *kelalim* (principles) and *kechaloto* ("when He had finished speaking").

17 Joseph Albo, *Sefer ha-ʿikkarim: Book of Principles*, ed. and trans. Isaac Husik, Philadelphia, Jewish Publication Society of America, 1930, vol. III, article 23, p. 203.

18 Judah ha-Levi, *The Kuzari*, introd. Henry Slonimsky, New York, Schocken Books, 1964, part 3, para. 35, pp. 166–7.

19 Ibid., p. 168.

20 Ibid., para. 73, p. 193.

21 Ibid., para. 41, p. 173.

22 Ibid., paras. 65–7, pp. 186–91.

23 For an extensive bibliography, see Yehuda Even-Shmuel (ed.), *Sefer moreh ha-nevuchim*, Jerusalem, Mossad Harav Kook, 1946, and more recently, Sarah Klein-Braslavi, *Peirush ha-Rambam le-sipur beriʾat ha-ʿolam*, Jerusalem, Ha-ḥevra le-ḥeker ha-mikra, 1978.

24 Judah ha-Levi, *The Kuzari*, part 1, para. 89, p. 62.

25 Bachya Ibn Paquda, *Duties of the Heart*, trans. Moses Hyamson, Jerusalem, New York, Feldheim Publishers, 1978, 2nd treatise, ch. 5, p. 163.

26 Moses Maimonides, *Guide for the Perplexed*, trans. M. Friedländer, 2nd edn, New York, Dover Publications, 1956, p. 5.

27 Ibid., p. 2.
28 Moses Maimonides, *The Mishnah of Avoth*, introduction in Paul Forchheimer (ed. and trans.), *Living Judaism*, New York, Feldheim publishers, 1974.
29 Maimonides, *Guide for the Perplexed*, p. 3.
30 Nissim ben Reuben Gerondi, *Derashot*, Jerusalem, 1960, p. 28.
31 For examples in other cultures, see Ricoeur, *The Conflict of Interpretations*.
32 Maimonides, *Guide for the Perplexed*, ch. 1, p. 14.
33 Ibid., p. 5.
34 Ibid., p. 4.
35 Isaac Abravanel, *Peirush al neviʾim ʾaharonim*, Jerusalem, Torah va-daʿat, 1957.
36 E. Shmueli, *Don Isaac Abravanel ve-geirush Sefarad*, Jerusalem, Bialik Institute Press, 1963.
37 Ibn Ezra, in Jacobs, *Jewish Biblical Exegesis*, p. 13.
38 Ibid.
39 See Peretz Sandler, "Le-beʿayat pardes" in A. Biram (ed.), *Sefer ha-yovel le-Eliahu Auerbach*, Jerusalem, Kiryat Sefer, 1955. This paper includes excerpts from W. Bacher, G. Scholem, and Bachya ben Asher, pp. 222–35.
40 F. Lachover and Y. Tishbi, *Mishnat ha-Zohar*, 2nd edn, Jerusalem, Bialik Institute Press, 1957, vol. I, p. 145.
41 S. Freud, *Moses and Monotheism*, New York, Vintage Books, 1955.
42 Benedict Spinoza, *Theologico-Political Treatise*, trans. R.H.M. Elwes, New York, Dover Publications, 1951, p. 103.

3   Song of Songs – a paradigm of cultural change

1 It should be remembered that the Septuagint incorporated the Song of Songs into the Holy Scriptures, perhaps not too long after the Great Assembly. In the Septuagint the word "love" is translated not *eros*, as a literal rendition might require, but *ágápe*, grace, a pure and holy love that is free of any trace of physical passion. The word *ʾamanah* ("from the top of Amana," 4.8) was read *ʾemunah* (i.e. faith – "from the beginning of faith" – *"apó archés pisteos"*). It is possible that the author of the apocryphal Second Book of Esdras (also known as the Fourth Book of Ezra), already viewed the Song of Songs as a Prophetic and allegorical work when, speaking of Israel, he wrote: "Out of all the flowers of the whole world you have chosen one lily . . . From all the birds that were created you have named one dove" (2 Esd. 5.25–6). See A. Kaminka's remarks in the introduction to his commentary on Song of Songs in A. Kahana (ed.), *Torah, neviʾim u-ketuvim*, Tel Aviv, Mekorot, 1930, vol. VI.
2 Moses Mendelssohn, *Torah, neviʾim u-ketuvim*, Jerusalem, 1974.
3 Haim Shelli, *Mehkar ha-mikra be-sifrut ha-haskalah*, Jerusalem, 1942, pp. 3ff. See also studies by Peretz Sandler, especially his entries in the *Encyclopaedia ha-mikraʾit*, Jerusalem, Bialik Institute Press, 1940–88.
4 David Baumgardt in the entry "Herder," *Encyclopaedia Ivrit*, Tel Aviv, Encyclopaedia Publishing Co., 1962, vol. XV, p. 197.
5 Johann Gottfried Herder, *Sämmtliche Werke*, Stuttgart and Tübingen, 1829, vol. XVII.
6 Ibid., p. 218: "Dies Volk war dichterisch selbst in seinem Ursprünge."
7 Ibid., p. 220.
8 Ibid., p. 223.
9 Herder too confronted the full severity of doctrinal tradition, for the Protestant religion by no means endorsed a secular interpretation of the Song of Songs. A humanist reformist theologian named Sebastian Castello had been expelled from the Calvinist city of Geneva for having dared to claim that the Song of Songs was a "colloquium Salomonis cum amica quad Sulamitha" (1544). It was not without an inner conflict that Herder himself resolved this dilemma. He had read the Song of Songs attentively and had consulted ancient and modern commentaries. Finally, however, no interpretation seemed to him more authoritative than the simple, literal text which, he felt, had been much distorted by others. See the introduction by Gillis Gerleman in M. Noth and H.W. Wolff (eds.), *Das Hohelied, Biblischer Kommentar*, Neukirchen, 1965, vol. XVIII.
10 Solomon Loewisohn, *Melitzat Yeshurun*, Tel Aviv, 1944.
11 Simon Bernfeld, *Mavo le-kitvei ha-kodesh*, Berlin, Dvir, 1923, vol. III, p. 142.

12 Ibid., p. 143. See also more recent commentaries: Mordechai Halter, *Shir ha-shirim*, Tel Aviv, 1960, and Eli'ezer Levinger, *Shir ha-shirim*, Jerusalem, Ha-ḥevra le-ḥeker ha-mikra, 1973.

13 In Kahana, *Torah, nevi'im u-ketuvim*, vol. VI, p. 4.

14 *Abot de-Rabbi Nathan*, trans. and comm. Anthony J. Saladrini, SJ, Ph.D. dissertation, Yale University, 1971, version A, ch. 1, p. 5: "Until they were included in the writings, Proverbs, Song of Songs, and Qohelet (were regarded as worthy) of being suppressed."

15 Wherever the Sages refer to a book as "rendering the hands unclean," they mean that the book is holy. The wording "Holy Books render the hands unclean" refers to an ancient Jewish idea that holiness causes impurity. The prototype and chief source of this strange *halachah* is found in the ceremony of the red heifer (Num. 19), where all participants in the sacred ceremony were rendered ritually unclean and required purification. The ruling on holy books rendering the hands unclean was one of the eighteen *gezeirot* (decrees) formulated by the House of Shammai and enacted by the Hillelites. See also tractate *Sab.* 14.

16 *Midrash shir ha-shirim zuta*, Solomon Buber edn, p. 4.

17 Most of the references to Song of Songs are found in the two Talmuds and in two *midrashim: Shir ha-shirim rabbah*, also known as *Midrash ḥazit*, and *Midrash shir ha-shirim zuta*, also known as *'Aggadat shir ha-shirim*. *Shir ha-shirim rabbah* was apparently compiled from various *midrashim*, perhaps in the eighth century. *Midrash shir ha-shirim zuta*, believed to have been composed in the ninth century, was edited and published by Solomon Buber (grandfather of Martin Buber).

18 *Midrash Song of Songs Rabbah*, trans. Maurice Simon, London, Soncino Press, 1939, 1.10.

19 Ibid., 1.1.

20 *Midrash shir-ha-shirim zuta*, 1.1.

21 *Midrash Song of Songs Rabbah*, 1.12, *Midrash shir ha-shirim zuta*, 1.1.

22 Abraham Ibn Ezra, *Commentary on the Canticles*, ed. and trans. H.J. Mathews, London, Trubner and Co., 1874, p. 10.

23 Much has been written on this subject. See H. Shirman, *Hashirah ha-Ivrit bi-Sefarad u-ve-Provence*, Jerusalem, Bialik Institute Press, 1954, introd., pp. 26–8. In his book on the art of Hebrew poetry, later translated into Hebrew under the title *Shirat Yisrael*, Moses Ibn Ezra announced he would let himself be guided by the Koran and by Arabic works of poetry and philosophy in pointing out the glories of Scripture and other writings of our ancestors.

24 Levi ben Gershon (Gersonides), *Peirush al ḥamesh megillot*, Koenigsberg, 1760 (reprinted in Israel without indication of place and date).

25 Ibid., 5.2. Issac Hirsch Weiss in *Dor dor ve-dorshav*, New York and Berlin, Plaut and Pinkus Publishers, 1924, part 5, p. 111, commented that we can only wonder at Gersonides' lack of poetic appreciation, how he failed to realize that his interpretation stripped the songs of all their poetic beauty, and how he could imagine that his commentaries were any closer to the text's literal meaning than the *midrashim* he so disparaged. Weiss sees no superiority in a philosophic re-creation of the text over an *aggadic* one.

26 Levi ben Gerson, *Peirush al ḥamesh megillot*, 4.2.

27 Ibid., 7.1.

28 Ibid., 15.1.

29 Ibid., 22.1.

30 Ibid., 7.2.

31 Moses Maimonides, *Guide for the Perplexed*, trans. M. Friedländer, 2nd edn., New York, Dover Publications, 1956, ch. 51, p. 387.

32 Ibid., end of ch. 51. Commentaries in this vein were made by Sa'adiah Ga'on, Joseph Ibn Caspi and the said Joseph Ibn Aknin in his *Peirush shir ha-shirim – hitgalut ha-sodot ve-hofa'at ha-me'orot*, ed. Abraham Halkin, Jerusalem, 1964.

33 Maimonides, *Guide for the Perplexed*, ch. 54, p. 396.

34 Ibid., p. 395.

35 Ibid., p. 396.

36 *Zohar ḥadash*, 63, Livorno, 1845.

37 *Zohar*, Exodus, 18b, trans. Harry Sperling, New York, Rebecca Bennet Publications, vol. II, p. 60.

38 Ibid., 143b, vol. III, p. 5.
39 Ibid.
40 Naḥmanides' commentary to the Song of Songs, first Introduction, 1. This work is included in many editions of the Hebrew Bible, such as the Mikra'ot gedolot editions.
41 Moses Isserles, Torat ha-ʿolah, part 3, 83, Tel Aviv, D.E. Eilbloom, 1970.
42 Moses Alschech, Sefer Shoshanat ha-ʿamakim, Zolkiew edn., 1755. It is worth mentioning that the author confesses in his introduction that he had been uncertain how the Song of Songs was to be interpreted, literally or mystically. He decided to follow both approaches with the result that the reader finds him alternating back and forth between traditional Talmudic exegeses and allusions to Mystical interpretations.
43 As hinted in the Zohar ḥadash and in Midrash shir ha-shirim zuta, 1.1.

4 The commandments in Israel's cultures

 1 The text of the two Chief Rabbis appeared in the journal Yavne, vol. III, nos. 7–12, Jersualem and Tel Aviv, April, 1949.
 2 The concept of the "yoke of mitzvot" and the "yoke of Torah" in Talmudic literature will be further examined later on. It is useful to mention here that Ben Sirah (Ecclesiasticus, c. 190 BCE) still employed the concept "yoke" in the general sense, as in this piece of advice: "Buy for yourselves without money, bend your neck to the yoke, be ready to accept discipline; you need not go far to find it" (Ecclus. 51.25, 26). But in a later apocryphal work, the Apocalypse of Baruch, the concept of the yoke already emerges: "I see many of Thy people who have withdrawn from Thy covenant and cast from them the yoke of Thy Law" (Baruch 41.3), ed. Revd Canon R.H. Charles, Society of Promoting Christian Knowledge, London, 1918, p. 58. These are later sayings and some scholars read them as warnings to the early Christians; in any event, these metaphors already manifest the influence of the Talmudic ontology.
 3 Yeḥezkel Kaufmann, The Religion of Israel, trans. and abr. Moshe Greenberg, Univ. of Chicago Press, 1960, p. 171.
 4 Ibid.
 5 Ḥaim Tchernowitz, Toldot ha-halachah, New York, 1938, p. 137.
 6 E.E. Urbach, The Sages, trans. Israel Abrahams, Jerusalem, Magnes Press, 1975, vol. I.
 7 Mekilta on Exod. 23.20 in Jacob Z. Lauterbach (ed.), Mekilta de-Rabbi Ishmael, Philadelphia, Jewish Publication Society of America, 1935, vol. III, ch. 5.
 8 Mekilta on Exod. 20.23 in Lauterbach, Mekilta de-Rabbi Ishmael, vol. II, p. 279.
 9 Mekilta on Exod. 20.2 in Lauterbach, Mekilta de-Rabbi Ishmael, vol. II, p. 229.
10 Isaak Heinemann, Taʿamei ha-mitzvot be-sifrut Yisrael, Jerusalem, Mossad Harav Kook, 1942.
11 Ibid., p. 34.
12 Mekilta on Exod. 31.14 in Lauterbach, Mekilta de-Rabbi Ishmael, vol. III, p. 200.
13 As cited in Urbach, The Sages, p. 99.
14 Sifre on Deut. 32.14, para. 317.
15 Midrash Genesis Rabbah 49b, trans. H. Freedman and Maurice Simon, London, Soncino Press, 1939.
16 See Rabbi Isaac's statement in Midrash Exodus Rabbah, Exod. 28.6, trans. S.M. Lehrman, London, Soncino Press, 1939, p. 335. For a detailed discussion, see also Abraham J. Heschel, Torah min ha-shamaim be-'aspaklariah shel ha-dorot, London and New York, Soncino Press, 1965, vol. II, ch. 4, which provides references and bibliographical indications that are beyond the scope of our work.
17 M. Rosenbaum and M.A. Silberman (trans. and annot.), Pentateuch with Rashi's Commentary, London, Shapiron, Valentine and Co., 1930.
18 Midrash Song of Songs Rabbah, trans. Maurice Simon, London, Soncino Press, 1939, 5.14, para. 2, p. 246.
19 Gedaliahu Alon, Meḥkarim betoldot Yisrael, Tel Aviv, Ha-kibbutz ha-me'uḥad Press, 1958, p. 239.
20 Ibid.
21 Yeshaʿayahu Leibowitz, Yahadut, ʿam yehudi u-medinat Yisrael, Tel Aviv, Schocken, 1975,

p. 21. See also Leibowitz's articles on the theology of the Halachah in *Bitzaron*, Jan.–Feb. 1978.
22 Sa'adiah Ga'on, *Book of Doctrines and Beliefs* in Alexander Altmann (ed.), *Three Jewish Philosophers*, New York, Atheneum, 1969, Prolegomena, para. 4, p. 44.
23 Ibid., p. 45.
24 Moses Maimonides, *Guide for the Perplexed*, trans. M. Friedländer, 2nd edn, New York, Dover Publications, 1956, part 1, ch. 32, p. 43.
25 Sa'adiah Ga'on, *Book of Doctrines and Beliefs*, ch. 3, para. 1, p. 93.
26 Ibid., para. 2, p. 96.
27 Ibid., p. 97.
28 Ibid., p. 98.
29 Ibid., para. 3, p. 104.
30 Ibid., para. 5, p. 110.
31 Ibid., para. 6, p. 113.
32 Ibid., ch. 4, para. 1.
33 Maimonides, *Guide for the Perplexed*, introduction, p. 6.
34 Ibid., part 1, ch. 1, p. 14.
35 Ibid.
36 Ibid., part 3, ch. 54, p. 395.
37 Ibid., p. 397.
38 Ibid., ch. 51, p. 384.
39 Moses Maimonides, *Mishneh Torah*, Jerusalem, Boys Town Jerusalem Publishers, 1965, Book of Knowledge, end of Laws of Repentance (*Hilchot teshuvah*), ch. 10, p. 93a.
40 Maimonides, *Guide for the Perplexed*, part 3, ch. 26, p. 310.
41 Ibid., ch. 27, p. 312.
42 Ibid., ch. 51, p. 389.
43 Ibid., p. 390.
44 Ibid., ch. 32, p. 323. Friedländer's translation speaks of "the prudence and wisdom of God," "His wisdom and plan," and "the Divine plan." We have replaced his cautious wording with what we consider a more accurate, though clearly bolder, rendition. Maimonides spoke of God's "cunning" and "stratagem," shocking as these terms may appear. Compare also Shlomo Pines' translation of *Guide for the Perplexed*, Chicago, Univ. of Chicago Press, 1963: "the deity's wily graciousness and wisdom" (vol. II, p. 524), the "divine ruse" (ibid., p. 527).
45 Maimonides, *Guide for the Perplexed*, part 3, ch. 32, p. 323.
46 Ibid., p. 324.
47 Ibid.
48 Ibid., p. 325.
49 Maimonides, *Mishneh Torah*, "Book of Knowledge," pp. 48a–48b.
50 Ibid., ch. 2, 7, p. 49b.
51 Maimonides, *Guide for the Perplexed*, part 3, ch. 28, p. 315.
52 Falaquera's (or Palquera) commentary appears in many Hebrew editions of the *Guide*.
53 Judah ha-Levi, *The Kuzari*, introd. Henry Slominsky, New York, Schocken books, 1964, part 3, para. 19, p. 157.
54 F. Lachover and Y. Tishbi, *Mishnat ha-Zohar*, 2nd edn, Jerusalem, Bialik Institute Press, 1957, vol. II, p. 382.
55 Ibid.
56 Ibid., p. 386.
57 G. Scholem, *Devarim bego*, Tel Aviv, Am Oved, 1977, p. 177. See also Y. Guttmann, *Beḥinat Kiyum ha-mitzvot*, Jerusalem, Makor, 1978, ch. 4, on the difference between a religion of redemption and a religion of *mitzvot*, and on the Sages' attitude toward Gnostic sects in the matter of *mitzvot*.
58 In the introduction to the section on the Written Torah, *Shnei luḥot ha-berit*, Josepov edn, 1878, p. 26.
59 Joseph Gikatila, *Sefer sha'arei 'orah*, Jerusalem, Bialik Institute Press, 1970, part 1. In this spirit, the Maggid of Mezeritz later declared: "Through faith you can address the Blessed One and lead Him as you please."

5   The threefold tension in Jewish history

1   Leo Baeck, *The Essence of Judaism*, Frankfurt-on-Main, J. Kaufmann Verlag, 1936, p. 66.

2   Ronald R. Dudley, *A History of Cynicism*, London, Methuen Co., 1937. E. Shmueli, "Modern hippies and ancient Cynics," *Journal of World History* (UNESCO), 3, XII, Neuchâtel, 1970. The Tanna'im's attitude toward the Cynic philosophy, which gained wide appeal at that period, has yet to be adequately studied.

3   It has been rightly stressed by scholars that Israel's election and separation was conceived primarily in relation to God, not in relation to other nations, with whom Israel had to deal on a daily basis in matters of subsistence and security.

4   U. Cassuto, *A Commentary on the Book of Genesis*, Jerusalem, Magnes Press, 1961, Part 1: "From Adam to Noah."

5   Samuel A. Loewenstamm, "Haviv adam shenivra be-tzelem," *Tarbiz*, 27, 1, 1958.

6   Yehezkel Kaufmann, *Toldot ha-'emunah ha-Yisraelit*, Tel Aviv, 1948, book 1, vol. III, p. 196. Also in book 2, vol. 1.

7   Issak Heinemann, *Darchei ha-'aggadah*, 2nd edn, Jerusalem, Magnes Press, 1954, see especially chs. 5–9.

8   *Mekilta* on Exod. 20.11 in Jacob Z. Lauterbach (ed.), *Mekilta de-Rabbi Ishmael*, Philadelphia, Jewish Publication Society, 1935, vol. II.

9   Herbert Danby (ed.), *The Mishnah*, London, Oxford Univ. Press, 1933.

10   Hanoch Albeck (ed.), *The Mishnah*, Bialik Institute Press and Dvir, order *Nezikin*, tractate *Sanhedrin* B, p. 182.

11   Talmud scholars have established that the authentic version of this *mishnah* indeed was, "If any man saves alive a single soul," etc. This is the version found in the Munich manuscript and in the Jerusalem Mishnah, as also in the first Venetian printed edition, which was later copied by the Cracow and Krotoshin editions. But most editions of the Mishnah contained the version, "If any man saves alive a single soul *in Israel.*" Needless to say, the adoption of one or another version has important legal ramifications: does the saving of a Gentile's life warrant desecration of the Sabbath? This question was debated in the Rabbinic culture, resulting in opinions that were generally unfavorable, sometimes downright harsh, to Gentiles, as, for example, the words of Rabbi Samuel Eliezer Edels (1555–1631), whose famous commentary, *Hidushei halachot*, accompanies most editions of the Talmud, in the commentary to *San.* 37a:

This is intended to teach you that any man who saves one soul in Israel, and it is intentionally specified "one soul in Israel," in the singular form, as this is the image of God, the Singular One of the world, and Jacob's form [i.e. Israel] is His likeness . . . but Kuttim [i.e. Gentiles] do not have the form of man, only the form of other creatures, and whoever brings about the loss of a soul among them does not lose the world, and whoever saves a soul among them neither adds nor diminishes anything in this world.

Rabbi Shne'ur Zalman of Ladi, author of the *Tania*, and Rabbi Israel Meir Cohen of Radun, the *Hafetz Haim* (*Mishnah berurah, Orah haim*, 30, 8, Tel Aviv, Pardes, 1955) also accepted this *mishnah* in its later, anti-Gentile, version. They permitted healing the Gentile sick on the Sabbath "for the sake of peace" and in order not to incur ill-feeling. This problem has arisen again in the State of Israel regarding the ministering of medical treatment to Arabs, and was brought before Chief Rabbi Untermann for judgment. See a collection on this subject in Rabbi A. Waldenberg, *Responsa tzitz Eli'ezer*, Jerusalem, part 8, ch. 6.

12   Moses Maimonides, *Mishneh Torah* Jerusalem, Boys Town Jerusalem Publishers, 1965, Laws of Forbidden Foods (*Hilchot ma'achalot 'assurot*), 17, 9–10. We should note here and also later on, when we inquire into Maimonides' *halachic* rulings pertaining to relations between Jews and Gentiles, that his views were strongly influenced by the Jerusalem Talmud, i.e. by those Palestinian Tanna'im and 'Amora'im who shaped the Jewish attitude toward Gentiles in the Land of Israel prior to the destruction of the Second Temple and shortly thereafter.

13   The first opinion is A. Buechler's, the latter is G. Alon's. According to Buechler, the notion of the ritual uncleanness of Gentiles was unknown in Israel until the close of the Second Temple period when the eighteen *gezeirot* (decrees) were enacted. Non-Jews were deemed

unclean because of their Gentileness. But this rule carried no practical consequences as uncleanness for all but priests was a term applicable only in the Temple itself and in Temple-related matters. Alon disagrees entirely both with Buechler's concept and with his details. In Alon's opinion, the uncleanness of Gentiles was rooted in ancient traditions, dating long before the destruction. "The halacha that ordains uncleanness for non-Jews led to definite consequences in the transactions between Jews and other peoples." See Gedaliahu Alon, *Jews, Judaism and the Classical World*, Jerusalem, Magnes Press, 1977, chapter on "The Levitical uncleanness of Gentiles," p. 148.

14 *Sifre* Deut. 51. Other sources relating to Israel's boundaries can be found in the Jerusalem Talmud, *Shevi'it* 6b, 31, 3, in the *Tosefta*, *Shevi'it*, and in a mosaic inscription on the floor of a synagogue in the Beit She'an Valley.

15 I Macc. 15.33–4.

16 See S. Klein, *Eretz Yehudah*, Tel Aviv, Dvir, 1939, and *Eretz ha-galil*, Jerusalem, Mossad Harav Kook, 1945; A. Buechler, *Am ha-'aretz he-gelili*, Jerusalem, 1962; S. Safrai, "Miztvot shevi'it ba-metzi'ut shele'ahar hurban bait sheini," *Tarbiz*, 4, xxxv, 1966, pp. 304–28.

17 Cicero, *Pro-Flacco*, trans. Louis E. Lord, Cambridge, Mass., Harvard Univ. Press, 1967, vol. X, p. 441.

18 It is indeed with this thesis that Maimonides opens his *Guide for the Perplexed*, although the first chapters attempt precisely to remove any incorporification of God.

19 Henri Bergson, *The Two Sources of Morality and Religion*, trans. R. Ashley Audra and Cloudesley Brereton, London, Macmillan and Co., 1935.

20 Judah ha-Levi, *The Kuzari*, New York, Schocken Books, 1964, part 1, paras. 26–7, p. 47.

21 For more on the "racial theology," see Y. Baer on Judah ha-Levi and on Don Isaac Abravanel, both in his *History of the Jews in Christian Spain*, trans. Louis Schoffman, Philadelphia, Jewish Publication Society of America, 1961, and in *Galut*, trans. Robert Warshow, New York, Schocken Books, 1947. See also Baer's Hebrew article on Don Isaac Abravanel's attitude to problems of history and politics, *Tarbiz*, 3–4, viii, 1937, pp. 241–59. See also Menahem Stein, *Dat va-da'at*, Cracow, Miflat, 1938, p. 178, and E. Shmueli, *Don Isaac Abravanel ve-geirush Sefarad*, Jerusalem, Bialik Institute Press, 1963, p. 123.

22 As quoted in Nahum N. Glatzer (ed.), *The Judaic Tradition*, Boston, Beacon Press, 1969, pp. 395–6.

23 Moses Maimonides, *Guide for the Perplexed*, trans. M. Friedländer, 2nd edn, New York, Dover Publications, 1956, part 2, ch. 25, p. 200.

24 Ha-Levi, *The Kuzari*, part 1, para. 115, p. 79.

25 Moses Maimonides, *Epistle to Yemen*, ed. Abraham S. Halkin, English trans. Boaz Cohen, New York, American Academy for Jewish Research, 1952, p. xi.

26 Ha-Levi, *The Kuzari*, part 4, para. 23, p. 227.

27 Maimonides, *Mishneh Torah*, Book of Knowledge, Laws Concerning Idolatry and the Ordinances of the Heathens (*Hilchot 'achum*), ch. 11, 1, p. 78b. See also note 12 above.

28 Ibid. ch. 10. 6, p. 78b.

29 Ibid., Laws Relating to Moral Dispositions and to Ethical Conduct (*Hilchot de'ot*), ch. 4. 4, p. 55a.

30 E. Shmueli, *Beit Yisrael u-medinat Yisrael*, Tel Aviv, Yavne and the Cleveland College for Jewish Studies, 1966, p. 380. See also the last chapter of this book.

31 See P. Sorokin's arguments on this issue in *Social and Cultural Dynamics*, London, 1937. vol. I, ch. I and vol. III, ch. 15.

32 See M. Buber, *Pnei 'adam*, Jerusalem, 1962, p. 382. In the essay on "The nature of culture" Buber discusses contradictions in culture by presenting a number of dualisms: culture has two faces, a creative face and a traditional one, an arena for personal creative initiatives, and integration with the endeavors of past generations, with the generality. These two faces of culture, revolutionary and conservative, initiating and preserving, each had its own historic value, Buber thought, but only the combination of the two had the value of culture. The cultural creation gives form and permanence to the flux of life, thereby creating a world of things that have an independent existence, outside of life and above it. A third type of dualism is growth and form, growth and consciousness. Form grows by itself, as it were, out of nature, but there is also a directing and inventive consciousness. Clearly, these types of dualisms are not the kind of tensions we are discussing here, but they are

useful in understanding the entire humanistic concept of culture. Our conception of culture, which is neither humanistic nor anthropological-sociological, as explained in chapter 1, is therefore quite different from Buber's ideas on this matter.

33 *Mekilta* on Exod. 13.17 in Lauterbach, *Mekilta de-Rabbi Ishmael*, vol. 1, p. 173.

34 A. Roberts and I. Donaldson (eds.), *The Ante-Nicene Fathers*, rev. A. Cleveland Coxe, Grand Rapids, Wm. B. Erdman Publisher, reprinted 1977, vol. 1, p. 217.

35 On this see the writings of my teacher Yeḥiel Michael Hacohen Guttmann, especially in *Beḥinat kiyum ha-mitzvot*, Breslau, 1931, ch. 1.

36 H.N. Bialik, *Devarim shebeᶜal pe*, Tel Aviv, Dvir, 1935, vol. 1, p. 225.

6   Historical knowledge in the service of faith

1 On Vico's work and the controversy it engendered, see F. Nicolini, *Commento Storico alla seconda Scienza Nuova*, Rome, 1949–50; A.R. Caponigri, *Time and Idea; The Theory of History in Giambattista Vico*, London, Routledge and Kegan Paul, 1953; I. Berlin, "The philosophical ideas of Giambattista Vico" in *Art and Ideas in 18th Century Italy*, Rome, edizioni di storia e letteratura, 1960; A. Momilgliano, "Vico's Scienza Nuova," *History and Theory*, The Hague, 1966, vol. v. This wide acceptance of historical perspective is not an indication of general agreement. Many readers, including social scientists, philosophers, and writers, shared the dissatisfaction which Nietzsche had already expressed in his 1873 essay on the utility and harm in history: "Vom Nutzen and Nachteil der Historie für das Leben." All three forms of historiography – the monumental, the antiquarian, and the critical – present numerous dangers to the welfare of men and nations; the latter have need, at times, of oblivion. Nietzsche warned against the "hypertrophy of the historical sense." His comments there on the "historical" and the "super-historical" pointed to a problem which later became the focus of the "historismus" debate, i.e. the dependence of values on the historical process, as explained by Troeltsch, Croce, Meinecke, and in our century, by Mannheim, Popper, and others. The weariness of history and the withdrawal from its burdensome heritage do not, of course, weaken the tie to history. For Vico, at any rate, the historical persepective was still a newly discovered triumph.

2 Moses Maimonides, *The Mishnah of Avoth*, end of ch. 1, in Paul Forchheimer (ed. and trans.), *Living Judaism*, New York, Feldheim Publishers, 1974.

3 2 Chron. 16.11; I Kgs. 22.39, 46, and many similar verses. Biblical historiography is not our subject here, nor do we deal with the writings of Josephus Flavius. Space limitations impose brevity, especially in matters that have already been adequately treated by many scholars.

4 On metaphors of time, see Frank E. Manuel, *Shapes of Philosophical History*, Stanford Univ. Press, 1965; R. Nisbet, *Social Change and History*, New York, Oxford Univ. Press, 1969. Nisbet described and analyzed the evolution of organological metaphors in European historical awareness. We know that Israel was viewed as one body both in the Talmud and in the Mystical culture. The organological metaphor is also very prevalent in the National-Israeli culture.

5 Benzion Dinur, *Dorot u-reshumot*, Jerusalem, Bialik Institute Press, 1978, p. 87. Dinur deals here with the historiographic fragments in the Talmudic literature, and mentions, *inter alia*, notebooks kept by Sages, records of the ancient *yeshivot* and of the presidents, historiographic *halachah* and historic *midrash*.

6 Ibid., p. 162. Isaak Heinemann cited many examples of this phenomenon, but used a different terminology to describe it.

7 All Talmud scholars have dealt with this matter, thus we only mention briefly Joseph Klausner, Gedaliahu Alon, A. Buechler, for their works on this period, Saul Lieberman for his studies on the Jerusalem Talmud and the *Tosefta*, and his method of dating the composition of tractates and *midrashim* based on variations in language, style, concepts, details of daily life, general prevailing conditions, and the influence exercised by Greek culture; lastly, Yitzhak Baer for his articles on the historical foundations of the Halachah, *Zion*, xxvii, Jerusalem, 1962, on Jerusalem during the Great Revolt, *Zion*, xxxvi, 1971, and others.

8 Much has been written about this ruling from the legal viewpoint. See Shmuel Shilo's *Dina*

de-malchuta dina, Jerusalem, Academic Press, 1974, and his article on the legal basis for the rule *dina de-malchuta dina*, in *Mishpatim*, II, Jerusalem, 1970. Nahum Rakover in "Dina de-malchuta dina," *Hagut*, Jerusalem, 1978, p. 75, points out the alien origin of this ruling, which confers legal validity upon a foreign law having no Jewish source and superseding explicit *halachah*. The article discusses the scope and effectiveness of this ruling from a legal viewpoint, but does not explain the historical conditions which occasioned it. A number of other scholars who have studied this ruling have also ignored history, e.g. M. Silberg, *Hok u-musar ba-mishpat ha-ʿivry*, Jerusalem, Magnes Press, 1952.

9 *Midrash Genesis Rabbah*, 78, trans. H. Freedman and Maurice Simon, London, Soncino Press, 1939.

10 Gedaliahu Alon, *Toldot-ha-yehudim be-Eretz Yisrael bi-tekufat ha-Mishnah veha-Talmud*, Tel Aviv, Ha-kibbutz ha-meʾuhad, 1958, vol II, p. 119.

11 Tractate *Semahot* 2, 9, trans. D. Zlotnick, New Haven and London, Yale Univ. Press, 1966, p. 35. In contrast to the permission, authorized in *Bab.K.* 103a, "to steal past customs."

12 On Rab and Shmuel and the new Persian kingdom see J. Neusner, *History of the Jews in Babylonia*, Leiden, E.J. Brill, 1965, part 1, "The Parthian period"; 1966, part 2, "the early Sassanian period". See also Neusner's essay "The religious uses of history" in *History and Theory*, The Hague, 1966, vol. v, p. 153.

13 There is a great difference in the art of narration and the attitude toward events and reality, but the purpose is identical. Again, it is not our intention to discuss here Biblical historiography. A separate study is required to compare it with Talmudic historiography.

14 Hermann Cohen, *Religion of Reason*, trans. S. Kaplan, New York, Frederick Ungar Publishing Co., 1972. A good number of Talmud scholars in both eastern and western Europe have written in this spirit of "idealization," a trend typified, for example, by E.E. Urbach's *The Sages*, trans. Israel Abrahams, Jerusalem, Magnes Press, 1975, a case of idealization, but not without insistence on proper testimony and evidence, as Hermann Cohen required.

15 Thucydides astounded and inspired his readers with the completely novel approach to historiography proclaimed in the introductory statements to *History of the Peloponnesian War*, trans. Sir R.N. Livingstone, London, Oxford Univ. Press, book 1, para. 22, p. 44:

With reference to the narrative of events, far from permitting myself to derive it from the first source that came to hand, I did not even trust my own impressions, but it rests partly on what I saw myself, partly on what others saw for me, the accuracy of the report being always tried by the most severe and detailed tests possible. My conclusions have cost me some labour from the want of coincidence between accounts of the same occurrences by different eyewitnesses, arising sometimes from imperfect memory, sometimes from undue partiality for one side or the other. The absence of romance in my history will, I fear, detract somewhat from its interest; but I shall be content if it is judged useful by those inquirers who desire an exact knowledge of the past . . . My history has been composed to be an everlasting possession, not the show-piece of an hour.

On the rigorous requirement for truthfulness and supporting documentation, compare Josephus Flavius' opening paragraphs in *Against Apion, or On the Antiquity of the Jews*: "My first thought is one of intense astonishment at the current opinion that, in the study of primeval history, the Greeks alone deserve serious attention, and that the truth should be sought from them, and that neither we nor any others in the world can be trusted." But scholars have justly remarked that Josephus uncritically accepted the historical evidence of "the two and twenty [sic] (books which) contain the record of all time," *Josephus*, trans. H. St. J. Thackeray, London, William Heinemann, 1926, vol I, pp. 65, 179.

16 These statements paraphrase the Sages. See *Midrash Genesis Rabbah*, 68.11; 74.11, 68.1; *Midrash Deuteronomy Rabbah*, 11.11; 1.31.

17 *Mekilta* on Jethro, tractate *Bahodesh*, 1 in Jacob Z. Lauterebach (ed.), *Mekilta de-Rabbi Ish-amael*, Philadelphia, Jewish Publication Society, 1935, vol. II, p. 194: "You were unwilling to be subject to God, behold now you are subjected to the most inferior of the nations, the Arabs. You were unwilling to pay the head-tax to God, "a beka head" (Exod. 38.26), now you are paying a head tax of fifteen shekels under a government of your enemies."

18 M.H. Amishai (Moshe Maisels), *Mahshavah ve-ʾemet*, Tel Aviv, Mitzpeh, 1939, vol. II,

pp. 302, 303. One need not agree with the conclusions of this thinker in order to be impressed by what he describes as the past's sheer weight, or the "weariness" of the past, a theme widely trumpeted by Nietzsche and, later on, by members of George's circle in Germany and elsewhere down to our own times (in Hebrew literature, by Berdyczewski). See n. 1, above. An abridged version of this book exists in English, but it does not include the sections on Talmudic Judaism cited above. M. Maisels, *Thought and Truth*, trans. A. Regelson, New York, Bookman Associates, 1956.

19 Rabbi Yoḥanan lamented: "The hearts [i.e. the intellectual powers] of the ancients were like the door of the Ulam [one of the chambers constituting the Temple, twenty cubits wide], but that of the last generations was like the door of the Hekal [only ten cubits wide], but ours is like the eye of a fine needle" (*Erub.* 53a). Similar sayings are frequent in the Talmudic literature. For further reading on the notion of decline held by Roman writers, see R. Starn, "Meaning-levels in the theme of historical decline," in *History and Theory*, The Hague, 1975, vol. XIV. Tacitus has even the notorious Nero complaining of the decline of Roman youth: "Quin, si qua in parte lubricum adulescentiae nostrae declinat, revocas, etc.," in Tacitus, *Annales*, XIV, 56.

20 See Louis Ginzberg's study on tractate *Tamid* in *Al halachah va-ʾaggadah*, Tel Aviv, Dvir, 1960. The study attempts to demonstrate that this tractate was not part of Yehudah ha-Nassi's (*Rabbi*) Mishnah, did not come under his redactorial hand, and when certain additions and revisions were removed from it, "this tractate constitutes the earliest Tannaʾitic composition, and although its structure is similar to that of the Mishnah, it is nonetheless different from *Rabbi*'s Mishnah in its method and language," ibid., p. 61.

21 Haim H. Ben-Sasson, "Li-megamot ha-chronographia ha-yehudit shel yemei ha-beinayim u-veʿayoteha" in *Historionim va-ʾaskolot historiot*, lectures delivered at the seventh convention of the Historical Society of Israel, Jerusalem, 1962.

22 For more on the Karaites, see history books by Graetz, Dubnov, and Salo Baron, whose fifth volume of *Social and Religious History of the Jews*, New York, Columbia Univ. Press 1937, devotes some 100 pages to the subject, including detailed bibliographical notes. On the Karaite conception of history, see also Raphael Mahler, *Ha-karaʾim*, trans. E. Shmueli, Tel Aviv, 1949. On p. 214, Mahler cites a statement of Sahl ben Mazliaḥ, a militant Karaite opponent of traditional religious authority: "Know, our brethren of Israel, that each one of us will be judged for his own deeds, and our God will not heed the apologies of he who argues: 'Thus acted our fathers,' just as He paid no heed to the protestations of Adam . . . For our blessed Lord has said: 'Be not like your forefathers'." This indeed is a declaration of radical rebellion against the traditional conception of history.

23 See A.M. Habermann (ed.,) *Gezeirot Ashkenaz ve-Zorfat*, introd. Yitzhak Baer, Jerusalem, Tarshish Books, 1945. On the different reactions to persecutions, see the collection *Milḥemet kodesh u-martyrologia be-toldot Yisrael uve-toldot ha-ʿamim*, lectures delivered at the eleventh convention of the Historical Society of Israel, Jerusalem, 1967.

24 Abraham Ibn Daud, *Seder ha-kabbalah* in A. Neubauer (ed.), *Seder ha-ḥachamim ve-korot ha-yamim*, Oxford Univ. Press, 1938, vol. I, p. 80. See his discussion there of the Karaites.

25 Moses Maimonides, *Guide for the Perplexed*, trans. M. Friedländer, 2nd edn, New York, Dover Publications, 1956, part 3, ch. 14, p. 278. Far-reaching consequences, particularly characteristic of this culture, derive from this statement.

26 Moses Maimonides, the Essay on Resurrection in Abraham Halkin and David Hartman, *Crisis and Leadership*, Epistles of Maimonides, Philadelphia and New York, Jewish Publication Society, 1985. We read there even harsher expressions (p. 212):

When I learned of these exceedingly deficient folk and their doubts, who, although they consider themselves sages in Israel, are in fact the most ignorant and more seriously astray than beasts, their minds filled with the senseless prattle of old women and noxious fantasies, like children and women, I concluded that it was necessary that I clearly elucidate religious fundamentals in my works on law.

On a slightly higher level, in Maimonides' view, are history books:

The third category comprises the talk that is undesirable. Man derives no spiritual benefit from it, yet it is also no sin or transgression. Of this kind is most of the talk of the common

people, about events past and present, such as how such-and-such a king conducts himelf
at home in his palace, or about the cause of somebody's death, and how a certain person
grew rich. The sages call this "idle talk."

Maimonides, *The Mishnah of Avoth*, 1, 17, in Forchheimer, *Living Judaism*, p. 46.

27 Moses Maimonides, *Mishneh Torah*, Book of Knowledge, Laws Concerning Idolatry and the
Ordinances of the Heathens, A, 2, pp. 66b–67a, and similarly in *Guide for the Perplexed*, part
1, ch. 63, we hear that the Patriarchs "guided their fellow-men by means of argument and
instruction," p. 94.

28 Salo Baron, "The historical outlook of Maimonides" in *History and Jewish Historians*,
Philadelphia, Jewish Publication Society, 1964.

29 Aristotle, *De Poetica*, trans. Ingram Bywater, 1451, ch. 9 in Richard McKeon (ed.),
Introduction to Aristotle, New York, Random House, 1947, pp. 635–6. In Aristotle's view,
history over-shadows the essential, the "generalities," and highlights instead the
insignificant, i.e. the details which do not demonstrate the generalities, as we heard in
Maimonides' remark above. For this reason poetry is more philosophical and more
important than history:

From what we have said it will be seen that the poet's function is to describe, not the thing
that has happened, but a kind of thing that might happen, i.e. what is possible as being
probable or necessary. The distinction between historian and poet is not in the one writing
prose and the other verse – you might put the work of Herodotus into verse, and it would
still be a species of history; it consists really in this, that the one describes the thing that has
been, and the other a kind of thing that might be. Hence poetry is something more
philosophic and of graver import than history, since its statements are of the nature of
universals, whereas those of history are singulars. By a universal statement I mean one as
to what such or such a kind of man will probably or necessarily say or do – which is the aim
of poetry, though it affixes proper names to the characters. (ibid.)

One can hardly claim that Greek historiography in fact exemplified this idea. Herodotus
and Thucydides may have sought to clarify general and typical ideas, but in their quest for
essence and for necessary laws they did not neglect the phenomena, events and
contingencies of history.

30 Maimonides, *Guide for the Perplexed*, part 3, ch. 50, p. 382. Perhaps this argument was
made primarily in order to explain in what respect the laws of Moses were superior to the
laws of the surrounding Gentiles. "His apologetic purpose forces him to resort to history
and to discuss the heathen practices of the ancient Near Eastern peoples"; Shlomo Pines,
Bein Maḥshevet Yisrael le-maḥshevet ha-ʿamim Jerusalem, Bialik Institute Press, 1977,
p. 163.

31 See S. Rawidowicz' article on Saʿadiah Gaʾon in *Knesset le-zecher Bialik*, Tel Aviv, 1939, and
in English, see his essays on Saʿadiah in *Studies in Jewish Thought*, ed. Nahum N. Glatzer,
trans. Lawrence V. Berman, Philadelphia, Jewish Publication Society, 1974, pp. 227–68;
Pines, *Bein Maḥshevet Yisrael le-maḥshevet ha-ʿamin*, has a chapter on the philosophical
sources of *Guide for the Perplexed* dealing with Maimonides' historical conception. See also
Salo Baron, n. 28, above.

32 I.H. Weiss, *Dor dor ve-dorshav*, New York and Berlin, 1924, part 5, p. 245. The traditional
education in the German communities up until the Emancipation, when coupled with a
rationalism that disdained history, was apparently responsible for this reaction from
Mendelssohn: "What do I know of history? All that bears the name history . . . has never
entered into my head; and I constantly yawn whenever I need to read anything historical."
Cited by S. Baron in *Social and Religious History of the Jews*, New York, Columbia Univ. Press,
1937, vol. II, p. 218.

33 Abraham Ibn Daud, *The Book of Tradition*, trans. Gerson D. Cohen, Philadelphia, Jewish
Publication Society of America, 1967, p. 3. The reliability of Ibn Daud's work was
questioned by many. Ḥaim Joseph David Azulai (the Ḥida) detected many errors in this
work and advised readers not to rely on it. "I noted on the page one word, 'lehadam' [i.e.
nothing of the kind] or 'untrue'."

34 *Seder ʿolam rabbah* ("The Great Order of the World"), the first attempt to establish a

sequential chronology of Biblical events since the creation of the world, dates from the second century CE. It ends with events dating from the period of Alexander the Great and the Bar Kochba revolt (132–5 CE). *Seder ʿolam zuta* ("Brief Order of the World") is of uncertain date, and carries its chronology up to Jewish Babylonia of the sixth century CE.

35 See Starn, "Meaning-levels in the theme of historical decline." The Platonic and Aristotelian theory of cycles also did not postulate, so it appears to scholars today, absolute cyclical regularity.

36 Ginzberg, *Al halachah va-ʾaggadah*, p. 254.

37 *Midrash Leviticus Rabbah*, 27, London, Soncino Press, 1939.

38 Ibid.

39 We recall Reish Lakish's well-known saying: "What is the meaning of the verse 'This is the book of the generations of Adam' [Gen. 5.1]? It is to intimate that the Holy One, blessed be He, showed him [Adam] every generation and its thinkers, every generation and its sages" (*San.* 38b). The entire chain of transmission is foreseen in all its details. This predestination, where the foreknowledge determines the development, was greatly overstated by the author of *Seder ʿolam rabbah* in his conclusion. However, the problem of predestination, which includes also the belief in reincarnation, a distinct belief in prefiguration, is not our concern here.

40 N. Rotenstreich, *Bein ʿavar le-hove*, Bialik Institute Press, Jerusalem, p. 59.

41 Isaak Heinemann, *Darchei ha-ʾaggadah*, Jerusalem, Magnes and Massada, 1960, p. 177.

42 J.B. Bury, *The Idea of Progress*, New York, 1932, p. 21–2.

43 N. Rotenstreich, *Zeman u-mashmaʿut*, Tel Aviv, Sifriyat Poʿalim, 1974, p. 46, seeks to contradict J.B. Bury's opinion that the idea of providence and the idea of progress are antithetical, by citing proof from the Kabbalah regarding the lengthy process of the soul's purification, an image which couples providence with progress. This is subject-matter for further study.

7   Historical consciousness in the Emancipation culture

1 The words of Ps. 146.7 *lehatir ʾassurim* ("to set prisoners free"), were read *lehatir ʾissurim* ("to permit the forbidden").

2 Many scholars have written on the ending of the Jewish Middle Ages and the beginning of the new era. See Benzion Dinur, *Bemifneh ha-dorot*, Jerusalem, Bialik Institute Press, 1955, in a chapter devoted to the question of redemption at the beginning of the Haskalah; Jacob Katz, *Tradition and Crisis, Jewish Society at the End of the Middle Ages*, New York, Free Press of Glencoe, 1961; Efraim Shmueli, *Massoret u-mahapecha*, New York, Sefarim, 1942. For an economic analysis of the emergence of the Emancipation culture, see Raphael Mahler, *A History of Modern Jewry 1780–1815*, New York, Schocken Books, 1971.

3 Zvi Locker, "Me-ʿadat ʾanussim li-kehilat kodesh", Jerusalem, *Zion*, 1–2, XLII, 1977, p. 76.

4 This formulation is cited by M. Kayserling in *Moses Mendelssohn, sein Leben und seine Werke*, Leipzig, Hermann Mendelssohn, 1862, p. 568, para. 57.

5 Moses Mendelssohn, *Gesammelte Schriften*, 1844, vol. V, p. 494.

6 Mendelssohn in a letter to the theologian Johann David Michaelis, *Gesammelte Schriften*, vol. III, p. 366.

7 Ibid., p. 360.

8 Herz Homberg (1749–1841) served for a number of years as a tutor in Mendelssohn's home and also participated in the latter's exegesis, the *Biʾur* to Deuteronomy. From 1787–1806 he served as a state-appointed inspector-general of Jewish schools in Galicia. Another of his catechisms, *Imrei schefer*, Vienna, 1808, admonishes its young readers to obey the monarch's commands, whether good or bad, because "the Holy One, blessed be He, by His holy will seats kings on their thrones, they are His kingdom's agents for dispensing justice on earth and leading the nations in righteousness."

9 Heinrich Graetz, *History of the Jews*, Philadelphia, Jewish Publication Society, 1956, vol. V, p. 289.

10 Moses Mendelssohn *Gesammelte Schriften* (Jubilaeumsausgabe), Berlin, Akadademie Verlag, 1930, vol. VII, and S. Rawidowicz' introduction there, p. xvi.

11 A reference to the modern reformers, in a letter to Immanuel Wohlwill (Immanuel Wolf), April 1, 1823.

12 Some twenty-five years later the first Leipzig Israelitic Synod (June 1869) adopted L. Philippson's proposal that the law of Moses be viewed as emphatically and fundamentally addressed to the modern secular state. On the polemics surrounding this idea see M. Maas, *Die Religion des Judentums und die politisch-sozialen Prinzipien unseres Jahrhunderts*, Leipzig, 1870. See also W. Guenther Plaut's English translation of documents originating from the Leipzig Synod, *The Growth of Reform Judaism*, New York, World Union for Progressive Judaism, 1965; Max Wiener, *Jüdische Religion im Zeitalter der Emanzipation*, Berlin, Philo Verlag, 1933; Albert Lewkowitz, *Das Judentum und die geistigen Strömungen des 19. Jahrhunderts*, Breslau, M. und H. Marcus, 1935; Oskar Wolfsberg, *Zur Zeit-und Geistesgeschichte des Judentums*, Zürich, Verlag Die Gestaltung, 1938.

13 Lazarus Bendavid, *Etwas zur Charakteristik der Juden*, Leipzig, J. Stahel, 1793.

14 I have enlarged the discussion upon trends and changes in the American Jewish community in my book *Beit Yisrael u-medinat Yisrael*, Tel Aviv, Yavneh and the Cleveland College of Jewish Studies, 1966, and thus limit my discussion of the Emancipation to pre-Holocaust Europe.

15 Aḥad ha-ʿam, *Selected Essays*, trans. Leon Simon, Philadelphia, Jewish Publication Society of America, repr. 1962, ch. "The spiritual survival,' pp. 275–6.

16 Leopold Zunz, *Gesammelte Schriften*, Berlin, L. Gerschel, 1875–6, part 1, p. 59. See also the introduction to his work *Die Gottesdienstlichen Vorträge der Juden*, Berlin, A. Asher, 1832.

17 Immanuel Wolf, "Über den Begriff einer Wissenschaft des Judentums," *Zeitschrift für die Wissenschaft des Judentums*, London, Leo Baeck Institute Yearbook II, 1957. For excerpts in English, see Michael M. Meyer, *Ideas of Jewish History*, New York, Behrman House Inc., 1974.

18 Haim Naḥman Bialik, *Ketavim*, Tel Aviv, Dvir, 1935, vol. II, essay on the Science of Judaism, p. 195.

19 Simon Dubnov, *History of the Jews*, trans. Moshe Spiegel, South Brunswick and New York, Thomas Yoseloff, 1967–73, vol. V, p. 100. Criticism was also voiced by Ismar Elbogen in his outline of a century of the Science of Judaism, "Ein Jahrhundert Wissenschaft des Judentums," in the jubilee volume published on the fiftieth anniversary of the Berlin *Lehranstalt für die Wissenschaft des Judentums*, Berlin, Dvir, 1922–4, part 2.

20 Gerschom Scholem, *Devarim be-go*, Tel Aviv, Am Oved, 1975, ch. "Reflections on the Science of Judaism," pp. 388ff. In a later appraisal of the Science of Judaism, similar, though somewhat tempered views are expressed; see G. Scholem, *The Messianic Idea in Judaism*, New York, Schocken Books, 1971, ch. "The Science of Judaism – then and now," pp. 304–13.

21 Scholem, *Devarim be-go*, pp. 388ff.

22 Ibid.

23 Ibid., p. 396. Similarly, Y. Barzilay took sharp issue with Scholem's essay in *Hadoar*, XXIV, 1978.

24 Nathan Rotenstreich, *Tradition and Reality: The Impact of History on Modern Jewish Thought*, New York, Random House, 1972, ch.3, "The Science of Judaism."

25 Zunz, *Die Gottesdienstlichen Vorträge der Juden*, p. 496.

26 On the development of the Science of Judaism in western Europe before the Holocaust, see S. Federbush (ed.), *Ḥochmat Yisrael bemaʿarav Europa*, Jerusalem and Tel Aviv, Ogen and M. Neuman, 1958. Needless to say, not all the important scholars can be mentioned here. I merely note that the beginnings we have described bore prolific fruit in the following generation.

27 Isaac Baer Levinsohn, *Teʿudah-be-Yisrael*, Vilna, R.M. Romm, 1855, pp. 31ff. The program proposed by Ribal (Levinsohn's acronym) resembles, both in its general outline and in its details, the program of western Maskilim for the improvement of education and the melioration of life in Europe. Most of the qualities characterizing the Emancipation culture are to be found in the opinions and aspirations expressed by Ribal.

28 See Aḥad ha-ʿam's correspondence, *Igrot Aḥad ha-ʿam*, Tel Aviv, Dvir, 1960, vol. I, p. 18.

29 The assumptions of naïve historical realism, or "objectivism," as Husserl and other phenomenologists termed it, raise questions concerning cognition and knowledge in the

social sciences and history which are beyond the scope of this work. For modern philosophers of history who have dealt with these fundamental issues, see the first two notes to chapter 1, and my articles in English: "Objectivity and perspectives," *Zeitschrift für philosophische Forschung*, Meisenheim/Glan, 1979; "How is objectivity in the social sciences possible?" in *Crossroads of Modern Thought*, Tel Aviv, Eked, 1984, p. 179.

30 Ranke's famous statement that the historian wishes to know "wie es eigentlich gewesen" has been much interpreted and discussed. Ranke himself was perhaps more "biased" than any historian of comparable note. Popes and kings generally emerge from his descriptions decked with multiple virtues, while rebels against authority are portrayed as odious evildoers. Politically, Ranke was a staunch conservative, taking sharp issue with the tenets of the French Revolution. He was a life-long supporter of Prussian authoritarianism, and after the revolution of March 1848 sided with Friedrich Wilhelm IV against the popular clamor for a democratic constitution. His studies tend to steer clear of problematic social and economic issues in order to tread safely "between the drops." His attitude toward the Jews was an equally "cautious" Christian conservatism. See T. Von Laue, *Leopold Ranke, the Formative Years*, Princeton, 1950; H. Liebeschutz, *Ranke*, Hist. Assoc. G. 26, 1954.

31 Salo W. Baron, *History and Jewish Historians*, Philadelphia, Jewish Publication Society, 1964, p. 260. Geiger emphasized that with all due respect to objectivity, it was necessary to take a stand in the matter of Israel's uniqueness, election, and destiny. The new objectivism aspired to rationalism and universality, thereby presenting a difficult challenge to both religious and national Jewish particularity. Were not the laws of world history equally applicable to Jewish history? This question was a major preoccupation.

32 I have chosen to enlarge on Jost partly because he is less well-known than some other historians, but also because his views are characteristic of the speculation on the nature of Judaism found in this Jewish Science.

33 Heinrich Graetz, *Darchei ha-historia ha-yehudit*, Jerusalem, 1969, p. 252.

34 Ibid., p. 275.

35 Dubnov, *History of the Jews*, vol. I, introd.

36 I.M. Jost, *Allgemeine Geschichte des Israelitischen Volkes*, Leipzig, C.F. Amelang, 1850, vol. I, p. 2. For the English rendition cited here, see Meyer, *Ideas of Jewish History*, p. 177.

37 Jost, *Allgemeine Geschichte des Israelitischen Volkes*, vol. II, p. 238.

38 Ibid., vol. I, p. 5. For English extract, see Meyer, *Ideas of Jewish History*, p. 179.

39 Jost, *Allgemeine Geschichte des Israelitischen Volkes*, vol. IV, p. 103. On the development of this idea in the nineteenth century, see Raphael Mahler's study on "Religious sects and cultural currents in Dubnov's view of Jewish history" in S. Rawidowicz (ed.), *Sefer Shimʿon Dubnov*, London and Jerusalem, Ararat, 1954. The idea that the religion of precepts had safeguarded the nation's survival became a cornerstone of functionalist sociology. Aḥad ha-ʿam also made this the foundation of his philosophy.

40 "Forschen und wandern, denken und dulden, lernen und leiden," H. Graetz, *Geschichte der Juden*, Leipzig, Leiner, 1888–1909, vol. IV; introd. English extract in Meyer, *Ideas of Jewish History*, p. 229.

41 Dubnov, *History of the Jews*, vol. I, p. 26.

42 Ibid., p. 27.

43 Graetz, *History of the Jews*, vol. III, p. 127.

44 Dubnov, *History of the Jews*, vol. II, pp. 412ff.

45 Ibid., vol. III, p. 645.

46 Graetz, *Darchei ha-historia ha-yehudit*, ch. "The rejuvenation of the Jewish race," pp. 103ff.

47 Ibid., pp. 123ff. in a chapter devoted to the development of the Messianic belief. S. Ettinger's introduction outlines developments in Graetz's views, including his views on the Messianic issue, pp. 34ff.

48 Ibid., p. 125.

49 S. Dubnov, *Sefer ha-ḥayim*, Tel Aviv, 1933, p. 280.

50 Dubnov, *History of the Jews*, vol. V, p. 859.

51 Wilhelm von Humboldt, *Über die Aufgabe des Geschichtsschreibers*, Leipzig, Insel Verlag, (no date), pp. 28–9. English version quoted here is cited by Baron in *History and Jewish Historians*, pp. 244–5 to illustrate Humboldt's influence on Jost.

52 On idealism's ability (or inability) to explain historical events, see the writings of Karl

Popper, R.G. Collingwood, Charles Beard, Carl Becker, Karl Mannheim, and subsequent discussions of these works. A later and far more sophisticated example of an idealistic interpretation can be found in Benedetto Croce, *History of Europe in the Nineteenth Century*, trans. Henry Furst, London, G. Allen and Unwin, 1934. See also E. Shmueli, "Croce on history and liberty," introduction to the Hebrew edition of Croce's work, Jerusalem, 1961.

53 Graetz, *Darchei ha-historia ha-yehudit*, p. 171.

54 Ibid., p. 57, This translation from Meyer, *Ideas of Jewish History*, p. 221.

55 Ibid. English citation from Meyer, *Ideas of Jewish History*, p. 224.

56 Ettinger's introduction to Graetz, *Darchei ha-historia ha-yehudit*, p. 15. Similar comments were made by Dinur on Dubnov.

57 Dubnov, *Sefer ha-ḥayim*, p. 290.

58 Dubnov developed this theory in "Letters on ancient and modern Judaism," 1897–1907, reprinted in *Nationalism and History, Essays on Old and New Judaism*, New York, Atheneum, 1970, and he never deviated from it. The theory, as it emerges from these "Letters," is discussed in Jakob Lestschinsky's article "Autonomy and the letters on ancient and modern Judaism" in Rawidowicz, *Sefer Shimʿon Dubnov*, pp. 166–93.

59 Benzion Dinur, *Dorot u-reshumot*, Jerusalem, Bialik Institute Press, 1978, p. 261.

8   The struggle for self-affirmation

1 As evidenced by the writings of the founders of Zionism and the architects of the modern resettlement of Israel, that entire new leadership élite which set out to lay the foundations for the new culture. The founders of modern Hebrew literature belong to this group.

2 Yeḥezkel Kaufmann, *Golah ve-nechar*, Tel Aviv, Dvir, 1929, vol. I, p. 1. The rendition of these citations in English is from Laurence J. Silberstein, "History and ideology: the writings of Y. Kaufmann," unpublished Ph.D. dissertation, Brandeis Univ., September 1971.

3 Joseph Klausner, *Historia shel ha-bait ha-sheni*, 2nd edn, Jerusalem, Aḥiʾassaf Publishers, 1950, p. 261.

4 Benzion Dinur, *Dorot u-reshumot*, Jerusalem, Bialik Institute Press, 1978, essay on the uniqueness of Jewish history, pp. 3ff.

5 Ibid., p. 4.

6 Ibid., p. 14.

7 See chapter 7 above, p. 184.

8 Klausner, *Historia shel ha-bait ha-sheni*, introduction.

9 Yeḥezkel Kaufmann, *Religion of Israel*, trans. and abridg. Moshe Greenberg, Univ. of Chicago Press, 1960, p. 1.

10 Dinur, *Dorot u-reshumot*, p. 31.

11 Ibid., p. 30.

12 Ibid., p. 31.

13 This point is leveled not only against historical idealism and historical materialism, but also against modern attempts to deny man's historicity by attribution of immutable cognitive structures, as in structuralism. See Walter Falk, *Vom Strukturalismus zum Potentialismus, ein Versuch zur Geschichts und Literaturtheorie*, Freiburg, München, Alber Verlag, 1976.

14 I refer to the Renaissance theory of perspective which heralded and accompanied the scientific representation of the world and created "realism" or "the new point of view" about which art historians have written extensively. See Jacob Burckhardt's beautiful chapter in *Der Cicerone*, Basel, 1860, II, p. 793 and E. Panofsky, "Die Perspektive als Symbolische Form", Vortraege der Bibliothek Warburg, 1924–5, Leipzig, 1927. Leonardo da Vinci explained how, aided by perspective, the new art would henceforth establish painting and sculpture on the foundations of the exact sciences, Treatise on Painting, in J.P. Richter, *The Literary Works of Leonardo da Vinci*, London, 1883.

15 Isaac Abravanel, *Maʿayanei ha-yeshuʿah* (commentary on the Prophets and the Hagiographia), Tel Aviv, 1960, p. 372, and elsewhere in his commentaries.

16 Abravanel's commentary to Deut. 26, *ki tavo*.

17 See W.H. Walsh, *An Introduction to Philosophy of History*, London, Hutchinson Univ. Library, 1967. See also W.H. Dray, "Point of view in history," *Clio*, 2, VII, 1978, n. 13 on

the debate about perspective and the possibility of a super-perspectival truth and the sub-perspectival fact.

18 Leon J. Goldstein, "History and the primacy of knowing," *History and Theory*, Beiheft 16 titled "The construction of the historical past," The Hague, 1977, p. 31.

19 Ibid., p. 32.

20 Gerschom Scholem, *Devarim be-go*, Tel Aviv, Am Oved, 1975, p. 402, and see ch. 7, p. 183.

21 In his preface to Dinur's *Dorot u-reshumot*, p. xvii.

22 Benzion Dinur, *Israel in the Diaspora*, Philadelphia, Jewish Publication Society of America, 1969, p. 4.

23 As cited by Josephus Flavius in *Antiquities of the Jews*; see *Josephus*, trans. Ralph Marcus, Harvard Univ. Press, vol. III, 1943, p. 509, ss. 115–16. On the Jewish dispersion in the Second Commonwealth, see S. Baron, *Social and Religious History of the Jews*, New York, Columbia Univ. Press, 1937, vol. I, pp. 128ff, and B. Dinur, *Dorot u-reshumot*, pp. 176ff.

24 Gedaliahu Alon, *The Jews in Their Land in the Talmudic Age*, Jerusalem, Magnes Press, 1984, vol. II, p. 757.

25 Dinur, *Israel in the Diaspora*, p. 3.

26 Alon, *The Jews in Their Land*, p. 225.

27 This Judah Ḥassid (Segal) ha-Levi (*c*.1660–1700), Sabbatean preacher and leader of the first organized Ashkenazi immigration to Palestine, is not to be confused with Judah ben Samuel he-Ḥassid (*c.* 1150–1217), prominent medieval scholar and leader of the Mystical movement of German-Jewish pietism (Ḥassidei Ashkenaz), mentioned later in this chapter in connection with Baer's assessment of that movement's impact on Spanish Jewry.

28 Benzion Dinur, *Bemifneh ha-dorot*, Jerusalem, Bialik Institute Press, 1955, p. 13.

29 Dinur, *Israel in the Diaspora*, p. 90.

30 Dinur, *Dorot u-reshumot*, p. 130.

31 Ibid.

32 Dinur, *Israel in the Diaspora*, p. 54.

33 Dinur, *Dorot u-reshumot*, p. 10.

34 Ibid., p. 147.

35 Philo, *Flaccus*, trans. F.H. Colson, London, Heinemann, 1941, vol. IX, p. 327.

36 Yitzhak Baer, *A History of the Jews in Christian Spain*, trans. Louis Schoffman, Philadelphia, Jewish Publication Society of America, 1966, vol. I, p. 1.

37 Yitzhak Baer, *Yisrael ba-ʿamim*, Jerusalem, Bialik Institute Press, 1955, p. 117.

38 Baer, *History of the Jews in Christian Spain*, p. 243.

39 Yitzhak Baer, "Ha-megamah ha-datit ha-ḥevratit shel *Sefer ha-ḥassidim*," *Zion*, III, 1938, p. 21.

40 Ibid., p. 50.

41 Baer, *History of the Jews in Christian Spain*, pp. 244–5.

42 See especially pp. 98 and 243 on the "Ashkenization" of Spanish Jewry.

43 Isaac Hirsch Weiss, *Dor dor ve-dorshav*, New York and Berlin, Plaut and Minkus Publishers, 1924, part 5, p. 213.

44 Ibid.

45 Yitzhak Baer, "Ha-historia ha-ḥevratit ve-hadatit shel ha-Yehudim," *Zion*, III, 1938, p. 280.

46 Ibid.

47 Ibid., p. 279.

48 Eliezer Eugen Täubler (1879–1953) was one of the last historians to write about the eternal Jewish essence in the tradition established by the Emancipation culture. Täubler was a scholar of the Graeco-Roman world, who spent his final years in teaching Bible and Hellenistic literature at Hebrew Union College, Cincinnati. Before World War I he founded and directed the Gesamtarchiv der deutschen Juden and later the Berlin Lehranstalt (later Hochschule) für die Wissenschaft des Judentums, where his lectures were attended by both Dinur and Baer, an influence which may perhaps partially explain the absence of proper perspective in their writings. A sample of Täubler's historical viewpoint, as set forth in his 1938 essay "Future and past": "Normalization does not offer a solution to the enigma of Jewish history." Everything that established Israel's uniqueness is outside the norm of

other nations. Behind the uniqueness of Israel's destiny there lies the uniqueness of its essence, and behind the latter – the uniqueness of ideas and forces that created this essence and directed its special development. The problem of the Jew's future is not the striving for a national and political norm. His course in the future will be determined by the law that has directed it hitherto. The essay, which appeared in the Schocken calendar for 1938–9, is cited by his widow, Dr. Selma Stern-Täubler in S. Federbush (ed.), *Hochmat Yisrael bemaᶜarav Europa*, Jerusalem and Tel Aviv, Ogen and M. Neuman, 1959, p. 261. This statement has the unmistakable ring of the metaphysics of Humboldt, Ranke, and the German idealists (see chapter 7).

49 Baer, "Ha-historia ha-hevratit ve-hadatit shel ha-Yehudim," p. 294.

50 Ibid., or in another formulation there: the inner forces "always seek to revert to their essential bent," as though they operated by their own special gravitational pull. In the final analysis the struggle of these forces is part of a destined "revolutionary renascence of all mankind."

51 Yitzhak Baer, *Galut*, New York, Schocken Books, p. 122.

52 On Buber and his attitude to the *halachic* commandments, see E. Shmueli, *Morashah u-maᵓavak ba-shirah uva-hagut*, Tel Aviv, Yahdav, 1978, pp. 265ff.

53 Baer, "Ha-historia ha-hevratit ve-hadatit shel ha-Yehudim," p. 294.

54 As for Christianity, Baer believed that the Sages of the Mishnah and their adherents were in fact better Christians than those who declared themselves true followers of the teachings of Jesus. Jesus himself spoke like a Tannaᵓitic Sage. Baer dismisses Christianity's claim to the inheritance of true Judaism ("Israel of the spirit") by turning the argument around: Jesus and the apostles resembled the early pietists who, like the Sages of the Mishnah and like pietists throughout the ages, were the ones who realized in practice Christianity's widely touted ideals of justice, charity, equality, humility, simplicity, and loving-kindness. In a number of his writings Baer sharply condemned instances of Christian nefariousness. See, for example, the conclusion of *A History of the Jews in Christian Spain*.

55 Klausner, *Historia shel ha-bait ha-sheni*, vol. I, p. 10.

9   Conclusions and implications

1 An example where the theory of cultures may shed new light is the Hellenistic-Roman culture at the end of the Second Temple period and the centuries immediately thereafter. Apocryphal literature, the Dead Sea Scrolls, and numerous archeological findings provide evidence that diaspora Jewish communities before the Common Era and until approximately 200 CE – during the period of the Second Temple and after its destruction – did not conform to the mold of Pharisaic Judaism (the Talmudic culture in our terminology, or "normative Judaism," as it is often called). Diaspora communities did not live according to the laws of the Torah as interpreted by the Sages. We must remember that only the Bible was available in Greek, not the Mishnah and the *midrashim*; the Sages' words were thus inaccessible to most diaspora Jews, and the latter had more in common with the general Hellenistic culture of their Graeco-Roman environment. Relics of their art contain many pagan symbols, and some scholars attribute the introduction of such symbols into Christianity to the influence of Hellenistic Jewish converts to the new faith. But even Jews who did not defect from "Judaism," i.e. from the law of Moses as they understood it and from the destiny of their people, are known to have produced mask and graven image, and on the synagogue walls no less, for what they must have considered the greater glory of heaven. Not only human and animal figures were depicted, but even female nudes, as in the mural of Pharaoh's daughter at the synagogue of Dura Europos. And not only paintings adorn Jewish holy places in the diaspora, but also relief carvings of human and animal figures. Pagan symbols were also found in a sarcophagus at the Beit Sheᵓarim necropolis in northern Israel. Erwin E. Goodenough cites numerous examples of human nudes in painting and sculpture in his monumental work, *Jewish Symbols in the Greco-Roman Period*, New York, Pantheon Press, 1953, vol. III, nos. 136 and 789.

It is interesting to study this syncretism in antiquity during a twilight inter-culture period – before the Talmudic culture had gained complete ascendance over Jewish life, when its claim to the legitimate, and exclusive, inheritance of the Biblical culture was not yet universally recognized. The extent of acculturation is evidenced, for example, in the widespread use of Gentile languages and names, almost reminiscent of that practice in the Emancipation culture of the nineteenth century: During the festival of Sukkot, in the year 13 BCE, nine leaders of the community of Cyrene in North Africa convened for a meeting in their synagogue. Seven had Greek names, one had a Roman name, and only one participant bore a Hebrew name. In this meeting they decided to render honor to one of their peers at every convocation, and at the beginning of each month to crown him with an olive garland and confer upon him an honorary medal. It was further decided to record this decision on a marble plaque to be placed in a suitable site within the municipal amphitheater. See ibid., vol. II, p. 145. The Sages, we know, disapproved of theaters and forbade them to Jews, but the Jews of this and other Hellenistic cities purchased special seats for themselves and their households in the circuses and theaters of the pagans; ibid., vol. I, p. 22, and vol. III, p. 144.

2 For more on the emergence of the Rabbinic culture, its position in Israel today, and the whole issue of legitimation and modernization in contemporary Jewish thought, see E. Shmueli, Ha-yahadut bein samchut le-hashra'ah, Tel Aviv, Sifriat Poálim, 1988.

3 On the principles of faith in the Middle Ages, see E. Shmueli, Don Isaac Abravanel ve-geirush Sefarad, Jerusalem, Bialik Institute, 1963, pp. 116ff.

4 Solomon Schechter, Studies in Judaism, Philadelphia, Jewish Publication Society, 1908, first series, p. 147 on "The dogmas of Judaism."

5 Post-Holocaust Jewish theological writings deal at length with the possibility of faith in Israel's chosenness during and after the catastrophe. See Arthur Cohen (ed.), Arguments and Doctrines: Reader in the Aftermath of the Holocaust, New York, Harper and Row, 1970, and Emil Fackenheim's essay there. See also E. Fackenheim, "Philosophy and Jewish existence in the present age," published in English in the journal Da'at, I, Bar-Ilan Univ. Press, Winter 1978, wherein he charges philosophy with insensitivity to the particular sufferings of Jews in our era. The article presents the position of a religious Jewish thinker, albeit not a traditionally Orthodox one. See also E. Fackenheim, To Mend the World: Foundations of Future Jewish Thought, New York, Schocken Books, 1982.

6 Hermann Cohen, Religion of Reason, New York, F. Ungar Publishing Co., 1972.

7 Moses Maimonides, Guide for the Perplexed, trans. M. Friedländer, 2nd edn, New York, Dover Publications, 1956, part 3, ch. 34, p. 329.

8 For a discussion of "ideas" and "essences" in the light of the phenomenology of Husserl and his disciples, see E. Shmueli, "Critical reflections on Husserl's philosophy of history," Journal of the British Society for Phenomenology, I, II, January 1971; "Consciousness and action," in A.T. Tymieniecka (ed.), Analecta Husserliana, Dordrecht and Boston, 1976 vol. v; "Husserl's transcendental subjectivity and its existential opponents," Telos, 6, Buffalo, NY, Fall, 1970; Crossroads of Modern Thought, Tel Aviv, Eked, 1984.

9 Michah Joseph Berdyczewksi, Baderech, vol. II, p. 47, English trans. in Arthur Hertzberg, The Zionist Idea, New York, Atheneum, 1976, p. 301.

10 Ibid.

11 Abraham Isaac Kook, Orot-ha-kodesh, part 2, in Ben Zion Bokser (trans. and ed.), Abraham Isaac Kook – The Lights of Penitence, Lights of Holiness, The Moral Principles, Essays, Poems, London, Spek, 1978.

12 This subject has been widely discussed in modern Jewish thought. See formulations by Eliezer Schweid in Ha-yehudi ha-boded veha-yahadut, Tel Aviv, Am Oved, 1974, pp. 105ff.

13 Midrash Psalms 146.

14 Cohen, Religion of Israel, p. 343.

15 Moses Isserles, She'elot u-teshuvot, Amsterdam, 1711, siman 7, p. 4, b. See also Ben-Zion Katz, Rabbanut va-ḥassidut, Tel Aviv, Haskalah, 1956, pp. 14–30, and H.H. Ben-Sasson, Hagut va-hanhagah, Jerusalem, Bialik Institute Press, 1960, p. 14.

16 Much has been written in recent times on interpretations of the past. Mordecai M. Kaplan's view is of particular interest, because Kaplan saw in Judaism not merely a religion in the narrow ritualistic sense, but a "Jewish civilization." He wished to expand the concept of Judaism and illustrate its luster in wider areas, in order to render it appealing to its alienated sons. Kaplan advocates complete separation between religion and state in favor of a free association of believers who mutually strengthen each other by developing their

moral fiber, an activity which the author also calls redemption. Personal salvation and Israel's redemption receive much attention in Kaplan's system, as in our own study. But Kaplan eliminates from Judaism the pragmatic-technical dimension of ontology, including that which Jews have created with other nations in the sciences, arts, and literature. "Jewish civilization" thus encompasses only creations unique to the Jewish spirit: religion, Torah, and tradition, the Science of Judaism, Hebrew language and literature, and Jewish art. See Mordecai M. Kaplan, *Judaism as a Civilization*, New York, Macmillan, 1934. Modern interpreters of Jewish culture include M.H. Amishai (Maisels), S.H. Bergman, S. Rawidowicz, and N. Rotenstreich. In recent years Eliezer Schweid has dealt with this subject, first in his above-mentioned book (n. 12), and later in *Emunat ʿam Yisrael ve-tarbuto*, Tel Aviv, 1977. Also noteworthy are the efforts of Alexander Barzel in *Lihiyot Yehudi*, Tel Aviv, 1978, to prove the force of seven basic ideas operative in Jewish history, a modern transposition, if you will, of theological "essence" into contemporary language and needs.

INDEX

spread of 14, 27, 152, 221
see also sectarians
Kashvut 96
Katz, Ben-Zion 273 n.15
Katz, Jacob 267 n.2
Kaufmann, David 186
Kaufmann, Yeḥezkel
  and essence of Judaism 2
  and German Bible criticism 63, 209
  on Judaism's failure to spread 128
  on religion of Israel 86, 87, 119, 120,
    121, 209
  on uniqueness of Jewish history 204
  works of 261 n.6, 270 n.2, 270 n.9
Kayserling, M. 267 n.4
Keller, A.G. 3, 42, 255 n.34
Kimḥi, David 53
Kirkisani, Jacob 154
Klausner, Joseph 142, 205, 208, 218, 233,
  265 n.7, 270 n.3
Klein. S. 262 n.16
Klein-Braslavi, Sarah 256 n.23
Kli golah, see instrument of exile
Klopstock, Friedrich Gottlieb 67
Knesset Israel, see Congregation of Israel
Kohut, Alexander 186
Kook, Abraham Isaac 245, 273 n.11
Koraḥ 50, 146
Koran 73
Krauss, S. 186
Krochmal, Naḥman 2, 3, 186
Kroeber, A. L. 41
al-Kumisi, Daniel 154
Kunitz, Paul G. 255 n.29
The Kuzari (Judah ha-Levi) 55–6, 130, 256
  n.18

Lachover, F. 257 n. 40, 260 n.54
Lachrymosity of Jewish historiography
  165, 183, 231
Lamentations, Book of 83
Language
  and experience 5, 17–8, 31
  and historical facts 214–5
  Jewish systems of 5, 31
Lau, T. von 269 n.30
Law, *see* Halachah, Oral Law
Lazarus, Moritz 87
Leadership, *see* authority
Learning, *see* scholar(s), Torah,
  transmission of
Lebensohn, Adam ha-Kohen 73
Legitimation
  via exegesis 26–30
  Poetic-Philosophic 99
  Talmudic 90, 93–7
  see also authority

Leibniz, G.W. von 216
Leibowitz, Yeshaʿayahu 2, 96, 259–60
  n.21
Leipzig Israelitic Synod 268 n.12
Lenzen, V.F. 252 n.1
Leonardo da Vinci 270 n.14
Lestschinsky, Jakob 270 n.58
Levi ben Abraham 72
Levi ben Ḥama, Rabbi 93
Levinger, Eliʿezer 258 n.12
Levinsohn, Isaac Baer (the Ribal) 186, 268
  n.27
Lewkowitz, Albert 268 n.12
Lewy, Israel 186
Lieberman, Saul 49, 50, 256 n.5, 263 n.7
Liebeschutz, H. 269 n.30
Literal meaning, *see* peshat
Livy 153
Lobkowicz, Nicholas 254 n.21
Locker, Zvi 169, 267 n.6
Loewenstamm, Samuel A. 261 n.5
Loewisohn, Solomon 67, 257 n.10
Luckman, Thomas 252 n.1
Lucretius 162
Luria, Issac (the Holy Ari) 78, 134
Luria, Solomon (the Maharshal) 246
Lurianic Kabbalah 78, 110
Luzzatto, Samuel David 106, 186
Lycurgus 67

Maas, M. 268 n.12
Maʿaseh bereshit (Creation mysticism) 77,
  97, 110
Maʿaseh merkavah (*merkavah* mysticism) 77,
  97, 110
Maccabees, *see* Hasmoneans
Mahler, Raphael 34, 265 n.22, 267 n.2,
  269 n.39
Maimon, Solomon 172
Maimonides, Moses (Moshe ben Maimon)
  and apologetics 8, 266 n.30
  on authority of sages 101, 155, 161,
    265
  and *Book of Harmony* 57
  on commandments 100–6, 136, 156
  and commentary on the Mishnah 54,
    156
  controversy over 22, 72
  on converts 130–2
  and courtly culture 105
  Epistle to Yemen 7, 131 (cited) 262, n.25
  Essay on Resurrection 155 (cited) 265
    n.26
  on Gentiles 125, 131–2
  on God 1, 76, 101–4, 119, 262 n.18
  on golden mean 105
  and heumeneutic rules 54